Richard J. Woods, O.P.

The Spirituality of the Celtic Saints

ORBIS BOOKS

Maryknoll, New York 10545

The Catholic Foreign Mission Society of America (Maryknoll) recruits and trains people for overseas missionary service. Through Orbis Books, Maryknoll aims to foster the international dialogue that is essential to mission. The books published, however, reflect the opinions of their authors and are not meant to represent the official position of the society.

To obtain more information about Maryknoll and Orbis Books, please visit our website at www.maryknoll.org.

Library of Congress Cataloging-in-Publication Data

Woods, Richard, 1941-
    The spirituality of the Celtic saints / Richard J. Woods.
      p. cm.
    Includes bibliographical references and index.
    ISBN 1-57075-316-4 (pbk.)
    1. Christian saints, Celtic. 2. Spirituality – Celtic Church. I. Title.
BR754.A1 W66 2000
270'.089'916–dc21

99-087442

For my maternal grandparents,
Angelus ní Powers and Edward Corcoran,
who kindled the flame,
and
Austin Flannery, O.P.,
Fr. Brian Jones,
Anthony Ross, O.P., and
Dom Sylvester Houédard, O.S.B.,
who fanned the fire:
Slainte an bhradain chughat!

Contents

Introduction

In Search of Celtic Saints

> O amazement of things — even the least particle!
> O spirituality of things!

> — WALT WHITMAN, "Song at Sunset,"
> *Leaves of Grass*

Not long ago, one of my Dominican friends was preaching in Oxford on March 1, the feast of St. David, the national patron of Wales. In the course of his homily the preacher remarked that despite hundreds of years of Christianity, David was the only canonized saint produced by that nation. Having been on the Isle of Môn, now known as Anglesey, the Island of Ten Thousand Saints, having made retreat on Caldy Island, where Saints Samson and Illtud lived and, it is said, David himself sought refuge, and having squinted across a brazen sunset sea at Bardsey Island, where still more thousands of Welsh saints are buried, I took occasion later to disagree with him, producing the names of several more renowned Welsh (or, more properly, early British) saints from the hallowed pages of the *Oxford Dictionary of the Christian Church* — Beuno, Deiniol, Dubricius, Illtud, Samson, Teilo, and Winifred (to whom could be added the irascible Gildas and many more).

"Ah," he replied with an unanswerable distinction, "but David is the only Welsh saint listed in the *Roman* calendar." He might have added that *Dewi Sant* is the only "Red Letter" Welsh saint in the Anglican calendar as well.[1]

And there lies the rub. Admittedly, Ireland has done somewhat better than Wales, with a handful of saints officially included in the Roman calendar, notably Patrick (who was British), Brigid, Columba (Columcille), and Columban. But Scotland has only Queen Margaret — and she was

1

half-English and half-German (St. Andrew the Apostle, the national patron, was presumably Jewish). Unlike Agatha, Lucy, Cecilia, Anastasia, Cosmas and Damian, and the others who enjoy "universal" relevance because of a presumptive connection with the ancient church of Rome, the rest of the named Celtic saints — several hundreds of them — are considered to be of merely local significance.

And yet Ireland has been known throughout the world as the Isle of Saints and Scholars since the eleventh century.[2] It was they, in Thomas Cahill's perhaps exaggerated estimation, who "saved civilization."[3] Moreover, to this day hundreds of place names in Ireland, Wales, and Cornwall recall their origins as "cells," or churches, of saints, and Scotland's major cities, as well as Iona, are particularly remembered for their patron saints. Celtic saints' names dot the map of continental Europe as well, where many are still honored by annual festivals. (See the appendix, p. 185, for a calendar list, woefully incomplete, of the major saints of Ireland, Scotland, Wales, and Brittany.)

Given the resurgence of interest in saints and sanctity in recent times, as well as the presence of millions of second-, third-, and fourth-generation descendants of Celtic immigrants throughout the world, not to mention the current Celtic revival in the arts, habitual negligence of the Celtic saints and their spirituality seems more and more like oversight. And a mystery. Why should thousands of early Christian saints in the Celtic lands have been so effortlessly overlooked in the first place?

The answer to that question is complex and fascinating and will engage us in what I hope will be a profitable side-exploration of Christian history and spirituality. But the immediate occasion of this book lay in still another friendly quibble a few years after the first, when I reviewed Robert Ellsberg's generous and fascinating literary calendar, *All Saints*, which provides surprisingly apt candidates, both traditional and contemporary, for spiritual reading every day in the year.[4] I complained (in an Irish journal, to be sure) that only seven Celtic saints, ancient and modern, were to be found in its five hundred ample pages — Patrick, Brigid, Columcille, and Columban, plus the medieval theologian Duns Scotus (but not Richard of St. Victor), the Welsh poet George Herbert (but not Henry Vaughan), and the Irish Benedictine John Main (but not Dom Columba Marmion). After working on another project for Robert, he invited (or perhaps I should say "challenged") me to develop a book on the spirituality of the Celtic saints for Orbis Books — an opportunity I found irresistible, having pursued the saints in literature, pilgrimage, and prayer for some twenty years.

Fine books on Celtic saints have been available for many years, some of them remarkably rich and readable, such as Mary Ryan D'Arcy's *The*

Saints of Ireland[5] and Eoin Neeson's *The Book of Irish Saints*.[6] (There is also a somewhat sentimental classic by Aloysius Roche bearing the revealing title *A Bedside Book of Irish Saints*).[7] Others are dense scholarly tomes, such as Charles Plummer's classic volumes in Latin and Irish — in the latter case accompanied by an English translation for those whose command of Middle Irish is as frail as mine.[8] (For further references, see the list of publications appended on p. 227.) But with the remarkable exception of James F. Kenney's monumental *Sources for the Early History of Ireland,* first published in 1929, these are now long out of print and often hard to obtain even in libraries.[9]

As I pondered the field of more recent publication on the Celtic saints, I discovered that popular accounts focused on only a few men and fewer women — from a dozen to perhaps twenty in all. Most report traditional events taken from the medieval Lives, which can be very misleading if taken at face value. On the other hand, a number of excellent scholarly studies have appeared recently that not only examine the Lives in detail as literary works in their own right, but also uncover the historical figures with sometimes startling results. These, however, tend to be specialist studies which are of interest primarily to other scholars in the field (and will also be found listed in the bibliography).

At the same time, depictions of "Celtic spirituality" have been filling publishers' lists for several years, as the "Celtic" cultural revival invigorated that industry as well as the fields of popular music and film. John O'Donohue's *Anam Chara: Spiritual Wisdom from the Celtic World* soared to the top of best-seller lists on both sides of the Atlantic.[10] Almost anything with the word "Celtic" attached to it has become uncommonly marketable. The latest catalogue from a major book club to reach my overcrowded mailbox includes, in its merchandise pages, a Celtic letter opener (silver-plated, nontarnish finish), a leather Celtic address book (for Celtic addresses?), and a Celtic body-decoration kit, including a "full range of Celtic images, from snakes to birds to interlocking circles and more."

"Irish," as university students in Oxford and Chicago tell me, "is in." Not many years back, *Riverdance* became an overnight international phenomenon. Irish-flavored "pubs" are wildly popular among young people throughout Europe and the United States. The arts are also favored. Irish poet Seamus Heaney's Nobel Prize was considered by many to be long overdue. Currently featured among acclaimed productions in Chicago theaters are Frank McCourt's *The Irish and How They Got That Way, Flannagan's Wake,* and two plays by Martin McDonagh, *The Cripple of Inishmaan* and *The Beauty Queen of Leenane.* The same is true of other cities in the United States and England. As I write, several new Irish films are scheduled to open within the next few weeks, following hard on the heels of *Waking Ned Devine* and *This Is My Father.*

But "Celtic" means much more than "Irish." And while the burgeoning Irish film industry is achieving international acclaim, Scottish and Welsh films such as *Rob Roy, Trainspotting,* and *The Englishman Who Went Up a Hill but Came Down a Mountain* have also claimed critical and popular attention. More to the point, the Lives of the Celtic saints embrace a whole family of men and women from all the Celtic-tongued nations.

So, in a word, between the painstaking investigations of scholars and the enthusiasms of popular culture there seems to be room for another look at the spirituality of the Celtic saints. In this book, however, I do not propose merely to provide another catalogue of well-known figures from Ireland, Scotland, Wales, and the European continent, much less an anthology of their lives. Several works of both kinds are more or less readily available, among them volumes by Allchin, Macquarrie, Minton, Ní Mheara, Pennick, Sellner, Sharpe, Wallace, and Webb (for which, and others, again consult the bibliography). Rather, I intend to explore the spirituality of the Celtic saints as revealed in their lives — not only written Lives from the dusky past of the twilit years of first millennium, but accounts from a variety of sources as well as reports from more recent times.

As a consequence of my own search for the saints and scholars who made the Celtic lands a lamp of learning and holiness during the Dark Ages, and managed to "save civilization" in the process, several topical areas emerged which proved to be of contemporary as well as ancient concern, and in the final chapter I will address these briefly — issues of social justice; the status of women in Celtic life and spirituality; the importance of art, literature, and music; and what is now generally referred to as "ecology," the place and value of the natural environment. To these must be added one of the perhaps surprisingly characteristic dual aspects of Celtic spirituality, the art of blessing and its perhaps surprising correlative, cursing. We still have something to learn from our ancient brothers and sisters.

Calling a book *The Spirituality of the Celtic Saints* may seem innocuous enough. But in some circles it is likely to be considered presumptuous, since among academic writers, the meaning of "spirituality" itself is hotly debated, and for some time scholars have expressed doubts about whether "Celtic" really refers to anything other than a group of languages, not to say whether we can learn much, if anything, about the saints in question from the records of their lives, assuming that such persons existed in the first place. I shall return in the first chapter to the problems surrounding "saint" and "Celtic" (including whether we can really speak of a Celtic culture or a Celtic church, much less a Celtic civilization). Here I would like to offer a few suggestions about the term "spirituality," at least what I mean by it.

After three decades of study, reading, discussion, and teaching in the field, I have come to think of spirituality as a set of related meanings rather than a single notion, much less a clear and distinct Cartesian idea.

The word itself has a curious history, one that begins in English early in the sixteenth century. Although "spiritualities" had been in use in English for a century to distinguish the properties of the church from those of the king and secular landowners ("temporalities"), around the year 1500 it was reintroduced from the French *spiritualité* to refer to "the quality or condition of being spiritual," that is, concerned with the things of the spirit as opposed to material or worldly interests.[11]

By contrast, from a biblical perspective, "spirit" is, first of all, the grounding attribute of the human person, a perception reflected in the origin of the notion in ancient Hebrew culture as "the breath of life" and a direct gift from God — *ruach*. Translated by Greek-speaking Jews a few centuries before the time of Christ as *pneuma,* to the Romans it was *spiritus;* both words meant pretty much the same as the Hebrew: "air," "wind," and "breath." As the fundamental metaphor for the transcendent dimension of human nature itself, the biblical notion of "spirit" can be described in J. A. T. Robinson's memorable words, "that in virtue of which [a person] is open to and transmits the life of God."[12]

"Spirituality," then, refers first of all to that "respiratory" dimension of personality that is receptive to God, our openness to what would later be called "grace." But it is likewise the capacity to *respond* to God and the gift of life. At the risk of quoting myself, I therefore suggest that at root "spirituality" means "the intrinsic, self-transcending character of all human persons and everything that pertains to it, including, most importantly, the ways in which that perhaps infinitely malleable character is realized concretely in everyday life situations."[13]

Spirituality in this primary sense is intractably individual, referring to what is most characteristically human about each of us. In the end, it is the story of our life as a whole as we have directed it toward the realization of our deepest longings and highest aspirations. But all life is shared in community, and each of our spiritualities reflects the social character of all human experience, specifically that of those specific communities into which we are born, in which we live, mature, and eventually die.

Thus it is also accurate to speak of collective or corporate *spiritualities* that embody the beliefs, values, goals, and paths of development that have formed in communities of men and women of various kinds — geographical, cultural, social, ethnic, and intentional. It is not misleading to refer to Protestant spirituality, Buddhist spirituality, Franciscan spirituality, Korean spirituality, or, in a still wider sense, women's or children's spirituality. In this respect, "Celtic spirituality" does mean something, even if it might be more appropriate to refer to "Celtic spiritualities," given the considerable variations that exist among peoples identified in whatever way as Celtic.

In most recent literature, such spiritualities are generally assumed to be Christian, but that assumption is, of course, historically relative. It has also been largely a factual situation for the last millennium and a half, and so it is possible to agree with Oliver Davies when he writes,

> Cultures, while differing from one another, also exist within a broader intercultural network of dependencies and continuities. To the extent that cultural identity is a vital ingredient in individual identity, and therefore a determinant in the way that we, as individuals, respond to the Christian calling, it is legitimate to speak of a national or ethnic spirituality, linked to the horizons of a specific culture.[14]

And while he is specifically referring to Welsh spirituality, his observations are equally applicable to Irish, Scottish, Manx, and Breton cultures:

> Such a spirituality must certainly be seen within the parameters of spiritual forms which are more generally common to the Celtic peoples as a whole and whose origins lie in the interaction of original Celtic primal or tribal religion with the young Christianity.[15]

As we turn to the saints of the Celtic traditions, we may expect, then, not to encounter stock characters in some uniform system of religious beliefs and observances, but rather considerable variation in personality, character, situation, and expression. Consequently, our task becomes trying to determine not only their individuality, but also what they might have held in common within the broad context of young and vital Christian churches.

As to the further question of why Celtic spirituality and the Lives of its saints should be of any, much less intense, interest today to scholars and the wider public, it seems evident that re-visioning Celtic Christianity provides an alternative, both historically and currently, to the imperial, Greco-Roman models of the church that have dominated Eastern and

Western Christianity since the era of Constantine. But not an alternative church.

Like Zen and Tibetan Buddhism, by its very differences from the "mainstream" tradition, the spirituality of the Celtic churches reveals the strengths and weaknesses of the larger system in a different light. And like marginal forms of religions elsewhere, it has intrinsic value worth reconsidering as Christians ponder the likely demands of the third millennium upon forms of participation, authority, leadership, interreligious dialogue, prayer, social action, and personal spiritual development.

A word of thanks is in order at this point to those who have aided and abetted me in the present enterprise, notably Robert Ellsberg and Michael Leach at Orbis Books, who proved to be patient and supportive when a variety of unexpected demands on my time and energies prolonged the completion of the manuscript beyond all our hopes. A special word of thanks is due John Eagleson, whose diligence and acuity prevented a host of major and minor problems. I trust that their confidence in the project will prove to be warranted. I am also deeply aware of my debt of gratitude to the researchers and scholars whose works have provided me with seemingly immense resources. Retrospectively, I am particularly awed by the work of Mary Ryan D'Arcy, whose superb book, *The Saints of Ireland,* was first drawn to my attention by Dr. Eoin McKiernan, the founder and former director of the Irish American Cultural Institute in St. Paul, Minnesota, who was so helpful to me when I was there in the mid-1980s. Repeatedly, I found myself returning to her as an almost infallible guide when perplexed by inconsistencies and conundrums discovered in the pages of the recognized authorities. (I hasten to add that any errors of fact or interpretation in the following pages are my own responsibility.) Over the years, brief encounters with very memorable figures, most now at rest in the place of their resurrection, also sped me on my way even when I was not sure where the path would lead. Among them, I owe a debt of lasting gratitude to Dr. Brian O Cuiv of the Institute for Advanced Studies in Dublin, Drs. Liam and Máira de Paor, Dr. Francis Byrne at the University of Dublin, and Dr. Theo Moody, the great historian of Northern Ireland. Finally, I wish to remember my beloved grandmother, Angelus ní Powers Corcoran, born in Tyrrellspass, County West Meath, in the year of Our Lord 1884, who first awakened my interest in and love for Ireland and all things Irish.

ONE

The Celtic Saints

Their Lives, Spirituality, and Legacy

> ... who with Saturn old
> Fled over Adria to th' Hesperian Fields,
> And ore the Celtic roam'd the utmost Isles.

— JOHN MILTON,
Paradise Lost (1667), 1, 521

Today the phrase "Celtic saints" invokes half-legendary images of ancient figures such as Patrick, Brigid, and Columba; bishops, monks, and nuns both austere and adventuresome; and perhaps even wandering sages and missionaries, rather than martyrs such as Oliver Plunkett, resolute founders and educators like Nano Nagle and Mother McCauley, reformed alcoholics like Matt Talbot, a hidden poet like Anne Griffiths, or a young lay missionary like Edel Quinn. Such modern and even contemporary figures deserve the epithet no less than their forebears and in some instances probably more so. Yet the fixed image of the "Celtic saint" remains an iconic figure of a remote age, and most likely a monk, a nun, or a bishop. And so it is with the dawn of Celtic Christianity that our story also begins.

This is only just, for the mantle of sanctity that extends from the first centuries of the Christian era to our own era is in some measure seamless, and the patterns of holiness were fixed early. But for over the last fifty years and more, a quiet revolution has been underway in the scholarly study of the lives of the Irish saints in particular and of the Celtic saints in general. Until then, much of the material in the Latin and Irish Lives tended to be taken more or less at face value, perhaps barring some of the wilder anecdotes. Oxford professor Richard Sharpe observes that the great historian of Irish monasticism, Msgr. John Ryan, was the last of the "old school" in this regard,[1] but among more popular writers, the Lives have continued to be accepted at least in digest form as biographical memoirs if not exactly historical documents.

The work of Sharpe in particular, but also of Kathleen Hughes, G. H. Doble, and Wendy Davies in Wales, Alan Macquarrie in Scotland, and a growing number of younger scholars, has also shown that the purpose of the Lives was far broader and also more defined than that of merely recording wondrous deeds of saints long dead. Their Lives put forth claims not only for preeminence among competing monastic traditions, but for grants of land as well. They are, in addition, compilations of spirituality and even philosophy. (Joseph Falaky Nagy's brilliant *Conversing with Angels and Ancients* [1997] is of exceptional importance in this regard.) And while the Lives may not shed accurate light on the particular period in which their subjects flourished, they supply valuable information about the times in which they were written.

It is well to bear in mind, however, that even when fraught with later concerns for precedence and property rights alien to the work and interests of the ancient saints themselves, and overlaid with miraculous legends intended to add luster to the holiness and fame of their subjects, the saints' Lives nevertheless point to men and women who were not fictional creations, but real founders and leaders, and whose memory was sacred to those who came after them. That memory may have been embellished to the point of incredibility, but it rested on fact, made the more memorable by its very embellishment. Thus, knowing *how* to read the Lives of the Celtic saints makes a difference.

Moreover, some of the accounts were written within living memory of their subjects, such as the Life of Ciarán of Saighir, which was composed by one of his fellow monks. The Life of Déclán was compiled from recollections of his disciples, and the Lives of Abbán and Columban were written within fifty years of their deaths.[2] And so we may even use some of the Lives as lenses to peer back into history at the lives and times of these remarkable people, provided we remember to adjust the magnification carefully. We are likely to find as a result true saints, not less but more appealing when shorn of some of the later if excessive glory granted them by a grateful posterity. And they still have something to teach us.

Holiness: What Is a Saint?

Holiness as a personal quality or condition can be distinguished from both the collective holiness of the community and, more importantly, the corporate holiness of institutional roles or offices. Thus, the pope and the Dalai Lama are referred to as "His Holiness," but in neither case does the title imply that the current bearer need be in fact a living saint. They may well be, of course.

In the Christian tradition, the meaning of "saint" (Greek: *hagios,* Latin: *sanctus*) has developed over the centuries from a designation for the members of the local church (e.g., Acts 9:13, 32, etc.; Rom. 1:7; 15:25, etc.) and the entire Christian community (e.g., 1 Cor. 1:2; 14:33, etc.; Eph. 2:19; Col. 1:26) to the medieval conception of a peerless miracle-worker and charismatic champion of the faith, to the more or less modern notion of an imitable model, designated by church officials as an exemplar of heroic virtue.[3] All these notions can be found in the somewhat circular dictionary definitions of "saint": "Holy, canonized or officially recognized by the church as having won by exceptional holiness a high place in heaven and veneration on earth."[4] "Holiness" is subsequently defined as "the quality or state of being holy — used as a title for various high religious dignitaries." And "holy," in turn, means "exalted or worthy of complete devotion as one perfect in goodness and righteousness."

Despite such conciseness, or because of it, comparative hagiology has become both impoverished and ambiguous in the Christian West. With the translation of the Hebrew Scriptures into Greek in the third century B.C.E., the single term "saint" (*hagios*) with its occasional gender-specific vernacular substitutes, "holy man" and "holy woman," had to serve for a variety of terms. For Jews, *qadosh, hasid, tsaddik,* and *shalem* each conveyed a distinctive nuance of personal holiness, to which may be added *talmid hakham,* "the pious scholar," and *yashar,* "upright," which also convey a nuance of saintliness.

Qodesh usually refers to a sacred place or thing and is the preferred term for the divine Otherness of God, which can be communicated by exposure or contact. In this regard, the derived term *qadosh* includes angels, human saints, and holy things, such as a sanctuary. *Hasid* comes from the verb *hasad,* "to show oneself kind or merciful" and refers to a godly person, someone preeminent in goodness, both merciful and reverent. *Tsaddiq,* meaning "just," "lawful," or "righteous," conveys the moral sense of legal purity. In later Judaism, *tsaddik* becomes the term of choice for "saint."[5] The term nearest the holistic concept of saint is, perhaps, *shalem,* which comes from the word *shalam,* "complete" or "finished," and connotes the qualities of friendliness, fullness, prosperity, justice, peaceableness, serenity, and wholeness.[6] It is related to the familiar term *shalom.*[7]

But even in the early Christian era, *hagios* could still refer indifferently to both human and angelic beings, as well as to God, to both the living and the dead, and to individuals in their own right as well as being members of the elect community. And scholars of religion such as Gerardus van der Leeuw and Rudolf Otto reminded us early in this century that from a phenomenological perspective the sacred or numinous transcends the personal sphere, pertaining even primarily to the perceived property or properties of objects, places, events, and times surcharged with a mysterious force or power that both allures and threatens.[8] Such holiness is contagious, infecting those who draw near to the Sacred Other regardless of their intelligence, social standing, or even moral qualities. In this regard, as Richard Kieckhefer observes, "The saint is a figure whose very being exudes power. His or her potency is often manifested in miracles associated with his or her body or grave; the person of the saint is a relic."[9]

It is now also commonplace to remark that in English as well as Romance languages, the root of the words of "holy" and "whole" are the same — on one hand the Germanic form *hál,* which means "entire" or "complete," and, on the other, the Indo-European radical *sa-,* which appears in words such as "sacred," "safe," "salvation," and "savior," and conveys the sense of integrity. (It also appears in "sane," "sanitary," and "preserve.")[10] To "hallow" and to "consecrate" mean approximately the same thing.

But contrasting views of holiness as "Otherness" and wholeness as "perfection," that is, completeness, constitute a real polarity in spirituality and theology which manifests the tension between sanctity as a numinous quality distinct from virtue and as the epitome of virtue. For older writers such as Josef Goldbrunner and a host of more contemporary authors, holiness simply *is* wholeness: it represents the fullness of the life God intends for human beings to enjoy, the fulfillment of the covenant promises.[11] Conversely, "transcendentalists" continue to argue that holiness has nothing to do with wholeness, which is taken to refer exclusively to the intensity of one's relation to God: "that one passes through all the stages of spiritual development does not necessarily mean that one is intensely holy, a saint. It merely means that one is quite healthy psychologically. Holiness and psychological wholeness are not absolute correlates."[12]

In some respects, the concept of holiness entertained by those responsible for selecting candidates for canonization in the Roman Catholic Church strives to combine the contrasted notions. Kenneth Woodward writes, for instance,

> The Congregation for the Causes of Saints is quite precise in its understanding of holiness. Holiness is the grace of God operating

in and through human beings. [But] . . . Holiness is manifested by a two-tiered structure of virtues: the three supernatural (so called because they are infused by grace) virtues of faith, hope, and charity (love of God and of neighbor), and the four cardinal moral virtues (originally derived from the ethics of Aristotle) of prudence, justice, fortitude, and temperance. Since all Christians are expected to practice these virtues, a saint is someone who practices them to a "heroic" or exceptional degree.[13]

Holiness and Wholeness: Reflections of Ancient Wisdom

Interpreting these different concepts of holiness not so much as exclusive categories but as poles between which personal saintliness and official sainthood exist in a creative and interactive field of divine energy permits us to readmit the nuances of ancient biblical tradition. The choice of the single Greek term *hagios* to represent *qadosh, hasid, tsaddik,* and *shalem* was not in itself faulty, for the former word comes from a more primitive term, *hagos,* which means "an awesome thing" and therefore "sacred" in the sense of "physically pure, morally blameless, or ritually consecrated." It could refer therefore to a variety of manifestations of divine power, including human moral excellence. Nevertheless, restricting the scope of the sacred by reducing so many aspects of saintliness to *hagios* also introduced considerable and enduring ambiguity into the discussion of divine and human holiness. Was a saint holy because she or he worked miracles, or did they work miracles because they were holy? Are miracles even important?

Despite the limitations of using *hagios* to refer indifferently to the many-sided phenomenon of sanctity, the richness of the Hebrew sense of personal and corporate holiness survived in the early church. To begin with, the original designation of "saint" was applied to the living members of the church regardless of their hierarchical status or likelihood of suffering a violent death for their faith.[14] Gradually, however, the ordinary notion of "saint" became associated with the ability to perform miracles as a sign of God's particular favor and indeed presence in the life of the favored man or woman. The only claim to holiness in some later accounts of saints' lives is in fact their ability to perform miracles, which is accepted as proof that they were especially close to and favored by God. Because of their proximity to God and their role as intermediaries, the auxiliary or "helping" function of such saints occupied pride of place in the ordinary lives of Christians. This would become especially characteristic of Celtic Christians, for whom saints were, perhaps above all, wonder-workers, channels and dispensers of divine energies.

Wherever people find solace and encouragement in stories of heroic valor, such narrative symbols are likely to exercise a powerful influence, especially in the face of institutional lethargy or, worse, persecution. It was not by chance that the consolidation of episcopal and papal power in the twelfth and thirteenth centuries coincided with the monopolization of canonization by the bishops and papacy and the subsequent deemphasis on the wonder-working, *qodesh* aspect of saintliness in favor of the moral view, the *tsaddik* or *hasid* aspect, the saint as model for virtuous emulation:

> The thrust behind papal canonizations was to present the faithful with lives worth imitating, not saints to be invoked for miracles and other favors. In this respect, the division between official and local or popular saints reflected the mounting tension within the church between the saint as exemplar of virtue and the saint as thaumaturge or wonder-worker.... The point at which the elites differed from the masses was the significance of miracles in establishing sanctity. Whereas the latter considered miracles as preemptive signs of the presence of holiness, the former regarded them "as effects of a moral conduct and spiritual life *on* which only the church could pass judgment."[15]

Nor is it unlikely that an emphasis on obedience and humility was of perceived benefit to a burgeoning theocratic bureaucracy.

In any case, at least in western Christianity, the tendency of church leaders since the Middle Ages has been to regard outstanding virtue, which is to say moral excellence, as superior to miracles.[16] Celtic Christians, on the other hand, delighted in miracle stories, finding in the deeds of the saints evidence of the reality of grace and the power of intercession, even apart from virtues such as kindness, mercy, and general benevolence. And they were also smashing good yarns.

Texts and Scholars

As a branch of textual scholarship, the study of hagiography ("holy biography") possesses its own criteria, procedures, and expertise. It has also generated a considerable body of literature in recent times, one that appears to be growing exponentially. At the same time, saints of all kinds (like angels) have recently acquired a new measure of popularity outside the academy. In both respects, the lives of the Celtic saints have emerged as a particularly rich resource, not only as an aspect of the resurgence of recent interest in all things Celtic, but also because they provide a large number of relatively early texts relevant to Christian history at an especially important period of development, the so-called Dark Ages.

The modern Irish word for "saint" is *naomh* (which is pronounced, varyingly, "nahv"). Unlike the Romance and Germanic languages, which differentiate between "sacred" and "holy," Irish usually renders "holy" by the cognate *naofa*. (*Naofacht* means both "holiness" and "sanctity," and the word for "hagiography" is *Naomhsheanchas,* or "saint-story.") Conversely, the Welsh *sant* is derived from the Latin *sanctus,* like the English "saint." But in both Celtic languages, the connotations of these terms are subtly different from the ordinary meaning in English and Latin-based languages.

In many respects, the early Celtic tradition resembled Hebrew and early Christian views of holiness and sanctity. This is especially true of the early British tradition in which generations of families entrusted by custom with the care and defense of the local church were known collectively as "saints," without undue regard to set standards of individual morality.[17] Nevertheless, individuals renowned for their virtue were also venerated as saints, even while living. (Today, of course, following the advice of Herodotus, "Call no man happy until he dies," we consider it impertinent to designate someone a saint until that person is safely entombed.) Miracles attesting to their closeness to God were expected and, when not sufficiently apparent, were in many instances generously supplied by later biographers. Or, rather, hagiographers.

Recounting the stories of the early saints was of great importance in a strongly oral culture such as prevailed in the Celtic realms before the coming of Christianity and to a considerable degree long afterward. The pagan Celts, at least their learned classes, the druids and poets, were not illiterate; some knew even Greek and Latin. But they resisted writing, lest the treasures of memory be lost. (Socrates put forward a similar argument in Plato's *Phaedrus,* 275b.) Gradually, however, the written word acquired luster among the recently converted Celts of Britain and Ireland, not least because of the cargo of precious texts — the Holy Scriptures — brought by the early missionaries. Soon, Christian monks began transcribing the ancient verbal lore of the pre-Christian Celts — "the Great Pagan Classics" — as well as committing to writing the stories of their own heroes, the saints.

Following continental models such as the Life of Martin of Tours (316–97) by Sulpicius Severus, the earliest Lives of the Celtic saints were written in Latin. Later in the Middle Ages, vernacular Lives were composed, although Latin continued to be employed, sometimes within the same sentence. In general, the Lives also followed a set pattern, much as did the Lives of illustrious figures from the classical past (and, nearer our own time, as do cowboy movies and "thrillers").

First of all, the saint will have (or be given) distinguished, even royal ancestors. His or her birth will be accompanied by some sort of miraculous sign, often a vision experienced by the saint's mother. After a sometimes astonishing childhood, the budding saint will be sent to a holy and famous teacher to be educated. Throughout the saint's life, angels will appear at important moments, providing necessary advice and protection. The saint will of course perform miracles, often including raising people from the dead (and sometimes striking them dead, blind, dumb, etc.). In the case of a male saint, he will make a visit to the pope, an archbishop, or a council and as a result be ordained a bishop or archbishop. (Female saints are usually made abbesses.) Toward the end of the saint's life, the saint will be warned of his or her impending demise, including the date, time, and circumstances. In some instances, a vision of the saint's entry into glory will be granted to another saint some distance away.[18]

The spirit of both Latin and vernacular Lives is much the same, although the later the Lives were committed to writing, the more extravagant were the deeds attributed to the saintly figures portrayed. Thus the tendency toward hyperbole and theatrical excess that characterizes many of the saints' Lives, especially the later vernacular ones, warrants approaching them with a measure of caution. It also prompts us to consider the nature of the Celtic spirit itself.

The Celts:
Their Character, Quest, and Realms

Julius Caesar restricted the term *Celtae* to the peoples of middle Gaul, and even those ancient writers who included tribes in northern Italy and Spain in its orb did not use it of the British or Irish. The word "Celt" was first employed in English by the naturalist Edward Topsell only in 1607, and its modern use as a linguistic term dates only from about 1700. And even though "Celtic" has acquired a considerable panache in popular culture surpassing its use (and mispronunciation) as a title for basketball and soccer teams, it has once again become fashionable in academic circles to deny that the term refers to much more than a set of related languages. Celtic consciousness, art, culture, music, and, of course, spirituality are suspect, sometimes urged to the sidelines of respectability as linguistic epiphenomena or dismissed entirely.[19]

As with most academic obsessions, there is a nub of wisdom in this new-found recalcitrance. It is surely more usual as well as accurate (and safer) to speak of Irish whisky, Scots porridge, Welsh rarebit, Cornish game hens, and Manx cats than to invoke some pan-Celtic mythos transcending the ethnic and cultural characteristics that differentiate a wide variety of peoples, sometimes stridently, on the playing field, in the pub and classroom, and in history.

On the other hand, "Celtic" obviously means more than a group of related languages. Here, popular imagination may be more truthful than scientific precision, for the cultural and spiritual aspects of life in the lands where Celtic languages are (or were) spoken share elements of a common vision, an attitude toward life, perhaps indefinable but real enough to be recognizable, even as spirituality. As Oliver Davies observes,

> Although there is an erroneous tendency in much popular literature to speak of a single "Celtic" culture or civilization as if this were a homogeneous whole, it is the contention of the present author that Celtic language cultures during the early Middle Ages exhibit common patterns of religious sensibility and belief which are supported both by geographical proximity and by elements of a common cultural inheritance.[20]

An ancient Indo-European people of the European heartland, the *Keltoi* (as they were called by the Greeks) fanned out from their original homeland early in the first millennium before the Common Era in a centuries-long migration which took them as far east as Scythia, south to Italy, west to Gaul and Spain, and eventually north to Britain and Ireland.[21] They were first mentioned by Greek geographers and historians at the beginning of the sixth century before the Common Era, when Hecateus of Miletus referred to Narbonne as a Celtic town. Sixty years later, Herodotus reported Celtic encampments on the upper Danube and in Spain.[22] The origin of the term remains obscure.

After the sack of Rome by the Senone Brennus in 387 B.C.E. and in view of Celtic support of Hannibal (c. 216 B.C.E.), the Celts quickly became the chief target of Roman antagonism. By a series of decisive battles the legions drove the Celts from the Italian peninsula by the end of the third century B.C.E. They continued the pressure for the next two centuries, until Celtic tribes occupied only the fringes of Europe — the Galician area of northern Spain, northern and western Gaul, Ireland, Britain, and the Caledonian highlands of the fierce, outlandish *Picti,* "the painted people" or, in Irish, *Cruithin,* who may have been only part Celtic.[23]

In his famous and self-serving *Gallic Wars,* Julius Caesar described his relentless subjugation of the Gallic Celts. His later imperial successors, Claudius, Hadrian, and Antoninus Pius, followed Caesar's example, subduing and "Romanizing" the major British tribes, establishing a western capital at Eboracum (York). In 122 and again in 142, the Romans built walls across northern Britain and Caledonia to keep the Picts and invading Irish Scots at bay. But the legions never crossed the "Western Sea" into Ireland. Archeology has shown that Roman traders, on the other hand, seem to have cultivated commercial contacts in southern and eastern Ireland, which might well have introduced Christianity there at an early date.

For two hundred relatively peaceful years Celtic Britain enjoyed the status of a Roman province, during which Christianity established itself more or less as it had throughout the rest of the empire. But beginning in 383, the legions were gradually withdrawn from Britain in order to protect Italy from increasing attacks by Vandals and Visigoths. In 410, the year Alaric's Visigoths sacked Rome to the scandal of St. Augustine (among others), the remaining troops were recalled, leaving Britain open to inevitable attacks from the pagan Irish and Picts as well as new invaders from the east — Jutes, Saxons, and Anglians.

In 476, with the ignominious deposition of the last Western emperor, Romulus Augustulus, by the German mercenary Odoacer, the Western Empire came to a quiet if dismal end. The church of Rome also went into organizational decline, largely because it had adopted the legal and governmental structures and even the territorial divisions of the empire.[24] (Even the term "diocese" originally referred to an administrative unit of civil government.)

The fifth century of the Common Era thus ended in political chaos, ecclesiastical disintegration, and disrupted lines of trade and communication. Later historians would see it as the beginning of "the Dark Ages." But two events had occurred earlier in that century that would not only transform Celtic Christianity, but eventually contribute to the recovery of Western civilization as a whole.

The first took place in 431 when Pope Celestine sponsored a minor mission to Ireland in response to reports that the Pelagian heresy was spreading from Britain. The mission was led by a prelate named Palladius, who seems to have had minimal success, and died shortly afterward, possibly in Britain. The following year, an even less auspicious mission was entrusted to an eager but untested Briton named Patricius. Then, a few decades after Patrick's unexpectedly successful career ended with his death, monasticism erupted in the Celtic churches. From those two sparks grew a blaze of evangelical energy and scholarship that would in time banish the darkness of the age.

Celtic Christianity

Medieval legends claim that the original Christian foundation in Britain was made in the first century by Joseph of Arimathea at Ynis Witrin (Glastonbury), and that his young grand-nephew, a lad named Jesus, might have traveled there with him to "walk upon England's mountains green." According to less romantic archeological evidence, Christianity came to Britain sometime in the second century and to Ireland by the fourth century, most likely as a consequence of trade with Roman Britain.[25]

The churches that grew up in Britain and Ireland endured for a very long time. If an "official" terminal date can be identified, their history as distinctive and to some extent independent bodies came to an end in 1152 with the Synod of Kells. But even when the Celtic church of Northumbria fell under English control after the Synod of Whitby five hundred years earlier, the British church was older than any Protestant denomination today and claimed to be as venerable as any patriarchate of East or West. And even the reforming Synod of Kells, which ended certain abuses and integrated the Irish church structurally with the continental church, left intact many of the characteristic features of Celtic Christianity. Some survive to this day.

During the second half of the nineteenth century, in the wake of Catholic emancipation in Ireland, the Oxford Movement, and renewed claims of papal supremacy under Pius IX, Protestant scholars emphasized the divergence of Celtic and "Roman" practices in the seventh century as evidence of a form of "proto-Protestantism" squelched by the Roman party led by St. Wilfrid at the Synod of Whitby in 663–64. Despite later partisan interpretations (including that of the Venerable Bede, writing only a century later), the conflict between the Celtic monks and the English clergy can hardly have turned on whether or not the Celtic churches were "Roman," however. Virtually the *whole* Western church was Roman.[26] Whitby resolved a struggle between competing political factions: that the king of Northumbria decided the case was not lost upon Abbot Colmán and the monks of Lindisfarne, some of whom were themselves English.[27] Significantly, the sections of the Irish church that had not adopted the new methods of computing the date of Easter and other reforms instituted in the sixth century did so almost at once. Within a century, the British church had done so as well, if reluctantly. But if unity with Rome was not in contention, as J. F. Webb aptly put it,

> What were the features of the Celtic Church that made it so obnoxious to the supporters of Rome? Not doctrinal unorthodoxy. There is no mention of dogma or theology in their quarrels, be-

cause the Celts were as much part of the Catholic Church as anyone else. The term "Celtic Church" is misleading because it suggests a separate denomination in the post-Reformation sense; in fact the Celts were completely Catholic in their views on the papacy.... Their differences were ritual and administrative, and had arisen because geographical remoteness favored the lingering on of practices elsewhere superseded, and encouraged the growth of local customs.[28]

The Miracle of Monasticism

Although monastic spirituality came to Britain and Ireland from Gaul, particularly Lérins, Tours, and Auxerre, its original home and character were Egyptian.[29] The familial, democratic, and decentralized character of North African Christianity must have endowed its monasticism with particular appeal to the Celts. For six hundred years, their churches were typified by its spirit, but one expressed in unmistakably Celtic fashion.[30]

At the height of their development in the eighth and ninth centuries, "families" of Celtic monasteries extended from Iceland to Italy. Resembling settlements or small villages, many monasteries admitted both men and women, married lay persons as well as celibates, and a variety of support personnel. Some abbots were married, and leadership was often handed down through families for generations. (In Ireland, the term *apad,* adopted from the Greek *abbas,* was displaced as a title of authority in the Middle Ages by *airchinnech* [*erenagh* in English], the term for a lay custodian. Lay abbacy was one of the abuses of the Celtic church particularly targeted by reformers such as the Céli Dé in the eighth century and St. Malachy of Armagh and St. Laurence O'Toole in the twelfth.)

Among the more austere monks, especially in periods of reform, the life-style was coenobitical, that is, the monks lived in separate cells or huts but participated in common prayer, meals, and other functions. However, there was also a tendency among the more rigorous ascetics to become hermits in the strict sense, separating from human company to undergo what came to be called the "green martyrdom," living in a remote, isolated place (*disert*) alone with God.

This quest for an intense, self-sacrificing form of Christian testimony was further expressed by the "white martyrdom," voluntary exile and death in an alien land out of love for the homeless Christ.[31] Renunciates like St. Columbanus and his companions who undertook such a life of perpetual pilgrimage came to be known as *peregrini pro Christo.* Sometimes these wanderers would simply set themselves adrift at sea in rudderless curraghs to go where the winds would carry them.[32] Others, like Columban and his disciples, had specific objectives in mind, among them the conversion of barbarian Europe.

Both the stable monks and the *peregrini* were very often capable scholars, poets, and artists. They copied, studied, and commented upon Scripture, but also pursued grammar, rhetoric, and even the works of classical pagan poets, especially Virgil and Horace. And while they preserved the writings of the Latin Fathers (Ambrose, Augustine, Jerome, Cassian, and Gregory, among others), the monks also saved for subsequent generations the prehistory of Ireland and its mythology: the Book of Invasions, the Ulster Cycle, the Fenian Cycle, and the Four Branches of the Mabinogi, among other sources, creating the earliest of all nonclassical European mythologies.[33] The great nature poetry of Ireland and Wales (and some of its love poetry) was also largely the creation of monastic hermits.[34]

Because the origins of British and Irish monasticism were largely Eastern, it proved to be fertile ground for theological and even philosophical thought as well as a tendency toward mysticism — the perception of the presence of God in the Word, worship, and the world of nature — that found expression in both prose and poetry as well as sculpture, metalwork, and painting, especially the "illumination" of manuscripts. It is not surprising that through his translations, an itinerant Irish scholar, John Scottus Eriugena, would introduce the mystical theology of Dionysius the Areopagite, Gregory of Nyssa, and Maximus the Confessor into the Latin West in the ninth century.

In time, the mystical and scholarly tradition of Celtic monasticism produced other outstanding figures in medieval theology, philosophy, and spirituality: Alcuin, Sedulius Scottus, Duns Scotus, Richard of St. Victor, and Peter of Ireland, St. Thomas Aquinas's first tutor, among them. But above all, the monasteries produced saints. And because scholarship, literature, and the arts flourished in the monasteries, they also produced the largest collection of saints' Lives in the early Christian church.

The Lives of the Celtic Saints: Texts and Transmission

Great saints appeared in the springtime of the Celtic church, during its flowering, and even during its decline. There exists a surprisingly considerable body of hagiographical lore concerning these redoubtable British and Irish figures. Although largely compiled in the Middle Ages, much of the source material is of greater antiquity.[35] Excepting the *Confession* of St. Patrick, which is not a "Life" in the hagiographical sense of later accounts, the earliest of these is probably the Life of Columbanus, written by an Italian monk of his monastery at Bobbio, Jonas of Susa, around 641, about twenty-five years after the saint's death. Cogitosus's Life of Brigid was written about 650 and was referred to as an exemplar by Adomnán in his Life of Columcille (ca. 679).[36] Together with the Lives of St. Patrick by Tírechán and Muirchú, these are the oldest of the Irish Lives, dating from the seventh century. After that, the literary floodgates opened widely.

Over a hundred Latin Lives and about sixty vernacular Lives have survived the ravages of time and human malice. Most of them are copies found in Europe, the originals having been lost in the wholesale destruction of manuscripts during the Viking raids and especially during the Reformation, when opposition to the cult of saints reached particularly violent proportions. (Ireland was not the only nation adversely affected by Protestant zeal. As Canon G. H. Doble observed, "The Reformation destroyed nearly all the liturgical books of Wales.")[37] Other factors contributed to the disappearance of liturgical, hagiographical, and cartulary manuscripts, including accident, civil discord, and ordinary attrition. The fact remains that only four Lives survived in Ireland itself, despite the overwhelming number of Irish manuscripts discovered elsewhere.[38]

U.S. President Harry S Truman once quipped, "study men, not historians." In this he echoed both Emerson, for whom "there is properly no history, only biography," and the great English historian Thomas Carlyle, who stated flatly, "Biography is the only true history." Such views would have found hearty endorsement among the Celtic Christians of the Middle Ages. But biography can be historically misleading if not approached as an account of human lives viewed in terms of purposes likely to be of greater moment to the biographers than to those they describe.[39]

Clearly, in regard to the Celtic saints in particular, relating history accurately, in the sense of punctiliously recording dates, places, persons, and events, was not of foremost interest to their biographers, nor, we can surmise, their readers. But what *was* the point of penning so many saints' Lives and, in fact, inventing them in some cases, if not to relate the history of the churches, perhaps not in terms of chronology, but certainly those of individual spiritual achievement?

The temporal gulf that distances the Celtic saints from the textual accounts of their lives presumably, if imperfectly, separates early fact from later fantasy. In bridging that gap by means of imaginative discourse, the saints' biographers initiated a conversation between long-departed holy men and women and their own generation and even with readers of later periods. By thus overcoming chronology, the Lives of the saints are able to unveil depths of meaning latent in *three* sets of lives. For behind the texts stand real persons, both the saints and their biographers, whose efforts set in motion the temporal and spiritual process that culminates in *our* reading and appropriating the texts. It is in this threefold dialogue that we encounter the spirituality of the Celtic saints.

Source Work

Most recent work on the Celtic saints has understandably focused on textual criticism, which has been a pressing need in all areas of hagiography but especially in Celtic studies, where the field may be white for harvest, but also mined with prodigious difficulties. Not least of these is determining the purpose of the saints' Lives when they were written down.

Since the 1940s, critical scholars such as Ludwig Bieler, G. H. Doble, Kathleen Hughes, Richard Sharpe, and Alan Macquarrie have alerted us to the fact that surprisingly mundane objectives lay behind many of the saints' Lives. Monastic scribes often freely invented events to score points against competing monastic groups, or to convey symbolic but pointed claims to disputed territory, or to serve warning to potential despoilers by recounting the woeful fate of those who earned the post-humous enmity of the great founders who continued to watch over their *familia*. Indirectly, of course, the Lives thereby provide valuable historical information about the times, places, and persons of the period in which were written, as we have noted.

But as Joseph Nagy has most recently argued, the Lives also contain a view of life and of the world as well as a vision of the overriding supernatural reality that shines through the *gesta* and *verba sanctorum*. In a word, the spirituality of the Celtic saints still radiates to some extent from the biographies by which these great men and women were remembered and their exploits preserved, embellished, and enlarged upon by a grateful progeny. The texts themselves speak.

But "texts" are more than manuscripts. The memory of the saints is also preserved in names — inscriptions on stone slabs and *ogam*-posts, but particularly in place names of wells, churches, and monasteries, even towns and seaports where God's friends lived, preached, and wrought their miracles of pastoral care. As Róisín Ní Mheara has recently shown, it is possible to trace the routes of Celtic evangelization through Brittany, Burgundy, Belgium, Germany, Austria, Switzerland, and Italy by studying the names of ancient towns and villages.[40] Within their churches and monasteries will also be found images and relics of the wandering saints of the early Middle Ages, who returned the light of faith to regions darkened by centuries of warfare and devastation.

In addition to biographies, inscriptions, place names, and images, evidence of the spirituality of the Celtic saints can be gleaned from a wide variety of other sources — archeology, art history (such as the study of stone crosses, manuscript illumination, and metalwork), and liturgical books such as monastic rules, missals, hymnals, calendars, martyrologies, and penitentials.[41] There are, beyond all that, ancient laws,[42] oral traditions, poetry, legends, secular literature, and the historical record contained in the various Annals of Ireland and Britain — year-by-year lists of notable social events, deaths, battles, and natural wonders, whether calamities like earthquakes and plagues or marvels, such as eclipses, comets, and similar terrestrial and extraterrestrial happenings.[43] Against all these the witness of the hagiographical manuscripts must be sifted, weighed, and measured.[44]

"Critical" history was not an invention of the eighteenth century, however. Efforts to chart and interpret human activities accurately can be traced back at least to Herodotus. Suetonius and other writers of antiquity provide authentic detail about important figures of the past, no matter how politically or personally tendentious their descriptions now appear. In the Christian church, before Bede there was Eusebius and the long tradition of *Acta* — the deeds of apostles, the passion of the martyrs, and the testimony of confessors. Such accounts are not biographies in the modern sense, for they are intended to edify as well as inform, to extol and model behavior as well as to describe it. To say that they often take liberties with fact is an understatement. But, once again, simply because such texts, including the Lives of the Celtic saints, are largely didactic documents does not rob them of all historical value.

For many reasons, Ireland, Wales, and Scotland never produced a Bede, a historian in the mold of Eusebius who set out to chart the entire saga of the English church from its most remote (and fanciful) ancestry to the present. In one sense, it was unnecessary. In the Celtic realms the Lives of the saints, taken as a whole, recounted the history of the church in Britain and Ireland in vast and intimate detail. As for Carlyle, biography for them was true history. On the other hand, the penalty for entertaining this sprawling and holy saga was considerable incoherence. Despite the work of later annalists and scribes, the chronicle of the saints (much less Celtic "history" as a whole) hardly achieved transparency even to those who lived within a span of three or four centuries. Bede himself knew nothing of Patrick or Kentigern, and Adomnán had not heard of Ninian.

Establishing the historical reliability of ancient references is, needless to say, notoriously difficult and, in some quarters, suspect. Careful scholarly scrutiny of a variety of sources over the past century has shown that a number of early "saints" are largely creatures of fiction or so laden with the preoccupations of later writers as to be practically unrecognizable. Under the reducing lens of cautious historiographers, renowned figures such as Patrick, Ninian, Brigid, and Columba may now appear in a less heroic not to say magical light, but it is also a much more human one. As Canon D. H. Doble wrote over fifty years ago,

> These Lives were written centuries after the period in which the saints lived, when the true story of what they did had been almost entirely forgotten. As they stand, they are not historical. But if we treat them primarily as literary problems and try to see how and why their writers put them together, we shall not be labouring in vain; we shall obtain some valuable evidence about the church and people in Celtic countries in the early Middle Ages, and we may even indirectly learn something about the Age of the Saints.[45]

We may, that is, learn something about the *spirituality* of those influential figures. For cautious scholarship does not necessarily *reduce* the heroic to the mundane, much less vaporize it. Just as Heinrich Schliemann was able to find Troy in 1871 by paying attention to ancient literary markers without diminishing Homer, so Leslie Alcock, John Morris, and a number of archeological and textual rebels reclaimed "King" Arthur from the realm of myth and literary fantasy without injury to the delights of Malory or T. H. White. Similarly, "real" saints in their ordinary garb can be even more inspiring to twenty-first century readers than when clad in the embellished vestments of cult without sacrificing the charm of the ancient and medieval stories, which possess their own point and purpose. The all-too-human Patrick emerging from the work of Bury, R. P. C. Hanson, de Paor, and others is a far more appealing and even awesome figure than the vengeful demigod portrayed by Tírechán or in the *Tripartite Life*.

T W O

The Saints of Celtic Britain

To begin at the beginning is not to begin with Ireland, which entered the Christian fold about two centuries after the church was established in Roman Britain. In neither instance can a particular date be assigned, nor is it known who first evangelized these Celtic islands — exactly. As noted in the previous chapter, medieval legends attributed the founding of the church in Britain to Joseph of Arimathea, who by that time was accepted as the grand-uncle of Jesus. Supposed to have been a tin trader, Joseph would have had reason to travel to Cornwall, one of the richest sources of tin in the ancient world.[1] On one of his trips there, so the legend goes, he brought his young grand-nephew along, as recalled in the eighteenth century by the visionary poet William Blake in his famous hymn from *Milton:*

> And did those feet in ancient time
> Walk upon England's mountains green?
> And was the holy Lamb of God
> On England's pleasant pastures seen?

Added around 1230 to William of Malmesbury's *De Antiquitate Glastoniensis Ecclesiae* (c. 1130), the legend holds that after the crucifixion and resurrection of Jesus, Joseph returned to Britain, bearing, it was believed, cruets containing the blood and pericardial fluid that poured from Jesus' side when he was pierced by the soldier's lance. Later generations would identify the sacred vessels with the Holy Grail. Joseph built and dedicated to the Mother of Jesus a small chapel on an island in a tidal mere known as Ynis Witrin, or the Isle of Glass.[2]

Over centuries of catastrophe and development, from this humble chapel rose the premier religious house of England, the great Benedictine abbey of St. Peter and St. Paul, where, it was also believed, Arthur and Guinevere were buried. Glastonbury was, after all, also known as Avalon, that is, Ynis Affalach, or the Isle of Apples. Not too surprisingly, in 1191 monks of the abbey unearthed a tomb containing the remains of a tall man and golden-haired woman. Inside the oak coffin was a lead cross bearing the Latin inscription, "Here lies the famous King Arthur, buried in the Isle of Avalon."[3] The bodies were removed to a new grave, but in 1539 the bones were scattered by order of Henry VIII at the dissolution of the monastery. Joseph of Arimathea himself was believed to have been buried on Hamdon Hill, a few miles away at Monacute.[4]

Near the monastery, just outside the town of Glastonbury, a tall hill rises five hundred feet above the plains of Somerset. Known as the Tor, it is believed to have been the site of an ancient Celtic temple of the god Nodens. Here, a church was built and dedicated, as was often the case in such circumstances, to the archangel Michael. By the Middle Ages, both Glastonbury Abbey and the Tor were also associated with St. Patrick, who was said to have climbed the Tor in the mid-fifth century. At the summit, he and his companion found the ruins of an oratory and writing that claimed Saints Phagan and Deruvian built it in honor of St. Michael.

Archeological evidence for Christian occupation at Glastonbury can be dated from only about 600, however, when the Celtic monastery was under the care of the abbot Worgret. There are also traces of a tenth-century monastery on the Tor, and a monastic settlement may have been built there as early as 650. In 704, the monastery at Glastonbury became Saxon under King Ina. It was destroyed by Vikings a century later, but the monastery was eventually rebuilt by King Edmund, who appointed St. Dunstan abbot in 988.

Although a natural structure, the Tor is circumscribed by an ancient maze, which was believed to mirror another maze inside the great, presumably hollow hill.[5] In Welsh legend the Tor is the abode of Gwynn ap Nudd (who may be the same as Gwydion, Nudd being a later version of Nodens), the king of Faery and lord of Annwn (the Underworld). In the medieval Life of St. Collen, Collen, a seventh-century abbot of the Celtic monastery, is taken inside the Tor to the court of Gwynn.[6] When Collen makes the sign of the cross, everything vanishes. But in later folk belief, Gwynn and Arthur still ride together on the wild hunt from Cadbury Hill to Glastonbury Tor accompanied by the Cwm Annwn, the hounds of hell.

Early Christian Britain

Christian missionaries to Britain did most likely come to Gaul and Britain along routes favored by Roman wine merchants and tin traders.[7] However they arrived, early Christian communities were in existence in southeastern Britain by the middle of the third century, and perhaps even earlier. According to Gildas, writing pretentiously enough sometime in mid-sixth century Wales, the first missionaries arrived during the reign of Tiberius, who died in the year 37.[8]

Writing in the eighth century, Bede also claims an early Christian presence. He incorporates into his *Ecclesiastical History* the story of Lucius, a legendary second-century British king who became Christian by petitioning Pope Eleutherius in the year 167.[9] Anthony Birley, in *The People of Roman Britain,* cites archeological evidence, such as the SATOR wordsquare at Manchester, found at a second-century level, which supports the idea of such an early presence of a Christian community in Britain.[10] Elsewhere in the first part of the third century, Origen of Alexandria referred to British Christians, and a few years later, Tertullian quipped that "parts of Britain inaccessible to the Romans were under the sway of Christ." Birley also enlists several early saints' Lives and martyrologies which suggest that by the end of that century, the church was considered well established. Continental testimony exists for the presence of British bishops at the Council of Arles in 314 and the Council of Rimini in 359.[11]

The First Celtic Martyrs

Some scholars have suggested that the reputed protomartyrs of Britain — Alban, Julius, and Aaron — were executed early in the third century.[12] Bede, however, maintains that the martyrs suffered toward the end of the century under the Emperor Diocletian. Here he is following the opinion of his British predecessor, Gildas, who referred to "the nine-year persecution by the tyrant Diocletian" and names "'*sanctum Albanum Verolamiensem . . . Aaron et Iulium legionis urbis,*' and almost certainly because he knew no more names, 'other citizens of either sex *diversis in locis*' — 'in various other places.'"[13]

In either case, all early writers concur that Christianity came into Britain under Roman occupation and that a number of Christians died for their faith. According to most accounts, Alban was beheaded at Verulamium, now called St. Albans, about 287. His cult was well established by 429, when St. Germanus of Auxerre first visited Britain. But the earliest account of Alban's martyrdom is that of Gildas, writing about 540. By the time St. Bede wrote his *History of the English Church and People* (c. 731), a shrine and church had been erected to Alban's memory.

Bede provides a suitably ornamental version of Alban's death in chapter 7 of his great historical saga. While still a pagan, Alban sheltered a fugitive Christian priest. Observing the priest at his prayers and vigils, he was moved to emulate the Christian's faith and devotion. After a suitable period of catechesis, Alban was baptized. When it became known that he was sheltering a Christian priest, soldiers were sent to search his house. Alban quickly exchanged garments with the priest and surrendered himself in place of his guest. Taken before a magistrate, Alban refused to offer sacrifice to idols. He was scourged to shake his resolve, but Alban remained firm. Finally, the judge ordered him to be beheaded. The other martyrs remembered with Alban, Julius and Aaron, were citizens of Caerleon who were executed about the same time. The feast day of all three is celebrated on June 20.

Not much more is known about the lives of early Christians in Britain, although archeological evidence suggests that some were comfortably well off. Pagan and Christian motifs mingle without concern in floor mosaics and decorations of the fourth-century villas. Even after the legions were withdrawn beginning in 383 and definitively in 410, Christian communities continued to exist in relative if diminishing security, as reflected in Patrick's account of his childhood in his *Confession,* one of the most important historical documents of the age. But some insight into the spirituality of these British Christians can be inferred in the writings of their most famous contemporary, an expatriate lawyer and theologian whose doctrine had enormous and lasting influence in Britain, Ireland, and southern Europe, much to the dissatisfaction of Jerome and the bishops of North Africa, most notably Augustine of Hippo.

The Perils of Pelagius

Like the other churches of the postclassical world, the Celtic churches had their differences with doctrines and practices identified with the church of Rome. Only one seemed sufficiently discordant to be branded as heretical, despite Bede's later suspicions about Irish deviations concerning the dating of Easter. It took its title from an itinerant teacher, preacher, and pamphleteer named Pelagius Britto (c. 360–c. 430), who seems to have been a well-born British layman who came to the study of theology from law.[14]

Resonating strongly with certain characteristic elements of Celtic culture and temperament, Pelagian teaching holds that human beings can achieve a state of spiritual perfection that amounts to at least virtual sinlessness, *inpeccantia.* That, of course, is the goal of most Christian exhortation from the writings of the New Testament to the present. Pelagius did not espouse impeccability, it should be noted. For him, sin and evil are real and present dangers; moral failure is always possible, if not inevitable. But the optimistic Pelagius was not at all comfortable with the grim notions of original sin and predestination to damnation emanating from the beleaguered dioceses of North Africa. Needless to say, his contrarian views, although more traditional than the innovations of Augustine and pervasive in the Celtic realms, sounded strangely in the ears of the dour Jerome and, of course, Augustine himself, whose Manichaean-tinted pessimism became more pronounced as he watched the City of Man crumble around him.

In astonishing streams of diatribe, personal invective, and ad hominem arguments, the Latin Fathers accused Pelagius of diminishing or even dispensing with the necessity of divine grace. What Pelagius actually taught was that human perfection was a possibility, and because God intended human beings to achieve their full measure of maturity, striving for such perfection was morally obligatory.

The Celtic peoples, pagan and Christian, seem to favor a grand and heroically austere spirituality (a characteristic that found expression in the life of Matt Talbot, among other recent Irish saints).[15] Not surprisingly, Pelagius's doctrine was popular among his countrymen and in Ireland. Patrick himself, Gildas, and other Celtic writers and teachers undoubtedly manifest "Pelagian" influence. In its orthodox Christian expression, this "heroic spirituality" would reach a pinnacle of development among the rigorously ascetical and saintly Célí Dé, or "Culdees," of the seventh century and later. Pelagius's doctrine was more explicitly defended in Sicily and Palestine. Eventually, however, the implacable enmity of the North Africans engineered its condemnation by several local councils, an imperial decree, and finally in 431 the Council of Ephesus.

Pelagius himself appears to have lost interest in debating his opponents and vanished into obscurity sometime after 418, perhaps returning to his native land. In any case, the reported prevalence of his doctrine in Britain prompted Pope Celestine in 429 to inaugurate a mission to expunge the now odious teaching from both Britain and Ireland. According to Prosper of Aquitaine, he placed a formidable and eminent bishop in charge of the British mission, St. Germanus (378–448), leader of the monastic school at Auxerre and teacher of Celtic saints such as Patrick, Illtud, and Brioc.

Germanus of Auxerre

St. Germanus may have been from Britain, for he was remembered there and in Ireland under the names Morgan and Garmon.[16] Accompanied by St. Lupus of Troyes, he arrived there in 429 or 430. According to the Life of Germanus by Constantius of Lyon,[17] the holy man was met at St. Albans (Verulamium) by a well-organized assembly of pro-Pelagian Romano-Celtic aristocrats. The verbal contest was hardly an easy one.

But Germanus and Lupus seem to have prevailed, if only for a time, for ten years later Germanus had to pay a return visit to disabuse the British aristocrats of their residual fondness for the teachings of their countryman.[18]

In the midst of Germanus's efforts at reevangelization, news came of a raid by Picts and Saxons. Germanus seized the initiative and led the supposedly timorous Britons into battle, endowing them with courage with the battle cry "Alleluia," thus contributing the "Alleluia Victory" to the legends of history. But this fleeting conflict with marauding pagans also provided an ominous indication that British Christians faced a much greater danger than that of overweening spiritual pride. The tide of history had turned.

From the vantage point of hindsight, Pope Celestine's decision, or perhaps afterthought, to authorize a less ambitious anti-Pelagian mission in 431 to the scattered Christians of Ireland in the person of St. Palladius is of even greater importance than the mission of Germanus. For although Palladius seems to have failed where Germanus (more or less) succeeded, he was followed a year later as leader of the Irish mission by one of Germanus's former disciples, an obscure, middle-aged, undereducated British priest named Patrick.

The *Llans* of Wales

As the native British (Welsh) Christians were pushed farther toward the Irish Sea by the pagan invaders, they relied more heavily on the characteristic features of Celtic church order rather than imperial administrative structures. In some respects, these resembled the semi-independent, local assemblies of the Irish monastic communities. But in other respects they differed very notably.

Although the church of Celtic Britain was organized along episcopal lines, as indicated in the ill-fated meeting between Augustine of Canterbury and the Celtic bishops and abbots in 603, the basic unit of the Christian community was the *llan* (plural, *llanau*), which shares some features with the Irish *cill,* the habitation of a well-known saint.[19] Just as the prefix *Kil-* still graces hundreds of Irish place names commemorating local saints, so the *llans* of Wales left their mark on the names of villages throughout the country: "All that now remains of most of the ancient *llanau* are parish churches built many centuries after these *llanau* were founded. The *Handbook* of the church in Wales lists over 430 parishes with *llan* as an element in their names, yet knowledge of the *llanau* they developed out of is very scanty indeed."[20]

Rather than a place, a *llan* was a region composed of districts of as many as three hundred inhabitants. A typical *llan* might include seven such districts. Much as the Irish monasteries were presided over with increasing frequency in the Middle Ages by lay abbots (*erenagh*), the Welsh *llanau* became the heritage of certain families, which were both guardians and administrators. As in the early churches of Palestine and the Diaspora, these were families of *saints*.

One of the most interesting of these families was that of St. Elen, the fourth-century wife of Maximus (Magnus Clemens), the usurper emperor who left Britain in 383 to embark upon a brief if stormy reign on the way to Rome.[21] (In later Welsh legend, Maximus is remembered as Macsen Wledig.) Elen, said to be a British princess and even the daughter of "old King Cole," that is, Coel, was later confused with St. Helena, the consort of Constantius Chlorus and mother of Constantine the Great, because one of Elen's sons was also named Constantine. When Maximus was killed in battle in 388, it is likely that Elen returned to Britain, where she became (as so often happens) the stuff of legend.

In addition to *llanau*, Wales had many important monastic centers, such as Llanilltud Fawr (Llantwit Major), Ynis Byr (Caldy Island), Llandaff, Llanelwy (St. Asaph's), and the great abbey at Bangor Iscoed, which reportedly numbered two thousand monks in its heyday. As elsewhere in the Celtic realms, hermits also figured prominently in the British church. In all these hallowed reaches were to be found men and women of learning and holiness, the saints of Celtic Britain.

Martyrdom did not cease in Britain with the departure of the legions, of course. In coming years, hundreds of British Christians, including monks and nuns, were massacred by the invading Saxons, Irish pirates, Picts, and other pagans. Bede records that Ethelfrith, king of Northumbria, slaughtered twelve hundred monks of Bangor Iscoed because they had prayed against him and cursed him at the Battle of Chester.[22]

With the coming of the eighth century, Viking raids added countless unnamed dead to the cloud of witnesses who gave their lives for their faith. In later centuries, as elsewhere, even Christians were not above killing each other in the name of doctrinal orthodoxy and conflicting allegiances.[23] Most early British saints are, however, monks, nuns, and bishops — pastoral leaders, missionaries, and contemplatives.

The Saints of Britain and Wales

Vae victis! Livy said: Woe to the conquered. Among their chief woes is doubtless that noted by the nineteenth-century American poet, feminist, and abolitionist Lydia M. Child: "their tyrants have been their historians!" It is thus not too surprising that so few Celtic saints grace the

Roman calendar, for Ireland, Wales, and Scotland were each subjected by their Anglo-Saxon and Norman neighbors to centuries of military conquest and cultural suppression, not least of which was religious intolerance. And the conquerors wrote the history. From a Celtic perspective, calling Augustine of Canterbury "the Apostle of England" has much in common with naming the New World for Amerigo Vespucci. As Thomas Cahill writes,

> Aidan, Columcille's beloved disciple and first abbot of Lindisfarne, has far better claim than Augustine of Canterbury to the title Apostle of England, for, as the Scottish historian James Bulloch has remarked, "All England north of the Thames was indebted to the Celtic mission for its conversion."[24]

Of many hundreds of saints of early Britain and Wales, as of other Celtic lands, all that remains to posterity is *nomina nuda,* the bare names. Not even legends survive. But Latin and later Welsh Lives exist for a number of them — including Ninian, Germanus, Cadoc, Illtud, Samson, David, Gildas, Padarn, Caradoc, Teilo, Tydecho, Beuno, Winifred, Maclovius (Malo), Paul Aurelian (Pol de Léon), Collen, and Winwaloe (Guénolé).[25] Still more names are known because they find mention in these ancient manuscripts.

The earliest of the post-Roman saints of Britain, and the fountainhead of the mission to the Picts, is Niniau (or, as he is now remembered, Ninian). Although his life is clouded by a paucity of factual information and later legendary accretions, such as his acquaintance with St. Martin of Tours (in honor of whom he or one of his successors named his church), Ninian (360–432) was undoubtedly a historical figure and one of pivotal importance to the British church.

Ninian: Father of Faith

Ninian is first mentioned by Bede, who claims him as a bishop and a Briton trained in Rome, but does not say he was a monk or founded a monastery.[26] He was born in Cumbria about the year 360 and was ordained bishop in 394, possibly in Rome, perhaps by Pope Siricius. His mission to Britain brought him to the southernmost tip of Galloway, now known as the Isle of Whithorn, where he landed in 397 and built a church at Rosnat called Candida Casa ("the White House"). From this evangelical base, Ninian and his disciples preached the gospel to the Southern Picts, those southeast of the Highland line. He is said to have died about 432 and was buried at Rosnat.

Although archeologists believe that Whithorn's earliest settlers did not arrive before the sixth century, "internal evidence of Patrick, Bede, the eighth-century poem, and Pictish archeology, points to a date for Ninian and his mission within the termini c. 461/493 (?) and 563," or roughly within several generations of the traditional date.[27] This would still allow for the Irish tradition that claims that St. Énda (c. 450–535) was for a while a disciple of Ninian. Ninian's feast day is August 26.

After Ninian, the mists of antiquity begin to dissipate sufficiently to allow us to at least glimpse a number of early British saints and even to establish some of the lines of tradition by which monastic "families" extended over several generations. Among the more notable saints of Celtic Britain are Illtud, Dyfrig, Teilo, Samson, Cadoc, St. David, the patron of Wales, his mother, St. Non, and a host of other saints of later times, such as Asaph, Gildas, Beuno, and Winifred.

Illtud

Illtud (450–535) was one of the earliest and foremost of the great monastic saints of Britain, certainly a larger-than-life figure as portrayed in the Life that was written about him hundreds of years later.[28] Like Pachomius over a century before, he was said to have been a soldier and a married man. Converted to the "life of the angels," he separated from his wife as well as his previous career, strongly reproving her when she attempted to contact him afterward. (The callousness he shows her, however hyperbolic and most likely only a later addition to the story, nevertheless testifies to the generally low esteem in which women were held among early Christian Celts — contrary to the popular notion of proto-feminism found in some recent literature.)

Illtud is claimed to have been one of the three eminent students of Germanus of Auxerre alongside Patrick and Paulinus. (In other accounts, he is said to have been a disciple of Cadoc.) His own disciples included Dyfrig, who succeeded him at the monastic school later named for him, Llanilltud Fawr, still known in its abbreviated Latinized form as the town of Llantwit Major, and (perhaps improbably) Gildas.

Even more practical than Benedict, his Italian contemporary, Illtud had agriculture on his mind, devising new ways of irrigating wasteland, improving cultivation, plowing, and even providing other monastic settlements with seed.[29] His previous military training would have supplied him with engineering skills useful in laying out plans for *llans,* as well, which in many respects resembled fortified camps. But there is evidence both in the Life and in his influence on a subsequent generation of saints that Illtud was a man of deep prayer and wisdom. He is remembered in Brittany as well as Wales, most likely because of the influence of a fellow student under Germanus, St. Brioc.

Dyfrig

Known by the Latin version of his name, Dubricius, Dyfrig is known to later ages only indirectly, but his importance is not diminished by the loss of a written Life.[30] He is mentioned in many others and even figures in Tennyson's *Idylls of the King* as Dubric, the "chief bishop of Britain," who crowns Arthur. As Bishop of Llandaff, he is also associated with Caldy Island (Ynis Byr), off the southern coast of Dyfed, where he seems to have had a retreat. His dates are uncertain, but he is generally thought to have died sometime toward the end of the fifth century.

Among Dyfrig's students are found several of the premier saints of Britain — Teilo, Samson, and Paul Aurelian, the Apostle of Brittany, who founded the monastery which became the diocese of St. Pol-de-Léon.

Teilo

Teilo, whose name is preserved in several *llans,* succeeded Dyfrig as bishop of Llandaff sometime toward the end of the fifth century (the date commonly given is 495, which would suggest a likely date for Dyfrig's death).[31] According to his biographer, Geoffrey of Llandaff, Teilo studied under Paulinus at Llandeussant. His own monastery, Llandeilo, became one of the more important places of learning in Britain. One of Teilo's illustrious disciples was the Irish monk St. Boite, who would become the founder of the great monastery known as Monasterboice.[32]

After Teilo died, according to the *Vita Sancti Teliaui,* a dispute arose among the various monasteries with which he was associated as to where he should be buried. The quarreling monks suddenly fell into a deep sleep. On awakening, they discovered three identical bodies. Without further disagreement, the bodies were buried in Llandaff, Llandeilo, and Penally.[33] (The miraculous multiplication of bodies was not uncommon in legends of the saints and solved the difficult problem of several churches laying claim to the relics. An almost identical tale is related about a dispute a few years later over the remains of St. Beuno.) Teilo's feast day is celebrated on February 9.

Samson

Another disciple of Dyfrig, Samson (c. 485–565) founded the monastery at Dol in Brittany and another at Pental, near Rouen. His Life, possibly the earliest of the British saints' Lives, was written around 610 by a Breton disciple at the request of the abbot and bishop of Dol, Tigernomalus.[34]

Samson seems to have served as abbot of an Irish monastery for a while, but was appointed abbot of Illtud's great monastery at Llantwit Major by a synodal decree and consecrated bishop in 521. Some years later, Samson was led by an angelic voice to cross the Severn estuary into Cornwall (a path that would be followed by many Irish and British missionaries in the future). There he founded four monasteries. Eventually, he migrated to Brittany, where he devoted the remaining years of his long life to founding more monasteries, beginning with Dol. He is also remembered on Jersey, Guernsey, and the Isles of Scilly, off the Cornish coast, where he may have spent some of his considerable evangelical energy.

One of the more interesting and probably factual stories about Samson concerns his efforts to obtain the release of a Breton prince named Judwal, whose father had been assassinated in a conspiracy between some Breton nobles and Childebert I, the Frankish king in Paris, who was holding Judwal captive. By means of display of miraculous power (and the threat of an impressive curse), Samson freed the prince, who returned to Brittany to exact appropriate revenge for his father's murder.

A once important saint from the early period about whom little is now known was Euddogwy (Latin, Oudoceus), who was believed to be the nephew of either David or Teilo. The *Vita Beati Oudocei* was written by a Norman cleric who was the author of the Book of Llandaff,[35] but the information from his Life, according to Canon Doble, is "completely legendary."[36] Even less is known about St. Dwynwen, a fifth-century patron of "true lovers," who was credited with conveniently restoring a dead suitor to life.

But with David of Menevia (520–88), a new chapter in British hagiography opens. For here is a figure not only larger than life in some respects, but one recognized in his own time and afterward as a saint of truly international significance. He was also the first of the saints of Britain to be formally canonized.

David of Menevia

St. David's life conforms in detail to the expected pattern of medieval saints' lives, which is to say that little historically reliable information survives about him. It also suggests he was considered so vitally important in the Middle Ages as the first "archbishop of Wales" that his Life became the model for many others.[37]

Although the circumstances of his birth may seem tawdry by modern standards, David was endowed by them with a noble ancestry stretching back to the hero of the north, Cunedda. In the more elaborate version of his life, his mother, St. Non, a nun, was ravished by King Sant of Ceredigion (Cardigan) — not an uncommon event in the lives of some illustrious saints. After suitably miraculous interludes, David was born at Henfynyw (Old Mynyw) in Cardigan and grew to manhood under the tutelage of Saints Guistilianus and Illtud. According to later tradition, Non was of Irish birth, christened Melane. She was given shelter by St. Ailbe of Emly, who baptized David at sea. Later Non became a recluse in Brittany on the banks of the river Elorn. Her grave, Dirinon, "the place of the nun," became the site of pilgrimage and was still frequented by Welsh travelers as late as 1577, when her remains were transferred to a special chapel. A holy well and oratory in the area are also dedicated to her memory.[38] It was also believed that Sant, suitably repentant, retired to a hermitage. He may be the St. Sant later venerated for his holiness of life.

According to his eleventh-century biographer, the monk Rhigyfarch, David next spent ten years at Llandeussant with St. Paulinus, another of Illtud's pupils and thus of the line of St. Germanus of Auxerre. Having chosen the life of a monk, David was guided by an angel, as the story goes, to begin a monastery at "New" Mynyw (Menevia) in the "vale of Rosina" at the very tip of the Dyfed peninsula. He would, in time, be credited as the founder of twelve monasteries, including Glastonbury, but the most famous remained Mynyw, later claimed to be the primatial see of the Island of Britain. For when on pilgrimage to Jerusalem, according to one medieval biographer, David was consecrated bishop. (Rhigyfarch claims, more plausibly, that David was elected bishop by popular acclaim at a synod held at Brefi during a crisis brought about by a reappearance of the Pelagian heresy.)

In any case, David was hardly the "priest-king" of later medieval fantasy, but, like Martin of Tours, remained a monastic figure. With a sapling as his crosier, he went about his pastoral work summoning his followers by ringing his hand bell, "Bangu" — "the dear loved one." His garb was also simple — animal skins in mild weather, with a few furs added in winter.

Not surprisingly, David's rule was austere, scandalizing the censorious but more liberal Gildas. Called "the Life of Water (*aquatica vita*)," because it forbade meat and wine, the monks' diet was restricted to fish (since they live in water), bread, vegetables, and, of course, water. Alcohol in all forms was forbidden. Animals could not be used even for plowing. Personal property was outlawed, including all monetary gifts to the monastery. Penance was prescribed for so much as referring to a book as "mine." At times, like other Celtic saints, David and his monks prayed standing up to their necks in sea water.[39]

Despite Gildas's (and our) misgivings, such ascetical heroism was not undertaken out of spiritual pride or because of some misguided notion of reparation. Like their earlier contemporaries in the deserts of Egypt and Syria, the Celtic monks perfected their singleness of devotion in such ways, repellent as they may be to modern sensibilities. As often seems the case with saints, they found such extreme practices helpful in overcoming distractions during long hours of prayer and meditation. We can only assume that their powers of concentration were proportionately strengthened.

David's reputation as a teacher of sanctity spread widely. Monks from Ireland, including St. Finnian of Clonard, crossed the sea to live under his direction, often for years. When David died at Mynyw in 588, St. Kentigern was at the monastery of Llanelwy, where in a vision he saw David's soul escorted into heavenly glory by angels.[40]

Unlike most Celtic saints, David was formally canonized by Pope Callistus II in 1120 (and thus merits his status as a "Red Letter" saint and enlistment in the Roman canon). In 1181, at the height of the struggle for supremacy between the churches of Wales and England, a great cathedral was begun at Mynyw, now called St. David's. There his bones were placed in a special tomb where they still lie amid the peaceful ruins. (Rivaling pilgrimages to the tomb of Thomas Becket at Canterbury, two pilgrimages to David's shrine were counted the equivalent of one pilgrimage to Rome.)

Behind the tales and political maneuvering inserted into the Lives of St. David lies the story not only of a real and captivating Christian leader, but also of a nation struggling to preserve its political and religious independence. In his own day, David reaffirmed unity of belief and holiness of life in the midst of disruption and doubt. Caught between political and ecclesiastical encroachment by Irish colonists on one side and land-hungry Anglo-Saxons on the other, he brought the disparate churches of western Britain into real communion.

Cadoc

A contemporary of St. David, Cadoc is said to have been a friend of the bard Taliesin and the "soul-friend" or spiritual mentor of St. Gildas as well as the founder of the great monastery of Llancarfan near Llantwit Major.[41] Associated with some of the exploits of Gildas's father, Caw Prydyn, Cadoc is also alleged to have lived for a time in Ireland at the monastery of St. Mochuda (Carthage) in Lismore and to have founded a monastery on the banks of the Liffey. On returning to Britain, he was accompanied by St. Finnian, later the abbot of Clonard and "teacher of the saints of Ireland." Other monasteries which he is claimed to have founded were at Cambuslang and Bannock.[42] Both aristocratic and lenient like his disciple Gildas, Cadoc was the author of an early Penitential. According to what is most likely an inflated account of his death by Lifris of Glamorgan, he was martyred in Italy on his way home from a pilgrimage to Jerusalem.

Gildas the Wise

Towering above other figures from the middle period of early Celtic Christianity is one of Britain's few historians. Like St. Bede, his English counterpart two centuries later, he was also recognized as a saint. Claimed as a disciple of Illtud, St. Gildas (c. 497–570) is remembered for his own writings as well as his influence on the churches of both Britain and Ireland.[43] His surviving works include *The Ruin of Britain* (a title variously given as *De excidio et conquestu Britanniae* ["On the Ruin and Conquest of Britain"], *De excidio Britonum,* or *De excidio Britanniae*), a number of letters, a fragment of a very early Penitential (the so-called Rule of Gildas), and a poetic *Lorica.*

Possibly of Pictish ancestry, Gildas was born in a northern British colony in what is now Clydesdale, Scotland, from where his family migrated to Môn (Anglesey), a large island just across the Straits of Menai in North Wales. His father was supposedly Caw Prydyn, an associate of St. Cadoc, Gildas's first teacher and spiritual guide. But if Gildas studied under Illtud, that would place him in the south. In any case, he seems to have become a monk, although some authorities believe he was a layman who married and reared a family. According to later legends, his brother Huail was an amorous rival of Arthur, who had him executed, thus earning Gildas's lasting enmity. (In Caradoc of Llancarfan's twelfth-century Life of Gildas, however, Arthur lays siege to Maelwas, king of the Summer Country, who had abducted Guinevere and was holding her in his castle atop Glastonbury Tor. The stalemate is broken only by the intervention of Gildas and the abbot.)

Gildas's *Ruin and Conquest of Britain* is a sustained diatribe against the secular and religious leaders of the recent past and Gildas's own day. He accuses them of responsibility for the pagan invasion because of a general decline of morals following the temporary halt of the Saxon onslaught following the Battle of Badon (c. 516). His book is written in a learned, admittedly pretentious, and frequently bombastic style reminiscent of the poet Virgil (whom he happily plundered): "Britain has priests, but they are fools; very many ministers, but they are shameless; clerics, but they are wolves all ready to slaughter souls. They do not look to the good of their people, but to the filling of their own bellies."[44]

While a reformer and stern critic of lax morals among the clergy, Gildas was not an extremist. He criticizes St. David's regimen for its severity, and also found Irish practices excessive. His own Rule (the so-called Penitential, one of the earliest) is comparatively mild.

That Gildas might frequently have been on the receiving end of criticism is suggested by his development of the charm-like metrical prayer or hymn used to ward off danger. Older than the "Breastplate" of St. Patrick, Gildas's *Lorica* may be the first work described by that term.[45] In true Celtic fashion, this protective prayer is threefold — an invocation of the Trinity, the saints, and angels for protection; a catalogue of the parts of the body to be shielded; and another corporeal inventory with additional petitions for safekeeping. (Compare the "Little Lorica" in *The Ruin of Britain:* " . . . my two sides are protected by the victorious shields of the saints; my back is safe at the wall of truth; my head as its helmet has the help of the Lord for its sure covering. So let the rocks of my truthful reproaches fly their constant heights.")[46]

In 565, according to the Welsh Annals, Gildas is said to have visited Ireland on a pastoral mission of arbitration, apparently resulting from a dispute between ascetics and less extreme monks. But he is also credited as championing the Roman style of tonsure and especially the new method of determining the date of Easter devised early in the sixth century by Dionysius Exiguus. Both his letters and Rule seem to indicate a continuing interest in the Irish church in later years.

Toward the end of his life, Gildas is believed to have traveled to Morbihan, in southern Brittany, where he founded a monastery at Rhuys, later known as St. Gildas de Rhuys. The Welsh Annals state that he died in 570.

Other saints of the later part of the sixth century include Asaph and Deiniol. Asaph (fl. 570) is said to have become a disciple of St. Kentigern when, according to later tradition, the latter was in exile from Scotland at Llanelwy (later called St. Asaph). When Kentigern was recalled to Scotland, Asaph succeeded him as head of the monastery and became the first British bishop of the see of Llanelwy. His feast day is observed on May 1. St. Deiniol (or Daniel) was probably the founder of the monastery of Bangor Fawr ("Great Bangor") and according to tradition was consecrated first bishop of Bangor by St. Dyfrig in 516. Among other churches dedicated to Deiniol is one at Hawarden, Clwyd. He died sometime around 580. Deiniol's feast day was celebrated on September 11.

Although his historical existence is factual, St. Beuno (d. 640), the abbot of Clynnog, became the focus of many later legends.[47] A contemporary of Cadwallon the Younger of Gwynedd (d. 634), he was the nephew of St. Cadoc. He is credited with the foundation of a number of monasteries in the kingdoms of Clwyd and Gwynedd. But his most famous exploit concerns his niece, St. Winifred (Gwenfrewi), the patron saint of North Wales.[48]

Pursued by Prince Caradoc ab Alaog of Hawarden, who was intent on wedding or ravishing her, Winifred sought refuge at Beuno's church. Just as she reached the door, Caradoc struck off her head with his sword. According to the legend, Beuno replaced her head on her body and restored her to life. A miraculous spring appeared at the site of the miracle. Later, Winifred founded a nunnery there. She is said to have died (naturally) around 650. Her relics were removed to the Abbey of Shrewsbury in 1138.

Beuno was considered to be a powerful opponent of other royal figures, having cursed Cadwallon for cheating him and similarly deprived the sons of King Selyf of their royal inheritance. After Beuno's death, a dispute arose among the monasteries he founded over where his body was to be buried. A deep sleep overcame the mourners, and when they awakened, they found three identical coffins before them. And thus Beuno was buried at Clynnog Fawr, Nevern, and Bardsey Island.[49] His feast day was observed on April 21.

A host of other saints have been honored among the churches of Wales, including Afan, Brioc, Cadfan, Caradoc, Curig, Doged of Llanddoged, Dogfael, Einion, Padarn, Pedyr, Severa, Tydecho, Tysul, and Sant.[50] Cornwall (Cerniw) had its own particular saints as well. Eleanor Duckett notes that among them, Petroc is remembered by the town name of Padstow, "Petroc-stow," St. Carantoc is similarly honored at the village of Crantock, and Mawgan is remembered at Mawgan Porth near Newquay.[51] Piran is celebrated as the patron saint of miners.

The Road to Whitby

Beginning late in the fifth century, waves of invading Angles, Jutes, and Saxons relentlessly drove Christian Celts to the west and north as well as south to Armorica or Brittany (Britannia Minor). Respite was won for a generation by a series of battles in which the legendary war chiefs Ambrosius Aurelius and Arthur "Pendragon" stemmed the tide of invasion. They could not reverse it, but the delay enabled Christian missionaries from Ireland and Iona, as well as native British monks, to begin the slow, dangerous process of evangelization. Irish monks were especially successful in the kingdom of Northumbria, where the mission of St. Aidán radiated from Lindisfarne. By the end of the century, assistance was also sent from Rome. In 597, the year St. Columba died on Iona, the monk Augustine was sent from Marseilles as emissary of Pope Gregory the Great to inaugurate the conversion of the Anglo-Saxons. Arriving in

Kent, he found an abandoned church at Canterbury, which he made his headquarters. But Augustine's success was limited to the southeast, and he died only seven years later.

Unsure of himself and inflexible in dealing with others, Augustine's bad manners botched his best chance to harmonize his missionary efforts with those of the British church at a pivotal meeting in 603 with representatives of the bishops and major monasteries. Differences in liturgical practice between the Celts and the Roman mission produced additional friction, as it had elsewhere.

In 601, Pope Gregory had dispatched another monk, Paulinus, to assist Augustine's mission in southern England. When King Edwin of Northumbria, who had seized the crown of Northumbria, married Ethelburga of Kent in 625, Paulinus accompanied her north. Edwin was duly converted and appointed Paulinus bishop of York. But in 633, after Edwin's death in battle with the British chief Cadwallon, Paulinus returned to Kent with Queen Ethelburga. King Oswald, who had become Christian under the tutelage of the monks on Iona, reclaimed the crown of Northumbria and sent to Iona for a leader capable of reviving the missionary work Paulinus had begun. Aidán was eventually selected. Made bishop in 635, he established his see not in a city, but on Lindisfarne, an island off the coast of Northumbria. There he also founded a school that included among its pupils twelve English boys who would in time become leaders of the English church. Among them were Chad, his brother Cedd, Wilfrid, Cuthbert, Ecbert, and Eata — all future bishops and saints.

Oswald died in battle in 642 and was succeeded by the saintly Oswin of Bernicia. In 651, Oswin was betrayed and killed by his cousin, Oswy. Aidán died, it is said, of grief, only a few days later. His successors, Saints Finan (d. 661) and Colmán, were also Irish monks of Iona, and their custom was Celtic. In this they were followed by King Oswy, now king of Northumbria and a Christian. But the queen, Eanflaeda, was from Kent and followed the custom of Canterbury, where the newer Roman methods of calculating Easter and administering the rites of baptism and tonsure were in force. Colmán resisted the efforts of Eanflaeda and her Kentish followers to replace the Celtic practices, but the English faction had a powerful champion in Wilfrid, who had accepted the new Roman customs when studying at Canterbury many years before.

In 663 King Oswy convened a synod to resolve the conflict, which only superficially concerned disputes over the calculation of the date for Easter and the shape of the monastic tonsure. The deeper struggle was that between Canterbury and Lindisfarne for ecclesiastical dominance (as it would be between Canterbury and St. David's in the west). The site

Oswy chose for the debate was the double monastery at Streanaeshalch, later called Whitby by the Danes, which had been founded in 657 by the formidable abbess St. Hilda (614–80) with the assistance of Bishop Colmán.[52]

A member of the Northumbrian royal family, Hilda had been baptized by Paulinus of York in 627. In 649, Aidán had consecrated her abbess at Hartlepool. Sympathetic to the Celtic tradition, Hilda sided with Colmán and Oswy against Wilfrid and the queen. Colmán argued that Celtic practices were based on the ancient custom of the Apostle John. A skilled debater (unlike his Irish opponent), Wilfrid retorted, just as erroneously, that the Roman usage was that of St. Peter and cited the Council of Nicea. Overwhelmed by this appeal to authority, Oswy conceded, lest he be found, as he said, resisting the keeper of the keys of heaven.

Colmán's dilemma was not posed merely by his reluctance to relinquish an ecclesiastical custom hallowed by centuries of Irish tradition. A more important issue, one significantly overlooked in most discussions of the Synod, is whether a secular ruler had in fact the authority to decide a purely ecclesiastical dispute. By agreeing to the debate, Colmán as well as Wilfrid perhaps implicitly acknowledged that authority. Colmán may also have counted on Oswy's ruling in favor of the Irish tradition followed by his court. That does not alter the fact that the king was exerting authority where it could be plausibly, if not entirely safely, contested.

Streanaeshalch was far from being Canossa, however. Faced with the perhaps unexpected verdict in favor of the English delegation, the Irish saint chose to resign his see. With his Irish disciples and thirty English monks, he left Lindisfarne for Iona and ultimately Ireland. He was succeeded as bishop by another of Aidán's pupils, the great (and thoroughly Celtic) Cuthbert, who may have been Irish himself.[53] Oswy, Hilda, Cuthbert, and many other adherents of Celtic custom obediently adopted the practices of the English church, no doubt to the dismay of native British Christians in the west who were engaged in a far more desperate struggle to preserve their lands and way of life.[54]

In Ireland itself, where the primacy of Rome had been neither doubted nor imposed, conversion to the new method of calculating Easter, and presumably the form of tonsure, had been accepted in the south as early as 634. Early in the next century, the Irish of the north also acceded.[55] In the end, perhaps the Synod of Whitby was not the decisive event Bede thought it was.[56] But although the Irish church would maintain its Celtic character and spirituality for many centuries more, the Synod of Whitby raised a rock against which it, too, would eventually founder: the supremacy of the English church in what were about to become "the British Isles."

But that was yet to come. In the early centuries of the Celtic churches, there was considerable exchange between the Irish and British monastic traditions, despite the differences that would increasingly distance them from each other linguistically. Latin remained a useful medium of conversation and writing, and the long sojourns of Irish monks in Britain and British monks in Ireland and Scotland undoubtedly meant that the dialectical differences could be surmounted.

Birinus, who some scholars claim to have been Irish, evangelized Wessex.[57] Among undoubtedly Irish saints in Britain, Finnian of Clonard and many other young Irish monks came to study with Illtud, Dyfrig, Samson, and David. St. Domnoc, a member of the royal O'Neill clan, is said to have studied under David and then returned to Ireland, where he became a hermit at Tibraghny in Kilkenny. (Domnoc seems to have been the beekeeper at Menevia. As he was departing for Ireland, the bees swarmed about his curragh despite his efforts to send them back to their hives. Finally, David blessed him and the bees and sent them all to Ireland. And it is said this is how honey first came to the monasteries of Ireland.)[58]

The Irish prince Columba and his followers undertook life-long pilgrimage from Ireland to evangelize the Picts of western Scotland. Aidán, Colmán, and perhaps Cuthbert were only three of the more famous immigrants who traversed the northern arc from Ireland to Iona and then crossed the rolling lowlands of Pictland to preach the gospel in the central and eastern parts of Northumbria.

Irish monks were also active in the south. St. Fursa, who was born in the west of Ireland about 575, evangelized East Anglia. The son of a prince of Galway and nephew of St. Brendan of Clonfert, Fursa became a monk on Inchiquin, Brendan's island. About 631, King Sigebert, who had been converted by Columban while in exile among the Burgundian Franks, invited Fursa to East Anglia. Accompanied by his brothers, St. Faolán Ultán, St. Gobain, St. Dicuil, and others, Fursa settled at Cnobbersburg (Burgh Castle), near Yarmouth, where Sigebert himself retired in time to end his days as a monk.

Famous for his visions, which Bede narrates, Fursa probably influenced Dante's depictions of heaven and hell in the *Divine Comedy*. After some twelve years as abbot, Fursa left Faolán in charge and set out on a pilgrimage to Rome. He never returned to England, remaining among the Franks as a missionary. After establishing a monastery at Lagny, near Paris, at the invitation of Erchonwald, Clovis's majordomo, Fursa died in 648 at Mazérolles and was later entombed at Péronne.[59]

The presence of numbers of British and even English monks in Ireland is also evident from accounts associated with "Mayo of the Saxons," as well as incidents in the lives of various saints such as Gildas and Ecbert. It has often been assumed that all the founders of the great Irish monastic traditions were themselves Irish. But as Alan Macquarrie writes, for instance, "It has been shown that 'St. Finnian of Moville' was probably not a native Irishman who came to Scotland to study, but a Briton who worked as a missionary in Ireland in the middle of the sixth century."[60] A whole monastery was established in Mayo for the English monks of Lindisfarne who departed after the Synod of Whitby.

St. Gerald of Mayo (d. 732), the son of an Anglo-Saxon king, was one of the English monks at Lindisfarne who accompanied Colmán to Iona and then to Ireland.[61] He is held to be the founder and first abbot of the monastery of Mayo. The most remarkable item in his Life concerns a recurrence of plague in 664, which came about when the joint high-kings, Diarmait and Blaithmac, convened the nobility of Ireland to resolve the problem of over-population. At Tara, the nobles proposed to call on God to send a pestilence upon the lower classes in order to reduce their numbers. Féchin of Fore approved of the proposal, but Gerald opposed it. Féchin and his party "fasted against God" to obtain their demand. The pestilence resulted, killing multitudes, including Féchin himself and many nobles and ecclesiastics. Gerald, however, was spared.[62]

British saints undoubtedly evangelized Scotland as well. Although Kentigern, the patron of Glasgow, is generally considered to have been an Irish Scot, he may well have come from Britain, as his name (Cyndeyrn) suggests. His seeking refuge at Llanelwy when driven from the region of Glasgow would thus stand to reason, unless it is pure fantasy (as some commentators believe). Being British would also account for his visionary connection with the death of St. David.

The greater number of British missionary saints traveled south, however, where ties of language and kinship established a natural connection. As Saxon pressure pushed the native Celts from their traditional homelands in the midlands of Britain, many migrated from Wales and Cornwall across the Muir Nicht, or Southern Sea (*Mare Austrum*), to Armorica. With them they took the memory of their saints, and other saints followed them who are still remembered in the names of towns, churches, wells, and rivers, among them Samson, Non, David, and Paul Aurelian with his Irish companion, Mawes. Illtud's name can be found at Lanildut in Finistère and the chapel of Loc-Ildut in Sizun; relics are located at Landebaeroin and Coadout. Landévennec was founded by Guénolé, Alet by Malo, Trécor by Tudwal. Dedications to Brioc can be found in St. Brieuc-de-Mauron and St. Brieuc-des-Iffs in Brittany, as well as at Caulnes in Côtes du Nord, where he is patron of the diocese of St. Brieuc.[63] Other British saints remembered in Brittany include Meugan, Cybi, Carranog, Cadog, Brioc, Dochau, Padarn, Pedroc, Sithney (Sidney), and Tysilo.

Conclusion

The gradual assimilation of the Celtic church in Britain by the Anglo-Saxon church centered on Canterbury, which gradually emerged as the primatial see of England. But the hard-won "triumph" of the English church over the native Celtic church was not to endure. With the conquest of England by William of Normandy in 1066, the structure, style, and, above all, the leadership of the church was quickly converted to Norman-French. William replaced English bishops everywhere with picked supporters, drawing on the Benedictine abbeys of the north, particularly Bec, from which he plucked both Lanfranc and then Anselm for starters. Both were shrewd and capable administrators, saintly, and learned. Anselm in particular ranks among the greatest of the medieval thinkers. But to expect that the high-born French-speaking Norman abbots would fail to grasp the character and spirituality of the Celtic churches is not to underestimate them. The pattern had been set long before. Needless to say, the struggle for supremacy continued, as St. David's and Llandaff strove against the claims of Canterbury.

As for the spirituality of the many and remarkably different saints of Britain and Wales, in most respects they resemble their kindred in Ireland, Scotland, and Brittany. Resolute, sometimes impetuous, and often driven to extremes of devotion and self-sacrifice, they were great lovers of God and neighbor, at least those who left them in peace. Their awareness of God's proximity found expression in the arts as well as narrative: manuscript illustration, poetry, metalcraft, and the sculpture of stone crosses. Much of their art was lost in the course of religious persecution and calamity over the coming centuries, but the joyful experience of God's radiant presence in Creation and human experience has been captured in much of surviving poetry of the Middle Ages and after.[64]

In terms of its teaching, Oliver Davies aptly epitomizes the genius of both the ancient and modern Britannic and Welsh spiritual tradition:

> It is Trinitarian, Incarnational and cosmic; and thus, in a profound sense, creationist, embracing multiplicity, physicality and universality. In addition, it is a form of Christianity which affords a special value to the creativity of the poet as one who both instructs the people and speaks before God on their behalf, and yet who also in himself embodies the inspirational power of art which is the sublime gift of God. It is above all here, in the implicit notion of

a poetic priesthood in which the poet — touched by a particular grace — speaks in and for the spiritual community, that we find the most distinctive aspect of the Welsh tradition.[65]

Indeed, the spirituality of Christian Britain remains a living tradition, linked over the centuries to the present in the lives of famed and unknown saints, preachers, and poets. Today, moreover, the eighteenth-century hymns of Ann Griffiths and the poetry of David Jones (Gwenalt), Saunders Lewis, and R. S. Thomas in our own century, no less than the great legacy of church music, art, and literature of the past, clearly belong not merely to Wales and Cornwall, but to the whole Christian world.[66]

Early Christian Ireland

Patrick, Brigid, and Columba

Bernard Lonergan once observed, as I recall, that for the Irish, every-thing comes in threes (including God). That might explain better than the story of the shamrock how Christianity, with its concept of the tri-une God, found comparatively quick acceptance among the Hibernian Celts.[1] It might also help explain why Ireland has three principal pa-trons — Patrick, Brigid, and Columba (Columcille). But Ireland honors hundreds of other saints, whose memories are preserved in textual Lives, place names, and legend. Such a cloud of witnesses is inevitably plural-istic and wildly diverse, as might be expected. But most of the known saints are monks, bishops, and nuns. Women and lay people are woefully underrepresented, not least because the hagiographers were invariably monks. This uneven distribution is not a particularly Irish phenomenon, as Kenneth L. Woodward has amply demonstrated in regard to Christian saints in general.[2] And it is worth noting in this respect that the spiritu-ality of early Ireland is not much different from that of other Christian lands in the medieval period.

However that may be, Ireland became Christian if not all at once, over a comparatively short period and relatively bloodlessly. That Christians were killed in early Christian Ireland we know from Patrick's *Letter to the Soldiers of Coroticus*, but only rarely because of their faith. On the other hand, it has been supposed that Palladius, Patrick's predecessor, may have met a martyr's death,[3] and, according to the prologue of the *Senchas Már*, the "Great Collection" of legal tradition, Patrick's charioteer, Odrán, was killed in a random act of murder by an agent of King Laoghaire as a test of Patrick's faith.[4] Thousands of Christians would also die at the hands of the Vikings as well as pagan raiders and even their own kinsmen. Others, like Faolán and Kilian, would perish as missionaries among barbarians in Europe. Despite all that, Ireland is not famous for the "red martyrdom," but rather, from the earliest times, for being the land of saints and scholars.[5]

Sources of Sanctity

The major sources of Lives of early Irish saints are three fourteenth-century Latin collections. The most important is the *Codex Salmanticensis,* now at the Royal Library in Brussels, which contains forty-seven complete or fragmentary lives of Irish saints.[6] The *Codex Kilkenniensis* exists in two manuscripts now in Dublin and contains twenty-eight Lives. Two copies of the *Codex Insulensis* are in the Bodleian Library, Oxford, and two in Dublin, copies of a lost original. These collections contain thirty-eight Lives, some of which repeat those in the *Codex Kilkenniensis.*[7] The two collections from these Latin and Irish saints' Lives edited by Charles Plummer early in this century remain standard resources.[8]

The fifteenth-century Book of Lismore contains a number of saints' Lives in Irish, which were edited and translated by Whitley Stokes.[9] Other materials are found in the *Silva Gadelica,* edited and translated by Standish H. O'Grady,[10] and single editions of the Lives of Patrick, Brigid, Columba, and other saints.[11] The indispensable modern reference for the Lives of the Irish saints is still James Kenney's monumental *Sources for the Early History of Ireland: Ecclesiastical* of 1929, reprinted in 1997 by the Four Courts Press, Dublin, the first part of a projected two-volume encyclopedic catalogue of manuscript materials. Regrettably, Professor Kenney did not live to complete the second volume of secular materials.

The Pre-Patrician Saints of Ireland

Embedded in the tradition of the early Irish saints is the belief that four bishops besides Palladius preceded Patrick, testifying significantly if perhaps vaguely to the presence of a Christian community in Ireland from the fourth century or even earlier. A late legend holds that an Irishman named Altus serving with the Roman army in Palestine witnessed the crucifixion of Jesus and returned to Ireland as its first evangelist.[12]

Pre-Patrician missionaries from Britain and Gaul almost certainly established small communities, even monastic settlements, along the southeastern coast, in what is now Wicklow, Wexford, and Waterford. But in 431 the deacon Palladius, thought by many to have been Germanus's assistant, was sent by Pope Celestine I as first bishop of Ireland, according to Prosper of Aquitaine. Prosper himself was vehemently anti-Pelagian and even very cross with those he considered semi-Pelagian, such as John Cassian. He does not, however, seem to worry about Ireland's susceptibility to heretical doctrine so much as its need for evangelization. Pope Celestine, on the other hand, had reason to be concerned with the influence of Pelagius in both Britain and Ireland. Pelagius's doctrine seems to have been well-known to later Irish scholars, including *peregrini* such as Faustus of Rietz and St. Columban. Thousands of citations from Pelagius's commentaries on Scripture and other works are found in sixth- and seventh-century Welsh and Irish manuscripts.[13]

However they came, evidently Christians were in Ireland as much as a century or more before either Palladius or Patrick arrived. Thus later hagiographers faced the delicate problem of interlarding the earlier traditions with the exploits of Ireland's most famous saint, a task they accomplished with sometimes startling results. Of the four traditional pre-Patrician saints of Ireland, only two are likely to have exercised their ministry before 432: Déclán of Ardmore in County Waterford, near Youghal Bay, and Ciarán of Saighir, near Birr in County Offaly. Ailbe, the patron saint of Tipperary, and Ibar of Begg-Eri (Beggery Island), Wexford, seem to have lived at the same time as Patrick or, like Énda, just afterward.[14]

Déclán of Ardmore

Déclán, whose feast is remembered on July 24, is believed to have been a prince of the Déisi (clans) of Munster, many of whom were expelled from Ireland in 368.[15] The events narrated in the medieval Life[16] are clouded by standard hagiographical attributes: his foreshadowed birth, a trip to Rome where he is consecrated bishop by the pope, his possession of a magical bell by which he summons a ship to return him to Ireland, and, on occasion, his raising the dead. Déclán's principal church was at Ard-Mór, in Waterford.

At one point, the Life of Déclán portrays Patrick coming to his assistance when Déclán's preaching was rejected by the pagan Déisi. Like Ailbe, Ciarán of Saighir, and Ibar, Déclán resisted Patrick's unwarranted intrusion into his affairs, but in the end he, like the others, "came to be of one mind with him."[17] In short, the Patrician churches led by Ard Macha (Armagh) eventually prevailed over the older churches of the south. But the proverb endured, "Let Déclán be the Patrick of the Déisi, let the Déisi be with Déclán till doom."[18]

Ciarán of Saighir

Like Déclán, Ciarán of Saighir was of royal lineage and born in Munster, on Clear Island, the southernmost point of Ireland.[19] Like Déclán, he was also made a bishop in Rome after years of study at St. Martin's monastic settlement in Tours. On his return to Ireland, Ciarán became a hermit in what is now County Offaly. Like St. Francis of Assisi, he is especially associated with wild animals who were his earliest "monks" — among them a hawk, a fox, and a boar.[20]

True to form, Ciarán raises the dead and utters powerful and effective curses as needed. His monastery at Saighir became the "place of resurrection" of the Kings of Ossory. Nearby, his mother, St. Liadan, founded a monastery of nuns. Ciarán of Saighir is sometimes identified with St. Piran of Cornwall (the patron of miners), where he is supposed to have migrated and died and where Piran's feast day on March 5 coincides with his.[21]

Patrick: The Apostle

While hundreds of the names of lesser-known saints have come down to us in the Lives and other ways of remembrance, Patrick, Brigid, and Columcille are *the* saints of Ireland. While neither the first nor the last of even the major saints, their reputation and popularity remain truly global. Two of this holy trio represent the finest flower of Celtic monasticism — Brigid of Kildare and Columba (Columcille) of Í (or Hii, or Iona, as it was later called). But the greatest of these is Patrick.

Patrick's mission to Ireland may have been instigated by Germanus when he received news of Palladius's death.[22] It has also been surmised that Patrick was commissioned by a group of British clergy and was, after some acrimony, consecrated a bishop — perhaps irregularly. Accompanied by several companions, probably British monks ordained as secular clergy, Patrick's first attempts at conversion seem to have met with meager success. Eventually, however, he was able to establish Roman diocesan structures, including a hierarchy of bishops, priests, and deacons, but it is unclear whether he founded any monasteries.

Like St. Paul, Patrick seems to have avoided evangelizing in areas already known to be Christian, mainly the southeastern coastal areas associated with Ailbe, Ciarán, Declán, and Ibar. His field of endeavor was the northern and central portions of Ireland, and he seems to have made his primary foundation at Ard Macha, near the ancient "capital" of Emain Macha.

He was most likely born in northwestern Britain at the very end of the fourth century.[23] The date of his birth has been hotly contested for centuries. Some Annals give 396 as his birth date, placing his mission between 432 and the reputed date of his death, March 17, 461.[24] In his *Confession*, Patrick tells us that he was the son of a Roman Celt, a deacon and minor public official named Calpornius, himself the son of a priest, Potitus. (A later Life claims that Potitus was the son of a deacon named Odissius, and that Patrick's mother was named Concessa. He is also provided a sister, Lupaid, who figures prominently in his later story.) The family most likely lived among other Romanized Celts in northern Britain, the region known as Rheged, despite a tenacious claim that he was born in what is now Scotland.[25]

When he was about sixteen, Patrick was captured by Irish raiders along with many "thousands" of other British Christians, including his sister and brother according to later accounts. He was later sold to a local chieftain, Miliucc, for whom he tended flocks on Sleamish Mountain in County Antrim. A nominal and only half-educated Christian, Patrick tells us that in the six years of slavery that followed, he learned to pray and eventually experienced moments of divine presence that enabled him to survive. When he was about twenty-two, he heard a voice in a dream urging him to escape. Traveling on foot some two hundred miles, he came to a port where a ship was ready to sail, probably somewhere along the coast of Wicklow or Wexford.

With difficulty, he secured passage as a member of the crew. After landing most likely on the coast of Gaul, now increasingly ravaged by Vandals and Huns, the traders and their companion traveled inland for twenty-eight days, possibly with a consignment of wolfhounds. At one point, only Patrick's prayers saved them all from starvation, for they soon came upon a small herd of swine. Eventually, Patrick obtained his freedom, and, after several years of wandering, made his way back to his parents' home in Britain.

He was not to stay. One night in a dream he heard voices calling him back to Ireland. He seems next to have sought and obtained permission to evangelize the pagan Irish and was most likely sent to Auxerre to study under St. Germanus, who had been commissioned to oversee the Celtic churches. But Patrick's mission to Ireland seems to have begun before he had completed his studies because of the early death of Palladius, who had been sent as a bishop to the Irish "believing in Christ" in 431.

Even though Patrick still lacked some of even the rudimentary theological training of the clergy of his time, Germanus ordained Patrick deacon, priest, and finally bishop. His mission did not begin, however, without opposition from some of the British clergy, who objected to his lack of proper preparation. (Toward the end of his life, their opposition would resurface, piercing the aged missionary to the heart and occasioning his rough, magnificent *Confession*.) In any event, accompanied by several monks ordained as clergy, Patrick set out for the land of his former captivity in the year of Our Lord 432.

At first Patrick's mission, like that of Palladius, was hardly a triumph. According to later accounts, he first set out to convert his old master, Miliucc, who not only refused to see Patrick, but burned his house down around himself in protest. Patrick's first significant convert seems to have been a local chief named Díchu, who gave him a barn at Saul in County Down for his first church.

Later traditions find Patrick (implausibly) confronting the high king of Ireland and his druids on the Hill of Tara in County Meath. Arriving on the eve of Easter, which coincided with the vernal equinox, Patrick lit a fire on the Hill of Slane, some miles away but apparently visible at that distance, in serious violation of the law of the land. King Laoghaire's druids warned the king that he must extinguish it or it would burn forever, displacing the native cult. Brought to Tara, Patrick engaged in a brief war of words and signs with the druids. The king was sufficiently impressed that he granted permission for Patrick to evangelize throughout the land.

Symbolic or not, Patrick's struggle against the druids won him converts and enabled him to establish a number of churches, eventually selecting Ard-Macha (Armagh) for his headquarters. For as long as forty years, he labored to win the pagan Irish to Christ. By the time of his death, the church was solidly if not yet widely established in the midlands and the north. Following the model he had brought from Britain and Auxerre, Patrick instituted diocesan structures, including a hierarchy of bishops, priests, and deacons. He seems not to have founded monasteries, although he may have established some houses for nuns, as reflected in this famous passage from the *Confession:*

> Among others, a blessed Irishwoman of noble birth, beautiful, full-grown, whom I had baptized, came to us after some days for a particular reason. She told us that she had received a message from a messenger of God who admonished her to be a virgin of Christ and draw near to God. Thanks be to God, on the sixth day after this she most laudably and eagerly chose what all virgins of Christ do. Not that their fathers agree with them; no — they often even suffer persecution and undeserved reproaches from their parents; and yet their number is ever increasing.

If not nuns, such women may well have served in a ministerial capacity.[26]

The Welsh annalist formerly known as Nennius lists Patrick's death in 457. Irish Annals give the date of his death as 493, but many historians still accept the traditional date of 461. He did not die at Armagh, however, but at the site of his first church, Saul, and was buried at Downpatrick.[27] (Conflicting legends have Patrick buried at Glastonbury, among other places, where thousands of Irish pilgrims traveled throughout the Middle Ages.) His successors strove to consolidate his foundations, and Rome probably assisted in some measure. John Morris observes that "half a dozen Irish bishops are recorded in the generation after Patrick's death, each established in a separate kingdom, most of them resident within walking distance, or a short drive, of a royal center."[28] But the struggle to preserve Patrick's accomplishments would be difficult and, in the end, depend less on diocesan structures than the peculiar genius of a spirituality Patrick awakened among his new converts.

Writings

Patrick's own spirituality is best known from two documents from his own hand — a pained and angry letter of excommunication sent to the soldiers of an impenitent Christian king in Britain, Coroticus, who had attacked and enslaved some of Patrick's converts, and his *Confession*, composed toward the end of his life as a final statement of fidelity to Christ and the church.[29]

Since Patrick was a Romanized Celt, his spirituality was not wholly alien to the pagan Irish. But as a slave, he came to know God ever more deeply in the great natural beauty of the land as well as the austerity of his condition. Through dreams and visions, the divine Spirit informed his inner life, which he nurtured by prayer and the study of Scripture. He felt Christ present in the assurance of grace:

> I saw him praying in me, and he was as it were within my body, and I heard him above me, that is, above the inner man, and there he was praying mightily with groanings. And meanwhile I was stupefied and astonished, and pondered who it could be that was praying in me. But at the end of the prayer he spoke as if he were the Spirit. And so I awoke, and remembered that the Apostle says, "The Lord is our advocate, and prays for us."

It is customary among scholars to regard Patrick's Latin with condescension, if not contempt. Although he was born and reared among provincial Celtic Britons and his Latin reflected his early schooling, or lack of it, he was familiar with contemporary literature and was, as Nora Chadwick wrote, "no isolated rustic, but...a partaker in the cultural thought of western Europe of his own day."[30] In her recent analysis of the form and content of Patrick's writings, Sr. Máire de Paor has demonstrated that Patrick was a skillful rhetorician, structuring his work in a subtle as well as vigorous style by no means inferior to other compositions of the time.[31] Self-deprecation and protestations of clumsiness were an expected aspect of well-mannered prose and no doubt reflect something of Patrick's natural modesty. But the directness and force of his words, especially the Letter to the soldiers of Coroticus, reveal the author as a man of resolution and courage as well as honesty.

In addition to the *Letter* and the *Confessions,* some sayings attributed to Patrick may well be authentic. One of the most interesting asserts the close connection between the Irish church and Rome: "The church of the Irish [*Scotorum*], or rather of the Romans; in order to be Christians like the Romans, you should chant among yourselves at every hour of prayer that praiseworthy cry, Kyrie eleison, Christe eleison. Let every church which follows me chant Kyrie eleison, Christe eleison. Thanks be to God."[32]

The Legend

Much of the rest of what is known about Patrick is seen through the magnifying lenses of folklore and legend. Over the centuries tales grew in proportion as his importance developed in the minds of hagiographers. Eventually, he appears in the joint guise of a semi-divine pagan hero, a Hebrew prophet, and a Christian wonder-worker. In Muirchú's Life, when Coroticus (Corictic) scorns Patrick's repeated demands to free the Christian slaves he has captured and make amends for those he killed, the stubborn and presumably Christian king turns into a fox and runs into the forest, never to be seen again.[33]

Although there are accounts of miracles and dramatic if improbable encounters between Patrick and the druids, pagan chiefs, and people of Ireland in the Lives by Bishop Tírechán and Muirchú,[34] the ninth-century *Tripartite Life of Patrick* set the tone for many of the outlandish exploits of the later Lives. Kathleen Hughes comments,

> It shows us a saint protecting his own, extracting privileges, quick to revenge injuries, a devastating curser. It does not present a morally elevating picture of Patrick. The saint sulking on the mountain top "in evil mind" and brow-beating the angel to wring greater benefits from God is poor spiritual teaching. As Sechnall rightly remarks of his colleague, there is very little charity. We see Patrick driving his chariot three times over his sister Lupaid for her unchastity, but it is she who prays that he will not take heaven from her lover and his offspring. [...] Angels serve Patrick, even performing menial jobs like cleaning the hearth for him.[35]

But, she is quick to note, "The writer is presenting the dignity and power of Patrick, and if he belittles Christian teaching it does not seem to matter."[36] For his real intention is consolidating the authority of the Patrician church, particularly Armagh, against the rival authority of Kildare, Ard-straw, Clonmacnois, and, ultimately, Iona. In the later Lives of Patrick, as in many other saints' Lives, property claims are made and validated symbolically: Patrick visits Ailbe and Déclán and requests or even offers assistance, but what is at stake is the relationship between their respective monasteries centuries after they were dead and buried.

As Patrick grows in importance, stories testify to his power and great-ness by showing him awakening the dead, including the long-dead pagan masters, to interrogate them about points of law and history. Sometimes he even baptizes them. He is capable of striking his opponents dead with a word and restoring health, sight, and wholeness to the infirm. He not only drives the ancient serpent from this new Eden; like Marduk, he confronts the mother dragon in her watery lair and subdues her. All is preserved in the memory of places and peoples.

Patrick's Purgations

The Irish penchant for rigorous austerity is associated with St. Patrick in three northwestern sites: Croagh Patrick in County Mayo, Lough Derg in Donegal, and St. Patrick's Bed on Maumeen Mountain in Connemara. Each represents a confluence of Christian and native Irish spirituality and none of them was probably ever seen by the historical Patrick. But to this day, the major sites of penitential pilgrimage in Ireland are Croagh Patrick and St. Patrick's Purgatory in Lough Derg. It was there, according to tradition, that Patrick prayed, fasted, and, like Jesus in the wilderness, overcame the forces of evil.

Croagh Patrick. Many thousands of pilgrims make the arduous climb to the summit of this volcanic cone in Mayo, often crossing the loose scree and precipitous ridges barefoot, especially on the last Sunday in July. According to tradition, in the year 441 Patrick fasted on the moun-tain, known locally as The Reek, for forty days and forty nights. From here he also banished the snakes from Ireland. But its pre-Christian an-cestry is much older, as are some of the austerities connected with it, such as the circumambulations, now centered on the statue of Patrick (seven times) and the oratory (fifteen times). "Reek Sunday" itself coincides with the ancient harvest celebration of Crom Dubh.

According to the *Tripartite Life,* while Patrick fasted and prayed on the mountain in order to wrest guarantees from God for his followers and the people of Ireland, God sent an angel to dissuade him. When that failed, God prompted clouds of blackbirds to harass him. Refusing to leave, Patrick dispersed his attackers by singing cursing psalms at them and ringing his bell. His diligence was amply rewarded when an angel appeared to announce that God would grant his petitions: he would be able to save souls, no Saxons would ever dwell in Ireland, and the Irish would remain faithful to Christ until the Day of Judgment.

Lough Derg. Patrick's combat with evil was not finished on Reek Mountain. The great serpent known as the Devil's Mother escaped to Lough Derg in Donegal, where he confronted and overcame her by more prayer and fasting.

Although Patrick's connection with Lough Derg rests solely on legendary grounds, each summer several thousand pilgrims devote three days to prayer and fasting on bread and black tea on a small island now called St. Patrick's Purgatory. Apparently, the "founder" of the Purgatory was the British saint Dabeoc, who migrated from Wales in the fifth or sixth century and who established a monastery on the island.[37]

Despite repeated and ultimately draconian efforts by the Protestant English to suppress pilgrimages to the site, Patrick's faithful followers have continued their trek and penances there for over fifteen hundred years. The church on the island is now a basilica.

The Heritage

In his captivating if not always entirely cautious exaltation of early Christian Irish contributions to European culture, *How the Irish Saved Civilization,* Thomas Cahill makes the extraordinary claim that Patrick was "virtually the first missionary bishop in history."[38] While hyperbolic, considering the failed mission to Ireland credited to Palladius and the presence of pre-Patrician Irish saints, the fact remains that Patrick presents an astonishing figure, unmatched in his missionary zeal since the early Christian era of the Apostles and first disciples of Jesus. The force of his spirit would affect the faith of all Europe and eventually the whole Christian world.

But at the time of his death, Patrick's achievements remained tentative. A new effort was sorely needed, one that would preserve Patrick's struggling young churches and also advance his program of conversion, as he had advanced those of his predecessors. That far-reaching development was the product of a spirit different from Patrick's but compatible with it, the genius of Celtic monasticism.

Patrick, after all, was himself a Romanized British Celt, trained, moreover, in the continental, more "Roman" church of Gaul, with its emphasis on episcopal authority and diocesan structure. The organizational form of the church Patrick bequeathed to Ireland was, accordingly, diocesan and episcopal. But the infrastructure of imperial administration that supported the churches of Gaul and Britain, enabling them to survive in the aftermath even of the collapse of the empire in the fifth century, was lacking in Ireland. Neither civil nor ecclesial Roman forms of government had touched Irish shores or penetrated the upper reaches of Alba (Scotland) before the mission of Palladius, whose failure to introduce the latter as the basis for a resilient church community seems evident. Nor did Patrick's efforts establish a lasting episcopal-diocesan structure. A different model was needed, one more suited to the social and political channels of the Irish people, especially in the face of a resurgent paganism.

An Irish solution to an Irish problem presented itself in its distinctive monastic structure and spirituality, one established by a handful of saints, principal among them Énda of Aran, Brigid of Kildare, and Finnian of Clonard. Within a century of Patrick's death, a wave of missionaries followed them from Ireland to spread the gospel to Scotland, Northumbria, and mainland Europe from Brittany and the Low Countries to Germany, Denmark, Switzerland, and Italy. By the twelfth century, Irish cloisters were established as far away as Russia.

Irish Monasticism

Celtic monasteries predate those of Benedict, and perhaps those of Cassian and Honoratus as well. The first small communities may have been established early in the fourth century near outposts of Roman Britain in Cornwall, Wales, and southern Scotland by refugees or pilgrims from Egypt and Palestine. The more proximate source was Gaul, particularly the monastic schools of Lérins, Tours, and Auxerre. The form of British and Irish monasticism was therefore Eastern, but its language and liturgy were Latin.

The story of Irish monasticism in particular is neither uniform nor placid.[39] Periods of growth and high spiritual attainment were followed by decline and renewal. Especially noteworthy in this regard is the movement known as the Céli Dé, the Servants of God, who flourished in the eighth and ninth centuries.

Although several methods of approaching the beginning and growth of Irish monasticism have been offered, Cardinal Tomás Ó Fiach plausibly suggests that the movement developed over four generations. The first founders were more or less contemporaneous with Patrick: Énda of Inish-Mór and Finnian of Clonard, as tradition maintains. Énda (450–535) was reputed to have been a disciple of Ninian at Rosnat, although his monastery was independent and fundamentally original. From his monastery at Killeany, a second wave of founders spread monastic life eastward: another Finnian, who may have been British, went to Magh Bile (Moville) on Strangford Lough, Eugene to Ardstraw, and Tighernach to Clones.

Finnian of Clonard (d. 549), who derived some monastic features from Britain, became the "teacher of the saints of Ireland," sending out the next group of saintly monastic founders, who are known collectively as "the Twelve Apostles of Ireland": Ciarán the Elder to Saighir; Columba to Derry (546), Durrow (556), and Iona (563); Ciarán the Younger to Clonmacnois (about 550); Brendan to Clonfert (554 or 559); Molaise to Devenish; Cainnech (Canice) to Aghaboe; Mobhí to Glasnevin; Colmán (or Colm) to Terryglass; Sinell to Cleenish; Brendan (the Elder) to Birr; Ninidh to Inismacsaint; and Ruadán to Lorrha in north Tipperary, where the famous Stowe Missal was written. (In fact, such as we know it, Ciarán of Saighir was even earlier than Finnian. The names of the "Apostles" were also variable. Sometimes Finnian himself is included, along with Comgall of Bangor, and others.)

A third generation of foundations was independent of Clonard: Bangor, founded by Comgall (d. 603), Glendalough, by Kevin (d. 618), Tuam, by Jarlath (c. 550), and Cork, by Finbarr (Bairre), around 623. Still another monastic tradition was that founded primarily by and for women: Kildare was established by Brigid early in the fifth century, Killeevy by Monenna before the end of the fifth century, Killeedy in County Limerick by Íte around 550, and Clonbroney in County Longford by Samthann in the seventh century.

By the end of the seventh century thousands of monastic sites existed in Ireland, of which hundreds of their ruins can still be found. Among some of the more famous are Déclán's monastery at Ardmore, County Waterford; Armagh, County Armagh, Patrick's chief establishment; Cashel, County Tipperary; the Dingle Peninsula, where solitary hermits built their distinctive "beehive" cells, Scelig Mhichíl (Skellig Michael), and Church Island, all in County Kerry; Kells, County Meath, a Columban foundation; Kilmacduagh, County Galway; Inishmurray and Sligo Abbey, County Sligo; and Monasterboice, County Louth, the site of Muiredach's cross. Later medieval establishments include Mellifont, County Louth (1142–1539, refounded in 1938); Jerpoint Abbey, near Thomastown, County Kilkenny; and Ennis Friary, Ennis, County Clare.[40]

Reflecting the tribal character of Celtic society, Irish monasticism was inescapably political. But although many of the Irish founders were of royal blood, such as Énda and Columba, little if any aristocratic distinction between the monks and other members of the monasteries or even those outside ordinarily intruded on their life. Having royal connections often helped during tense moments of confrontation, but tribal enmities also proved perilous in times of conflict.

Generally, Celtic monasticism tended to be decentralized, pluralistic (if not exactly democratic), and loosely organized. Some monasteries admitted both men and women, married lay persons as well as celibates, and a host of artisans and other workers. In some instances, abbots were laymen and even married. Leadership could be handed down through families for generations.

Unlike the Benedictine tradition of the south, rules varied from monastery to monastery. Monks often wandered from one to another seeking a compatible form of life. (As elsewhere, however, wandering monks or "gyrovagues" were frowned on by the jurists.) If they failed to find one, as in the story of Brendan of Clonfert, they could always begin their own monastery and frame still another rule. Consequently, dozens of Latin and Old Irish and Latin monastic rules existed, attributed to saints from Ailbe to Columban, although almost invariably composed by later disciples.[41] The rules consist largely of metrical and therefore more easily remembered maxims concerning (among other things) prayer, perseverance, silence, mutual service, the sacraments, reverence, diet, mutual dependence, and moral behavior, including that of the wider monastic group, even nobles and kings. As a whole, they provide a surprisingly inclusive glimpse of the spirituality of early Christian Ireland up to the medieval period.

As monasteries outgrew their boundaries, a group of monks or nuns would be sent out to establish "daughter" communities. At the height of their development in the eighth and ninth centuries, the resulting networks, or *familiae,* of Irish monasteries stretched from Iceland to Italy. The form of life tended to be coenobitical, that is, the monks lived in separate cells or huts but shared worship, meals, work, and other activities. But the more austere ascetics tended to become hermits, separating themselves from common life to live in remote, isolated places alone with God: "the green martyrdom." Such austerity also found expression in the "white martyrdom," voluntary and permanent exile in imitation of the homeless Christ. As in the lives of Columban and his followers, this often meant a life of perpetual pilgrimage.

Life in a Celtic Monastery

Structurally, Celtic and especially Irish monasteries resembled settlements or small villages surrounded by a wooden palisade or stone wall. At first, the monks lived in small "cells" constructed of wood or wattle-and-daub. Several might share the same cell if large enough. Communal buildings — the church, refectory, and guest house — occupied another section of the enclosure. A third portion was given over to buildings needed by craftsmen and farmers, including individual and family living quarters.

Politically, the monastery was governed by an abbot or abbess (*apad,* and later *comarba,* or "heir" of the founding saint) assisted by a principal minister (in fact a vice-abbot, *tánaise apad*). A group of older members served as a council, giving advice and assistance when needed. Among them were the guestmaster, the cook or cellarer, the infirmarian, the porter, and the teams of copyists. The steward, or *oeconomus,* supervised the monastery's material resources.

In some monasteries the diet was spare and restricted, as at Menevia. Bread, fruit, vegetables, fish, honey, and water were common staples. The more austere rules were vegetarian and nonalcoholic. Others permitted the consumption of meat as well as wine, beer, and mead.[42] Monastic clothing consisted of a white linen or woolen tunic, accompanied in severe weather by a coarse cloak and hood. The monks usually wore sandals for journeying, but otherwise went barefoot.

The daily schedule in an Irish monastery was a rhythmic sequence of prayer, work, study, and penitential practices. The ordinary worship included the canonical "hours" of psalms and readings and the Eucharist, which was not celebrated daily, but once or twice a week. Long litanies or *loricae* were composed by monkish poets, probably for processional usage. In the course of time, many acquired almost magical significance as charms to ward off evil. A superb and famous example is *The Deer's Cry,* attributed to St. Patrick, but in fact a much later composition.[43]

Work consisted of agriculture — sowing, weeding, harvesting, milling, and storing — as well as brewing and animal husbandry, such as tending flocks. Monks would also have been weavers and machinists, making and repairing their own tools. But unlike the Benedictines, the Irish monks did not consider manual work to be part of the *opus Dei.* Despite the edifying tales in the Lives of the founding saints, as the monasteries grew more prosperous and powerful, the monks delegated such labor to the lay *manaig,* or monastic clients, in order to devote themselves to prayer, study, and pastoral care. While prayer was of paramount importance, especially the chanting of the psalms, study was valued greatly in the life of the monastery, as was copying manuscripts: the Scriptures, the commentaries of the Fathers, even the classical Latin poets, Horace and Virgil especially. The copyists also preserved the ancient mythology of their pagan ancestors. Liturgical books were of particular importance. Early British texts were almost wholly destroyed during the religious strife of the sixteenth and seventeenth centuries, but surviving Irish liturgical works include the Stowe Missal, the Book of Armagh, the Book of Deer, the Book of Dimma, and the Book of Mulling. Personal devotional literature of both monks and lay people has also survived, including the small "pocket gospels" intended for travel.

Penitential practices also figured prominently in the spirituality of these ancient saints. In addition to fasting and silence, they restricted the hours of sleep and engaged in physical austerities such as the *crosfigil* (praying for an expended period with their arms outstretched), or repeated genuflections, or praying submerged in icy water up to their necks. "Castigation" or the "discipline," a ritual beating with switches or a strap, was administered daily, except for Sundays and major feasts. Repugnant to Christians today, monks included, such austerities would have been considered an ordinary part of religious life in that tougher, more heroic age.

Although attracted to the wilderness and *diserts* of solitary communion with God, Irish monks were not antisocial. Even their asceticism accomplished a missionary function by its very example. Active missions to pagan areas of Pictland, England, and the European mainland began as a form of solitary witness rather than an attempt at direct evangelization. Imitation succeeded, and as Christianity spread northward and eastward from Ireland and Wales, a true missionary impulse developed. By the ninth century, wandering scholars had succeeded the missionaries, returning the light of learning as well as faith to much of postimperial Europe.

Preaching and pastoral care were important spiritual activities for the monks. The thirteen sermons of St. Columban may not be typical of preaching in the seventh century, but there is no particular reason apart from his genius to assume they were unusual. Stories abound of saints — both men and women — attracting large numbers of people to hear them preach by ringing the hand bells they carried with them for that purpose. Spiritual direction and the administration of the sacraments occupied much of their time. The *anamchara,* or "soul-friend" — confessor, advisor, and mentor — was an indispensable companion on the spiritual journey, especially for monks and nuns. In the Martyrology of Oengus the Culdee, St. Brigid tells a young monk whose *anamchara* has recently died, "anyone without a soul-friend is a body without a head; eat no more until you find a soul-friend."

Confessional practice was of special importance to the monks, who eventually developed the Penitentials in order to foster an equitable system of penances. In all monastic traditions, great emphasis was placed on charity, especially kindness and hospitality to the poor, sick, and suffering, who often resorted to the monasteries in times of famine, injury, and illness. Such devotion to the poor was conspicuous in the lives of the great saints.

Monasteries served as schools, for many noble families as well as common people fostered their children to the saints for their schooling, particularly sons and daughters who were destined for life in the church.

Monasteries were also home to works of art, some of them brilliant and precious, including the carved stone crosses that marked various boundaries inside the monastic enclosure. Metalcraft from the eighth and ninth centuries reached a high degree of perfection as seen in the surviving chalices, crosiers, jeweled book covers, and shrines for the bells, bones, and belts of sainted founders.

The greatest of the artistic achievements of the monasteries are the metalwork and especially the illuminated manuscripts of the seventh and eighth centuries, whose calligraphy, illuminations, and portraiture rank among the art treasures of the world. The Book of Durrow, the Book of Kells, the Lindisfarne Gospels, and the Gospels of Chad, among others, represent only a few of the hundreds of similar, perhaps even greater works irretrievably lost to accidents of time, the predations of pirates, and the deliberate destruction undertaken by the iconoclastic English Puritans of the seventeenth century.

Decline and Fall

Plundering attacks on the monasteries were not new when the Vikings first appeared in Irish waters during the final years of the eighth century. Pagan Irish, Pict, and Saxon pirates had attacked them for centuries. Even Christian chieftains attacked monasteries for political reasons or simply for booty. As early Christian Ireland had neither banks nor police, monasteries were often utilized by their neighbors for storing valuables as well as grain. Of course, highly ornamented liturgical vessels, book covers, crosiers, shrines, and reliquaries were of special interest to the Vikings. The monasteries suffered greatly from such attacks, and countless monks and nuns were killed. But the monasteries survived. The Vikings themselves hardly even merit mention in the Lives of the saints. The decline and fall of Irish monastic life had other, more ordinary causes. Prosperity was not least among them.

The growth in worldly wealth led inevitably to worldly greed and ambition. A martial age was tempted to solve its problems by martial means. Battles between monasteries in Cork and Clonfert over disputed lands in Tipperary and between Durrow and Clonmacnois on issues probably of mere prestige supply tangible proof of decline.[44] In response to this even greater peril to the spiritual life of Old Ireland, a reform movement arose in the south that would, for at least a century, breathe new life into the monastic tradition.

God's Clients

The most auspicious reform movement in Irish monasticism is attributed to the Céli Dé (singular: Céle Dé), the "servants" or "clients" of God, anglicized as "Culdees."[45] Originating early in the eighth century in connection with Mochuda's monastery at Lismore, the movement was strongly influenced by St. Samthann, the abbess of Clonbroney. Other leaders included Ferdachrich (d. 747), the abbot of Darinis in south Munster, Mac Oige (d. 739), and especially St. Maelruain of Tallaght and his friend and fellow monk Mael-dítruib. According to Máire and Liam de Paor, "The Célí Dé were especially active in the south and east, and their chief centers were the monasteries of Finglas and Tallaght — 'the two eyes of Ireland' — both within a few miles of the present city of Dublin."[46]

The reformers were especially gifted poets. The great nature poetry of the early Middle Ages is largely a product of their influence. But their chief contribution was a determined spirituality that in resisting the increasing secularization of the monasteries, married monks, and strife between rival monasteries, returned to the austere spirit of the founding saints of centuries past.

Several Irish rules are attributed to the Célí Dé, and their influence was certainly felt in others, particularly the Rule of Mochuda (St. Carthage). *The Prose Rule of the Célí Dé* represents the daily customs of Tallaght transcribed some time after the death of Mael-ruain, about whom little else is known.[47] It begins with dietary regulations and the conduct of the refectory, testifying to their importance to the reform movement. There are prescriptions concerning confession and the role of the *anamchara*. A proponent of stability, Mael-ruain carefully regulated the practice of pilgrimage, guiding his monks away from the famous sites of Europe but rather to the north and west of Ireland. Liturgical practices were described in some detail, including the curious practice of treating a pregnant woman who is seriously ill by reading the baptismal rite over a bowl of water and giving it to the woman to drink. As the blessed water passed over the fetus it was "as baptism to it." Other matters include study and the payment of tithes and other fees. The overall thrust of the regulations is to reduce the control of lay stewards and clients over the life of the monastery. Another document from a later period, *The Monastery of Tallaght,* is less a rule than a journal of monastic observances in the *oentú* ("unity," or family of monasteries) belonging to Tallaght.[48]

Despite the considerable successes of the Célí Dé reforms in Ireland and Scotland, their period of influence was curtailed by the appearance of the Vikings at the end of the eighth century. According to Máire and Liam de Paor, the raids of the Northmen were directed chiefly against the monasteries, which had grown prosperous and often wealthy. But Tallaght and Finglas were among the first to be attacked.[49] While Tallaght endured, Finglas survived for only about a century. O'Dwyer notes that the first entry in the Annals of Ulster occurs in 763 and the final one in 867.[50]

According to John Ryan, the coming of the Vikings in 795 brought the reform movement to an abrupt end:

> Not one monastery in the land escaped, certainly not one of any prominence. Some ceased to exist. Others became wraiths or phantoms of what they once had been. The holding of two or more abbatial titles showed that the day had come when the abbot was not a monk at all. A number of monasteries survived rather as schools than as places of worship and prayer, with the abbot as headmaster.[51]

By the end of the first millennium, the decline and fall of the Celtic church was past remedy. Pressured relentlessly by Anglo-Saxon, Danish, and finally Norman invaders, the resistance of the British and eventually the Irish churches to domination by non-Celtic churches isolated them geographically and then turned them increasingly in on themselves. In Ireland, factionalism, favoritism, and ultimately political control had been reintroduced by war chiefs and then the Norman invaders from England. By the beginning of the twelfth century, the need for yet another and far more searching reform was clearly apparent. In promoting that reform, St. Malachy of Armagh and St. Laurence (Lorcan) O'Toole, the greatest and most saintly figures of the Irish church of the time, also supplied the death blow to the old Irish church and indeed to the Celtic churches as a whole.

Increasingly, hopes for reform had looked to the European mainland, where new orders of monks and soon, mendicant friars, were reviving the Christian church in ways Irish monasticism, exhausted by centuries of conflict and abuse, could not. Even before the Norman invasion, the church was reorganized into dioceses ruled by powerful and even saintly bishops. Continental monks, preeminently the Augustinians and Cistercians, were introduced from the mainland. Both processes were accelerated by the Anglo-Norman conquest that began in the later part of the twelfth century and continued into the thirteenth.

Over the next century, some of the old Irish monasteries became episcopal sees, others adopted the Augustinian rule, while still others were demoted to serve as parish churches. Several monasteries survive as towns even to the present day, such as Armagh, Kildare, Kells, Killaloe, and Derry. Others were gradually abandoned, including Clonmacnois, Durrow, Glendalough, Kilmacduagh, Nendrum, and Monasterboice.[52] But it would be true to say that in these new developments the light of learning and evangelical zeal carried to the wastelands of Europe in the seventh and eighth centuries had returned to Ireland four hundred years later. Had the last Irish monks been able to peer ahead into the coming centuries, they would probably have realized that as the ominous shadow of political and religious oppression loomed ever larger in the east, these new energies would be sorely needed for the survival not only of their way of life, but of the Christian faith itself as they knew it.

In the beginning, perhaps the greatest of the Irish monastic saints were granted prescience, for the foundations they created were solid and lasting. Patrick's life work, realized beyond expectation in the monastic tradition as a whole, attained its initial and most illustrious achievement in the first of the great abbesses, Brigid of Kildare, and the prince of Irish missionaries, Columba, who justly share with Patrick the dignity of national patronage.

Brigid of Kildare: Queen of the South

Known as "Mary of the Gael," St. Brigid of Kildare (ca. 450–525) is one of the most beloved of saints.[53] Her first biography was written in the seventh century, long after any reliable historical information had been displaced by tales of her remarkable powers and career, largely, it would seem, the product of the undeniable admiration in which she was held.[54]

Cogitosus and Ultán identify her father as Dubhthach, a pagan noble of Leinster. According to Cogitosus, her mother, Brocseach (or Brocessa), the daughter of Dalbronach, was of noble parentage, while Ultán and the later Latin Lives claim that Brocseach was a slave in the household of Dubhthach. She may have been both noble and a secondary wife, or *adaltrach,* which might account for her being "banished" to Faughart near Dundalk in County Louth before Brigid's birth in 457. In any case, Brocseach was a Christian, and Brigid seems to have been baptized at an early age despite being fostered to a druid as a child. She also seems to have been reared as a noblewoman for whom her father had planned a suitably dynastic marriage. But Brigid chose to dedicate her life to Christ as a nun. Cogitosus provides a suitably dramatic dispute with Dubhthach over the matter, which was decided by the king of Leinster, himself a Christian, in Brigid's favor. With seven other girls, Brigid was clothed with the veil of a nun.

In later accounts, Brigid was consecrated at Magh-Teloch by two bishops, St. Mel of Ardagh and St. MacCaille of Longford (d. 480, according to the Annals of Ulster). By accident, St. Mel mistakenly read over her the prayer for the consecration of a bishop. When St. MacCaille informed him of his error, Mel replied that it should stand, but that Brigid would be the only woman to hold the episcopal office in Ireland! Cogitosus may have known of this legend, and his introductory remarks describe her in plainly episcopal terms, but he adroitly avoids mentioning it or St. Mel, for that matter.

Brigid seems to have established her first house for her nuns near Croghan Hill, but having been given a tract of land by the king of Leinster, she moved it to Druim Criadh, in the plains of Magh-Life (the Liffey Valley). There she founded what would be the most famous monastery in Ireland near an ancient oak tree that might have formerly been sacred to the druids. Her monastery was thus known as Cell-Dara, "the church of the oak." (The tree itself is said to have survived to the tenth century.)

Kildare

According to a tale found in Gerald of Wales, Kildare had been a pagan sanctuary where a ritual fire had been kept perpetually burning by an order of virgins. Some scholars have suggested that as the last of this line, Brigid transformed the pagan sanctuary into a Christian shrine. However that may be, Brigid and her nuns inherited the sacred fire, which was surrounded by a hedge through which no male was allowed to pass. The fire was maintained until the suppression of monasteries during the Reformation.

Whatever its pagan origins, the Kildare Brigid founded was a double monastery, with herself presiding over the nuns as abbess while St. Conlaed was abbot of the monks. This tradition continued for centuries, according to the lists of succeeding abbesses and abbots, or *comarbai*, found in the Irish Annals. Moreover, the abbess of Kildare claimed to be head of all the nuns of Ireland, and Cogitosus claims that Conlaed was, in effect, bishop primate.

At Kildare, Brigid also founded a school of arts and letters, presided over by St. Conlaed, who had been a master craftsman before Brigid plucked him from his hermitage to be her co-founder. It produced its own Gospel Book, which, had it survived, would have at least rivaled the Book of Kells. Lost at the time of the Reformation, this great masterpiece was described in the twelfth century by Gerald of Wales, whose enthusiasm for the Book of Kildare overcame his habitual disdain for the Irish when he acclaimed it as so beautiful it could only have been the work of angels, as the legend of its creation affirmed.

As a Christian evangelist, Brigid seems to have traveled extensively in her chariot, founding churches and monasteries, obtaining freedom for captives, offering advice where it was wanted and probably where it wasn't. She negotiated the release of hostages, healed lepers, assisted the poor, and returned sight to the blind and speech to those who were dumb.

According to Cogitosus, Brigid herself was taught to read and write as a child. Her monastery was justly famous for its learning as well as the arts, which flourished under Conlaed. She also had a particular rapport with nature, from weather to plants and animals. Many of her reputed miracles involve the protection of flocks and even of wild animals.

Conlaed died some years before Brigid and was buried under a suspended silver crown on the left side of the high altar in the cathedral. When Brigid died, most probably around the year 550, she was buried in a casket of precious metals and jewels under a golden crown at the right of the altar, opposite Conlaed's tomb. Late in the ninth century, her relics (and presumably those of Conlaed) were removed to Downpatrick because of the threat of Viking raids. There they were interred in a tomb said to contain the bodies of Patrick and Columba. According to the *Catholic Encyclopedia,* in 1186 the relics were solemnly translated to Downpatrick Cathedral "in the presence of Cardinal Vivian, fifteen bishops, and numerous abbots and ecclesiastics."

In 1283, three Irish crusaders took the head (or hand) of St. Brigid with them as they departed for the Holy Land. They seem only to have reached Portugal, where a plaque in an ancient church in Lumiar records their burial. A relic of Brigid is preserved in a chapel dedicated there to her memory.

The Legend

Cogitosus seems to have been a monk at Kildare, who sometime in the mid-seventh century was assigned to compose a life of the foundress based on what materials he could assemble.[55] In fact, his biography is little more than a collection of miracle stories, of real value only for the light they shed on the church and secular society of his own time. Strikingly absent in his account is any mention of St. Patrick.[56] Most of the miracles Cogitosus reports might seem more appropriate for a fertility goddess than a nun, but that may well have been his point.[57] Her first miracle as a child was to produce a sudden supply of butter, saving her mother from shame. When she took the veil before Bishop MacCaille, she knelt to touch the wooden base supporting the altar. Miraculously, the wood regained its life, "as green as if the sap still flowed from the roots of a flourishing tree," and, by repute, cured infirmities and diseases of the faithful who touched it thereafter.

Brigid exercised particular power over natural events. Her crops remained dry in a rainstorm; at her prayers, a single cow produced an endless stream of milk; she was able to hang her cloak on a sunbeam.

When sheep were stolen from her flock to discredit her, the number was miraculously intact at the end of the day. She was able to transform water into beer and make salt from a stone. Like many Irish saints, she had a particular affinity with animals as well. At her behest, a wild boar joined her herd of swine, escaping hunters. Wolves also acted as swineherds for her.

Brigid's miracles of healing were as notorious as her nature wonders. Cogitosus describes breathlessly how, following the example of Christ, she opened the eyes of a person born blind. She cured a dumb child, healed the lame, and tended to lepers. Certainly questionable from a modern (and even ancient) point of view, however, is the account of her terminating an unwanted pregnancy. It seems that a young nun turned to her in distress when, as a result of a fall from grace, she found herself in the family way. Brigid prayed over her, "exercising the most potent strength of her ineffable faith," and the fetus disappeared. The miscreant nun was restored to both health and, through penance, her state in life. (Cogitosus's obvious approval of this procedure is reflected in other stories in the Lives of the Irish saints, such as Ciarán of Clonmacnois, who preserve women, often nuns, from shame and disgrace by "disappearing" the fetus. By contrast, in the *Tripartite Life*, when Patrick's sister Lupaid similarly sins, he runs her down three times with his chariot, presumably destroying her body to save her soul, but spares the life of her child and her lover.) But Brigid is also capable of punitive acts. When rustlers steal her cattle, the river rises against them and sweeps them away.

Among the series of tales about St. Brigid and various animals, at least one, as Kathleen Hughes observes, "does not seem to belong to a well-recognized folk-pattern, that of the king and the wild fox."[58] When a courtier sees a fox entering the king's hall, thinking it to be a wild animal, he kills it, unaware that it is the king's special pet, trained to do a variety of tricks. Furious, the king orders the man to be executed and his family sold into slavery. When Brigid hears of the harsh sentence, she harnesses her chariot and speeds to the palace to plead on the man's behalf. On the way, in answer to her prayers, God directs a wild fox to leap into her chariot and accompany her to the palace.

The king refuses to revoke his sentence unless the man produces another fox as cleverly trained as the one he had killed. When Brigid releases the fox she has brought into the court under her mantle, it performs all the tricks that the king's fox had done, amazing the audience. So the king relents and releases the man. Brigid had one more trick up her own sleeve, however. After the man had been released and she had returned to Kildare, the wild fox, oppressed by the noise and bustle of the court, made its escape. Although the fox was pursued by riders and hounds, Cogitosus happily concludes by telling us that it made fools of them all, "fled through the plains and went into the waste and wooded places and so to its den."[59]

Brigid's Legacy

Although Brigid was the special patron of Leinster, her popularity in Ireland soon rivaled that of Patrick himself, not least because of the great store of tales that grew up around her. Kildare grew to be the richest and one of the most powerful monastic churches until the Norman invasion. Because of the prominence Brigid gave learning, she became the special patron of scholars, especially those training to be priests. She is, in addition, the patron of poets, milkmaids, and a variety of other professions.

In Scotland, the Pictish war chief Nechtan-Mór declared Brigid patron of Abernathy in the sixth century.[60] She was likewise patron of the Clan Douglas, whose members were buried in the church dedicated to her. In the nineteenth century, Cardinal Moran was able to list more than twenty more dedications along the western coast and in the Orkney Islands. Alexander Carmichael discovered that she was one of the principal patrons of the people of the Western Islands. Brigid was also honored in England. Mary Ryan D'Arcy tells us that Gunelda, the sister of Harold of England, fled to Burgundy after the Battle of Hastings with a cloak once worn by Brigid. Nineteen pre-Reformation churches were dedicated to her, including St. Bride's in London's Fleet Street. Liturgical offices in her honor are found in several old European breviaries: Venice, Gein, the Lateran, and Quimper in Brittany. She was commemorated in Cologne, Maestricht, Mayence, Würzburg, Constance, Treve, Strasburg, and Paris. From Iceland to Italy, parish churches, hospitals, and chapels were dedicated in her name. In 1807, Bishop Daniel Dulaney of Kildare founded a teaching order in Brigid's honor, the Congregation of St. Brigid. Its members now minister in Ireland, England, Australia, New Zealand, and the United States.

For centuries among Irish Christians, making "St. Brigid's Crosses" has been an annual custom on the day before her feast day, February 1, which corresponds with Imbolc, one of the four great festivals of the old Celtic year. According to tradition, the custom commemorates the practice of St. Brigid herself, who once visited a peasant (or, in some versions, a chieftain) who lay dying. Lacking a crucifix, she wove a handful of rushes into a cross for him to hold.[61]

And in Ireland, a traditional greeting is still "Brigid and Mary be with you."

Columba: The Warrior Dove

Columba's name is variously rendered in classical and contemporary sources. Columba ("Dove"), his Latin name, is preferred in the earliest Latin Lives and seems to have been the form he used himself. His Irish nickname has been spelled Colm Cille, Colum-cille, and Columcille by various authors.[62] It means, as the Old Irish Life in the *Leabhar Breac* tells us, "Colum of the Church," an epithet he gained as a child because of his predilection for visiting the little church at Tulach Dubhglaise, near his birthplace. He was baptized Colum by the priest to whom he was fostered. But according to later writers his given name was Crimthann, which in Old Irish means "Fox."[63] Connections between the saint's name and animals were not missed by the early hagiographers.

Columba was born in 521 of a royal clan of the Uí Néill, according to later accounts in Gartan, County Donegal. His father, King Fedelmid, was descended from the legendary Niall Noigiallach ("Niall of Nine Hostages"). Columba's grandfather, Fergus, was the son of Conall Gulban, the eponymous ancestor of the Clan Connell, from whom the region of Tyrconnell was named. Eithne, Columba's mother, was said to be descended from Cathoair Mór, the most famous of the kings of Leinster. At the time of his birth, his half-uncle, Muirchertach mac Erc, was king of Tara. But Columba was destined for the church rather than kingship. We are told that an angel told Eithne that the son she would bear would be a prophet of God. At seven, according to his greatest biographer, the ninth abbot of Iona, St. Adomnán (or, in older works, Adamnán), he was fostered to a priest named Cruithnechin. When he reached his maturity, he went to Magh Bile in County Down to study under St. Finnian. Possessing keen poetic talent, Columba also studied for a time as a deacon in Leinster under the guidance of a poet named Gemmán. But under the younger St. Finnian at Clonard, he was later ranked as one of the "Twelve Apostles of Ireland."

Over his long life, he founded a number of monasteries for which he composed his own Rule, notably Dair-magh, "the Oak Plain" (or Durrow), around the year 546; Daire-Calgaich, "Calgach's Oak Wood" (Derry), in his ancestral territory of the north about 556; and Kells in County Meath sometime later.[64] In all, according to Reeves in his famous study of 1857, more than forty Irish churches, and fifty-six in Scotland in addition to Iona, comprised the *paruchia* of Columba or were later associated with his cult.[65]

In the year 563 Columba and twelve companions left Ireland for Í (Iona), an island off the Scottish coast, where he founded his greatest monastery.[66] There, despite journeys throughout Scotland and back to Ireland, he spent the remainder of his years, dying in 597. Alongside Patrick and Brigid, Columba is venerated as a national patron of Ireland and the principal patron of the churches of Derry and Raphoe. He is also one of Scotland's national patrons. His feast day is celebrated on June 9.

A Pilgrim for Christ

The reasons for Columba's exile have long been disputed. Adomnán tells us that he simply wished to be a pilgrim for Christ. In later accounts, this "white martyrdom" is imposed on him by a synod as an act of reparation for causing the Battle of Cuildreimhne. The story (now considered implausible) goes that on a visit to St. Finnian of Magh Bile, Columba secretly made a copy of a psalter. Finnian discovered the "theft" and demanded the return of the original and the copy as well. When Columba refused to relinquish the copy, Finnian appealed to the high king, Diarmuid, who ruled, famously, "To every cow her calf, and to every book its copy," thus establishing the principle of copyright protection. Already opposed to Diarmuid because of the king's execution of one of his protegés, Curan, the son of the king of Connaught, Columba appealed to his Uí Néill kinsman, and in the ensuing battle, Diarmuid was defeated. (A more likely explanation is that Columba raised a joint army of his own people and those of Connaught to avenge the prince's execution, his death having been an outrage against sanctuary and Columba's personal honor.) Columba was held responsible for the carnage in any case, and he chose exile as his punishment, vowing to convert as many Picts as the number of the fallen.

Although Columba's exploits were undoubtedly exaggerated by his biographers, if not wholly and increasingly invented as years went on, he was an outstanding figure — prince, poet, statesman, and apostle. (A number of Latin poems are ascribed to him, including the famous Altus Prosator.)[67] In time, his monastery at Iona surpassed even Armagh as the principal see of the Irish church and the hub of the missionary effort among the Picts of Scotland and the pagan English of Northumbria and Wessex. His story belongs as much to Scotland as Ireland and will be taken up again in that context. One of his later exploits concerned both countries, however, and occurred in Ireland.

In 575 (or, quite probably, a decade later), Columba made one of a number of return visits to Ulster for an important convention, or *mórdál*, held at Druim Cett, near what is now the town of Limavady, County Derry.[68] As his biographers looked back on it, Druim Cett marked the occasion of Columba's "saving" the poets of Ireland, who were threatened with extinction by royal decree. In fact, while Columba did intervene on behalf of the poets, other matters were of greater importance.

To begin with, it is likely that Columba came at the request of Aedán, the king of the Scottish kingdom of Dál Riada, as part of his entourage. Although interpretations of the events at Druim Cett vary, Columba had, it is said, three objectives in view: the release of Scandlán Mór, a young prince of the Osraige who was being held hostage under harsh conditions by Aedh, the *árd-rí*, or high king; assuring peace between the Dál Riada of Ireland and their kinsmen in Scotland — the main purpose of the convention; and the protection of the *filidh* (poets) from the banishment with which they were threatened because of the animosity of the nobility. Despite claims made by later writers, it seems clear that Columba was only partly successful in his quest. He did not secure the immediate release of Scandlán Mór, although the prince was eventually freed. But some kind of agreement was entered into by representatives of the Dál Riada from Scotland and the Northern Irish kingdom, and Columba's appeal was successful on behalf of the *filidh,* whose overbearing demands for hospitality and resort to satire had so irritated the nobles. The poets had to accept social and numerical diminishment, however, as well as mend their demanding ways. While Columba may not have played the key role in these events his biographers would have wished, there can be little doubt that his influence was felt keenly enough that Dallán Forgaill, the chief poet of Ireland, was moved to compose a formal eulogy in his honor.

The Life

We possess three Latin accounts of Columba's life, two by *comarbai,* or successor abbots at Iona: Cumméne Ailbe, the seventh abbot, who ruled from 657 to 669; and Adomnán, the ninth abbot, who ruled from 679 to 704. The third is a very brief account by Bede.[69] In addition, there is the old Irish Life of Columcille,[70] and the *Amra Coluim-cille* (*Hymn or Eulogy to Columcille*) composed by Dallán Forgaill after the convention at Druim Cett.[71] (The legend states that when the poet began his recitation, Columba stopped him, ordering him to finish it only after his death.)

The earliest account of Columba's life, that by Cumméne Ailbe, the great-grandson of a first cousin of Columba, was probably written in the second quarter of the seventh century and is known only from the extracts inserted into Adomnán's Life. It was less a biography than a chronicle of his miracles.[72] Of the four major works of early Irish hagiography, Adomnán's Life of Columba towers above the books of Cogitosus, Tírechán, and Muir-chú as narrative and especially as history, despite the inevitable admixture of saintly hyperbole.[73] Unlike other hagiographers, Adomnán does not advance territorial claims, although he includes accounts of Columba's foundations.

The Life was composed on Iona at the request of the monks around 690. Adomnán's sources, in addition to the oral tradition of the monastery, included the Life by Cumméne Ailbe and at least one other document. Adomnán names many of his oral sources, including Failbe, the eighth abbot; Oissene, a disciple of St. Fintan; Máel-Odrán moccu Rin, a priest of Derry; several old men who had information from Lugbe moccu Blai, a disciple of Columba; Finan, an anchorite of Durrow; Commán, the nephew of Fergno, the fourth abbot; and a monk, Ernene moccu Fir-Roide, a contemporary of Columba who lived long enough to talk with Adomnán.[74]

Less reserved than Adomnán's Life, the Old Irish Life contains, among other tales, an account of Columba's friendly quarrel with St. Ciarán of Clonmacnois, who was the son of a carpenter, as to which was the poorer. They are interrupted by an angel, who carries an axe, an adze, and an augur. The angel then reproves Ciarán for comparing himself to Columba, for while he had given up only his father's apron to follow Christ, Columcille had given up the kingship of Ireland.[75]

Columba's Death

A week before his death, Columba, now in his seventy-seventh year, had a vision of an angel in the monastery church on Sunday alerting him to prepare for his final day. The following sabbath he made a final tour of the enclosure, assuring himself that there was sufficient grain stored for the coming year. Adomnán tells us, in one of the most touching stories of any Celtic saint, that as Columba paused to rest on his way back to the monastery, the old white horse that carried the milk pails for the monks approached and laid its head against his breast. As if mourning, the horse seemed to weep. Columba would not allow his servant, Diarmuid, to drive the animal away, for God had, he said, revealed to it that his master was leaving. So he blessed the faithful horse as it turned away.

Columba then raised his hands in blessing over the monastery, predicting its future greatness. Returning to his cell, he resumed copying the Book of Psalms, stopping at Psalm 34, verse 10: "those who seek the Lord lack no good thing." After evening prayer, he rested for a time on the stone floor. He committed his final instructions to Diarmuid for the community: "Love one another without pretense. Preserve peace." Hearing the bell for the midnight office, he made his way to the church where, moments later, Diarmuid and the other monks found him dying before the high altar.

The Legacy

Following Columba's death, the influence of Iona and his other foundations expanded to dominate the churches of northern Ireland and southern Scotland. In Ireland, the Columban *paruchia* was ranked next in importance and dignity to Patrick's and that of Kildare. In the next generation, missionaries from Iona, led by Corman and then the great Aidán, set out to evangelize Northumbria and were active in Wessex. Other Columban missionaries took the gospel south to the European mainland.

Iona's fortunes fell during the Easter controversies of the late seventh century, largely because of the increasing pressure of the English church following the Synod of Whitby. Adomnán himself accepted the reforms around the year 690, but his efforts to win over Iona seem to have instigated a schism in the community. Only a minority of the monks supported him. In 692 and 697 Adomnán made pastoral visits to Ireland, where he died in 704.

FOUR

The Saints of Ireland

The names of the known saints of Ireland number in the hundreds.[1] Behind the details (some might say "clutter") added from the political and social agendas of the saints' biographers, the lives of real men and women can be detected. The best known can be grouped according to their dates.[2]

For the two centuries after Patrick, a number of Latin Lives describe the exploits of outstanding founders and early missionaries. But the largest group includes men and women of the sixth to the eighth centuries, when Christian culture especially flourished and the Irish seem to have taken it upon themselves to save civilization. After them, as the Viking terror ended the golden age of the Irish church, fewer but nonetheless great saints continued the saga, not least of whom were those formidable reformers, the Céli Dé. From the ninth to the thirteenth century, as wandering scholars and missionaries returned the light of faith and learning to Europe, decline perhaps inevitably occurred in Ireland itself as civil strife, invasion, and rebellion became the order of the day. That would remain the case for the next seven hundred years, but even during the coming Troubles, martyrs, scholars, and other saintly women and men would continue to grace the Irish church.

Saints of the Fifth and Sixth Centuries

Perhaps the earliest of the pre-Patrician saints, Ailbe was bishop of Imblech-ibair (Emly) and the apostle of Munster. Emly remained the church of the Munster kings of Cashel until Cashel itself was turned into an ecclesiastical capital and the king himself became a bishop.[3] As he is the principal patron of the diocese of Cashel and Emly, Ailbe's feast day is celebrated there on September 12.

The remaining pre-Patrician saint mentioned in the Life of Déclán is Ibar (or Ybar or Ibarian), who is remembered in Wexford for his monastery on Beg-Eri (Beggery Island) and particularly in connection with St. Monenna, who sought advice from him and direction for her nuns. According to legend, Patrick threatened to banish Ibar, who is said to have replied, "Wherever I shall be, I will call it Ireland." No Life has survived, but a brief lectionary account was published by the Bollandists.[4] Ibar's feast day was observed on April 23.

Several saints' names appear among Patrick's assistants. Of Benén (Benignus), Auxilius, Sechnall (Secundinus), and Iserninus, little is known.[5] Tassach and Assic (Asicus) were held to be Patrick's artificers (unless these are alternative names for one individual):[6] makers of altars, patens, crosses, croziers, shrines, even churches. Traditionally, Tassach became the first bishop of Raholp in County Down. Assic was the first bishop of Elphin in Roscommon, which in later years became an important art center.

One of Patrick's first converts according to later tradition, Erc was a young man in the retinue of King Laoghaire on the night Patrick dramatically announced his arrival by igniting the Paschal fire on the Hill of Slane.[7] When Patrick was summoned before the king, only Erc and the poet Dubhthach seemed aware that Patrick was a true holy man and rose to greet him. In later years, Erc became a priest and bishop. His church at Tralee became a school for other saints, among them, for a time, St. Brendan of Clonfert, whom Erc tutored as a child. As a monastic center, Tralee flourished for several centuries until subjected to repeated destruction by Viking and Norman raiders. Erc's feast day is on November 2.

One of the earliest of the nuns of Ireland was called Adhracht and is known in English as Attracta. According to tradition, she received the veil from Patrick himself and could have been the young noblewoman he remarks on in his *Confession*. She chose a site for a monastery where the poor and sick would find refuge. Known as Killaraght, "the cell of Adhracht," the hospice she established at Lough Gara in Sligo endured until the suppression of the monasteries in 1539.

She was especially venerated in Sligo, where Attracta's cross and cup were preserved throughout the Middle Ages by the O'Mochain family. Attracta is a secondary patron of the diocese of Achonry, for which Cardinal Moran drew up a special mass and office in her honor in the nineteenth century. Parishes named for St. Attracta are found in the United States and other countries where her memory traveled with settlers from Sligo.[8]

Énda of Aran: Father of Monasticism

Although Patrick alludes in his *Confession* (c. 41) to young men and women dedicating themselves to the life of religion, Irish monasticism effectively begins with Énda of Aran (c. 450–535). A warrior-prince of Oriel, he was the son of King Conaill Derg of Airgialla, and therefore a Pict. Énda's conversion seems to have occurred when his fiancée suddenly died. After he went through a long period of mourning, his older sister, Fáenche (Fanchea), a nun, upbraided him, persuaded him of the vanity of earthly loves, and sent him packing to Ninian's Candida Casa. After learning the rudiments of monastic life, Énda returned to Galway, where Oengus mac NadFraich, the king of Cashel (and husband of one of Énda's other sisters), granted him the Aran Islands for his monastic site. For Énda preferred the challenge of the harsh, lonely islands to the fertile enticements of the mainland.

Énda's way of life was austere and demanding, as might be expected of an ex-soldier like Pachomius of Egypt two centuries earlier. But his "school for saints" attracted a multitude of followers, among them Finnian of Clonard, Jarlath of Tuam, Carthage of Saighir, Ciarán of Clonmacnois, and even for a time, it is said, Columba of Iona. According to tradition, St. Brendan the Navigator paused at the beginning of his famed voyage to obtain Énda's blessing.

It is believed that Énda died in 535, a very old man. Although for some reason his feast day is not included in the calendar of the Irish church, he is remembered on March 21. Several manuscripts exist of the Life of Énda, which was composed later in the Middle Ages.[9]

His sister Fanchea was the abbess of a community of nuns at Rossory in Fermanagh, although when Énda established his monastic center on Aramór, she joined him there and with his help built the monastery of Killeany. There she died around the year 520. She is remembered on January 1.

Bishop Mel, by tradition a disciple of Patrick, and famous for his inadvertent consecration of St. Brigid, was the first abbot-bishop of Ardagh in Longford, where the cathedral still bears his name. Mel's wooden crosier, encased in a bronze, ninth-century reliquary, was discovered in the nineteenth century and is now preserved at St. Mel's College. His feast day is on February 7.

Another Patrician disciple, Mac Nessi or Mac Nessa, became the first bishop of Connor and is the principal patron of that diocese. He is said to have died in the year 514. Mary Ryan D'Arcy relates that a stone preserved in the wall of the basilica at St. Patrick's Purgatory, Lough Derg, commemorates a pilgrimage made there by Mac Nessi in the fifth or sixth century. His feast is observed on September 4.

Monenna

One of Old Ireland's most interesting women saints, Edana (or, according to several sources, Darerca, or possibly Sárbile) is known to posterity as Monenna, Moninne, or even Modwena because of the addition of the prefix *Mo,* a common Irish term of endearment found in many saints' nick-names.[10] She was apparently a Pict. The Martyrology of Oengus for July 6, her feast day, represents her as a grand-niece of Eochu, the ancestor of the ruling family of Dál Araidi, and eighth in descent from Fiacha Araide. In legend and popular tradition Monenna was believed to have received the veil from Patrick himself. At first she lived in her parents' home as a recluse. Later, she was associated with her uncle, St. Ibar, on Beggery Island, whose guidance she sought for her nuns, and with Brigid, who, according to the Annals of Ireland, sent her a gift of a silver shrine. If a late date is accepted for Patrick, all that could be possible for an old woman who lived until the year 517.

Having been warned by Ibar that after his death the rivalry of the monks on Beggery Island would imperil her monastery, Monenna and her followers migrated to Fochard, and then to Sléibhe-Cuilinn (Slieve Gullion) in Armagh. Cell-Sléibhe-Cuilinn, "the Church of the Mountain of Cuilenn," now known as Killeevy, became one of the more important women's monasteries in early medieval Ireland.

Despite her royal connections, Monenna was famous for her poverty, only some of which was deliberate; women had a much more difficult time obtaining and holding property and donations than did the monks. Manual labor was always a major element in the religious life of her nuns. After her death, her spade and hoe were revered with the same devotion given to the crosiers and bells of the male saints.

One of the more interesting stories about Monenna concerns St. Kevin of Glendalough, who succumbed to a temptation to attack and destroy her monastery when he learned that she had been praying with a reformed robber and his band. Monenna called his attention to the demonic source of his jealously, exorcised it, and drew him a hot bath to help him calm down.[11]

The Lives of St. Monenna. The principal Life is found in the Salamanca Codex, and the British Museum holds three manuscripts including an abridgment by John of Tynemouth of a version compiled by the abbot of Burton-on-Trent. There are also a number of editions.[12] The primitive Life may have been written in the first half of the seventh century, making it a contemporary of Cogitosus's Life of Brigid and Cumméne Ailbe's Life of Columba, and thus one of the earliest of the Irish *vitae.*

In honor of Monenna two extant Latin hymns were composed at Killeevy in the eighth or possibly seventh century. An appendix to Monenna's Life contains an account of a vision seen three days after her death by one of the sisters, in which the saint upbraids the nuns for already relaxing the Rule. There is also an account of a miracle that occurred during the rule of the third abbess to succeed her.

Derlasre, the abbess, was engaged in building a wooden church which needed only the large roof beam to complete it. After a long search, a suitable log was found on a nearby mountain top. But no one was able to remove it because of the difficulty of the terrain. In desperation, Derlasre sought the intercession of St. Monenna. The next morning the beam was found a short distance from the monastery. The builders searched for traces of the huge timber along the way, but saw only some broken branches at the level of the tree tops.

Monenna's Heritage. Despite fluctuations in fortune, Killeevy survived and sometimes flourished for some seven hundred years. During that time, Monenna's fame spread from Ireland to Scotland and England. In *Celtic Scotland*, W. F. Skene claims that Maiden Castle and also Edinburgh, commonly believed to refer to Edwin's Fort (Dun Edin), were named in her honor.[13] A St. Medana or Mo-Edana is commemorated in the Breviary of Aberdeen on November 19. Encouraged by the ancient Scottish connection, the English monks of Burton-on-Trent also claimed Monenna as their patron. As a fortunate consequence, most of the documents relating to her life and cult were preserved there.

Cannera

Another of the women saints of Ireland troubled by male misogyny is Cannera or Canair, whose memory is kept on January 28. Having lived as a recluse for many years at Bantry, on the southern coast of Munster, she was attracted by reports of the sanctity of St. Sénán's monastery on Scattery Island, off the coast of what is now County Clare, and traveled there to spend her final days. But Sénán held to his rule that no woman would ever enter the enclosure. Even after she crossed the water to the island on foot, he refused to let her enter, so the story goes. "Christ is no worse than you," she replied. "He came to redeem women no less than men." Sénán relented sufficiently to bring her the Eucharist as she lay near death in 530 and buried her on the coast as she had requested. Despite Sénán's misgivings, the tide never washed away her grave.

Cannera became a patron of sailors, who traditionally saluted as they passed her grave on the beach of Scattery Island and carried pebbles from the island to protect them from shipwreck.[14]

Buite

After studying for a time under St. Teilo at Llandaff, Buite (or Boite) led a party of sixty "holy men and virgins" to the east coast of Scotland, where they engaged in missionary work among the Picts. Their ranks included twenty "Germans," a term that probably means Anglians. Buite may have baptized King Nechtan Morbet when he was a boy in Ireland, the recollection of which gave rise to the later legend that he raised the dead king to life. Buite later founded Monasterboice (a name which simply means "Boite's Monastery") in County Louth. It was in fact a double monastery, but the women's and men's sections were separated by several miles.

According to the legend, as Buite lay dying on the day of Columba's birth, he predicted the birth of "a child illustrious before God and men." His feast day is remembered on December 7.[15]

Today, Monasterboice is justly famed for its two superb sculptured crosses. The larger West Cross, or Muiredach's Cross, has been dated about 923. It is named for the abbot who "caused this Cross to be made." Another famous abbot there was Flann, whose eleventh-century poems found in the Book of Leinster and other works are of exceptional interest.

Finnian of Clonard

Known as "the teacher of the saints of Ireland," Finnio moccu Telduib was born toward the end of the fifth century of a noble Leinster family. After being fostered to Fortchern, a grandson of the legendary King Laoghaire, Finnian became a disciple of a Wexford hermit, Coemhan. Next, he studied under St. Cadoc at Llancarfan in Wales and retained a life-long affection for (and correspondence with) his fellow pupil there, Gildas, whose reforming mission would bring him to Ireland several times in later years. Finnian may also have lived for a time at St. David's monastery at Menevia.

He founded his first monastery at Aghowle, County Wicklow, but established his major foundation at Clúain-Iráird (Clonard), "Erard's meadow," on the River Boyne in County Meath, around the year 520. Attracted by his reputation for holiness and learning (the Penitential of Finnian has been attributed to him),[16] hundreds of young men flocked to his side.[17] The most illustrious became known in later times as "the Twelve Apostles of Ireland": Columba of Iona, Ciarán of Clonmacnois, Brendan of Clonfert, Molaise of Devenish, Cainnech (Canice), Mobhí, Colum (or Colmán) of Terryglass, Sinell, Ciarán of Saighir, Brendan of Birr, Ninidh of Inismacsaint, and Ruadán.[18]

Several versions of the Life of Finnian have been preserved in Ireland, England, Brussels, and the Salamanca Codex. According to the Annals of Ulster, Finnian and several of his disciples perished in the great epidemic of 548–49. He is remembered on December 12. Clonard itself endured until the Reformation. Today, only a twelfth-century baptismal font and a few fragments from the latter days of the once-great monastery can be found imbedded in the wall of the Protestant church.

The Apostles of Ireland

In "The Twelve Apostles of Ireland," a short manuscript of the fourteenth or fifteenth century edited by Plummer in his collection of Irish Lives,[19] the entire group is gathered together as a kind of monastic Knights of the Round Table, when the vision of an "indescribably large flower" instigates the quest of the Land of Promise that sends Brendan of Clonfert on his seven-year trek. The rest of the story is an excerpt from the Life of Brendan. But clearly, the twelve great saints were regarded as a kind of fraternal community by writers of the Middle Ages.

Ciarán of Clonmacnois. Columba we have met already and shall encounter again from the perspective of the Scottish saints. Ciarán, his friend and sometimes holy rival, became one of the most honored of the Irish saints and founder of the great monastic city at Clúain-moccu-nois (Clonmacnois), whose ruins still keep vigil on the shores of the Shannon.

Ciarán was born in Roscommon around the year 512, the son of a carpenter. He was not, however, poor, much less a common tradesman, as might be inferred, but a member of the class of *soernemid*, which according to the "Law of Status" included the clergy, nobility, the learned, and owners of property. For a time, Ciarán was a disciple of St. Énda and visited St. Sénán's monastery on Scattery Island. He founded other monasteries, but his major achievement was the center of learning and holiness at Clonmacnois, although he lived only long enough to see it begun when he, like his master, fell victim to the "Great Mortality" of 548. Ciarán was known for his impetuousness and fiery temper, as well as his life-long friendship with Columba. He is also remembered for his affection for animals. Ciarán is the principal patron of the church of Ardagh and Clonmacnois. His feast day is observed on September 9.

Clonmacnois flourished for centuries as a monastic city of learning and sanctity, until burned by soldiers of Elizabeth during the Reformation. In keeping with Ciarán's example, the abbots of Clonmacnois were often selected from the families of tradesmen rather than the aristocracy.

Brendan the Sea-Farer. Brénainn (Brendan) is remembered throughout the Christian world as "the Navigator," although he traveled widely throughout Britain and elsewhere before undertaking his two famous sea voyages, after which he settled down (more or less) at Clúain-Ferta (Clonfert) in Galway, where he died about the year 580.[20]

Brendan was baptized by Bishop Erc, Patrick's early convert, who arranged for him to be fostered as an infant to the formidable St. Íte. At his maturity, he returned to Erc for further instruction but retained his affection for (and reliance upon) his foster-mother. Both Íte and Erc seem to have supported Brendan's wanderlust, which took him on visits to St. Énda on Aran-Mór, St. Jarlath of Tuam, and eventually to St. Finnian of Clonard, where he, too, was numbered among the Twelve Apostles of Ireland.

After a vision of a "Land of Promise" somewhere in the Western Sea that he experienced while on Slieve Aughty (according to account in the *Vita Brendani*), Brendan built three hide-covered curraghs and, with the blessing of St. Énda, sailed off into the Atlantic with ninety other monks.[21] After five years, they returned, having failed in their quest. After a forty-day fast and retreat and some good advice from St. Íte, Brendan had a large wooden boat constructed, which may have taken him and his crew of sixty as far as North America in their second, two-year pilgrimage.

The Legend of Brendan's sea voyage was one of the favorite works of the Middle Ages, surviving in more than one hundred Latin manuscripts and others in English, Spanish, French, German, Italian, and other languages. The *Navigatio* is almost pure fantasy, but as engaging as any contemporary science-fiction novel. Brendan and his monks encounter St. Patrick and Judas Iscariot, sea monsters, and a great whale that allows them to celebrate Easter annually on his back.

In one of their many adventures, Brendan's crew comes across an island inhabited by some devilish little folk who will forever after lurk in Irish memory. As they attempt to land, the harbor is suddenly filled with demonic figures in the shape of "dwarfs and leprechauns [*luchurpán*],"[22] whose faces are black as coal. Brendan ordered the crew to raise anchor, realizing that no one can land unless he is able to war against demons to the point of shedding his blood. They are unable to budge the anchor, however, and the boat is trapped for a week until the crew cut the cable and sail away.[23]

On his return, Brendan founded several monasteries, including Clonfert, which flourished until destroyed during the Protestant Reformation. He is also said to have established a monastery for women at Annaghdown, County Galway, where his sister Brig became abbess. Among his journeys, Brendan seems to have visited Columba on Hinba and Iona, Llancarfan in Wales, and may have accompanied St. Malo to Brittany.

St. Brendan is the principal patron of Kerry and the diocese of Clonfert. His feast day is celebrated on May 16.

Molaise. At least sixteen Irish saints share the hypocoristic, or "pet," name of Molaise, "my flame," from the Irish *mo* and *las.* Molaise of Daim Inis (Devenish Island) on Lough Erne, Finnian's disciple, is credited with becoming Columba's *anamchara,* although this honor is also attributed, confusingly, to another Molaise of Inis Muiredaig (Inishmurray), and both can get confused with St. Molaise or Laserian of Lethglen, who lived a generation later. Molaise of Devenish founded a church and monastic school on his island about 530 and died there in 564.

Canice of Kilkenny. Cainnech (or Canice, "Kenneth") was born in 517 of the Ciannachta tribal group of Dún Geimin in what is now Derry. From Clonard, he labored among the Picts in Scotland and the Western Isles, where according to Adomnán he visited Columba on several occasions. On returning to Ireland, he founded a major monastery at Achad Bó (Aghaboe) in Ossory where he is said to have died around the year 600. Cainnech is venerated in Kilkenny, where he founded a monastic church. He became the special patron of the city, which bears his name, and the splendid medieval cathedral is named in his honor. His feast day is celebrated there on October 11.

Colum of Terryglass. The son of Crimthann, a noble of Leinster, Colum (Colmán) studied as a youth under Finnian at Clonard. The story is told of him that one day St. Senach, who would succeed Finnian as abbot, found Colum kneeling with his hands outstretched and so absorbed in prayer that birds came and lighted on his shoulders. "It is he who will offer the Holy Sacrifice for me at my death," Finnian said on hearing of it.

Colum founded the monastery of Clúain Eidnech (Clonenagh), where his disciple St. Fintan became abbot. He also founded Iniscaltra (Holy Island) in the Shannon that became famous under St. Caimin. At some time Columba is believed to have visited him there. Near Iniscaltra was Tírdá-Glas ("the field of two streams"), a woodland retreat where Colum retired to pray in seclusion. Later, he founded a monastery on the site, not long before his death of the plague, recorded in the Annals of Ulster for 549. His feast day was celebrated on December 13.

Brendan of Birr. Little is known of Brendan of Birr, who, like Brendan of Clonfert, came from the line of Fergus MacRoy. (Birr is not far from Clonfert.) In the "Twelve Apostles of Ireland," it is he who is first chosen to go in quest of the Land of Promise. But because he was the oldest of the disciples, the choice fell to the younger Brendan. When Brendan of Birr died on Iona, according to some accounts in 571 or 572, his friend Columba experienced a vision of his friend's soul being escorted into heaven by angels. The following day, Columba offered a special Mass for him. His feast day is remembered on November 29.

The monastic school at Birr continued until the ninth century. There the beautiful Book of Gospels attributed to Abbot MacRegal was completed. It is now in the Bodleian Museum, Oxford.[24]

Ruadán (Rúán). Ruadán, whose Life is found in the Salamanca Codex, settled at Lothra (Lorrha) in north Tipperary, near the northern shore of Lough Derg. The most famous (if fictitious) incident in his career centers on the cursing of Tara and its resulting decline. A late medieval legend, the story goes that Aed Guaire, a king of Connaught, killed an emissary of the high king Diarmuid Mac Cerbaill (d. between 565 and 572) and then fled to Ruadán for protection. Violating monastic sanctuary, Diarmuid seized Aed Guaire and killed him. In retaliation (and perhaps desperation), Ruadán convoked an assembly of saints at Tara to curse Diarmuid and Tara itself.

Scholars alert us to the fact that no king of Connaught named Aed Guaire is known to history. Further, some of the saints supposedly involved in cursing Tara were either dead at the time or still in their childhood. Tara, moreover, continued to be a royal residence for nearly a century. Kenney tells us that Diarmuid's son and grandson succeeded him to the throne of Tara. References to the king of Tara in the Annals of Ulster for 670, 737, and 764 suggest that even if Ruadán and his fellow saints cursed the capital, their gesture had little effect. However, Tara may have been temporarily deserted after an outbreak of the plague in 664–65, during which the joint rulers, Diarmuid and Blathmac, both died.[25]

Ruadán himself died in 584. His feast day was celebrated on April 15. Lorrha continued to be a center of spiritual culture for several centuries. There in the ninth century the liturgical manuscript known as the Stowe Missal was composed. It is one of the most valuable resources on the liturgy of the ancient Irish church.[26]

The Lesser Apostles. Mobhí Clárainech ("the flat-faced") of Glas Noiden (Glasnevin) remains an obscure figure, but he is said to have died of the Plague that bore away so many of the saints beginning around 545.[27] Abbot Ninidh little is known other than that he founded a monastery at Inis Maige Sam (Inismacsaint) on Lough Erne. Sinell (or Senell) is also an obscure figure, whose name is remembered as the founder of a monastery at Clúain-Inid on Lough Erne.[28]

Íte: Fostering Mother

Next to Brigid among the sainted women of Ireland, Íte (c. 480–570) is surely the most irresistibly memorable. (She is also one of the four great

Irish women, along with Brigid, Monenna, and Samthann, of whom Latin Lives have survived.)[29] Again excepting Brigid, she is probably the best known as well, not least for the charming Old Irish poem attributed to her in the form of a lullaby to the infant Jesus, "Ísucán."[30] She is remembered as the foster-mother of the saints of Ireland, among whom St. Brendan figures most prominently.

Her name was actually Deirdre. She was born to a royal family of the south, in County Waterford. Her major foundation was the monastery church of Clúain-Credal in County Limerick. In time, it would come to be known as Cill-Íte or Killeedy. There many young boys and girls were fostered, including St. Brendan, with whom she retained a life-long spiritual relationship.

Asked by Brendan what three things were most pleasing to God, Íte replied, "a faithful heart, simplicity of life, and generosity with charity." When Brendan returned discouraged after his first voyage, she advised him that he had failed because he had sailed in a boat covered with animal hides. She told him to build a boat of wood, which he did, and sailed into legend (and very likely all the way to North America and back).

Devoted to the poor and oppressed, Íte would accept only small grants of land for her foundations. In her Life is also found the story of a young nun who became pregnant and fled the monastery. She gave birth to a son and soon fell into slavery. When Íte learned of it she sent word to Brendan. He secured her freedom and sent her to Íte, who welcomed her back into the community.

Íte also became patron of the Uí Connell Gabra of Munster, whose victory in battle over the Corcu Oche in 552 was ascribed to her prayers. According to the Annals of Ulster, she died in 570 or 577, "a tolerant, humorous old woman."[31] Some time after Íte's death, her monastery may have been taken over for a time by a community of monks, witness to the difficulty religious women faced in a culture where inheritance always favored males. But churches and schools are still dedicated to her memory from Cornwall to the United States. She is named in Alcuin's poem about the saints of Ireland. Her feast day is kept on January 15.

Other saints of the period include Comgall (516–603), a Pict of Dál nAraide who founded the great monastery at Bennchor (Bangor) on the southern shore of Belfast Loch around the year 555. There one of the few surviving works of the Old Irish liturgy, the Antiphonary of Bangor, was composed. According to tradition, Comgall's *anamchara* was St. Fiacre, abbot of Ullard, near Kilkenny.[32]

Bangor followed one of the most arduous of all the Irish rules, but nevertheless attracted zealous recruits such as Saints Columban and Gall, who spent twenty years there before departing as a missionaries to the European mainland. Bangor was also noted for its learning. In later years, Comgall visited Scotland, where he was on friendly terms with Columba and is said to have founded a monastery at Tiree. His feast day was observed on May 10.

St. Eoghan (Eugene) of Ard Sratha (Ardstraw) was a bishop and abbot who ruled one of the more influential monasteries of the sixth century. An alumnus of Candida Casa like Énda, Finnian of Magh Bile, Cairpre of Cúil Raithin (Coleraine), and Tighernach of Clúain Eois (Clones), his principal church at Ardstraw became a cathedral but was later included into the diocese of Derry. Eoghan died in 618. As the patron of the churches of Galway, Kilfenora and Kilmacduagh, and Derry, his feast day is celebrated on August 23.

St. Lelia, who is remembered especially in the city of Limerick, probably lived in the sixth century. Her name is preserved in the church-site of Killeely. Her feast day was observed on August 12.

Gobnait

Among the saintly women of Munster, pride of place very likely goes to St. Gobnait, who was, however, born in what is now County Clare. She is also remembered at Inisheer in the Aran Islands, where a church is named in her honor. Alerted by an angel to seek "the place of her resurrection," as the old Irish saints preferred, she traveled to Ballyvourney in County Cork, where she saw the sign the angel had foretold — nine white deer grazing in a meadow.

When St. Abáin (Abbán) came into the region, long associated with the Clan O'Herlihy, he chose Gobnait to preside over the monastery for women he founded there.[33] A number of miracles are attributed to her, including halting the progress of the plague by marking off the boundaries of the church and routing a troop of raiders by releasing her bees on them. Mary Ryan D'Arcy points out that "Gobnait" is the Irish equivalent of the Hebrew name Deborah, which means "honey bee."[34]

The place of Gobnait's resurrection has long been considered a healing shrine, where discarded crutches, spectacles, and other tokens are still left to testify to her enduring appeal. Her feast day was celebrated on February 11.

Colmán of Dromore

Colmán may be the name most frequently found among the Irish saints. Of more than two hundred instances, Colmán of Dromore stands out as one of the most influential bearers. A teacher of saints, he lived most of

his life in County Down. He was tutored in holiness by Ailbe of Emly and
Coelan of Nendrum, where he was for a time the teacher of St. Finnian
of Magh Bile. Churches in Scotland and Wales were named for him, and
he is listed in the rolls of saints in both Ireland and Scotland. Colmán
died sometime in the latter half of the sixth century. His feast day is
remembered on June 7.[35]

Iarlaithe (Jarlath)

Like Brendan of Birr and Brendan of Clonfert, Jarlath was a descendant
of Fergus Mac Roy, ancestor of many of the heroes and saints of Ireland. He was schooled by St. Sénán, the disciple of Patrick, and may have
studied under St. Énda as well. Later, Jarlath founded the monasteries of
Clúain Fois (Clonfuis) and Tuaim-dá-gualann (Tuam). At Clonfuis, his
pupils included Brendan of Clonfert and Colmán MacLenini of Cloyne.
At Brendan's advice, according to the traditional account, Jarlath traveled east to look for a site of a new monastery and the place of his
resurrection. He would know the place, Brendan promised, when his
chariot wheel broke. That came to pass at Tuam. There a great monastic
school grew up, celebrated in the Middle Ages for its art works. Jarlath is
recalled as both bishop and abbot. He died around the year 550. Jarlath's
feast day is celebrated on June 6, although he is listed in the Martyrology
of Oengus for December 26. He is patron of the church of Tuam.[36]

Finnian of Magh Bile (Moville)

Finnian of Moville was probably a British monk who traveled to both
Scotland and Ireland in the middle of the sixth century.[37] He is sometimes said to have studied under St. Énda on Aran-mór and also to have
tutored St. Columba, but it is easy to confuse him in both respects with
St. Finnian of Clonard. Both have also been credited with the brief Penitential of Finnian and with association with St. Gildas.[38] But by all
reports he became the abbot of Magh Bile (Moville) north of Strangford Lough in County Down. He is believed to have died in 579 and is
remembered on September 10.

Finbarr (Bairre) of Cork

The City of Cork was, by tradition, founded by Bairre or Finbarr,
who was born at Rath Raithleann. In search of solitude, he traveled
to Gougane Barra, a small island west of what is now Cork City, and
where annual pilgrimages are still made in his honor. Finbarr founded a
church in a marshy place (*corcaigh*) nearby, around which a city eventually developed. Finbarr died around the year 600. He is the patron saint
of Cork, and his feast falls on September 25.

Saints of the Seventh and Eighth Centuries

Kevin

One of the most famous saints of Leinster, Caoimhghin (Kevin) was born late in the sixth century.[39] In search of the contemplative life he retired to the valley of Glen-da-locha (Glendalough, the Glen of the Two Lakes) high in the Wicklow mountains.[40] Soon, however, reports of his holiness attracted men and women to follow him into his *dísert*. Because of the later eminence of his monastery, Kevin became the center of a host of legends.

Even after Kevin founded a monastery for his followers, he sought solitude for prayer and meditation. The third Irish Life[41] recounts how he spent the Lenten fast in a small hut made of wattles, open to the sky, with only a flagstone for a bed. Once during this period, as he lay in prayer with his arms outstretched, a blackbird built her nest in his open hand. When he became aware of her presence, he kept his hand in that position until she had hatched her eggs.

An angel came to him afterward and helpfully advised him to moderate his austerities and return to human society. Kevin replied that his pain was slight compared to the sufferings Christ had endured for his sake.

Animals figure prominently in the stories about Kevin. One of them concerns a monster in the lower lake that endangered pilgrims who came to Glendalough. Rather than killing it, the saint banished the beast to the upper lake, near his own cave. For this reason, the lower lake is known as the lake of healing.

Kevin's cave (or "bed") was inaccessible by land (and still is). But that did not keep admirers from pursuing him. One young woman named Kathleen, infatuated with the uncommonly handsome young monk, surprised him one day in his cave at prayer. Depending on what version one hears, Kevin either pushed her out of the cave or so frightened her that she fell backward out of it. According to one's preference for comedy or tragedy, the lovesick girl either retreated in disgrace or drowned, which would have required a rather determined effort on her part, as the lake is some distance from the foot of the nearly vertical hill. Kevin's own death is believed to have occurred in 611 or 612. He is the principal patron of Glendalough and one of the chief saints of Leinster. His feast day is celebrated on June 4.

Mochuda

Carthach (Carthage, or Mochuda, "my dear one," as he was more widely known) stands out as a genuinely remarkable character even among the Irish saints of the seventh century. He was the founder of two important monasteries and the focus of a tense conflict with monastic and secular rulers of northern Ireland.[42] The "son of Finall of the Ciarraige Luachra by race, of the Uí Ferba to speak precisely," Carthach was born in Kerry sometime in the mid-sixth century but migrated to the northern "half" of Ireland late in the sixth century, where he formed a monastic community at Rahen (or Rathan, now Rahan, near Tullamore in County Offaly).

The most memorable character found among Mochuda's monks at Rahen is Constantine, the son of Fergus, a Pictish king who abdicated his throne, became a monk in Ireland, but (as related in the twelfth-century Life of St. Kentigern by Jocelin of Furness) later labored as a missionary in Scotland and was martyred in Kintyre.[43] In the story of Mochuda, however, Constantine remains and eventually dies at Rahen, a friendly if somewhat thick giant of a monk with a voracious appetite and a prodigious temper, as becomes evident to Mochuda's persecutors. For in 636, according to the Annals, a confederation of the kings of Tara and Meath, together with (or stimulated by) the abbots of Clonmacnois, Clonard, and Durrow, decided to evict Mochuda and his monks from Rahen.

Territorial jealousy has traditionally been the motive ascribed to Mochuda's antagonists, for he was a southerner living in northern Ireland, and, worse still, his monks had a reputation for great holiness: "every third man of them held converse with angels." The more likely occasion was that Mochuda favored the "new" method of calculating the Easter cycle introduced in 525, which for a time divided the Irish church along north-south lines.[44]

For whatever reason, kings and abbots sought to expel Mochuda and his community from Rahen, as related in the medieval thriller *Indarba Mochuda a rRaithin* ("The Expulsion of Mochuda from Rahen"), which is found in the Martyrology of Oengus and other manuscripts. By a process of drawing lots, since no one wanted the onerous and even dangerous task of confronting the old man, a number of emissaries were selected to bear the bad news. Each faltered or, in some accounts, died, on approaching Mochuda, perhaps out of fear. Eventually the king of Meath grew impatient and ordered his troops to scourge Mochuda and his monks out of Rahen — not, however, until they had been routed several times by the gigantic Constantine.

Before leaving, Mochuda pronounced a terrible curse on his enemies (not an unusual safeguard in saints' Lives to remind potential marauders of the penalty for violating monastic integrity). The number of monks who left with him (not counting the dead, who rose from their graves at one point, wanting to follow their saint until placated by him) was said to be "seven and two score and eight hundred," a large but not impossible census, given the size of Irish monasteries of the time.

After a period of wandering, Mochuda and his monks were intercepted by the king of Munster, Failbe Flann, and his wife, who had a vision of "an innumerable flock of birds" coming to the place they were visiting, "and the leading bird alighted on the king." Failbe granted Mochuda the land on which they met, and the old man soon began to lay out the boundaries for a new settlement. As the story goes, he was approached by a nun named Cainell, who asked what he was doing. "The monks are making a fort [*liss* in Irish]," he replies. (In fact, the configuration of early Irish monasteries had much in common with fortified camps.) "That is a great [*mór*] fort indeed," Cainell said. "Then let that be its name," Mochuda concludes, "the Great Fort — Liss-mór."[45]

The old abbot did not live long at Lismore, however. His death is recorded for the year 637. But he assured that the monastery would always remain hospitable to the poor, the oppressed, and the infirm. The care of lepers was especially associated with both Rahen and Lismore, the history of which is recorded to the year 1156. According to Kenney, writing in the 1930s, "The leper colony is still remembered in local tradition around Lismore."[46] Mochuda is the patron of the diocese of Lismore and is commemorated on May 15.

Odrán (Otteran)

In some accounts, Odrán (Odhráin or Otteran) was one of St. Columba's companions (and some think his brother) on his mission to Iona in 563 and, according to tradition, the first to die there. According to the Middle Irish Life of Columba, Odrán volunteered for this honor as a sacrifice to hallow the foundation of the new monastery. (Nagy and others detect a residue of pagan lore here that is not too difficult to disengage from the rest of the narrative.)[47] The place where he was buried became known as Reilic Odráin, "Odrán's Cemetery." A more trustworthy account holds that Odrán was a pre-Columban saint (d. 549) who had founded churches on Iona, Mull, and Tiree and gave his name to the cemetery where he himself was buried.[48] In any case, many years later, after the Vikings had embraced Christianity, their kings and nobles were given burial there among royal Scots and Picts and the holy monks and martyrs. The Christian Norse of Waterford took Odrán for their patron saint. His feast day is celebrated on October 27.

Molaise (Laserian)

Laisrán moccu Imde (or Laserian) of Louth is associated with the monastic church of Leth-glenn (Leighlin, now in County Carlow), which was founded according to traditional accounts by St. Gobbán sometime in the fifth century.[49] Although venerated widely, Laserian is especially remembered in Carlow. In Scotland he is generally remembered by his hypocoristic name, Molaise ("my flame"), a common term of endearment for Irish saints, as we saw earlier.

The twelfth-century Latin Life, preserved at the Royal Library in Brussels, claims that he journeyed to Rome, where he was consecrated bishop by Pope Gregory. On a return visit, he was made (even more implausibly for the time) apostolic delegate to Ireland. Laserian also became, as befits a pilgrim to Rome, a proponent of the new method of dating the Easter cycle. According to the Life of St. Fintan (Munnu), Molaise attended the Synods of Magh Lena and Magh Ailbe, where it was decided that the "Roman" usage would prevail in Ireland. Molaise also figures in the Life of St. Moling.

Molaise's association with Scotland rests first on the belief that he was taken there by his mother as a child after the death of his father. He may also have lived for a time as a hermit on Holy Island, which lies in Lamlash Bay near the Isle of Arran in the Firth of Clyde. He died around the year 639 at Leighlin and was honored by one of the three most exalted burials in Ireland, next only to those of Patrick and Mochuda.[50] His feast day is celebrated on April 18.

In 1992, the Tibetan Buddhist community of Samye Ling purchased Holy Island as a spiritual retreat center and have, contrary to some expressed fears, preserved the ancient Christian character of the area associated with St. Laserian.

The names of scores of migratory Irish saints from the seventh century are found in the Annals and other sources for Ireland, Scotland, and Britain. Among them are found both women and men. Another saint named Modwena was a nun who lived in the latter part of the seventh century. When St. Hilda of Whitby died in 680, King Aldfrid of Northumbria, who had studied as a youth in Ireland, requested that Modwena succeed her as second abbess of Whitby. He also entrusted Modwena with the tutoring of his sister, Elflaeda, in order for her to be able to assume the role of abbess in due course. Once her task was accomplished, Modwena returned to Ireland.[51]

Moling (Mullen of Ferns)

St. Moling's fame rests on his now lost Yellow Book, but he was of note as a saint and monastic leader as well.[52] A number of his poems have survived, or are at least attributed to him.[53] He seems to have been reared at Ferns, having been rescued by the monks when abandoned as a baby. Later, he founded a monastic refuge, Techmolin (from *Teach Moling,* House of Moling), where he retreated in solitude and prayer. Directly chosen by St. Aidán to succeed him as bishop of Ferns, Moling distinguished himself in his pastoral responsibilities. In 693, Moling succeeded in freeing all of Leinster from the annual tribute of oxen claimed for centuries by the kings of Tara. Eventually, he was able to resign from Ferns and return to Techmolin (now St. Mullins in Carlow).

A number of stories are attached to the popular saint of Leinster. In one of them, his pet fox made a meal of one of the hens that belonged to the monastery. Accused of his crime by the monks, the fox replaced the dead hen with one from the nun's monastery. Moling reproved him gently, told him to return the stolen hen, and never to steal again. Astonishingly enough, that is what he did.

According to a story found in the Félire Oengusso, once Moling was at prayer in his church when he saw a young boy coming toward him, dressed in fine purple.

"Who are you?" Moling asks.

"I am Christ, the son of God," the youth replies.

"I know not that," Moling says. "When Christ came to converse with the Culdees, it was not in purple raiment or in kingly guise that he came, but in the guise of the unfortunate — a leper or someone ill."

One of the most touching stories attached to Moling involves the mad king Suibne (Sweeney), cursed for his violent temper and obstructions by St. Ronán Finn at the Battle of Magh Rath. But in spite of his horrible condition, or perhaps because of it, Suibne is sheltered and protected by Moling, to whom he dictates each evening what he has experienced on his forays into the wilderness. All comes to grief, however, when Moling's swineherd finds Suibne talking innocently with his wife and slays him, suspecting that the mad king was trying to seduce her.[54]

Moling died around the year 697, and his feast day is remembered on June 17. In the twelfth century Gerald of Wales mentioned seeing Moling's now lost Yellow Book. An illuminated Gospel Book named for him, the Book of Mulling, is later than the saint, but still one of the earliest Irish illuminated manuscripts. Originating in Techmolin, it was in the possession of the Kavanagh family of St. Mullins, near the monastic site, from which it passed into the hands of Art MacMurrough, and eventually to Trinity College, Dublin.

Molúa

Molúa (Lugaid moccu Ochae) seems to have come from the Corcu Oche, an ancient people of Munster who had been subjugated by the Uí Fidgente, a sept of the Eóghanachta.[55] His mother was of the Dál Birn in Osraige (Ossory). Two years before his birth in 554, his father's people suffered a great defeat through the prayers of St. Íte. Some of the ancient Lives maintain that Molúa was schooled under Comgall of Bangor and Finnian of Clonard. While that may be improbable, it is not contested that he founded a monastery at Druimsnechta (Drumsnatt) in Monaghan before establishing his major foundation, known afterward as Clúain-Ferta-Molúa (Clonfertmulloe, or Kyle) in Laois, as well as other churches.

Molúa's kindness both to human persons and animals is recalled with particular affection. According to the Félire Oengusso, when he died in 608, Mael-Anfaid, the abbot of Lismore, found a little bird wailing and lamenting. Intrigued, Mael-Anfaid vowed to fast until he learned the meaning of the bird's sorrowful cries. Eventually, an angel appeared to him and explained that he should fast and grieve no longer, "for Molúa mac Ocha has died, and therefore all living creatures bewail him. For never has he killed any animal, little or big; so human beings do not mourn him any more than do the other animals, including the little bird you saw."[56] Molúa's feast day is kept on August 4.

Animals figure largely in many saints' Lives. According to the Life of St. Colmán moccu Sailni (better known as Colmán Elo), both he and his monastery, Lann Elo, took their name from the swans who sang to the monks as they labored to build it.[57] His father's name is given as Beogna, his family being of the Dál Sailne, a branch of the southern Uí Néill. References in Adomnán's Life of Columba indicate that he spent some time at Iona, returning to Ireland the year of Columba's death (597). He settled for a while at Connor in Antrim, but eventually returned to Meath, where he founded the famous monastery of Lann Elo (Lynally, near Tullamore), not far from Durrow.[58]

St. Mochua, abbot of Tech-Mochua near Timahoe, County Laois, is said to be one of the three ex-warriors among the saints of Ireland (along with Énda and Comgall). Among other exploits, he is credited with curing Colmán Elo of a sudden loss of memory he incurred because of a sin of pride, and Munnu of his leprosy. He is believed to have died in the year 654.[59]

Aidán of Lindisfarne

Of the Irish monks who made the long journey to the northeastern coast of England to preach to the pagan Mercians, Bernicians, Deirians, and other Germanic invaders, Aidán was one of the earliest and the most revered.[60] He was born around the year 580. Having studied, it is believed, under St. Sénán on Scattery Island as a youth, Aidán went to Iona, where in time he succeeded Corman, the first missionary bishop to the Angles. Corman had responded to the appeal of King Oswald, who had converted to Christianity as a refugee on Iona in 616. But the irritable Corman found the English too stubborn to teach.

In his account, Bede reports that Aidán suggested that Corman's approach had been too harsh, and that a more kindly approach would have better results. His suggestion earned him a turn as a missionary bishop, and he succeeded remarkably well. He arrived on the coast of Northumbria in 635 and located his see at Lindisfarne rather than at the royal capital of Bamburgh.

Aidán's life was one of personal austerity, kindness to others, devotion to his flock, and skill in teaching. Twelve of his pupils became bishops and saints of Christian England, including Chad, Cedd, Eata (later abbot of Melrose and Lindisfarne and then bishop of Lindisfarne and Hexham), and Wilfred. Lindisfarne became the spiritual and artistic center of northern England. Hundreds of Irish and English monks were drawn there. Among its greatest treasures was the beautifully illuminated Lindisfarne Gospels, now in the British Library. Aidán died in 651, shortly after the death of his friend King Oswin, who had been assassinated by his cousin, Oswy, the king of Bernicia. Aidán's feast day is celebrated on August 31.

Adomnán

Born in 624, a generation after Columba's death, Adomnán, who was also known as Eunan, achieved just and lasting fame as the biographer of one of the three chief saints of Ireland and the original patron of Scotland. But Adomnán's other achievements transcend his important memoir. Of the family known as the Cenel Conaill, and thus a blood relative of Columba, he became the ninth abbot of Iona in 679 and remained abbot until his death there in 704. His role in the Easter controversies was pivotal. Unlike most northern Irish prelates, Adomnán accepted the new method of dating Easter introduced from Rome under Pope John I and added his considerable influence to sway the church of Northumbria and parts of Ireland to adopt it. He failed to win over his own monks, however.[61]

Adomnán founded churches in Ireland and Scotland, and in addition to his famous Life of Columba, he also wrote an important treatise on the Holy Land and drew up a code of civil and ecclesiastical law known as the Law of the Innocents, and sometimes the Law of Women, which is probably the first instance of human rights legislation in European history.

The Cáin Adomnáin contains a historical preface of legendary proportions, which describes the reasons why the extraordinary legislation was necessary and how it originated.[62] (The role Adomnán's mother plays in the story is especially noteworthy.) This section was most likely written in the ninth century, but includes important records, such as the list of Irish, Pictish, and Scottish kings, tribal chiefs, abbots, and bishops who ratified Adomnán's Cáin at the Synod of Birr in 697 and again in 727. The main body of the document itemizes the ecclesiastical punishments and monetary compensations for slaying or injuring women, children, or clerics. Finally, it specifies the periodic "dues" owed to Iona for accepting the Law and coming under its protection. (*Cáin* is not the ordinary term for "law," but, like the modern Irish word, means "tax," referring to the fees owed for the benefits derived from the law.)

Among other texts by or attributed to Adomnán are the *Canons,* or *Rule,* a collection of twenty Latin prescriptions that treat chiefly of acceptable animal foods. The third of Adomnán's writings is known as *De Locis Sanctis.* A Latin commentary on Virgil is also attributed to him.

One of the earliest and most influential travel journals of the Middle Ages, *The Holy Places* was based on interviews with a Gallic bishop named Arculf, who had been shipwrecked on the west coast of Britain while returning from a pilgrimage to Jerusalem. Adomnán reinforced the bishop's memoirs by drawing extensively on manuscripts in the monastery library, adding information from a number of authors on Sicily, Egypt, Tyre, Crete, and Constantinople.

Adomnán made a gift of the book to King Aldfrid of Northumbria, from whom copies passed into various English monastic libraries and eventually formed the basis of Bede's own treatise on the subject. From England and Ireland, copies made their way into continental libraries. Eoin Neeson points out that the account of the life of St. George in Adomnán's work effectively introduced his cult into England.[63]

Adomnán is the principal patron of the Diocese of Raphoe, Ireland, and was widely revered in Scotland. His feast day is September 23.

Dympna of Gheel

On the rocky coast of Achill Island, which protrudes into the Atlantic off the coast of Mayo, can be found a well and a chapel dedicated to St. Damnat (Damhnat, Davnet) or Dympna, sometimes spelled Dymphna. Not far away is a tower said to have been used by Grace O'Malley, the formidable "Grainne" of saga and ballad, the pirate queen of sixteenth-century Galway. The contrast between the two legendary women could scarcely be more complete.

The tale of St. Dympna is preserved in a thirteenth-century Life by a canon named Pierre of the church of St. Aubert, which was commissioned by Guido, the bishop of Cambrai.[64] The legend claims that Dympna was the daughter of a pagan Irish king of Oriel and his Christian wife. When she died, the morose king became fixated on his daughter, perhaps because she reminded him of her mother. He resolved to marry her. With the aid of her chaplain, Gerebern, and some attendants (including the court jester), the terrified girl fled and sought refuge at Gheel in modern Belgium, near the city of Antwerp. There she established a hospice for the poor and sick of the region, especially those troubled in mind. Eventually, her father learned of her whereabouts and pursued her to Gheel. Enraged by the young woman's adamant resistance, he killed both Dympna and Gerebern.

Miracles of healing were soon reported to have occurred at the site of the martyrs' deaths. Cures for madness and epilepsy were especially noted, and Dympna became the patron saint of those afflicted with mental illness. The memory of Saints Dympna and Gerebern is kept in Belgium, Ireland, and the United States, where there is a National Shrine of St. Dymphna in Massillon, Ohio. As patron saint of Clogher, her feast day is celebrated on May 15.

Fintan (Munnu)

As Molaise and Mochuda were champions of the new methods of dating Easter that perturbed the Celtic churches in Britain and Iona, so Fintan moccu Moie (or Munnu, as he was hypocoristically known) defended the older custom in the debates at the Synod of Magh Ailbe. According to a remark in the Life of Cainnech, Munnu seems to have been the son of a druid, Tulchan, with whom he visited Iona before Columba's death.[65]

He founded a monastery, Tech-Munnu, or "Munnu's House," a site now known as Taghmon near the modern city of Wexford. According to Adomnán, when Munnu returned to Iona after Columba's death, the abbot Baithine sent him back to Ireland. A number of stories cluster around the historical figure, including at least one attempted voyage to the Land of Promise. Munnu died in 635.

Another saint named Fintan is identified with the monastic church of Clúain Eidnech (Clonenagh, in Loígis, now County Laois). He was a disciple of St. Colmán of Terryglass but achieved his renown by the excessive austerities of his rule. Ryan relates that his monks "refused the use of any animal, and not a single cow. If offered a little milk or butter they refused it with thanks. Should it happen perchance that someone had brought milk into the place unknown to the stern abbot, the vessel upon discovery had to be broken at once."[66] The ordinary fare of the monks seems to have been wild herbs and greens, and like the great Welsh saints, they drank only water.[67]

Saints of the Later Period

Samthann

Samthann of Clúain Bronaig (Clonbroney) in County Longford, also known as Safan, was born of a noble family of Ulster. Although betrothed at one time, she chose to follow Christ as a nun rather than marry.[68]

Samthann's reputation is that of a wise, even shrewd judge of character and a practical administrator, a woman impatient of pious pretension. Two of her answers to questions about prayer have been preserved. Asked which is the most appropriate position for prayer, standing, sitting, or lying prostrate, she replied simply, "Each and all of them." And to a student who confessed his intention to give up his studies in order to devote himself wholly to prayer, she retorted, "How will you ever be able to learn to concentrate in prayer if you can't even keep your mind on your books?"[69]

Samthann is reported to have been a poet. She is mentioned in the Lives of other saints and finds a place in the list of saints in the Stowe Missal.[70] Her death is listed for the year 739, and her feast day was kept on December 19.

For several centuries Clonbroney remained one of the three primary monasteries for women. The death of the last abbess is recorded in the year 1160. Samthann's reputation continued to spread, however. She finds mention later in the Middle Ages with Íte and Brigid in an ancient litany in the Austrian city of Salzburg.

Malachy

The last, troubled years of the Celtic church were graced by the lives of two illustrious saints, both reformers, who contributed in no small way to the destruction of the last remnants of the old Celtic order, but who also provide a bridge to the new order of the High Middle Ages: Malachy of Armagh and Lorcan Uá Tuathail (St. Laurence O'Toole).

Máel Máedoc Uá Morgair (1095–1148) is probably best remembered throughout the Christian church and beyond for something he never did: utter mischievous prophecies about the end of the world.

Born in Armagh, Malachy (as he is more conveniently known to the non-Gaelic world) seems to have been the son of the chief man of learning (*fer légind*) and fostered by Imar Uá hAedhagáin (O'Hagan), a hermit and reformer.[71] He first comes into view in 1120, when Cellach (Celsus), the archbishop of Armagh, named Máel Máedoc as his vicar. He was selected for additional training in the politics of the reform movement at Mochuda's great monastery of Lismore. In 1129, shortly before his death, Celsus named Malachy his successor. A five-year struggle for control of the primacy of Ireland ensued. Malachy prevailed in the end, but immediately resigned in favor of Gilla-mac-Liag (Gelasius) of Derry and *comarba* of Columba.

Malachy continued his efforts at reform from his see at Bangor, and in 1139 journeyed to Rome to obtain recognition for the two archbishops of Ireland. The pope said that the request must come from a national synod, but appointed Malachy his legate to the Irish church. During his travels, he stopped at Clairvaux, where he met St. Bernard. The two saints became fast friends, and Malachy sought and obtained permission to introduce the Cistercian Order into Ireland. The first Irish monastery was established at Mellifont in 1142.

Five other houses were established in the following five years. Then, in 1148, a national synod of bishops at Inis-Patraic made formal application for papal recognition of the two archbishoprics. As legate, Malachy set out for France, where he planned to meet Pope Eugenius. He stopped at Clairvaux, where, exhausted by age and pastoral care, he died on November 2 in the arms of St. Bernard.[72]

Máel Máedoc Uá Morgair was buried at Clairvaux in front of the high altar. St. Bernard's second sermon on the death of his friend expresses the heart of Malachy's spirituality: "He was poor toward himself, but rich to the poor, a father to orphans, a husband to widows, protector of the oppressed. A cheerful giver, he never asked for anything and it embarrassed him to receive. He made no distinction of sex or age or condition or rank. He never failed anyone, for his heart overflowed with sympathy for all."

Five years later Bernard himself died and was buried in the same grave as his Irish friend. St. Malachy is the principal patron of the churches of Armagh, and of Down and Connor. His feast is observed on November 3.

Laurence O'Toole

Lorcan Uá Tuathail was born in 1128.[73] He spent many years as a youth as a hostage of Diarmait Mac Murchadha (Dermont MacMurrough), the king of Leinster who brought such calamity upon Ireland in the twelfth century. Around the year 1140, he entered the monastery of Glendalough, where he became abbot in 1153. In 1162 he was selected by the primate of Ireland, Gelasius of Armagh, to be archbishop of Dublin.

In the midst of chaos resulting from the Norman invasion, Lorcan took the lead in the Irish effort to control their expansion. In 1175, the Treaty of Windsor recognized Ruadri a Conchobair (Rory O'Connor) as king of Connaught and *árd-ri*, or high king, but the Normans largely ignored it. Lorcan's own brother was killed in battle with Norman knights in 1178. The following year, Lorcan attended the Third Lateran Council and was made papal legate for Ireland. On his return journey, while attempting to negotiate with Henry II of England at his court at Eu in Normandy on behalf of Rory O'Connor, Lorcan died on November 14, 1180.

In 1191 the process was begun for his canonization, which was granted on December 11, 1225. As stated in the Bull of Canonization of Pope Honorius III, Lorcan was a man "totally dedicated to God: indefatigable in his prayer, stern in his bodily penances, unstinting in his almsgiving." His heart is preserved at Christ Church Cathedral in Dublin, where he is the principal patron of the city. His feast day is celebrated on November 14.

With the passing of Saints Malachy and Lorcan, following the revolutionary synods of Rathbreasil (1110) and Kells (1152), which divided Ireland into dioceses for the first time since Patrick, it can safely be said that the history of the Celtic churches as distinct entities had come to an end. The spirituality of the Celtic saints is another matter entirely. And just as that spirit had survived the tremors and cataclysms that had shaken then toppled the old order, so it would survive the coming of the Normans, the Tudor period, the era of Cromwell, and all the rest. Malleable as gold and more precious, it assumed a variety of configurations. But, as always, it remained what it had always been — an exquisite sense of the nearness of God and the other world, a keen longing for communion with that great Oneness, a delight in the beauty and power of Creation, and the occasional responsive bout of exuberant asceticism. Above all, perhaps, was an awareness of the glory of the Word that found its many-splendored expression in poetry, story, tales, and song.

FIVE

The Scottish Saints

Archeological evidence for a Christian presence in the region north of Britain known to the Celts as Alba, to the Romans as Caledonia, and since the early Middle Ages called Scotland can be dated to a very early period.[1] But the presence of a recognizable church with a body of believers, at least a rudimentary clergy, and some kind of organization, not to say buildings and other concrete remains, does not appear until well into the fifth and sixth centuries.

At first, the church of the northern regions was largely a missionary frontier of the Irish church, particularly the monastic *paruchia* of Columba, which evangelized the southern and especially the northern Picts from its base at Iona.[2] The exception, of course, is the establishment of a Christian community at the southern tip of Galloway by the shadowy figure known as Ninian (or Nynia or Ninniau), whose church at Rosnat (Whithorn), Candida Casa, seems to have served as an early monastic school as well as a missionary outpost for the evangelization of the southern Picts. Whether Ninian enjoyed any real success in his mission is uncertain. Another exception is the British presence in the Christian kingdoms of Rheged, Strathclyde, and Manaw Goddodin, all of whom engaged the Picts and Scots in a complex series of political, military, and religious encounters ending with their eventual expulsion of the Britons by the unified Scots and Picts under Kenneth mac Alpin in 842.

Gradually the uneasy federation developed into a distinctive Celtic culture and ultimately a more or less unified realm that took its name from the dominant Irish tribe that had invaded four centuries before, the Scotti. A Scottish church distinct from the *paruchia* of Columba emerged in the troubled era following the Synod of Whitby, as Pictish kings such as Nechtan mac Derile seized the opportunity it presented in 717 to drive recalcitrant Irish monks back to their island headquarters and eventually to Ireland itself. By the tenth century, Scottish bishops and abbots ruled a church that looked neither to Iona nor to Canterbury for direction and was increasingly wary (as were the Scottish chiefs) of the territorial hunger of the kings and bishops south of Hadrian's Wall.

The Scottish church also looked increasingly to its own saints for spiritual inspiration and guidance. Early Scottish spirituality and the contours of its saints' Lives remain largely Irish in form and often in content, understandably enough. But a distinct Scots sanctity would soon emerge.[3] Its development was tied in many respects to the early history of the Scottish nation itself.

The Scottish Realm

Two events in Columba's life were of special significance in the formation of the kingdom of Scotland. In 574, contrary to his own initial inclination, he anointed Aedán mac Gabráin as king of Scots, inaugurating a tradition of ecclesiastical oversight despite the fact that he was not a bishop. Second, in 585 or shortly afterward, he accompanied Aedán to a great convention at Druim Cett in Ulster, at which the sovereignty of the Dál Riadan kings in Scotland was upheld against the claims of the Uí Néill kings.[4]

Eventually, the Scots lost control of the territories of Irish Dál Riada when Domnall Brecc was defeated in 637 at the Battle of Magh Rath. His subsequent defeat and death in battle against the British of Strathclyde in 642 prepared the way for Pictish ascendancy in the seventh and eighth centuries. Although Dál Riada came under the control of the Angles of Northumbria at that time, the victory in 685 of Bridei (or Bruide) over the Northumbrian king, Ecgfrith, reversed Anglian expansion north of Hadrian's Wall for several centuries.[5]

In 717, King Nechtan furthered eroded Irish influence by siding with the Northumbrian church against the supporters of the Celtic rites. Promising to build a stone church in honor of St. Peter, he banished the nonconforming Irish monks from his realm. By 741, the dominance of the Picts was completed when Oengus I (727–61) defeated the Irish Scots and took the crown of Dál Riada. The first king to rule over both Picts and Scots was probably Constantine I, the son of Fergus of the Cenel nGabráin (d. 820). The hegemony continued until 839, when a combined army of Picts and Scots was defeated by the Norse.[6] After a stormy period of sometimes savage infighting, a unified realm emerged again under the first figure who is known to history as king of Scotland,

Cínead (Kenneth) mac Alpin, who significantly removed the last relics of Columba from Iona to his new capital of Dunkeld in 844.

The Scottish church experienced its next period of growth under Constantine II, who reigned from 900 to 943, when he abdicated to join the Culdees at St. Andrews. When he died there in 952, because of the "tanist" system of succession Constantine was followed by his cousin Malcolm I, who died in 954. He in turn was succeeded as king of Scotland by Indulf, while Malcolm's son became king of Strathclyde. The alternating tanist system continued until the reign of Duncan, the grandson of Malcolm II (1005–34), who finally united the kingdoms.[7] His son, Malcolm III *Ceann Mór* (or Canmore, "great chief"), was king from 1058 until 1093, and kings of the house of Canmore ruled Scotland until 1256. By then, not least because of the efforts of Malcolm Canmore's saintly queen, Margaret, both the church and the realm of Scotland were united and, for many years to come, at least relatively secure.

How St. Andrew Came to Scotland

An important step in Scotland's acquisition of an enduring ecclesiastical and apostolic identity occurred with the accession of St. Andrew the Apostle as the national patron. The first church at the site that would be called St. Andrews was probably founded in the eighth century. The medieval cathedral and Augustinian priory were begun in 1160, and the former was consecrated in 1318. The largest church in Scotland, and the primatial see, it was destroyed in the Reformation but remains impressive even in its ruined state.

The foundation legend survives in two versions, both medieval.[8] Despite differences, each relates how the Pictish king Oengus I, son of Fergus (Onuist, the son of Uurguist), who had defeated the Irish Scots in 741, founded a church on the coast of Fife in thanksgiving for a victory in battle over the Anglians and dedicated it to St. Andrew. In the shorter version, Oengus (or Angus) had a vision of St. Andrew while campaigning in Mercia. After his victory, he vowed a tenth part of his kingdom to God and St. Andrew. Meanwhile St. Regulus, a monk in Constantinople, had a vision urging him to take the relics of St. Andrew and sail with them to a place called *Rigmond,* "the royal mount." He was eventually met on the coast of Fife by King Angus, who granted him the site, a third of his kingdom, and the headship over all the churches of the Picts. In the longer version, St. Regulus arrived with the relics at Kylrimont, at that time called Muckros. After a battle with Athelstan at the Tyne, Angus met him and granted Regulus (and

St. Andrew) a *paruchia* extending from the Firth of Forth to the Firth of Tay.

Surely closer to the facts of history is the account preserved by Skene and other scholars that "Regulus" was actually a sixth-century Irish monk, Riaghail, the abbot of Muicinish in Lough Derg, who became a missionary to the Picts at St. Cainnech's monastery at Rigmond. The relics of St. Andrew were most likely brought to Scotland by an eighth century abbot, another Irish monk, Tuathal or Tuathalán.[9]

Early Saints of Scotland

Many fewer saints' Lives exist for Scotland than Ireland or Wales partly because of the destructiveness of the Reformation period, but also because many of the earliest saints in Scotland were Irish or British missionaries. There were, however, early as well as later Scottish saints whose names and sometimes Lives have been preserved for posterity. Sources are regrettably scarce. One of the richest of them is the *Breviarium Aberdonense* (the Aberdeen Breviary) commissioned by William Elphinstone, bishop of Aberdeen (c. 1500), who wanted to assemble from a variety of sources, most now no longer extant, brief Lives of the Scottish saints for readings during the liturgy on their feast days. It was Scotland's first printed book, published in Edinburgh in 1509 or 1510, and contains accounts of dozens of obscure or otherwise unknown saints such as Cullen, Duthac of Tain, Fillan, Machan, and Mirren of Paisley, as well as their more famous colleagues — Adomnán, Blane, Colmán, Kenneth, Ninian, and others. Another resource is the collection known as *The Legends of the Saints,* formerly attributed to the medieval writer John Barbour (c. 1375), which contains a number of late vernacular Lives.[10]

Despite the obscurity that will probably always cloak his life, Ninian, as we have seen already, is celebrated as one of the original saints of Scotland for a number of reasons: his mission was to the southern Picts, Candida Casa was located in Scotland, and he is remembered there in a multitude of place names and churches. Candida Casa was, of course, an "international" school for budding monks, one particularly favored by Irish students, as we have seen.

Not surprisingly, Columba is the principal saintly figure in early Scottish history. But in addition to Ninian, several other pre-Columban saints are recalled in both legends and "harder" media — inscriptions, place names, and texts, often by incorporation into other saints' Lives. Two of the earliest and most important of these early saints of Scotland may have been Picts or possibly Britons: St. Serf and his fosterling, St. Kentigern (Mungo), the patron saint of Glasgow.

Serf of Fife

A late sixth-century figure (or, some scholars claim, as late as the ninth), St. Serf (Servanus) of Fife was the founder of Culross and, according to Jocelin of Furness's later *Vita Sancti Kentigerni* and the anonymous *Vita Kentigerni*, the foster-father and first teacher of St. Kentigern.[11] Serf's name is unique in the register of saints and was almost completely unknown in early Celtic literature and to Bede.[12]

According to later and wholly fictitious legends, Serf came from Canaan or Israel, a wandering monk who, before he found the place of his resurrection at Culross, had studied at Alexandria in Egypt, was elected bishop in Canaan (presumably somewhere west of Egypt), went to Jerusalem at the advice of an angel, and there was made patriarch. Seven years later, guided by the same angel, Serf departed for Rome, where he was soon elected pope (sadly unrecorded in any known source). After a pontificate of seven years, the angel led him across the Alps, where his disciples were attacked by a horde of demons but, protected by Serf's prayers, survived. Eventually, Serf (and presumably his companions) arrived in Scotland, where he was welcomed by Adomnán (anachronistically enough) and assigned the area of Fife for his ministry. Following a brief altercation with the local king, Brude the son of Davogort, and a second meeting with Adomnán, Serf succeeded in establishing Culross and went on to make another foundation at Lochleven. After a suitably miraculous apostolate, which included raising the dead, curing the blind, lame, and deaf, and (for good measure) slaying a dragon, Serf died on July 1 sometime around mid-century and was buried at Culross. In 1217, a Cistercian abbey was founded on the site.

The tradition that Serf fostered Kentigern is not found in the *Vita Servani*, but comes from other sources, primarily the Latin lives of St. Kentigern, for whose disciples the connection with Serf was evidently more important than it was for Culross. As with many other saints' Lives, the intent was, as Macquarrie states, "to set out the territorial and jurisdictional claims of an early Christian church or monastery there." And in fact archeological evidence supports the likelihood that "Culross was Serf's chief church and the site of his monastic school."[13] Other than that, Serf remains a figure obscured by entertaining legends.

Kentigern of Glasgow

Kentigern (or Cyndeyrn, c. 518–603) was historically a close contemporary of Columba.[14] According to the Latin Life by Jocelin of Furness, he was the child of a princess named Thenau (or Thaney, sometimes Thanog in Irish), the daughter of the king of Lothian and herself later sainted.[15] Because she was pregnant after having been raped by Prince Owen, her father attempted to dispose of her by driving her off a cliff in a cart. Surviving that, she was set adrift in a coracle, but that floated ashore at Culross, where she was soon rescued by St. Serf. Serf, moreover, accepted St. Thaney's child and fostered him, giving him the name Mungo, "dear fellow," which is how Kentigern is remembered in much of Scotland. (Whether or not the story of Kentigern's Moses-like rescue reflects historical fact, it may well be true that as a child he was fostered by Serf.)

A number of charming stories adorn his early life, such as his resuscitation of Serf's pet robin, which little Mungo's schoolmates, jealous of the affection shown him by their master, killed and blamed on him. In another anecdote, his hostile chums extinguished the sanctuary lights he was charged to maintain in order to embarrass him, but at his prayers heavenly fire ignited them again.

Later, Kentigern chose to work among the "Cathures" in the area which would in time become the city of Glasgow. In the historically unreliable but adventuresome Life written by Jocelin of Furness, after some years Kentigern was driven from Scotland by the pagan tyrant Morcant, who regarded with suspicion his considerable success in converting the people to Christ. Kentigern took refuge in Wales at Llanelwy (St. Asaph's), where he founded a monastery and became its first bishop. After the accession of King Redderch the Bountiful following the Battle of Ardderyth in 573, he returned to Scotland and labored among the Cathures until his death around the year 603.[16] His feast day is January 13.

Irish Saints in Scotland

Before, during, and even after the divisive events precipitated by the Synod of Whitby, Irish monks ministered extensively in the lands of the Picts and Scots. Among them are found several whose names and deeds are preserved in places and legends, as well as finding mention in other saints' Lives.

Among pre-Columban missionaries, Buite (or Boite), the founder of the great monastery at Monasterboice, seems to have led a far-ranging preaching mission among the Picts in Scotland, as we have already seen. The legend that Buite raised King Nechtan from the dead may refer to his having baptized the Pictish king years before when he was in Ireland as a child. But besides preserving the memory that the first missionaries who came to the Picts were Irish monks, the story also establishes "facts" about the deeds of land claimed by the monks' successors, for

Nechtan is said to have promptly endowed Buite with a castle and several other sites.[17] Buite himself is remembered in the church he founded near Nechtan's fort, Kirkbuddo, that is, Buite's Church.[18]

Another Irish saint, Cainnech, or Kenneth, of Aghaboe (517–600) is remembered for his missionary work in Scotland and the Western Isles by a host of place names. Cainnech also founded the important monastic center on the east coast known as Kill-Rigmonaig (Rigmond), which was changed to St. Andrew's when the relics of that saint were brought there in 736.

Adomnán claims that Cainnech visited Columba at Iona a number of times and accompanied him on several journeys, including the important embassy to King Brude. In one remarkable story of their friendship, Columba and some of his monks were returning to Iona when their boat was threatened with submersion by a sudden storm. The crew begged Columba to pray for their safe return, but he replied, "Today the duty of praying for your safety is not mine, but Cainnech's!" At that moment in Aghaboe, many miles away, Cainnech was moved by a sudden inspiration and dashed from the refectory to the oratory in such haste that he lost a sandal. He explained to his astonished monks, "This is no time to eat, when Columba's boat is in peril on the sea!" His prayers were heard, and the boat reached safety.[19] That we are perhaps not dealing with the plain facts of history is suggested by another story Adomnán tells of the time Cainnech left his staff behind on a visit to Iona, but it miraculously caught up with him before he reached Ireland.

A number of other Irish saints roughly contemporary with Columba figure prominently in the early history of the church in Scotland: St. Moluag of Lismore, St. Maelrubhi of Applecross, and the martyr St. Donnán of Eigg and his companions, all of whom labored for the conversion of the pagan tribes in the west and Western Islands.

A year before Columba and his monks sailed for Í, Moluag (or Molúa, from his Irish name Lugaigh plus the affectionate prefix, also known as Murlach) established a missionary base among the Picts at Lismore, an island in Loch Linnhe on the west coast of Scotland. A monk from Bangor, Moluag had been preceded by St. Comgall himself, who as a Pict was at an advantage in securing a welcome from the powerful King Brude. For years, Moluag labored among the Picts in the eastern, northern, and southern ranges of Alba, founding churches and monasteries. He died around the year 592 and is remembered on June 25.[20]

Maelrubhi was another monk of Bangor who followed Moluag's footsteps half a century later. Of mixed Pict and Scot parentage, he was born in Ireland around the year 642 and, like his predecessor, became a monk at Comgall's great monastery. He traveled to Alba, where he founded a

monastery at Applecross in Ross. From there, beginning in 673 he traveled throughout the Western Isles, where his name is preserved in almost
two dozen parish churches. Although not the first missionary to work
there, he is rightly considered the Apostle of Skye.[21] According to later
legend, he died a martyr at the hands of Viking pirates in 722. Like the
martyr Dympna, Maelrubhi also became celebrated in regard to curing
mental illnesses, especially at his holy well on Inis Maree in Loch Maree, not far from Applecross, both of which are named for the saint. His
feast day was observed on April 21.[22]

Donnán of Eigg was one of the Irish missionaries who preceded Maelrubhi to Skye. He was a monk of Iona who labored among the pagans
of the Western Isles, settling eventually at Eigg, which was under the
control of a pagan queen who terrorized the people with her bands of
sea-roving marauders. Irritated by the establishment of a group of Irish
monks, she ordered them all to be killed, despite the protests of the islanders. When the pirates approached, as the story goes, Donnán was
presiding at mass on Easter Sunday in the year 616. He asked that the
monks be allowed to finish their devotions. Then he and his fifty-three
companions were promptly massacred. (McNeill suggests that this may
have been the first appearance of Viking raiders in the Hebrides.)[23] All
their names are recorded in the Martyrology of Tallaght for April 17.

Despite the large-scale and lasting accomplishments of these and
other early Irish missionaries, none is remembered with the affection
and tenacity of the first abbot of Í and Scotland's first patron saint,
Colum of the Church. Although a prince of Ireland and a church-
man of considerable influence there, Columba's greatest contribution
to Celtic Christianity no doubt took place in Scotland where, in fact,
a greater number of churches were added to his *paruchia* than in his
native country.

Columba and Iona

Columba's achievements span the eighty miles between Ulster and Iona,
the tension between sixth-century Scots and Picts, and even the differences that separate today's Presbyterian Scots and the Catholic Irish. His
biographers suitably embellished his early life with miracles, such as how
he turned water into wine for St. Finnian when he was studying at Magh
Bile, or how, when he was being tutored by the poet Gemmán, a young
girl was murdered despite their efforts to shield her. Columba declared
that her assailant's soul would descend to hell as swiftly as hers as-
cended to heaven and the murderer dropped dead. But Columba's factual
accomplishments were miracle enough to earn him lasting renown.

His exploits in Ireland have been told elsewhere. In Scotland he is remembered for his missionary work among the Scots and Picts, his friendship with Aedán mac Gabráin, and his spectacular initial confrontation in 564 (probably as an ambassador of Aedán) with Brude mac Mailchon, the high king of the Picts, at his fortress near Loch Ness. As the story goes, when Columba, Comgall, and Kenneth approached the gates, they found them closed. Columba struck them with his staff, and to the astonishment of the Picts, they burst open of their own accord. Whether this incident is a pious legend or fact, Columba's embassy to Brude undoubtedly opened the gates to the conversion of the northern reaches of Alba and reduced the pressure on Christian Dál Riada.[24]

Columba had arrived on Í (later known as Iona) with his twelve companions in the year 563, although he may have founded a hermitage on nearby Hinba (identified as Colonsay or possibly Jura)[25] before establishing what would become one of the most important monasteries in the Celtic world. At the time, Í was part of the Irish kingdom of Dál Riada, ruled by his cousin Conaill. (Later accounts claim that he was given the island by Brude, which seems less likely, although Brude had by that time effectively reduced Conaill to vassalage, and he may have simply confirmed the grant.)

From his monastic headquarters on Í, Columba exercised considerable spiritual direction over the kingdom of Dál Riada, whose capital had been transferred from Ireland to Scotland generations earlier by King Fergus Mór. After Conaill's death, Columba had a series of religious experiences while in seclusion on Hinba. These persuaded him to accept (and anoint) Aedán mac Gabráin as king of Dál Riada rather than his favored candidate, Aedán's brother, Eoghan. The choice was truly providential, for it became a decisive moment in the early history of Scotland. The Scots of Dál Riada soon came to recognize Columba as their spiritual and ecclesiastical chief. (Columba's anointing of Aedán was the first in the British Isles, and the prototype for all that followed.)

The division of Dál Riada between Ireland and Scotland and especially the transfer of the capital to Scotland had provided an opportunity for northern Irish kings, particularly the Uí Néill, to demand tribute and even threaten Irish Dál Riada with annexation. At the Convention of Druim Cett, Columba most likely played a decisive role in preserving Dalriadan independence in Ireland for many years to come.

While Adomnán's Life of Columba is remarkably free of the usual stories about the acquisition of monastic territory (especially in the face of later disputes), an account is preserved elsewhere of Columba's saintly persuasion at work in the donation of land for the foundation of St. Drostán's monastery at Deer, in Buchan.[26] When Columba and

Drostán petitioned the *mormaer,* or steward, of Buchan, Bede Cruith-
nech, for the land, he refused to grant it. Soon, one of his sons fell
seriously ill. So Bede approached the saints to obtain a healing prayer and
offered them the land. At their prayers, the boy was restored to health.
The story may be fictitious, but it established an important connection
between the Mormaers of Buchan and the monastery of Deer.

One of the most intriguing tales about Columba concerns a monster
in Loch Ness that threatened one his monks, Lugne, whom Columba had
sent into the water to retrieve a boat from the farther bank. (This event
occurred on the famous journey to Brude's fortress.) Making the sign of
the cross, Columba held the monster at bay until Lugne returned safely.
The beast then slid back into the lake, if not, apparently, into oblivion.
(Recent commentators have expressed doubts whether this beast was the
"real" Loch Ness monster, however, since it behaved more like a typical
sea-serpent and also appeared in the wrong part of the lake.)[27]

Columba labored for the salvation of the Scots and Irish for thirty-
four years, returning, as we have seen, several times to Ireland, where
he still exercised considerable spiritual sway. All that time, according to
Adomnán, "he could not let even one hour pass that was not given to
prayer or reading or writing or some other good work. Night and day
he so unwearyingly gave himself to fasts and vigils that the burden of
each single work seemed beyond the strength of man. Yet through all
he was loving to everyone, his holy face was always cheerful, and in his
inmost heart he was happy with the joy of the Holy Spirit."

Years of ministry had tempered the fighting spirit and created one
of the most loving and lovable saints of Ireland and Scotland. As he
lay dying, his last instruction to his monks was that they "keep among
you unfeigned love with peace." Columba's spirituality as a *peregrinus
pro Christo* is admirably described in these lines from the Old Irish Life
cited on his feast day:

> a man leaves his fatherland completely in body and soul even as the
> twelve apostles left, and those of the perfect pilgrimage, for whom
> the Lord foretold great good when he said in the gospel: You have
> forsaken for my sake your country and your kindred, your wealth
> and your worldly happiness, that you may receive a hundredfold
> of good from me here in the world and life everlasting yonder after
> the day of judgment.
>
> Here, in truth, are they of the perfect pilgrimage, in whose per-
> son the prophet speaks: I give you thanks for it, O God. I have
> pilgrimage and exile in the world even as the elders who went
> before.[28]

Columba was buried on Í, but his bones proved as restless as the man himself. For many years, they lay quietly in the monastic cemetery under a simple marker. Then about fifty years after his death, his remains were removed and placed in a beautifully embellished reliquary that became one of the treasures of the monastery. Its legend was sufficiently well known that Í was raided many times by Vikings bent on plunder. Over the years, scores of monks died under their swords rather than reveal its location. What became of the reliquary itself is unknown, but it was widely believed that Columba's relics were eventually divided, some being taken back to Ireland, where according to tradition they were interred at Downpatrick, while the others were transferred to Dunkeld by Kenneth mac Alpin in 844.

Iona of the Saints

In his history of the English church and people, the venerable St. Bede recalls that the monastery on the island called Hii (or Í, or, by his time, Iona) was for a long time the chief of almost all others of the northern Irish as well as the Picts, and the abbots of Iona exercised spiritual jurisdiction over all their people.[29] The subsequent history of Iona concerns both Scotland and Ireland in different ways.

Only eighty miles from the Irish coast, Iona is a stony, windswept island, possessing enough fertile soil to support a few farms. It is just under three and a half miles long by about one and a half across. A mile-wide channel divides it from the much larger island of Mull, from which the modern traveler can take a ferry to visit the ancient site. The old buildings have long since vanished, but the Iona Community, an ecumenical Christian association founded in 1938 by the late George MacLeod of Fuinary, has carefully restored the medieval Benedictine monastery built over them.[30]

Two of the greatest artistic creations of the Western world had their origins on Iona, many believe at the hand of Columba himself, although they were finally products of the eighth and ninth centuries: the incomparable Book of Kells and the Book of Durrow. The famous "Battler," or *Cathach,* of the O'Donnells, now in the Royal Irish Academy, is a copy of the Book of Psalms also ascribed to Columba and long believed to be the book he copied from Finnian at Magh Bile.

The subsequent history of Iona alternated between calamity and recovery. Late in the seventh century, the divisions introduced by the controversies associated with the reform of the liturgical calendar led to a diminishment of Iona's prestige in both Scotland and Ireland, where the Patrician communities and Kildare became more prominent. In Scotland, weakened by internal dissension after Adomnán's acceptance of the reforms around 680, Iona's influence was further reduced by the domination of Rheged and Dál Riada by Northumbrian Angles. In 717, the Pictish king, Nechtan IV, made common cause with Northumbria, driving all the monks of Iona from his realms back into Argyll, as noted in the Annals of Ulster.

Through all of this, Iona retained its primacy among the many churches and monasteries of Columba's *paruchia* in Ireland and in Scotland. But in the ninth century, Viking pirates began their devastating raids on the monasteries of the western coast, sacking Iona in 795, 802, and 806, when eighty-six monks were murdered. In 814, the abbot Cellach transferred the seat of Columba's *comarba* to Kells. As the Viking terror continued, it was sometimes moved to other Irish monasteries offering even greater security. But despite the slow if inexorable erosion of Iona's influence and prestige, Columban monks retained a presence at the monastery, even after another massacre in 825, when the acting head of the community, an Irish monk named Blathmac, was hacked to death with his companions for refusing to disclose the hiding place of Columba's reliquary.[31] The monastery was attacked again as late as 986.

After Kenneth mac Alpin's accession around the year 843, Iona's influence increased for a while, although it never regained its stature as the foremost center of learning and art among the Columban monasteries. Pictish, Scottish, and even Norwegian kings were buried in its cemetery. In 980, the Norwegian Anlaf Cuaran (Olaf the Red), once king of Northumbria and subsequently of Dublin, who ten years earlier had looted the monastery at Kells, abdicated his throne and became a monk on Iona.[32] The abbey was restored by St. Margaret in the eleventh century and ultimately taken over by the Benedictines in 1202, who replaced the simpler Celtic buildings in the larger style of the continental monks. Iona's early history ended with the dissolution of the monasteries in 1539. Uniquely, because of the work of George MacLeod and the Iona Community, it was reborn as a center of Celtic monastic spirituality in the twentieth century.

Adomnán

A long series of saintly abbots succeeded Columba at Iona. The most famous of these was the ninth, St. Adomnán, Columba's chief biographer, whom we have met before. Irish-born, he was abbot of Iona from 679 until his death there in 704.

Like Columba, Adomnán was a diplomat as well as a scholar and poet. His Life of Columba is the masterpiece of early Celtic hagiography, one of the treasures of world literature. His other writings, as we have had occasion to note, were also influential. His efforts to protect women, children, and clerics from the horrors of combat created a milestone in the evolution of human rights legislation. Yet Adomnán failed in his bid to convince most of his monks on Iona to accept the revised form of the liturgical calendar and other reforms of the late seventh century.

He was, it is said, of the same royal blood as Columba, being born in Donegal of the Cenel Conaill in 624. Having achieved success and fame as the *anamchara* of Finachta, later the high king of Tara, where he is remembered in several memorials, Adomnán tutored the exiled Anglian prince Aldfrith, who lived in Ireland for some twenty years. In 679, Adomnán was elected abbot of the monastery on Iona, the ninth of that line, but he retained his important connections with both the high king, Finachta, and Aldfrith. This would be of great benefit when in 684 men of the Anglian King Ecgfrith of Northumbria raided the coast of Meath, taking a considerable number of prisoners. (Kenney suggests the otherwise unprovoked raid may have been in retaliation because the Irish were sheltering Aldfrith).[33]

A year later, Ecgfrith was killed in battle with the Picts (a penalty, Bede says, for his unholy action the previous year). When Aldfrith succeeded to the throne, Adomnán traveled to Bamburgh in 686 and obtained the release of the prisoners. He continued to maintain close relations with the Anglian court, and during a visit there a few years later was persuaded to adopt the reforms urged by the Roman clergy attendant on the king. Among them was Ceolfrith, the abbot of Jarrow (Bede's monastery). According to the ever supercilious historian, Adomnán "was earnestly advised by those more learned than himself not to presume to act contrary to the universal customs of the church, whether in keeping of Easter or in any other observances, seeing that his following was very small and situated in a remote corner of the world."[34] Although he extols Adomnán as "a wise and worthy man, excellently grounded in the study of the Scriptures," he adds, sorrowfully, that on his return to Iona the learned abbot failed utterly to win over more than a handful of his monks, still smarting more than a generation after the judgment at Streanaeshalch.

Bede next informs us that Adomnán then sailed to Ireland, "and by his simple teaching showed its people the proper time of Easter. He corrected their ancient error and restored nearly all who were not under the jurisdiction of Iona to Catholic unity, teaching them to observe Easter at the proper time."[35] Here, however, Bede's animosity led him astray. The southern Irish abbots and bishops had in fact adopted the new Easter cycle a century earlier. Adomnán's successes among the Irish would, moreover, have occurred among monks under Iona's jurisdiction. In any case, Adomnán undeniably became one of the chief proponents of the reform in the north of Ireland on his return there in 692 and 697. It was on this second pastoral visit to attend the Synod of Birr that he promulgated the famous Law of the Innocents, or Cáin Adamnáin.[36]

Adomnán died in 704 and is remembered on September 23.

Other Irish Saints in Scotland

A whole family of saints sired by Cellach (Kelly), a seventh-century king of Leinster, came to Scotland as missionaries. Cellach's son Comghan (Coman), his sister Kentigerna with her three sons, his nephew Fillan, and six others joined him in founding a monastery at Lochalsh in western Ross.[37] Kentigerna is known as the mother of saints, the most famous of whom is Fillan, and "Loch Lomond's Lady of Grace." After the death of her husband, Feredach, Kentigerna sailed with Comghan to Scotland. Several churches are named for her, but she is remembered as having become a recluse on a small island in Loch Lomond, sometimes called the Nun's Island, where a parish church was named for her. She died around the year 734.

Fillan (or Foillan) was a monk of Munnu's monastery in Wexford and seems to have preceded his mother and uncle to Scotland, where he was a hermit near St. Andrew's. When Comghan and Kentigerna arrived in Ross, Fillan joined them there. He is one of the most popular of the early saints, his name being preserved in many churches, fairs, a cave (consequently destroyed by Reformers in the seventeenth century), and several holy wells. Mary Ryan D'Arcy relates that the great Scottish hero Robert the Bruce had a special devotion to St. Fillan, having obtained a relic of the saint on the eve of the decisive Battle of Bannockburn in 1314. Having spent the night in prayer, Bruce later attributed his success in battle to Fillan's intercession. His abbot's staff and bell are still preserved.

Comghan is commemorated on October 13, Kentigerna on January 7, and Fillan on January 19. In Irish calendars the Daughters of Feredach are remembered on March 23.

One of the most celebrated of the Irish saints of Iona was the monk Blathmac, about whom Walafrid Strabo, the Benedictine abbot of Reichenau (from 838 to 849), wrote a Life in Latin hexameter verse shortly after Blathmac's death at the hands of the Vikings during their fourth raid in 825.[38] Like Énda and Columba, Blathmac was born of a royal Irish family but became a monk and later abbot in Ireland. Desiring to prove his love for Christ, even to the shedding of his blood, he obtained permission to move to Iona, for several decades a choice prey of marauding Vikings. There he joined the small community left to maintain the monastic presence on the island and carry on its pastoral commitments to the Christians of the western coast.

In due course, on a day when the abbot, Diarmuid, was away, Blathmac had a prophetic warning that an attack was imminent. At his direction, the monks quickly buried the precious reliquary containing Columba's bones. Blathmac offered the others the choice of remaining or leaving, and then returned to the duties of the monastery. The next morning, January 19, the Vikings attacked during the celebration of mass. They massacred the monks who had stayed behind, but offered to spare Blathmac if he would divulge the location of the great reliquary. He refused and was slowly hacked to pieces, Walafrid says, on the very steps of the altar. When the remaining monks returned, they buried Blathmac where he had died.[39] His memory is celebrated on January 19.

Other Scottish Saints

Because of the dependence of the Scottish and Pictish churches on Irish and British missionaries, the roster of native-born Scottish saints in the early Christian period is much shorter than the other Celtic nations. But as we have seen, there were a number of them. Their Lives are few, however. Exceptions are those of St. Catroe and, a century later, St. Margaret, one of Scotland's patron saints.

Among the earlier saints, Machar is said to have established a church in 594 at what is now Old Aberdeen. The cathedral that bears his name was begun in 1136. Conan, another native Scot, is remembered at St. Conan's Kirk on the shore of Loch Awe, near modern Oban. He was a pupil of Columba at Iona and is the patron saint of Lorn. St. Rule is associated with the area around St. Andrews.

Blane the Culdee

A younger contemporary of Columba and Kentigern, Blane was born about 565 near Kingarth, in Bute. He was the son of Aedán, an Irish king of Dál Riada. His uncle, St. Cathan, was the bishop and founder of the important monastery of Kingarth. But Blane was first educated under Comgall at Bangor and at Cainnech's monastery at Aghaboe before returning to Kingarth, where he eventually succeeded his uncle as abbot and bishop.

Blane evangelized large areas of Strathclyde, Perth, and the Pictish highlands of the north, in all of which he is remembered in church dedications and place names such as Kilblane (and Kilblain). But Blane's best-known foundation was in the valley above Dunagoil in Bute, which takes its name from him, Dunblane. Blane died around the year 590 and thus was too early to be part of the Célí Dé reform, but he is fondly remembered in Scotland as "Blane the Culdee." His feast day was observed until the Reformation on August 10 at St. Andrews, Dunkeld, and Argyll.

Like Kingarth, the monastery at Dunblane flourished for hundreds of years until, in 790, in the rule of the seventh abbot, the buildings were burned to the ground by Viking raiders. The cathedral church was rebuilt, however, in the twelfth century. Blane's bell is still preserved there.[40]

Kaddroe

While most of the missionary saints to the European mainland in the ninth and tenth centuries were Irish and British emigrés, one at least was a native Scot, although born of a princely Irish family. In *The Saints of Scotland,* Alan Macquarrie includes an account of the Life of St. Catroe (or Kaddroe), who traveled to Germany in 941 and became, in time, abbot of Metz.[41]

Kaddroe was born in 900 and was fostered as a youth by his uncle, a priest remembered as St. Bean (Beanus). He seems to have been trained for a time at Armagh, but having become a teacher at Bean's monastic school, Kaddroe eventually decided to become a pilgrim. Bean dissuaded him for a time, but Kaddroe and several companions left for the mainland in 941 after meeting with King Castantin (Constantine) II, who conducted them to Cumbria. The party traveled to York, where they were given hospitality by a king named Erik, whose wife seems to have been related to Kaddroe. From York, Kaddroe passed on to London, after which he was received by King Edmund of Wessex at Winchester and escorted to the Channel by the archbishop of Canterbury, Oda (941–58).

Befriended by a noblewoman named Hersent, the pilgrims were established in religious communities in Burgundy, where they were professed as monks. Kaddroe's appointment as abbot of Waulsort was confirmed in 946 by King Otto I, later the Holy Roman Emperor. Kaddroe's reputation and a few helpful miracles convinced the bishop of Metz, Adalbero I, of his sanctity, and in 953 Kaddroe was installed as head of the once famous but decayed abbey of St. Clement. He restored the abbey to its former glory, and his miracles and holiness grew apace.

Eventually Kaddroe was summoned to the court by the Empress Adelaide, mother of the future Otto II. Before departing, Kaddroe predicted that he would die before returning to Metz. After a lengthy stay at court, Kaddroe sought permission to return to Metz. But the empress urged him to stay on, which he did, working several miracles of healing. Adelaide eventually released him, but on his way back to Metz in 971, the aged abbot died. His body was carried on to Metz, where he was interred in the Church of St. Felix. In the year 991, the Emperor Otto III referred to him as "Cadroel of blessed memory." His feast day was observed on March 5.

Margaret the Queen

Scotland's first canonized saint and second patron was a laywoman, the daughter and granddaughter of kings, the wife of King Malcolm III of Scotland, and the mother of a brood of royalty, some of whom were uncommonly saintly if never sainted. She was not Scottish, but of English and German parentage.[42]

Margaret was the granddaughter of King Edmund Ironside, who was defeated in an intense conflict in 1014 by Canute the Great, the first Danish king of England. Edmund died in 1016. Rightly fearing for their lives, his sons Edward and Edgar fled abroad. Edward eventually arrived at the court of Hungary, where he married Princess Agatha, the daughter of the martyred king, St. Stephen. Margaret was born in 1046. When she was about ten, her father was recalled to England by St. Edward the Confessor, who had ended the Danish conquest, but he died almost immediately on his return. Margaret remained at the English court for the next ten years, until the defeat of King Harold by William of Normandy in 1066 overthrew the native regime. In 1068, Queen Agatha, her son Edgar, Margaret, and her sister fled to the court of Malcolm III of Scotland, who ruled from 1058 until 1093. Malcolm was quickly alert to the benefits of a tie by marriage to the now exiled English royal family, with whose help he had overthrown the regime of MacBeth.

Their marriage was not merely one of convenience, however. Malcolm and Margaret not only produced eight children, some of them as saintly as their mother; genuine love and affection existed between the royal couple. Malcolm cheerfully endorsed his wife's support of the poor and infirm as well as her generous grants to the Culdees, endowments to churches, and efforts at reforming clerical abuses. Among other accomplishments, Margaret was responsible for the rebuilding of Iona.[43] In 1070, by founding an abbey at Dumfermline, the ancient capital of Scotland, she also introduced the Benedictine Order into Scotland.

Far from being a Celtic-hating queen, Margaret seems to have learned enough Gaelic to communicate with the many hermits she visited (as well as the Scottish members of her own family). Her objections to practices in the Celtic church greatly resembled those of Saints Lorcan O'Toole and Malachy O'More a century later, among them secular control of churches, the neglect of celibacy among the clergy, and lack of participation in the sacraments. By strengthening the Scottish episcopacy, Margaret prepared the way for the strong and patriotic bishops of the fourteenth century who, siding with Robert the Bruce, consolidated ecclesiastical as well as national independence.

But like many saints before her, Margaret, even though a queen, had to confront the entrenched misogyny that often festered in the spirituality of male saints. According to Goscelin's Life of St. Laurence of Canterbury, written at the beginning of the twelfth century, when Margaret visited the church built at Fordoun to honor St. Laurence of Canterbury, she was warned by the canons that no woman was allowed to enter the precincts. Margaret replied that she intended only to honor and exalt the shrine, and went ahead. Suddenly, she was seized with severe pains and had to be rushed away. Later, she blamed herself for not observing the cautions and asked the canons to pray for her. Her gifts to the church were generous.[44]

Malcolm and Margaret both died in 1093, he in battle because of the treachery of false friends, she of grief four days later at the age of forty-eight. Despite several fluctuations in fortune, the descendants of Malcolm Canmore and Margaret eventually secured the royal succession over the tanist system, which led in time to greater political stability. Particularly under David I, Margaret's third son ("a sair [sure] saint for the crown"), the diocesan episcopate was extended and strengthened. Margaret was canonized in 1250. Her feast day is celebrated on November 16 in the Roman calendar.

Despite the revisionism that inevitably dogs the steps of scholarly examination, the essential witness of Margaret's holiness of life and the impact of her sanctity (as well as her political acumen) have survived recent analysis, as summarized in the concluding words of Derek Baker's fine essay:

> Margaret was a remarkable woman in a turbulent age and society, no more a saint, I would suggest, than her daughter or her youngest son, but no less, and like them in temper and attitude. If any final, definitive assessment must await the critical reappraisal of the sources, and in particular of Turgot's Life, and if her life was less dramatically and practically influential than is sometimes claimed, we may yet agree with Turgot, "Let others admire in others the signs of miracles; I esteem much more in Margaret the works of mercy. Signs are common to the good and to the bad, but works of true piety and love are peculiar to the good. . . . Let us more worthily hold her in awe, because through her devotion to justice, piety,

mercy and love we contemplate in her, rather than miracles, the deeds of the ancient fathers."[45]

Richard of St. Victor

Margaret would not be the last of the saints of Scotland, although canonizations would be rare in the wake of the religious conflicts of the Middle Ages and afterward. Among Scottish saints of the later medieval period, at least passing mention must be made of Richard of St. Victor and the great Franciscan theologian and philosopher Duns Scotus.

Richard (d. 1173) was a Scottish (or possibly Irish) canon regular at the Abbey of St. Victor in Paris, the greatest mystical theologian of his time. He followed in the spiritual tradition of Hugh of St. Victor, who died about a decade before Richard entered the abbey. Like the older mystic and theologian, Richard couched his teaching in the form of biblical allegories, but also wrote philosophical and scriptural commentaries. His most influential work was a pair of treatises on mystical contemplation, *Benjamin Minor* and *Benjamin Major* (also known as *The Twelve Patriarchs* and *The Mystical Ark*).[46]

Later, Richard was appointed prior of St. Victor's, but his later years were troubled by the financial irresponsibility of the abbot, who was removed from office in 1171, two years before Richard's death. Richard's teaching influenced a host of great theologians in the later Middle Ages, including St. Bonaventure, St. Thomas Aquinas, the author of *The Cloud of Unknowing,* Meister Eckhart and the Rhineland mystics, and, through Bernadino of Laredo, the great Spanish saints and mystics, Teresa of Avila and John of the Cross.

Duns Scotus

Born in 1266 in Littledean, Scotland (now known as Duns), John Duns was the son of Irish settlers who was tutored by his uncle, Elias Duns, a Franciscan friar, in Dumfries. After his admission to the Franciscans and his ordination in 1291 (on St. Patrick's Day), John was sent to Oxford and Paris to teach. In 1306, he successfully defended the doctrine of the Immaculate Conception against the Thomists in a famous disputation. Next sent to lecture in Cologne in 1307, he died suddenly on November 8, 1308. The case for his formal enrollment among the saints is being actively promoted.

Scotland also produced its quota of martyrs during the troubled and bloody Reformation period, not least of whom, from at least one perspective, was Mary Stuart, the last Catholic monarch of Scotland and mother of James VI, whose accession as James I of the United Kingdoms suspended Scotland's hard-won independence for the following four hundred years. During those long years, and especially in the nineteenth century, many saintly Scottish men and women, both Protestant and Catholic, renewed the ancient tradition of Kentigern, Columba, and Kaddroe, as Scots missionaries carried the gospel with them to Africa, Asia, Latin America, and wherever the Spirit led them.

SIX

Brittany and Beyond
The Pilgrim Saints

Since ancient times, land-based peoples have tended to regard the sea as a barrier to travel and communication. But as E. G. Bowen has shown in his important study, *Saints, Seaways and Settlements,* in the period between the end of Classical Antiquity, dated conveniently at 476, and the beginning of the Middle Ages, sometime after the Carolingian era, water routes were looked on by the Celts as highways connecting tribes and monastic *familiae,* especially where immigration had divided them across channels, estuaries, lakes, and the great ocean itself.[1]

Such a perspective did not so much ignore the very real dangers of travel by water, especially on the open sea, as it recognized the even greater dangers attendant upon travel by land, where hostile kings, bandits, roving bands of freebooters, barbarians, Vikings, and wild animals, not to say unpredictable weather and the ordinary hazards of misdirection, could prolong a journey greatly or end it violently. And the fact is that a sea route was also often the shortest distance between two points. Brittany provides a case in point.

Bound by the sea on two long coasts, it was a land known by a number of names in its long, colorful history. The early Celts and even the Romans called it Armorica, a name created from the word *ar,* "on," plus *mor,* "the sea." Later, after substantial migrations of Christian refugees from Britain and Cornwall in the sixth and seventh centuries, it was distinguished from "Greater Britain" as Britannia Minor ("Lesser Britain"), or simply Brittany. The French have called it Cornouaille as well as Bretagne, but it is known to its Breton-speaking Celtic people as Brezh. The Breton language is not derived from that of the ancient Gauls of Caesar's time, but has strong affinities with Welsh and Cornish because of the successful occupation by the refugees and colonists from the north fleeing the invading Saxons.

There were Christians in Brittany long before the tide of immigration began in the sixth century.[2] It was an ancient land even when the first missionaries arrived there, perhaps late in the third century. Pre-Celtic megalithic tombs and stone circles such as those at Carnac date back to the fourth millennium before the Common Era. England's Stonehenge, which uniquely resembles them, may have been constructed by immigrants from Armorica, but for what reason is still veiled in the mists of prehistory. A thriving Celtic culture based on sea trade existed along the coastal areas by the second century B.C.E. During Julius Caesar's protracted Gallic Wars, he battled and destroyed over two hundred ships at Quiberon Bay in 56 B.C.E.[3]

The origins of Christianity in Armorica are also veiled in legend, but it seems reasonably clear that organized communities were in place by the beginning of the fifth century.[4] By 450, the pressure of Saxon invasion had already begun to drive Christian Britons south across the *Muir Nicht* (the Southern Sea) to seek safety and new homes. Within a century, the trickle had become a flood. Still, the refugees and colonists seem to have been integrated into the sparsely settled peninsula without violence or even significant disruption. However, the language of Armorica would be forever altered by the new Celtic settlers, just as the name "Little Britain" proved to be permanent.

The immigrants were often led by priests or monks who settled at a site suitable for a church or monastic cell, an area that became known as a *plou,* or parish. (As with the Irish *cill* and the Welsh *llan, plou* became a prefix to a saint's name and thus fixed the memory of these religious pioneers.)[5] Still more saintly monks and priests came later to minister to the Christians who had already settled in their new homeland. Among them were Brioc (Brieuc), Tudwal, Mac Low (Maclovius or Malo), Samson of Dol, Mehan, Winwaloe, Paul Aurelian, and Gildas.[6] Both St. David (Dewi) and his Irish mother, St. Non, were also active in Brittany.[7]

The medieval Lives of the early Breton saints suffer from the same tendency that make the Lives of British, Irish, and Scottish saints unreliable as historical biographies — the desire to enhance the reputation of the saint by fanciful embellishment (often based on folklore), the need to provide a charter establishing ancient origins (preferably by a royal grant of land), and a very human interest in urging primacy or at least superiority in regard to the claims and pretensions of rival monasteries and churches. Nevertheless, some of the information contained in the Lives points to facts confirmed in other documents of the time, and details of both monastic and parochial life are often invaluable.

By far the more renowned saints of the Breton church were the British and Irish priests, monks, and bishops who led their flocks to safety across the Western Sea or the missionaries who followed them. Supported by a host of place names, their stories provide at least an outline of the early history of Christian Brittany and additional evidence of the sometimes astonishing spirituality of the Celtic saints.

British Saints in Brittany

We have already encountered a number of British (Welsh) missionaries to Brittany and beyond, including Paul Aurelian and Illtud. According to later accounts of his Life, Brioc of Cardigan (c. 440–530) was a descendant of Macsen Wledig (Maximus Magnus) and was first known as Tyfriog.[8] As a child, he was sent to Gaul by his parents for instruction by St. Germanus. He returned to Britain, where he remained for a number of years until bidden by an angelic revelation to return to the land of the Franks. Like most British missionaries, he went by way of Cornwall. Finally arriving in Brittany, Brioc founded an important monastery at Trécor (Tréguier). He also founded an abbey on the site of the present cathedral city of Saint-Brieuc, where he died around the year 530.

St. Tudwal, or Tugdual, who may have been Brioc's nephew, was his successor at Trécor. He is also remembered at nearby Lan Pabu by his hypocoristic name, Pabu, or "papa."[9] Although St. Illtud (450–535) may never have traveled to Brittany in person, he is remembered at Lanildut in Finistère and Loc-Ildut in Sizun, mostly likely because of later disciples who carried his memory with them as missionaries.[10]

Another early saint, Budoc, was the son of British (or possibly Irish) immigrants to Brittany who was nevertheless born at sea, where his mother (like too many other saints' mothers) had been cast adrift in a sealed cask. Rescued at Waterford, Budoc grew to young adulthood and then returned to Brittany as a missionary. There he established a monastery on the site of an abandoned Roman ruin on the island of Lavret near Plaimpol on the north coast, a few miles from St.-Pol-de-Léon. (McNeill points out that Bodoc is associated with St. Mawes or Modez, an Irish monk who founded a monastery on the Isle of Modez, off the coast of Léon, and is listed as a companion of Paul Aurelian.)[11]

Samson (485–565) was British by birth,[12] but he is remembered in Brittany as Samson of Dol. Four of the five early Lives of Samson were written by monks of Dol, the first of which may be almost contemporaneous with the saint himself (c. 610).[13] According to the primitive Life,

Samson first traveled to Ireland with some scholars who were returning from a pilgrimage to Rome. For a time, he seems to have lived at Dún Étair, atop the Howth Headland. He may have been briefly in charge of a monastery but was recalled to Wales to become abbot of Llanilltud, after which he journeyed to Cornwall and eventually to Brittany, where he founded the famous monastery at Dol and several others. Samson may have been present at a synod in Paris about 563 and is remembered on the Channel Islands and the Isles of Scilly.

Mehan (Méen), from Gwent, lived in the vast forested area of Brékelien (Brocéliande), later celebrated in Arthurian myth as the haunt of Merlin and Nimuë. From his hermitage there grew the abbey of St. Méen with its famous healing fountain.[14] St. David of Menevia, the patron of Wales (520–88), and his mother, St. Non, are also remembered in Brittany.[15] Other British saints are venerated by Breton place names and churches, including Winwaloe (Guénolé), Paul Aurelian (Pol de Léon), Mac Low (Maclovius, or Malo) of Llancarfan (490–565), the founder of Aleth (later St. Malo), and a host of others. Of these, Winwaloe may well be the most widely venerated.[16]

Winwaloe (Guénolé, or Guignolé), who died between c. 504 and 532, founded the important monastery of Landévennec in Finistère, at the tip of the Breton peninsula of Crozon, just across from Brest.[17] The son of a Welsh prince, Fracan, and his wife, Gwen, Winwaloe followed the path of so many Welsh monks to Brittany. He came ashore at Ploufragan (which is either named in memory of his father, or reflects the fact that his father led the missionary band). For a time, he studied under St. Budoc on Lavret Island, but eventually founded his own monastic center at Landévennec (a hypocoristic title taken from *Lan Towennoc,* "the church of Winnoc"). Perhaps because of his association with Budoc, the monastery maintained an Irish character and may have relied on the Rule of Columban.[18] (James Kenney relates that when in 818 Emperor Louis the Pious sought to impose ecclesiastical and political conformity on Brittany, he addressed his order enjoining the abandonment of Irish practices and the adoption of the Roman tonsure and the rule of St. Benedict principally to the abbot of Landévennec, Matmonoch. Even so, the monastery preserved its strong connections with both Ireland and Britain.) Winwaloe is remembered on March 3.[19]

Irish Saints in Brittany and Beyond

From the beginning, migrant Irish saints played a key role in the evangelization and pastoral care of Breton Christians. Many are remembered in the place names of churches, monasteries, and districts. One of the earliest was St. Ronán, a sixth-century saint whose parents were converted by St. Patrick. He was first a missionary in Cornwall in the company led by the Irish nun St. Breaca. He is said to have come to Brittany around the year 500 and is remembered in the region around Laon, where there is a village named St.-Ronán. There is another in Quimper, and in the parish of Lanrenan yet another village is called Laurenan. Ronán settled, finally, in a remote area overlooking the Bay of Douarnenez that came to be called Locronan, which is said to preserve relics of the saint. It also marks the circuit of Ronán's most lasting remembrance, a penitential route known as *La grande Troménie,* over which a long procession winds once every six years and which each true Breton is expected to join once in a lifetime.[20] (There is also a smaller, annual *Troménie.*)

Several curious stories about Ronán involve the wife of a local pagan farmer who becomes his nemesis. When a sheep belonging to the farmer, who was of help in setting up Ronán's hermitage in the forest of Nevet, is snatched by a wolf, Ronán commands the thief to return the animal unharmed. Grateful and amazed, the farmer becomes a Christian, but his wife, Keben, accuses Ronán of being a werewolf and deserving of death. When this plot fails, she conceals her husband's favorite child in a chest and accuses Ronán of stealing and eating it.

Subjected to trial by ordeal, Ronán is proved innocent when two savage wolfhounds loosed on him meekly drop to his feet after he blesses them with the sign of the cross. The child is found dead in the chest, but Ronán resuscitates it. For some years, he continues his ministry of healing and guidance until at a ripe age he decides to return to Ireland to die. Before he reaches a port, however, he dies. A cart pulled by four white oxen returns his body to the region of Nevet, where the right to inter it is disputed among bishops and local chiefs. The oxen are allowed to wander freely, fixing the path of the Troménie (*Tro Menehi,* "the sacred circuit"), before coming to a halt at the hermit's cell.

During the journey, the cart passed by Keben as she was doing her wash. Enraged, she hurled her beating-stick at the oxen, breaking off one's horn, which fell to the ground at the top of the next hill, where a station called "The Place of the Horn" was established. Nearby is another, "Keben's Cross," where the earth opened up and swallowed the vicious woman.[21]

James Kenney provides an annotated list of Irish saints, in addition to better-known missionaries, who traveled to Brittany.[22] Among them are Efflam, an Irish prince who is the subject of a twelfth-century Life. One of several Irish saints associated with dragons, Efflam is portrayed, like St. Michael, pinning one of the winged reptiles to the earth with his staff.[23] The story is told that he came to the aid of King Arthur, who had been fighting the dragon for three days. Arthur is near death from exhaustion and thirst when Efflam, newly arrived in a boat from Ireland, revives him with a spring of water and then drags the no doubt equally exhausted dragon into the sea, where he drowns it.

Efflam is also said to have been married, but before consummating the union with St. Enora, his wife, he determined to become a pilgrim for Christ. Enora followed him to Brittany in a leather currach, joined him at Plestin-les-Grèves, and died there in a little cell Efflam built next to his own. Efflam, one of the more popular saints of Brittany, died around the year 512.[24] He is venerated in the church of Plestin-les-Grèves.

Other Irish saints include Feock, an archbishop of Armagh, who is reported to have floated to Brittany on a stone; Leutiern (Lughtiern) of Brittany; Menulfus (Menore), who founded the monastery of St. Menoux in Bourges; Ninnoca; Osmanna, the patron saint of Féricy-en-Brie; Sunius (Sezney); Tenenanus (Tinodorus) of Uon; and Vougay (Vio), an archbishop. Kenney points out that the textual references are late and fanciful. Their historical value consists in establishing and maintaining a constant tradition of the close association of churches in Ireland, Britain, and Brittany from the fifth to the tenth centuries. Some of the accounts undoubtedly arose from church dedications, which are plentiful in those areas where large numbers of Irish immigrants settled.[25]

Over the next several centuries, wave after wave of Irish monks, nuns, and bishops washed up on the shores of Brittany, leaving in their wake a number of centers such as such as Locronan and Nantes. But there were far more numerous Irish foundations in the lands of the Franks, that is, modern Belgium, France, Germany, and northern Switzerland. In Belgium, there were, among others, Nivelles, Fosses, Waulsort, and Liége. In France, Irish monastic centers were established at Jouarre, Luxeuil, Meaux, Faremoutiers, Rebais, Jumièges, Soissons, Laon, St.-Gobain, Rheims, Lagny, Lure, St.-Ursanne, Angers, Tours, Fontaines, Auxerre, Péronne, Bordeaux, Bèze, Marmoutier, Remiremont, and Narbonne (to name only a few). Among German monasteries Erfurt, Aachen, Würzburg, Disibodenberg, Mainz, and Metz were Irish, and in Switzerland the areas around Lake Constance such as St. Gall, Chur, and Säckingen were haunted by Irish hermits. There were Salzburg in Austria and Aosta, Bobbio, Lucca, Rome, and Taranta in Italy.[26]

Fridolin

An early sixth-century missionary to Germany, St. Fridolin is remembered in an eleventh-century Life by the monk Balther.[27] One of the earliest of the Irish *peregrini,* Fridolin was attracted by the aura of the great theologian and church leader St. Hilary, who had become bishop of Poitiers in 350. Shocked to discover the ancient shrine ruined and in need of repair, Fridolin undertook its restoration. A strenuous opponent of still vigorous Arianism, Fridolin also labored among the Visigoths of the Aquitaine, recently subjugated by Clovis. In time, Fridolin's efforts were rewarded when he was appointed abbot of Saint-Hilaire, one of the principal centers of Christian Gaul.

Fridolin moved on during the reign of Clovis's son, Clothair I, traveling to Triers and Rheims and then south up the Rhine into what is now Switzerland. There he founded several monasteries in honor of St. Hilary, including the important houses at Chur and his most important foundation at Säckingen. A popular tale from this period concerns a dispute between Fridolin and the brother of Count Urso of Glarus, who had bequeathed the island of Säckingen to the saint after his death. Hotly contested by Urso's Alpine successor, Fridolin proved the legitimacy of his claim by raising Urso from the grave and prompting the cadaver to testify in court that he had donated the land. (This may be the first recorded instance of the use of "spectral evidence" in legal proceedings.)

Once in possession of the island, Fridolin employed his considerable engineering skills to drain the soil and prepare the foundations, even changing the course of the Rhine to secure the island to the mainland. (Besides establishing the monastery on a solid footing, his achievement earned Fridolin the title of patron of hydraulic engineers.) He died at Säckingen around 539 and is remembered with a high festival there on March 6. His monastery survived until 916, when raiding Huns destroyed it. In the eighteenth century, a large baroque church, Sanckt Fridolins, was built in his memory and now houses a small museum containing a number of relics from the original abbey.[28]

Columban: Apostle to Europe

Of all the Irish missionaries to mainland Europe, Columban (Columbanus) is one of the earliest, the most famous, and by all accounts the most amazing, being abbot, preacher, poet, scholar, theologian, prophet, and saint.[29] His Life was written by Jonas of Susa, an Italian monk of his monastery at Bobbio, who entered there only three years after Columban's death in 615. Composed between 630 and 641, it is thus the most nearly contemporary of all the Irish saints' Lives and remarkably free of additions from folklore and pious adulation.[30]

Columban was born about 543 in Leinster, somewhere near the Carlow-Wexford border. If Jonas supplies less than the usual wonders attendant upon a saint's birth, he at least informs us that Columban's mother dreamed shortly before the event that the sun would rise from her breast and illuminate the entire world with its rays.

His first studies were at Clúain-inis (Cleenish Island) on Lough Erne in Fermanagh, where St. Sinell was abbot, himself a disciple of Finnian of Clonard and one of the "Twelve Apostles of Ireland." Cleenish was already famous for its scholarly pursuits, and young Columban studied Latin grammar, rhetoric, geometry, and the Holy Scriptures. After his return to his home, if the legend can be credited, a near-disastrous attempt by a young woman to entice the handsome, rugged, and smart young scholar into marriage prompted Columban to announce to his mother his intention of becoming a monk. In the long tradition of distraught saints' mothers, she wept, pleaded, and ultimately threw herself across the threshold to prevent his departure. Undeterred, Columban stepped over her and found his way to Bangor, where Comgall had established one of the most austere and learned of all the Irish monasteries.

Columban devoted the next twenty years to advanced study and the practices of prayer and contemplation. During this time, he most likely composed the first of his many works, a commentary on the Book of Psalms, which has been lost, and several poems. At some point, prompted by an impulse of the Spirit, Columban decided to seek permission to travel to Gaul (or as it was now called, Frankland or France) as a pilgrim for Christ. Comgall, no mean missionary himself, gave leave not only to Columban, but for twelve companions to accompany him, including Deicuil (Deicola), who may have been his elder brother, Gall, and Potentin (later the founder of the monastery of Coutances in Normandy). Without a plan of action other than their trust in providence, the monks set out to find their destiny, forever turning their backs on Ireland.

They traveled first by boat to Cornwall, where two place names on opposite sides of the peninsula probably indicate their route — St. Columb Major and St. Columb Minor. Setting sail once more, the monks arrived at St. Malo on the north coast of Brittany, now Normandy. Additional place names in the region suggest that the monks stayed in the area for some time. Ultimately, their work became known to the Frankish court, and Columban was summoned to appear before King Gunthram of Burgundy, one of Clovis's grandsons.

Impressed by the evident piety and success of the Irish monks, the king offered them land to establish a monastery in the region of the Vosges in eastern Burgundy. Columban selected an abandoned Roman fort known as Anagrates, now the village of Annegray (the remaining church was destroyed during the French Revolution). At first refusing offers of assistance, the monks began restoring the walls and tilling the ruined fields. They would probably have starved had not the local farmers brought them cartloads of vegetables now and then. But the effort was successful, and Columban was soon able to branch out, making foundations at Luxeuil in 590, his most famous monastery in the north, and Fontaines in 592.

As Columban's influence spread, tension grew with the Frankish bishops who, although they might have been reprehensible in their neglect of pastoral duties, were keenly alert to the threat presented to their authority by an energetically apostolic and popular tribe of monks who functioned without their leave. One of the sticking points was the issue of the Celtic Easter, even at this early date. Never one to refuse a challenge, Columban penned a remarkably direct (some might say impertinent) letter defending the Celtic customs to Pope St. Gregory the Great in the year 600. Whether the pope responded is not known, but two years later Columban was summoned to a provincial synod at Châlons-sur-Saône. With typical self-assurance, the aging abbot thanked the bishops for their interest but declined to attend.

Despite Columban's years (he was now in his mid-sixties), he next found himself embroiled in the dangerous contest for the crown of Burgundy waged by descendants of Clothair I, Clovis's son. Gunthram of Burgundy had died in 592, his kingdom passing in 595 to his grandnephew, the young King Theuderic, whose brother Theudebert was nominally king of the East Franks, or Austrasia. In fact, both were very much under the domination of their grandmother, Brunhilde, widow of Sigebert I and mother of Childebert II, king of Austrasia and, for a brief time, Burgundy, but he also died in 595. For all her nominal Christianity, Brunhilde was undoubtedly one of the most savage and evil women of the age, ruling with an iron whim. She soon posed a major problem for Columban. (Among her other crimes, the old queen was responsible for the murder of St. Desiderius, the bishop of Vienne.)

At first, Theuderic was friendly toward Columban, as his father and uncle had been. But like others of the Merovingian line, he was weak, dissolute, and swayed by the lure of the moment, usually involving a love interest. Prodded by Columban to marry honorably, the young king took a Spanish princess as his bride, but Brunhilde was not ready to be shunted aside by a new royal dynasty. Deftly she engineered the downfall of the princess, who sacrificed her considerable dowry to return safely to Spain. Columban confronted the aging queen and resolutely refused to bless her two great-grandsons, both illegitimate, predicting that "sons begotten of harlotry shall never inherit the Frankish crown."

Brunhilde's hatred unleashed a storm of opposition, turning even Theuderic against his former friend. All the Irish monks were ordered to

depart Burgundy and Austrasia, leaving only the native monks to continue the work of evangelization (and maintain a Christian façade to
the realm). Driven from their monastery and forbidden assistance from
anyone in the two kingdoms, Columban and the Irish members of his
communities made their way to the coast, where at Nantes they awaited
a ship to return them, defeated, to Ireland. After a few miles, the aged
Deicuil could go no further and was allowed to drop behind, building a
small hut for himself in the wilderness. It was the year 610, and Columban himself was now nearing seventy. (Deicuil's refuge became, in time,
the monastery of Lure.)

From Nantes, Columban wrote a touching letter to his monks at
Luxeuil, appointing Athala as his successor and bidding them preserve
their peace and unity in love. Then, when a ship arrived, they set sail.
Almost immediately, the ship ran aground on a sandbar and could not
be budged till Columban and his monks were cast ashore by the captain,
who was then able (miraculously, some said) to continue his voyage. The
Irish monks made their way overland to Neustria, the kingdom of the
West Franks, and found temporary refuge at the court of Clothair II,
Theuderic's cousin but not his ally. The king offered Columban land for
a foundation, but the monks decided to venture on, intending to cross
the southern passes into Italy.

Their next stop was at the court of Theudebert, who proved a friend
and offered the monks land for an establishment in the lake district of
what is now northern Switzerland, the southernmost part of his realm.
They rowed their way up the Rhine, possibly chanting the famous boat
song found among the poems attributed to Columban. They eventually
settled in a promising area, but their fortunes turned sour when the
impetuous Gall seized the idols and offerings in the local pagan shrine
and threw them into the lake. The furious inhabitants beat Columban
and would have murdered Gall, had he not been a swift runner. Sadly,
the monks abandoned the area and, advised by a friendly priest named
Wilimar, whom they encountered further south, they began over again
near what is now the town of Bregenz on the Boden See.

Once again, however, the enmity of the pagan chiefs threatened their
mission and even their lives. To make matters worse, in 612 King Theuderic, spurred on by his grandmother, lured his brother into a trap and
took him prisoner, annexing Burgundy to the Kingdom of Austrasia. He
sent Theudebert to Brunhilde, who had him blinded, clothed in the habit
of a monk, and finally murdered. Fearing for their safety, Columban and
his monks left Bregenz and began their trek to Italy.

Soon, however, Gall fell behind, pleading illness. In the tenth-century
Life of Columban by Walafrid Strabo of Reichenau, but not in that by

Jonas, it is said that Columban distrusted Gall's reasons for staying behind and, as a penance, forbade him to say mass so long as Columban remained alive. It is a strange story and likely to be fictitious, even for an abbot as austere as Columban, given the desperate need for missionary priests in Frankland at that time. In any case, Gall remained near Bregenz, where the simple dwelling and church he built would someday become a great abbey and give its name to a city and a canton of Switzerland.

Columban and his remaining disciples, including the faithful Athala, who had joined him at the court of Clothair, went on to Lombardy, where they were warmly received by King Agilulf and Queen Theudelinda. Agilulf granted the wanderers enough land to build a new monastery at Bobbio on the river Trebbia, located between the cities of Piacenza and Genoa. They restored a ruined church and began the work of building.

Nor had Clothair II been idle. In 612, Theuderic died of a sudden illness, and with the aid of the Burgundians, Clothair engineered a revolt against the elderly tyrant, Brunhilde. She was seized, tried, and condemned for countless crimes, tortured for days, and then publicly executed in a dramatically brutal fashion, being dragged to death at the tail of a wild horse. Clothair next removed the royal heirs by intimidation and, when helpful, assassination, thus fulfilling Columban's unhappy prophecy. As king of all the Franks, Clothair II was now in a position to assist Columban, whom he had not forgotten. He invited the aged abbot to return to Luxeuil, but Columban declined, preferring the challenge of a new beginning, one which Clothair aided by gifts of gold.

Columban was now in his seventies, but his strength was hardly diminished. He threw himself into theological controversies, preaching and writing against the Arian heretics and upbraiding Pope Boniface IV.[31] He began adding to the collection of books and manuscripts that would someday make Bobbio the greatest monastic library in Europe, in some instances copying the books himself. Two years later, in 615, he died at the age of seventy-two or seventy-three. His feast day is celebrated on November 23.

By the end of the century, more than one hundred monasteries founded by sixty-three of Columban's disciples followed his Rule, the most successful monastic *familia* in Europe until it was supplanted by the more lenient Benedictine Rule. Over the centuries, the great library at Bobbio would also became a treasury of resources for the Ambrosian Library in Milan, as well as libraries in the Vatican, Naples, Vienna, and the Escorial.[32]

Columban Spirituality

To say that Columban's Rule was austere, even harsh by contemporary standards, is an understatement. Minor infractions such as talking without necessity, laughing or coughing in choir, and spilling a cup of beer were punished by fasting and additional labor, or by blows or strokes with a leather strap across the hand or the shoulders. Almost heroic standards of achievement were accepted by the monks who, after all, had courted struggle and difficulty to prove their commitment to Christ. The Pelagian influence in early Celtic spirituality lingered for many centuries. Or perhaps it would be more accurate to say that the robust, wildly generous quest for excellence that inspired Pelagius was still at work in the saints of the latter centuries, spurring them on to what seem to be nearly impossible accomplishments.

Conversely, their reliance on God's grace to overcome all obstacles amounted perhaps to presumption. But the middle centuries of the first millennium were difficult and demanding times. Despite that, or because of it, the appeal of the strenuous life of the monastic missionary led many hundreds of young and middle-aged Christians away from the relatively safe and beautiful homelands of Ireland and Wales across the channel into the wasted lands of the old empire. There semi-savage pagan tribes as well as wolves, boars, and other dangerous animals were a constant threat, and the terrain and weather itself created sometimes mortal peril. They came with joyful hearts, and Columban above all was known to be light-hearted and humorous, even playful in his addresses to kings and pontiffs, not to say his own disciples. He was no thug, but a man of poetic temperament and a classical education. The charm of his personality was sufficiently magnetic to attract many hundreds of recruits. Nothing was expected of them that he did not undertake himself, even into his seventh decade.

Above all, Columban was a man deeply in love with God and Christ. After thirteen hundred years, his writings still glow with a serene warmth and freshness that one might expect from the pen of Augustine or a late medieval mystic:

> God is everywhere, utterly vast, and everywhere near at hand, according to his own witness of himself; I am, he says, a God at hand and not a God afar off. The God we are seeking is not one who dwells far away from us; we have him within us, if we are worthy. For he resides in us like soul and body, if only we are sound members of him, if we are not dead in sins.... Who, I say, shall explore his highest summit to the measure of this unutterable and inconceivable being? Who shall examine the secret depths of God? Who

shall dare to treat of the eternal source of the universe? Who shall boast of knowing the infinite God, who fills all and surrounds all, who enters into all and passes beyond all, who occupies all, who transcends all? Whom no one has ever seen as he is? Therefore let no one venture to seek out the unsearchable things of God, the nature, mode and cause of his existence. These are unspeakable, undiscoverable, unsearchable; only believe in simplicity and yet with firmness, that God is and shall be even as he has been, since God is immutable.[33]

The Irish monastic influence in Brittany and France lasted for two centuries, although in 716, when St. Wynfrith (Boniface), the English bishop and missionary, arrived in Germany, he did his utmost to erase all memory of the generations of Irish monks who had prepared his way, not least of all by instructing him. Similarly, the Carolingian emperor Louis the Pious, Charlemagne's son, also sought to enforce conformity in 818 by requiring that Breton clergy abandon Irish practices in favor of the "Roman Easter" and tonsure, and that Columban monks adopt the Rule of St. Benedict. (Winwaloe's monastery at Landévennec, Louis's main target, nevertheless maintained close associations with both Ireland and Wales.)[34]

Even though the more lenient Benedictine way eventually replaced that of Columban, his memory never faded from the many lands he and his disciples had evangelized. Today, thirty-four parishes in northern Italy are still named in his honor.[35] Some say the family name of Christopher Columbus was ultimately derived from that of the Irish saint. In 1916, Columban's spirit was fittingly evoked when the St. Columban Missionary Society was founded by Bishop Edward J. Galvin and Fr. John Blowick. In 1922, it was augmented by the Missionary Sisters of St. Columban. Today, hundreds of Columban missionaries perpetuate the tradition of their great namesake by preaching the gospel, teaching, and healing in Africa, Asia, and Latin America.

Gall of St. Gall

Hundreds of other Irish missionaries migrated to Brittany, Frankland, and even Italy in the years that followed, if none could match the sheer energy and creativity of the great Columban. (Róisín Ní Mheara charts the course of over one hundred Irish *peregrini* in her excellent and colorful study, *In Search of Irish Saints*.) Among his companions, St. Gall, Columban's friend and disciple, perhaps comes closest, the patron saint of the canton that bears his name and indeed of all Switzerland.[36]

Although ill and no longer young when he parted from Columban (being only a few years Columban's junior), Gall made his way across the Lake of Constance seeking Arbon and his friend, the priest Wilimar, who nursed him back to health. When his strength was restored, Gall asked one of Wilimar's deacons, a young man named John, to lead him into the wilderness to find a place where he could settle. Undeterred by John's accounts of wild animals and wilder weather, Gall set out with his guide, stopping only when he stumbled and fell. Taking that for a sign, he announced, "Here I will stay."

With the assistance of Wilimar's workers, Gall constructed a hermitage. Gradually, the once fiery and impetuous preacher won the trust and affection of the local people, including the chieftain, Gunzo, who had threatened Columban and the others only a few years before. In time, Gall was offered preferments: the bishop's seat at Constance, the abbacy of Luxeuil. But the old man consistently declined.

In 615, Gall realized in a vision that Columbanus had died in Bobbio and immediately offered a requiem mass for his old friend and master. He then sent his deacon Magnoald to Bobbio to verify his vision. Weeks later, Magnoald returned bearing the sign of reconciliation and spiritual communion, Columbanus's *cambutta*, his pastoral staff, which he had left to Gall before his death.

Like many Irish saints, Gall displayed a great affection for animals in the wilderness. He is reported to have taught a bear to fetch firewood for him, for which the docile animal was rewarded with a loaf of bread. (I have been told that the bear-motif that appears on so many Swiss emblems in Bern and elsewhere may be a reminiscence of this helpful fellow.)

Finally, around 630 on a visit to his old friend Wilimar at Arbon to preach on the feast of St. Michael, Gall, now well past his ninetieth year, suddenly died. His body was returned to his monastic church on the River Steinach, where he was buried next to the altar. In the years that followed, Gall's hermitage grew into a monastery, which prospered greatly, attracting scholars and saintly monks from all over Europe. In time, it passed under Benedictine control but continued to enjoy the prestige and glory of the greatest of the Swiss monastic foundations. Like Bobbio, the monastery of St. Gall also became famous for its library.

Gall himself is remembered in the names of many churches in Switzerland and Italy, where his feast day is celebrated on October 16.[37] Sankt Gallen (in French, St. Gall) is now a manufacturing town in northeastern Switzerland, about forty miles east of Zurich. Famous for its textiles, embroideries, and laces, it still possesses an excellent municipal library, not the least heritage of its ancient Irish namesake.

Fursa and His Brothers

Fursa (Furseus or Fursey) was the third amazing Irish missionary of the seventh century, an evangelist of the interior wilderness as well as the spiritual wastelands of barbarian Europe, worthy of inclusion alongside Columban and Gall.[38] Born in Galway, some say at Tuam, about 575, Fursa was the nephew of Brendan of Clonfert and the elder brother of Faolán (Foillan) and Ultán, fellow pilgrims to England and the continent.

His younger years were devoted to training under St. Meldan on Inchiquin Island, one of Brendan's foundations. Later, Fursa built a monastic retreat where he and his companions lived for several years. One day, stricken by a sudden and serious illness, he had what to-day would be called a "near-death experience." Transported in spirit by angelic companions through purgatory and hell, he was intercepted at the very threshold of heaven in the throes of unutterable joy by two Irishmen who told him that he must return to his earthly life to preach and save men and women from the deadly fate of sin. When he awak-ened, Fursa was healed but also aware of the course his life would take thereafter.

For twelve years, Fursa preached the length and breadth of Ireland until he was so pressed upon by crowds eager to hear him preach that he decided to emigrate to East Anglia as a pilgrim for Christ. Accompanied by his two brothers, Dicuil, Gobán, and several other companions, Fursa was cordially welcomed by the pious King Sigebert I around the year 631. (Exiled as a youth to Gaul, Sigebert had been instructed by Columban and his disciples and would himself end his days as a monk.) The king offered the monks an abandoned fort, which Fursa soon transformed into a monastery — Cnobheresburg, Bede called it.

While preaching among the East Anglians, whose conversion is cred-ited to Fursa and his disciples, the Irish seer experienced further visions, some of which were transmitted in oral tradition even to the time of Bede, who describes them a century later in his great history.[39] After ten years, Fursa again grew weary of routine and constant activity and, committing the monastery to Faolán's care, retired into the fens to join Ultán in solitary contemplation as a hermit. But under the constant threat of attack by pagan Mercian soldiers of the savage King Penda (whose troops eventually killed Sigisbert and destroyed the Anglian kingdom), Fursa decided once again to travel. Leading a band of pilgrims, he set sail for Rome and wherever his destiny lay beyond it.

The pilgrims first came to land in Brittany, where Fursa preached in the distinct around Mayoc, where he is still remembered. Although invited to remain, Fursa pressed on into Neustria, where he came to the attention of the royal court in a remarkable manner. Pausing at the invitation of Duke Haimo of Ponthieu at his castle at Mazérolles, near the Sommes estuary, Fursa was able to revive the Duke's only son, who had succumbed to a sudden illness. Reports of the miracle reached the ears of the powerful mayor of the royal palace at Péronne, Erchonwald, who would bestow property for several Irish monastic foundations during his term of office. Impressed by the obvious holiness of his visitor, Erchonwald invited Fursa to remain in Péronne, but the aging monk declined in order to finish his pilgrimage to Rome. He left behind at the church the relics of Patrick and Meldan he had brought from Ireland and prophesied that his own body would someday lie there.

After visiting Rome, Fursa returned to Péronne, but rather than accepting the offer of a church in the capital, he was given title to land at Lagny on the Marne, not far from Paris. There, in 644, he began his third major monastic foundation. He was not to live much longer, however. In 649, now in his mid-seventies, Fursa died while returning from a visit to some Irish monks at Mazérolles. As he had foretold, his body was returned to Péronne for burial.

But like so many of his predecessors, even in death Fursa became the object of contention. Claims for the right to his body were made by Erchonwald, Haimo of Ponthieu, and a third noble, Berchar, the duke of Laon. A well-known solution was achieved in which Fursa's bier was hitched to a team of white oxen, who were then allowed to roam as they would. The procession made its way toward Péronne, where Fursa's mortal remains were enshrined with all due ceremony. His feast day is observed on January 16.

Although his own monastery at Lagny prospered until destroyed by Vikings in 880, Péronne flourished, attracting so many Irish pilgrims that it became known as *Peronna Scottorum* — "Péronne of the Irish." (In Ireland, it was called *Cathair Fhursa*, "Fursa's City.") Fursa's visions, *Fis Fhursa ar Ifreann*, with their graphic depictions of the next world, were translated into several languages and became favorite reading matter in the Middle Ages, long before Dante's *Divine Comedy* (which it is said they influenced).

Recalled in Suffolk, Fursa became the patron saint of Northampton. But in France, he became one of the most popular of all the saints. Among his devotees was St. Louis IX, who attributed his victory over English invaders in 1243 to Fursa's intercession. Again, after his safe return from the Crusades in 1256, King Louis caused a new abbey to be built over the ruins of the ancient monastery, which also had been destroyed by Viking raiders. In 1536, Péronne was delivered from a siege through the invocation of its saint. But while the abbey church of St. Peter, where Fursa had first lain, was spared the destructiveness of the French Revolution, the church of Saint-Furcy in Lagny was sold and demolished in 1792. Several relics were preserved at the church of St. John the Baptist, and in recent times the ancient façade of Saint-Furcy was restored along with the holy well attributed to the saint, both of which now border the municipal square in Lagny.[40]

Fursa's brothers, Faolán and Ultán, followed him to France.[41] After Penda's Mercians destroyed the Kingdom of the Angles, they salvaged all the books and manuscripts they could carry and followed Fursa's path to the continent. Received at the court of Clovis II in 649, the year of Fursa's death, the brothers were given leave to preach throughout the lower Rhineland, Flanders, and the lands to the east. Faolán is especially remembered in Belgium, where he founded a monastery at Fosses. There Itta, the wife of the mayor of the palace, Pepin of Landen, had donated land for a monastery between the Sambre and Meuse rivers. (Itta is even better known for founding the great double monastery at Nivelles, where her daughter, St. Gertrude, was abbess.) Ultán became abbot of Fursa's monastery at Saint-Quentin and then succeeded Faolán at Péronne when his brother began his new foundation at Fosses.

Returning from visiting Ultán for the feast day celebrations at Saint-Quentin in 655, Faolán and his three companions were attacked and killed by bandits in the forest of Seneffe, where the bodies were concealed. According to tradition, Ultán learned of his brother's death by means of a vision of a dove flying with blood-stained wings toward heaven. Two months later St. Gertrude herself was led to the place the martyrs had died. She recovered the incorrupt body of Faolán and returned the remains to Nivelles. Ultán remained at Péronne until his death there in 686.

Faolán is credited with introducing the cult of St. Brigid into Belgium, where "St. Brigid's Crosses" are still plaited for her feast day as they are in Ireland. Faolán and Brigid also share a stained-glass window in Aachen cathedral, and the two saints are linked in memorials as far away as Spain.[42] Faolán's feast day is celebrated on October 31, and Ultán's on May 2.

Fiacra, the Gardener of France

One of the most popular of the Irish saints in Brittany and France, Fiacra (c. 600–670) is thought to have come from Kilkenny.[43] He is usually portrayed with a spade, as is only fitting for the patron of gardeners. But it was as a healer that Fiacra (Fiacre, as the French would have it) was first known and long venerated. (Róisín Ní Mheara reports that in the earliest effigies, Fiacra is portrayed not with a spade, but with an abbot's staff, the Irish *cambutta*).[44]

From his first habitation in Brittany, where he was remembered by several place names, Fiacra came to the area of Meaux, northeast of Paris on the Marne. Here he is said to have established a garden where he cultivated flowers and especially healing herbs to attend to the needs of the infirm, particularly pilgrims to Rome, Tours, and other important religious sites.

The foundation legend of Saint-Fiacre-en-Brie explains the spade by telling how the bishop of Meaux, St. Faron, promised the saint as much land as he could ring with his spade in a day in order to accommodate the growing number of pilgrims and infirm seeking shelter at his hermitage.[45] As he dug rapidly to enlarge the church boundaries, a rift miraculously opened before his spade, indicating the path and actually creating it. But this was observed by a hostile woman of the region who denounced Fiacra before Faron as a sorcerer. Immediately ordered to stop, Fiacra sat sadly on a rock awaiting vindication. When the bishop found him, the stone seat had softened into a "chair." This and other signs convinced Faron of Fiacra's sanctity and the wickedness of the accusation by "La Becnaude," as she is called, whose features hardened and grew sharp as stone. Moreover, from that time forward, women would not be allowed to cross the trench into the sacred precincts of the shrine.

The story may account for the custom in later centuries that women never entered his cell or the village chapel where Fiacra was eventually buried, not even Anne of Austria, the queen of France, who made a pilgrimage to the saint's shrine in 1641, or Queen Mary of Modena, the wife of the exiled King James II of England. (The practice, not uncommon in monastic environs, may also account for the story. In either case, the ban lasted until the monastery was disbanded in 1760.)[46]

According to Martin Wallace, Fiacra became so well known for curing a certain ulcerous condition that it became known as "St. Fiacra's Disease."[47] By the thirteenth century, Fiacra's popularity had spread throughout France, where many churches are named in his honor. His relics were so prized that both Edward, the Black Prince (d. 1376), and King Henry V attempted to steal them for England during the Hundred Years War. Returning to England through Normandy, Edward left the portion of the relics he had removed on a church altar in Montloup, but on the following morning, no one could lift them from the altar. Edward's death shortly afterward was regarded by the French as divine retribution. Henry allowed his soldiers to pillage the monastery at Meaux because of the numbers of Irish who had fought on the side of France, but was himself felled by St. Fiacra's Disease and died on the saint's feast day in August 1422.[48]

Fiacra's shrine and memory were highly regarded by the kings and queens of France as well as by bishops, monks, and common folk. Late in the ninth century, an attempt was made to suppress all the Irish hospices, but in 846 the emperor, Charles the Bald, granted them protection at the request of Hinkmar, the archbishop of Rheims. Centuries later, Louis XIII is said to have died with a medal of Fiacra in his hand. The Irish saint's popularity survived even the ordeal of the French Revolution in a curious way. In Paris, four-wheeled horse-drawn cabs came to be known as *fiacres* because of their use at the Hôtel Saint-Fiacre, a point of departure in the seventeenth century for the healing shrine of the saint in Meaux. In Austria cabs are similarly known as *Fiakers* and, not by accident, Fiacra is the patron saint of taxi-drivers.

In Ireland, Fiacra's feast day is recalled on August 30 as the patron of Ossory.

The Blood of Witness

Sudden death stalked the early missionaries to Europe in a variety of guises. Ireland provided a number of martyrs even before the end of the fifth century. Fingar, a prince of Connaught, and his sister Piala were converts of Patrick who went to Brittany in the first wave of missionary enthusiasm and are remembered at Vannes. From there they went on to Cornwall, where they were martyred with other companions shortly after landing at the mouth of the River Hayle.[49] They were followed by St. Hia (Ives), another Irish pilgrim, a nun whose cell left her name forever on the spur of land where she chose to establish her hermitage.

Around the year 570, two sisters, Máire (Maura) and Brígit (Britta), and their brother, Espain, children (it is said) of King Ailill, were returning from a pilgrimage to Rome and the shrine of St. Martin at Tours when they were killed by pagans from the north. They are commemorated by churches at Ste.-Maure-de-Ourance, St.-Épain, and the town of Nogent-les-Vierges.[50] We have already encountered the story of St. Dympna and Gerebern, who are remembered by several church names in Belgium, particularly the St.-Dympnakerk in Gheel and the Augustinian abbey at Fingulo.[51] (The remains of Saints Dympna and Gerebern were discovered in the thirteenth century, at which time a hospital was begun in her honor.)

St. Kilian and his companions, Colmán and Totnan, were martyred in 689 by order of Geilana, the wife of Duke Gosbert of Würzburg. A native of Mullage, County Cavan, Kilian (640–c. 689) and the others became missionaries in areas of Germany still largely pagan. When Kilian objected to the marriage of Gosbert and Geilana because she was his dead brother's widow, the infuriated woman seized the opportunity for revenge when her husband was away. The remains of the martyrs were discovered fifty years later and reinterred in Würzburg. Despite his antagonism toward Irish customs, St. Boniface elevated Würzburg to the status of an episcopal see in 741 in honor of St. Kilian, building a cathedral on the site of the martyrs' deaths. It became one of the popular pilgrimage sites in medieval Germany and the repository of many Irish manuscripts. Kilian's feast day is kept on July 8.[52]

Heritage

The ancient faith nurtured among the Breton people by the labors and blood of British and Irish missionaries during the "Dark Ages" proved resilient. Even during the often fierce persecution of Christianity during the French revolutionary period, the Bretons clung as tenaciously to their faith as did Huguenots under Cardinal Richelieu or Catholics and Anglicans during the English Commonwealth and the era of the Penal Laws. Like the Irish, Welsh, and Scots, they also resisted efforts to outlaw and erode their native language.

The Breton people also retained their ancient seafaring ways into the modern era both in the fishing industry and as sailors, providing crews for the French navy. As pilgrims, many made their way to the New World, settling on the east coast of Canada, especially on Cape Breton Isle in what is now Nova Scotia. Expelled after the cessation of Canada to England in the eighteenth century, they made their way by ship and overland to the Louisiana Territory, where their faith, music, and cuisine have created a viable and vital culture among the "Cajun" people of the Bayous.

If it was often the initial point of landing, Brittany was but one of the lands to which the call of the gospel prompted Celtic monks from Ireland, Britain, and Scotland to leave their homelands and set off as pilgrims for Christ, devoting the rest of their lives to evangelizing and teaching the pagan tribes who had overrun the empire in the fifth and sixth centuries. As a spontaneous movement of the spirit, it was without doubt the first and greatest missionary impulse in Christian history, inexplicable in any terms other than the desire to win souls for Christ.

In later centuries, the ancient faith fared more or less well through the Reformation and Revolutionary eras, the oppression of Bismarck, the advent of Communism and National Socialism, and even modern materialistic atheism. Still, the names of the Celtic saints remain imbedded in the very fabric of the land, in churches, villages, wells, and caves. And where those wandering saints established their hermitages, oratories, monasteries, and churches, memory has survived in legend, art, and custom as well as the books and manuscripts they copied and left behind.

SEVEN

The Blessing and the Curse

Peering back in time to the origins of the Celtic churches, the Lives of their saints, and the evolution of their national identity provides only a partial glimpse of the sources of Celtic spirituality. The land, its climate, the music and poetry of the people, their languages themselves — all have had their role to play.[1] History itself, the long memory of struggles and achievements as the Celts sought to preserve their way of life from encroachment and suppression, also influences our perceptions. But the time of the saints did not cease with the end of the Celtic churches or even the Celtic nations as independent (and interdependent) communities of men and women who shared kinship, language, faith, and tribal heritage. Celtic saints and their spiritualities can be found in every era, differing as star from star in glory, yet linked by ties of tradition and aspiration to those who went before and those who follow after.

Despite immense differences between nations and cultures, commonalities are always present. Among them I would emphasize, first of all, the Word (and the word), the place of Scripture and also of poetry, prose, and song.[2] The earliest shreds of Irish and Welsh verse are, appropriately enough, found inked in the margins of church-related manuscripts: copies of the Bible, commentaries on Scripture, canonical tables, penitentials, and legal documents. Parchment was scare, and poetic inspiration fleeting.

Second, the monastic element in Celtic spirituality was formative for a number of reasons. The Celtic monks and nuns were not only heroes of the faith, but celebrated as poets, writers, preachers, and, in the end, saints and mystics. They sought the highest form of life, one dedicated to the quest for intimacy with God and service to their fellow human beings. They embodied the ancient ideal of the robust champion as well as the sage, witnessing in their austerity and eloquence the further reaches of human nature. They were not all brilliant, not all good; but those who were left an indelible mark on subsequent history and the consciousness of the Celtic peoples and to some degree the world. Above all, they loved the Word.

Third, the monastic and also the lay poets, who were no less capable of articulating a truly spiritual vision of life, drew much of their inspiration from nature or, as they would have seen it, Creation. The beauty of the land, the sky, the animals, and the many-splendored trees and flowers all spoke to them of God. Curiously, they seem not, as a whole, to have felt any need to allegorize nature or interpret it as a mere screen on which the abstract energies of God were projected to give color and form so that human minds could perceive them — and then, like the early Greek-speaking mystics, dispense with the lot in order to have "only God" at their contemplative disposal. Animals, trees, and the land itself, both enchanting and threatening in turns, were simply what they were and were celebrated as such. The olden Celts were, as we would say today, inalienably romantic, but they were also realists. The ever fascinating sea provided food and inspiration for the swirling spirals in Celtic art, but it could also rage and kill. It was not just a symbol.

Let us look a little more closely.

The Monastic Inheritance

If the spirituality of early Celtic Christians was more monastic in tone than that of their contemporaries elsewhere in postimperial Europe, that was because Celtic monasticism was much more a part of the ordinary life of the people than elsewhere. In this, the Celts were akin to the early Christians in Alexandria and Antioch, who saw in the desert *abbas* and *ammas* the fullest development of the Christian life. In both regards, the quest for solitude in order to pray and contemplate only attracted disciples seeking teachers more knowledgeable than themselves of the perils and promises of the spiritual life. In that respect, the distance between Énda of Arran or Kevin of Glen-da-locha and Antony of Egypt or Pachomius is not, in the end, very great.

For the Celtic monks in particular, sacred Scripture enjoyed pride of place in their spiritual quest. They not only studied Scripture, prayed with Scripture, and preached from Scripture, they copied Scripture and embellished the pages with some of the greatest art of the first Christian millennium. The Word was at the heart of everything.[3]

All the early literature of the Celtic churches, especially in Ireland, brims with scriptural citations. St. Patrick's professional and personal

apologia, like Augustine's autobiographical confession a generation before, is constantly punctuated with biblical comments and allusions.[4]
The magnificent Gospel Books of Kells, Birr, Durrow, Lindisfarne, and
others, undisputed masterpieces of the world's great art, may have been
used rarely for liturgical celebrations, although missals were created for
this purpose at a very early period. More likely, they were created to
embody the respect and devotion Scripture received at the hands and
hearts of the great monastic centers. They were shrines of the Word.

Scripture was similarly foremost in private devotion. Besides the superb monuments of calligraphy and portraiture in the form of the Gospel
Books and the grand missals made for liturgical use, Irish scribes created
small "Pocket Gospels" which could be taken on journeys or pilgrimage or simply used in the intimacy of one's cell. But the Word of God
was also subject to critical study, exegesis, and commentary by the
monks, for whom love of study was next only to love of God. Even the
major writings of Pelagius, a very early figure, consist mainly of biblical
commentaries, especially those on St. Paul's Epistles.[5]

A vigorous ascetical discipline, as we have already seen, also typified
the spirituality of Celtic monasticism from the beginning. In its extreme
forms, such asceticism may strike us today as pathological, although
in those heroic times it would hardly have appeared so. In any case,
extraordinary practices characterized only a minority of monks, largely
the Célí Dé.

Prayer, both public and private, mental and physical, was hardly of
less importance in Celtic spirituality than Holy Scripture. The formal
liturgy consisted of the mass, the sacraments, and, at least in the monastic
settlements, sung psalmody.[6] Even more than the Benedictines, Celtic
monks devoted many hours each day to chanting in common the praises
of God from the Psalter. In addition, many of the saints privately recited
the entire 150 psalms every day — by heart and, it is often affirmed,
standing up to their necks in seawater, lakes, or rivers. (No doubt an
effective way to concentrate the mind!)[7]

Among other forms of prayer, litanies, or *loricae,* were composed from
at least the sixth century, probably for processional usage. In the course
of time, many acquired almost magical significance as charms to ward
off evil. A superb and famous example is *The Deer's Cry,* attributed to
St. Patrick, but in fact a much later composition.[8]

Devotion to Jesus, to the angels and saints, and in particular to Mary
seems always to have been a principal feature of the prayer life of Celtic
spirituality, especially in Ireland, where Jesus was often referred to simply
as "the Son of Mary." Feast days were celebrated with particular exu-
berance, requiring a relaxation of the severe rule even of the ardent Célí

Dé, who were responsible for much of the revival of personal spirituality toward the end of the first millennium.[9]

As we have already seen, much of our knowledge of the early period of the Celtic churches comes from the scores of long and short biographies of saints written from the sixth century to the later Middle Ages. Hundreds, perhaps thousands of place names in Wales, Ireland, Scotland, and Brittany still testify to the enduring importance of areas associated with favorite saints. Often little else is now known of these revered men and women but their names, many but hardly all of which have been preserved in the Celtic martyrologies.[10]

The saints were not merely recalled as heroes of the faith, however. In a variety of ways, they remained real presences in the lives of their successors, ready to assist by their own prayers, and also capable of enhancing, protecting, and defending their *familia* and other clients in this life and the next by the power of their word, even from beyond the grave. Revered for their blessings, they were also feared for their curses.

Words of Power

Twin edges of the sword of invocation, blessing and cursing are properly understood only in combination, if not inseparably connected, especially in the lives of the Celtic saints in which they were integral and frequently decisive weapons in spiritual combat — at least in the minds of their later biographers. But each likewise manifests a distinctive aspect of Celtic spirituality that endures to the present.

Among the ancient Celts, the spoken word embodied power, the ability both to heal and to harm. One of the most dreaded imprecations, lasting well into the Christian era, was the poet's satire, a verbal weapon employed against inhospitality, meanness, or guile with sometimes lethal results. In a society that revered honor above all, a person could die of shame. Of equal potency, and even more greatly feared in later times, were the priest's curse and the widow's curse, which carried the force of divine vengeance in their wake.

Language, for the ancient Celts, was thus not merely a "means of communication" as it is for the modern world — the proper domain of grammarians, public relations experts, and textual analysts. Language was a mystery, the power of revealing and disclosing the depths of human and heavenly experience, one glorious facet at a time. It was the domain of poets, wizards, and priests. And still, among many Celts, remains so.

Of course, praise and blessing were not original developments in Celtic spirituality, but derive from a long tradition of prayer in the Hebrew and Christian ways of life in which God is extolled for the manifold gifts and care that shower upon humans and the whole of Creation. Yet the characteristic verbal sensibility of the Celts contributed a particularity of nuance that is as unmistakable as it is rich. As a result, few elements of Irish and Scottish spirituality are as typical as their blessings — and their negative aspect, cursings. The saints specialized in both.

The ordinary Irish words for "blessing" are *beannaím* and *coisricim,* the former of which comes especially close to the Latin *benedicere* and *beatus,* which in turn correspond to the biblical Greek *eulogeo, eulogia,* "to speak well." In English, however, the word "bless" comes from the Old English *bletsian,* which is related to "bleed," *bledan,* and ultimately to *blod,* "blood." For both animal and human blood were used from the dawn of humankind in ceremonies of consecration. To bless meant to mark with blood, to make holy, to sign, in Christian terms, with the bloody cross of Jesus.

But "bless" also came to mean "to make happy." In Scripture, it is used to translate *beatus,* where the Greek has *makarios.* All these words mean "fortunate" or "happy" in the sense of "blessed," but also and more importantly, they mean being close to God.[11]

Hebrew, like Greek and other languages, used several words to indicate what we translate as "blessing." The most common are *ashar,* "to be straight, or level," and especially *barak,* which means "to kneel," and from which comes the word for "blessing," *berakah.* The fundamental sense is to benefit someone, to praise, to prosper. For the Hebrews, from whom Celtic Christian spirituality drew much of its depth, blessing is a reciprocal act: we are blessed by God, and we bless God in return. But only God can truly bless: we bless when we extend God's blessing to each other and to the whole world of Creation. When we bless God we acknowledge God as the source of our life and welfare and the origin of all goodness and gifts. To bless is thus an act of giving thanks and praise, ultimately, therefore, of Eucharist. To experience woe is to lack and long for that intimacy and communion.

In Gen. 1:22, God blesses birds and fishes, and then blesses human beings (1:28; 5:2). Other animals were undoubtedly blessed in the original story. All are told to increase and multiply as part of this blessing. God blesses the Sabbath (Gen. 2:3) and makes it a day of blessing. God blesses Noah and his children and tells Abraham, "I will make of you a great nation, and I will bless you...and by you all the nations of the earth shall be blessed" (Gen. 12:2–3). But the Hebrews were likewise commanded in Deut. 8:10, "You shall bless the Lord," and they are promised a few verses later, "The Lord will bless you" (15:10). Over a third of the Psalms sing of blessing God for all the favors and gifts showered abundantly on us. Under the New Covenant the cup of blessing is, above all else, the blood Christ shed for the salvation of the world, and for this we praise and worship God.

In Scripture, "woe" ('*owy* in Hebrew and *ouai* in Greek, almost exactly the same sound) is an exclamation, a lament at being deprived of God's blessing or, worse, even being cursed, cast out of God's presence and grace. But woe is not the same as a curse or malediction, the pronouncement of a judgment against a person, a people, or the very land itself, as in Genesis 3, where God curses the serpent and then the earth because of human sin. Both beatitudes and woes are declarations, even litanies of such blessings or their lack. Scripture is full of them. There are twenty-six beatitudes in the Psalms, eight in Proverbs, and twenty-three in the other books of the Old Testament. There are lots of woes, as well. The Book of Jeremiah contains a whole catalogue of both. Luke gives us four of each. (Matthew later adds seven "woes" in chapter 23 which do not quite balance the beatitudes of the fifth chapter. But they still go together.)

In the end, all blessing simply means being close to God, declaring the proximity and reciprocity of all goodness in the divine bounty. Thus for St. Paul, every blessing flows from Christ, God's blessing itself, God's benediction on Creation and the divine presence made definitively visible and tangible. To the extent that we draw closer to Christ, the happier we become. Not merely receptively, but — and this is more important — actively. We bear blessing, like a tree planted near a source of water that continues producing foliage and fruit even in drought.

Like the ancient Hebrews, early Irish, Scots, Welsh, and Breton Christians realized from the depths of their souls that to remain joyful, to be able to sing and dance, to celebrate beauty and goodness in circumstances of deprivation, oppression, and infamy means to be raised to new life, to be in Christ, delivered from the power of sin and death. They understood Jesus' warning not to look to those who are wealthy, powerful, overfed, and carefree to understand happiness, but to look to the lives of those whom the world counts worthless or worse. For the seed of their bliss is hope, watered by faith in God's promises and the reality of the presence of the Holy Spirit in their midst.

Ancient Blessings: St. Patrick's Breastplate

Among the nearly countless blessings found in Celtic literature, the "breastplate" of St. Patrick, the "Lorica," or, as it is sometimes known, *The Deer's Cry* (*Fáeth Fiada*), is one of the most ancient and justifiably the most famous.[12] This magnificent prayer of blessing, a chant attributed to St. Patrick when he and his disciples slipped through a lethal ambush set by King Laoghaire, embodies almost every element of Hebrew and early Christian benediction. It begins with a profession of faith in the Trinity, no doubt evoking a lost and ancient creed: *Atomriug indiu niurt trén togairm trindóit....*

> I arise today
> Through a mighty strength, the invocation of the Trinity,
> Through belief in the threeness,
> Through confession of the oneness
> Of the Creator of Creation.

It then turns to Jesus, the source of all blessing through the mysteries of his life, death, and resurrection. But Jesus is the Lord of the Universe, illuminating the entire universe of God's handiwork, beginning with the celestial spirits and the great heroes of biblical tradition and continuing with the communion of saints:

> I arise today
> Through the strength of Christ's birth with His baptism,
> Through the strength of His crucifixion with His burial,
> Through the strength of His resurrection with His ascension,
> Through the strength of His descent for the judgment of Doom.

> I arise today
> Through the strength of the love of the Cherubim,
> In obedience of angels,
> In the service of archangels,
> In hope of resurrection to meet with reward,
> In prayers of patriarchs,
> In predictions of prophets,
> In preachings of apostles,
> In faiths of confessors,
> In innocence of holy virgins,
> In deeds of righteous men.

The world of Creation is now summoned to his assistance, recalling the order of the various beings' making and their dependence on God, a prayer of praise echoing in Celtic cadences the Canticle of the Three Young Israelites in the Furnace of Nebuchadnezzer:[13]

> I arise today
> Through the strength of heaven,
> Light of sun,

Radiance of moon,
Splendor of fire,
Speed of lightning,
Swiftness of wind,
Depth of sea,
Stability of earth,
Firmness of rock.

There follows what can only be interpreted as a thoroughly Irish paean of invocation and petition, best sung (as it often is):

I arise today
Through God's strength to pilot me:
God's might to uphold me,
God's wisdom to guide me,
God's eye to look before me,
God's ear to hear me,
God's word to speak for me,
God's hand to guard me,
God's way to lie before me,
God's shield to protect me,
God's host to save me from snares of devils,
From temptations of vices,
From every one who shall wish me ill,
Afar and anear,
Alone and in multitude.

Here the writer turns his plea for protective blessing against the forces of evil and sorcery that imperil the spirit:

I summon today all these powers between me and those evils,
Against every cruel merciless power that may oppose my body and
    soul,
Against incantations of false prophets,
Against black laws of pagandom,
Against false laws of heretics,
Against craft of idolatry,
Against spells of witches[14] and smiths and wizards,
Against every knowledge that corrupts man's body and soul.

Finally, the author turns back again to Christ, his shield, creating a magnificent trope on the thought of St. Paul in Ephesians 6:11–17, which rises to a climax of exultation before returning, splendidly, to his opening incantation:

Christ to shield me today
Against poison, against burning,
Against drowning, against wounding
So that there may come to me abundance of reward.
Christ with me, Christ before me, Christ behind me,
Christ in me, Christ beneath me, Christ above me,
Christ on my right, Christ on my left,
Christ when I lie down, Christ when I sit down, Christ when I
    arise.
Christ in the heart of every man who thinks of me,
Christ in every eye that sees me,
Christ in every ear that hears me.

I arise today
Through a mighty strength, the invocation of the Trinity,
Through belief in the threeness,
Through confession of the oneness,
Of the Creator of Creation.

Cherished down the centuries, this great litany of praise and protection is not only profoundly Christian, but deeply Celtic. It is especially and rightly noted for its appreciation of the divine presence shining forth from the depths of Creation itself, the miracle of nature ever close to the Celtic heart. In his sensitive and eloquent commentary, Noel Dermot O'Donoghue points out that the prayer "calls on all the elements to bless and protect human beings, as if there were something holy and powerful already present in the world of nature. And not only holy in some passive sense but living and responsive, just as the angels and saints, invoked elsewhere in the hymn, are living and responsive."[15]

A similar vision of the presence of God in all things (and the presence of all things in God) was preserved unbroken by the Celtic Christians of the Western Islands off the coast of Scotland over centuries of oppression and turmoil following the Reformation and the "pacification" of the Highlands imposed by England following the abortive revolution of 1745. In the nineteenth century, many of these prayers were recorded in the original Gaelic by Alexander Carmichael, who published them in two volumes in 1900.[16]

Invocations from the Hebrides

As an official in the Department of Customs and Excise, Carmichael had the opportunity to travel extensively in the Inner and Outer Hebrides. To his credit, his respect for the faith of the islanders, many of whom were still Catholic (and still are), earned him their trust. On at least one occasion, he refrained from publishing a prayer he had copied because the old man who had recited it to him worried that "outsiders" might ridicule his simple but eloquent "going-to-sleep prayer."

The prayers of the West Highlanders of the Outer Hebrides were strongly trinitarian and Christological. The mysteries of Creation, the redeeming death of Christ, and the healing, strengthening Spirit of God enter frequently into their thoughts, marveling, and blessings. A catholic richness pervades the celestial audience who accompany the crofters, herders, and fishermen throughout their daily work and rest. Chief among the Highlanders' favorite saints were Mary, Brigid (or, as she was more familiarly known, Bride), Columba, and, in a somewhat lesser role, Patrick. The archangel Michael figures prominently as the strong defender and the guide of souls at death. Named companions include the other great archangels of biblical and extra-biblical tradition, Gabriel, Raphael, Ariel, and Uriel, whose presence and intercession witness to the antiquity of islander beliefs.

God, Christ, Mary, the other saints, and the angels were almost tangible participants in the islanders' continuous dialogue of praise, petition, and thanksgiving. Despite the grim poverty and austere environment in which they struggled to survive, these humble Christians knew themselves to be surrounded by glory. But surprisingly lacking from their invocations are complaint, discontent, resentment, and especially guilt and fear. Carmichael may have idealized his informants to some degree, but it is unlikely that they would have deceived him completely over more than forty years of patient inquiry.

As might be expected, blessing was paramount in the spirituality of the island peoples, as in this simple May Day prayer:

Bless, O Threefold true and bountiful,
Myself, my spouse, and my children,
My tender children and their beloved mother at their head.
On the fragrant plain, on the gay mountain sheiling,
  On the fragrant plain, on the gay mountain sheiling.[17]

The daily round of work was the subject of many of the prayers of the Christian islanders. In this prayer at dawn, a housewife reflects on origins and sources as she kindles the hearth fire, casting her net of protection over the rest of her day and that of her family, friends, and neighbors in the presence of the heavenly court:

I will kindle my fire this morning
In presence of the holy angels of heaven,

In presence of Ariel of the loveliest form,
In presence of Uriel of the myriad charms,
Without malice, without jealousy, without envy,
Without fear, without terror of any one under the sun,
But the Holy Son of God to shield me.
God, kindle Thou in my heart within
A flame of love to my neighbor,
To my foe, to my friend, to my kindred all,
To the brave, to the knave, to the thrall,
O Son of the loveliest Mary
From the lowliest thing that liveth,
To the Name that is highest of all.[18]

Tending their flocks and fishing were two of the most important occupations on the Western Islands, and each was surrounded by a veritable stockade of blessings to protect those involved, both human and animal, as well as to ward off the manifold hazards of sea, weather, and predators.

Go shorn and come woolly,
Bear the Beltane female lamb,
Be the lovely Bride thee endowing,
And the fair Mary thee sustaining,
    The fair Mary thee sustaining.

Michael the chief by shielding thee
From the evil dog and from the fox,
From the wolf and from the sly bear,
And from the taloned birds of destructive bills,
    From the taloned birds of hooked bills.[19]

The poor fisherman was, on the day of a good catch, still far richer than his neighbors who might be sore pressed to provide a meager supper from the land. The prayer for success in fishing is also a promise of bounty to those less fortunate, a pledge to divine justice.

The day of light has come upon us,
Christ is born of the Virgin.

In His name I sprinkle the water
Upon everything within my court.

Thou king of deeds and powers above,
The fishing blessing pour down on us.

I will sit me down with an oar in my grasp,
I will row me seven hundred and seven strokes.

I will cast down my hook,
The first fish which I bring up

In the name of Christ, King of the elements,
The poor shall have it as his wish.[20]

Every detail of life was related to the all-present Spirit of God by these humble Christians. Milking the cows was one of the most important daily chores, one that could never be omitted. The affection of the Islanders for their cows is manifest in a number of blessings. Crooning to them to ease the milk was an ancient custom. Each cow might have her own croon, and Carmichael reports that sometimes unless the crooning was right, the cow might not give her milk. The following is a crooning blessing, a prayer over the work and over the cow herself.

Bless, O God, my little cow,
    Bless, O God, my desire;
Bless Thou my partnership
    And the milking of my hands, O God.
Bless, O God, each teat,
    Bless O God, each finger;
Bless Thou each drop
    That goes into my pitcher, O God![21]

At the end of the day, sleep was the special subject of blessing, in keeping with ancient Christian custom. Carmichael recorded a number of night blessings, including this in the familiar form of the Lorica.

I am placing my soul and my body
On Thy sanctuary this night, O God,
On Thy sanctuary, O Jesus Christ,
On Thy sanctuary, O Spirit of Perfect truth,
    The Three who would defend my cause,
    Nor turn Their backs upon me.

Thou, Father, who art kind and just,
Thou, Son, who didst overcome death,
Thou Holy Spirit of power,
Be keeping me this night from harm;
    The Three who would justify me
    Keeping me this night and always.[22]

Death was an ever present companion on the islands, where conditions were harsh. Still, a number of the island folk lived to be of considerable age. But in the end, death comes for all, and that inevitable visitation was kept before their minds by a number of prayers. One of the most famous is called "The Soul Leading." Carmichael explains that this blessing, also known as "The Soul Peace" or "Death Blessing," was intoned or sung over someone who was near death. The person who says it was called "soul-friend," and "will be held in special affection by the friends of the dying person ever after.... As the prayer is sung, the soul-friend makes the sign of the cross with the right thumb over the lips of the dying." The archangel Michael here fulfills his ancient role as the "angel of death," leading the soul into paradise.

> Be this soul on Thine arm, O Christ,
> Thou King of the City of Heaven.
>> Amen.

> Since Thou, O Christ, it was who bought'st this soul,
> Be its peace on Thine own keeping.
>> Amen.

> And may the strong Michael, high king of the angels,
> Be preparing the path before this soul, O God.
>> Amen.

> Oh! The strong Michael in peace with thee, soul,
> And preparing for thee the way to the kingdom of the Son of God.
>> Amen.[23]

Two of the most beautiful of the prayers of the *Carmina Gadelica* are "The Lightener of the Stars," a lyrical exclamation of sheer praise at the wonder of Creation, and a simple *lorica* Carmichael copied down from an old woman who dared to resist the demands of the Reformed preachers that she abandon the ways of the past. Both embody the heart of Celtic spirituality, the legacy of the great poetic saints of centuries past.

> Behold the Lightener of the stars
> On the crests of the clouds,
> And the choralists of the sky
>> Lauding Him.

> Coming down with acclaim
> From the Father above,
> Harp and lyre of song
>> Sounding to Him.

> Christ, Thou refuge of my love,
> Why should I not raise Thy fame!
> Angels and saints melodious
>> Singing to Thee.

Thou Son of the Mary of graces,
Of exceeding white purity of beauty,
Joy it were to be in the fields
  Of Thy riches.

O Christ my beloved,
O Christ of the Holy Blood,
By day and by night
  I praise Thee.[24]

Carmichael copied the following "breastplate" prayer, our last witness, from an old woman, Mary Macrae, in 1866. She had been a great dancer in her youth and loved to sing. When her "old-world ways" were abjured and condemned, she paid no heed, "singing her songs and ballads, intoning her hymns and incantations, and chanting her own mouth-music, and dancing to her own shadow when nothing better was available."[25]

God with me lying down,
God with me rising up,
God with me in each ray of light,
Nor I a ray of joy without Him,
  Nor one ray without Him.

Christ with me sleeping,
Christ with me waking,
Christ with me watching,
Every day and night,
  Each day and night.

God with me protecting,
The Lord with me directing,
The Spirit with me strengthening,
For ever and for evermore, Amen.
  Chief of chiefs, Amen.[26]

Although Carmichael and others translated the Gaelic prayers into what is in many cases obviously the smoother diction of late Victorian English, the sense if not the letter of the sharp-edged Celtic spirit survived, not least, I suspect, because Carmichael himself was a native speaker and without question still alive to the beat of the ancient rhythms of language and life. And if the "saints" are those who live the Christian life thoroughly, relating every moment of their waking (and sleeping) lives to the presence of the Holy around and within them, these wonderful proclamations of praise and protection echo the poetic appeals of Columba, Sedulius Scottus, and the great figures of the Celtic past. There is, however, another, darker facet of that holy consciousness, both ancient and modern.

The Art of Malediction

The way of blessing leveled the often-rocky path of the ancient Christian Celts, creating peace and an aura of protective love around family and friends. But the other side of the coin of protection was of particular if, hopefully, not equal importance: cursing. Like an ancient Hebrew prophet, the Patrick of the *Tripartite Life* and other later accounts blesses his converts and those who assist him, but roundly and vehemently curses those who thwart his plans. He raises the dead, but also strikes malefactors down with a word, often for what appear to be trivial reasons. His curse is powerful, even irresistible.

Of course, the Patrick of history also asserted his authority in stern words. One of the most precious documents of the fifth century, his Letter to the soldiers of Coroticus, protests his outrage over the Christian Briton's pirate attack on a group of recent converts, many of whom were killed outright, others captured as slaves. Patrick's invective swells like thunder, climaxing in an appeal to the soldiers to shun the chieftain if he fails to repent and release his captives. It is, simply, a decree of excommunication, perhaps the first of the great Irish curses.

History fails to record what impact Patrick's anathema had on the petty Christian king, who had, Patrick himself observes, scoffed at the grieved bishop's initial remonstrance. Later biographers supply the lack, however. Muirchú describes the amazing outcome in his Life of Patrick when the unrepentant Coroticus is transformed into a fox and disappears into the forest.

Whether for good or ill, Patrick's word was intensely effective, even magically so, as shown in his legendary and lethal encounters with King Laoghaire's hostile druids. Similarly, according to later accounts, Columba uttered mighty curses against his opponents, and we find the imprecations of offended saints like the combustible Ciarán of Clonmacnois reaching from beyond the grave to punish, sometimes mortally, those who slight their *familia* or devotees.[27]

In accordance with conventions of early medieval hagiography, not to say Celtic story-telling, such accounts are undoubtedly dramatic exaggerations, even if they were based on actual incidents. But they represent more than icing on the cake of hero-worship. As the eminent Celtic scholar Joseph F. Nagy has argued, these texts encode a significant testimony that in the cultural idiom of Ireland and Britain establishes the grounds of credibility. Above all, it is the power of the word, which is to say God's word, which is being manifested. In Celtic hearing, the truth is not so much embellished as enshrined in symbolic form. And the truth in these instances wears the countenance of justice.

The common Irish word *mallacht* ("curse") was based on the Latin *maledicere,* "to speak evil or harm" to someone.[28] Another term, *escaine,* is as old as the language itself. Both reproduce in their own idiom the biblical notion of the New Testament Greek words *anathema* and *katara.*[29] But behind the Christian tradition there lies an even more ancient legacy of prophetic retribution nowhere more forcefully expressed than in the famous (or infamous) "cursing psalms."[30]

Despite the central emphasis on love and peace in the Christian biblical tradition, the destructive and sometime lethal aspect of incurring divine vengeance, especially by withholding truth — the truth of things as well as human testimony — is hardly absent. Often it is conveyed indirectly, as in the parable of the fig tree found in Matthew 21:19 and Mark 11:13, or the story of Ananias and Sapphira in Acts 5:1–11 and of Elymas the magician in Acts 13:6–11. Merely altering the sacred text can evoke retribution, as in Revelation 22:18–19: "I warn every one who hears the words of the prophecy of this book: if any one adds to them, God will add to him the plagues described in this book, and if any one takes away from the words of the book of this prophecy, God will take away his share in the tree of life and in the holy city, which are described in this book."

Provoking the "wrath of God" by wanton acts of lying, deceit, or distortion of the truth does not justify wishing others harm, however: "bless those who curse you, pray for those who abuse you," Jesus insists in Luke 6:28 and elsewhere.[31] What then are we to make of the potent curses of Patrick, Columba, Mochuda, and others, maledictions that can bring death and disease upon those who obstruct the will of the saint? Tara itself was said (wrongly enough) to have been brought to ruin because of the curse of Ruadán and his companions. (It might be noted that the Irish are not the only Celtic saints with a penchant for effective cursing. In the case of St. Beuno, Oliver Davies writes, "The relatively brief account of his life records no less than four occasions on which Beuno curses someone with fatal consequences."[32] Teilo, among other Welsh saints, was feared because of his curses.)

Original Cursing

Among the Irish in particular, the curses of the priest, the poet, and the widow were especially dreaded. The deadly satire of the poets, one of the causes of their near-banishment at Druim Cett, had been curtailed by the compromise achieved by Columba, although the curse of a poet lingered as a reminder of their former prestige. Especially during the later Penal period, priests not only lacked status, but were outlaws and therefore helpless before the law. Fear of their curse was often the only restraint between them and the gallows.

As in the traditions of the ancient Hebrews and early Christians, widows were particularly vulnerable to misfortune, and thus deserving of special protection and assistance.[33] When no earthly assistance came to her aid in distress, she had only God and the saints to protect her. Incurring the widow's curse was thus to risk divine vengeance. But while the mere possibility of earning her malediction might serve to forestall injustice from other Christians, the ritual curse was her last recourse against those for whom the fear of God was of no consequence. It is said that the distressed woman would go to a public place where she would kneel and loosen her hair, and then utter an imprecation against her persecutors that cried to heaven for vengeance. Such lamentation, a public outcry for redress, was no mere pursuit of personal revenge, but a plea for social justice.[34]

Despite all that, the most potent curse was surely that of the great saints, whose care for their followers and even remote inheritors entailed punishing malefactors who threatened the monastic family as well as preventing wrongdoing by dint of the fear of incurring saintly wrath. In the later Lives, as noted earlier, Patrick was notorious for his curses. Native-born Columba came close in the craft of malediction. Even Adomnán records the story of the deadly judgment Columba pronounced on the murderer of the young woman he and old Gemmán had tried to protect when he was still only a deacon.

In later tales, Columba's ire was roused by a wide range of paltry insults, often with devastating consequences.[35] Sometimes the outcome of provoking the saint's displeasure was proportionately petty, as when on a journey through Tyrone, Columba desired to know the time of day, but the area lacked a cock whose crowing could assist. So Columba cursed the district, with the result that there would never be a cock there again.[36]

A more sinister tale involves the wife of King Aedh, who, because she mocked Columba's efforts at reconciliation at the Convention of Druim Cett, had the venom of her own mockery turned against her. She was, at the saint's pronouncement, changed into a crane.

Among the "great stories" of holy malediction we have already considered the cursing of Tara by Ruadán, Brendan of Birr, and other saints, the penalty for King Diarmuid's violation of sanctuary.[37] Even granting the implausibility of the event having ever occurred, not to mention its ineffectiveness if it did, the point was indelibly made — not even kings could violate with impunity the honor of God's saints and sanctuaries.

Another cursing story concerns one of the most memorable figures of Irish legend and literature, the mad king Suibne (Sweeney), whose arrogance and untrammeled temper ran afoul of a potent antagonist in St. Ronán Finn, the abbot of Druim-iskin.[38] By way of prologue, Suibne seized from Ronán a tunic he intended to be a gift. This act of injustice resulted in the king's being cursed by Ronán and the other saints of Ireland. Sometime later, just before the Battle of Magh Rath (Moira) in 637, Suibne heard Ronán's bell ringing in the forest and flew into a violent rage. He dashed into the woods and seized the saint, who had been praying the psalter. Suibne snatched the precious book and threw it into the nearby lake. Suibne was prevented from further violence only by the onset of battle preparations. Although Ronán's psalter was later retrieved by a helpful otter, that did not prevent the saint from bestowing a second curse on the intemperate tyrant.

The third blow fell when Ronán and his monks, attempting to prevent the battle and the inevitable carnage (in which, in fact, Suibne's Dál-nAriade was decisively defeated), blessed both armies with holy water. Considering himself mocked, Suibne hurled a spear, killing one of the monks outright. Another was saved when the spear glanced off his hand-bell. The monk then pronounced the third and most devastating curse on Suibne — that, like the spear, he would fly aslant (lose his mind) and one day die from a spear wound just as he had slain the innocent monk.

After the battle, Suibne did lose his wits, becoming a fugitive among the birds of the forest, shunning and being shunned by human society except for the protection and companionship offered by St. Moling. But even that gentle saint could not forestall forever the fulfillment of the saint's curse. In due course, Suibne was speared by Moling's own swine-herd, who found the mad king conversing with his wife and assumed the worst.

Still another saint whose curse was widely feared was Maignenn, whose church, Cill Maignenn, is remembered sadly in the name of the notorious Kilmainham prison in Dublin. But in one account, Maignenn provides a counterpoint to the custom of saintly malediction. When a thief made off with the cow belonging to a poor leper woman of Cill Maignenn, she appealed for redress to the monks. Appalled at the injustice and the violation of the sacred precincts, they rang their bells in unison and cursed the scoundrel — excepting only Maignenn. When questioned about his silence, he replied that he would have to bestow a blessing on the hapless thief, since no one else would offer so much as a prayer on behalf of one so roundly condemned to hell.[39]

All such stories have in common both the effort to redress gross injustice in the absence (or sometimes the presence!) of anyone capable of
enforcing moral or legal constraints and also at least the hint of the formal elements of excommunication — invocation to God for vengeance,
the ringing of bells, and the solemn pronouncement of judgment. Often
the imposition of anathema is preceded by other forms of holy coercion,
especially fasting, that most Celtic of persuasions and protests against
injustice right up to the present. The objective was to shame the perpetra-
tor into repentance, even by a fast unto death if necessary.[40] Sometimes,
however, the target of the stratagem countered by his own fast. Further, curse could be met by curse, as happened in the conflict between
St. Ruadán and King Diarmuid, who proved to be a formidable exponent
of the art.

In all likelihood, as Patrick Power and others have proposed, such
measures served multiple purposes during periods when might and right
were all-too-often indistinguishable and violence against the defenseless
all too common. They strengthened the moral authority of the church,
expressed in the indignation of its holiest representatives, who were
presented in a light no less powerful than that of the great heroes of
the pagan past.[41] Finally, when all other avenues of private and public protest had been exhausted, the curse remained for the powerless a
final recourse to God. And this reliance on divine retribution points to
a further dimension of the spirituality of the Celtic saints, their passion
for justice.

EIGHT

The Struggle for Justice

The frequently incendiary political character of Celtic civilization is central and important in all its manifestations, whether ancient or modern.[1] In particular, the prominence given to peacemaking and social justice in the Lives of the Celtic saints reveals them to have been pioneers in this area, and none more so than the great biographer of Columba, St. Adomnán, the ninth abbot of Iona. But his story, which involves the protection of the women of Ireland and noncombatants, has its necessary antecedents. It also has its consequences, as Ireland produced its quota of women saints, martyrs, and leaders over the following centuries.

Because of the tribal nature of the monastic settlement and indeed of Celtic life in all aspects, social involvement was as inescapable for the monks as it had been for the druids before them.[2] This social dimension was largely expressed in their devotion to pastoral care, particularly spiritual development among those who applied to them for advice and counsel. But, as we have seen in a variety of instances, engagement in the political process itself was commonly among the principal preoccupations of the saints, whether by voluntary instigation as with Columba or by reluctant inveiglement in the stories of Ruadán and Ronán.

If personal honor was the chief virtue and most prized quality among the Celts, the face it showed in their social life was *loyalty:* beyond doubt, beyond price, and beyond limit. Its dark, unforgiving shadow is revenge, for personal treachery is the greatest sin against the tribal way of life. In such a context, the most extreme expression of political action, or, rather, its failure, is violence, battle, or trial by combat, in which opponents strove against each other to determine by blood, if need be, how power should be allocated, disloyalty punished, and honor vindicated.

Not without cause, the Celts were perceived from the earliest times

161

as a hot-headed, quick-tempered people, as prone to reckless violence as to drunkenness. Early on, the ultimate symbol of valor was, after all, going into battle stark naked, armed only with sword and shield and the fierceness of battle frenzy. In early Christian Ireland, while the monasteries were vigorously Christian, they were also Celtic, and, at times, even monks went to war, as the various Annals and the later Lives of Columba testify. Nor were their weapons always those of the spirit. Even so, the task of promoting and preserving peace and justice frequently devolved to the monastics, both men and women, and especially the saints among them.

Despite notable achievements, Celtic civilization during the second half of the first millennium was hardly a halcyon era. But if in fact social reality fell short of the ideal, justice and charity were still the acknowledged hinges of political life in Christian Britain, Ireland, and Scotland. Distributive justice was prominent in the Celts' dealings with one another. Equality was a cherished value, if in a stratified and heroic culture women, children, serfs, and slaves lacked the rights, prestige, protection, and influence sought and enjoyed by males, unless they were of royal blood. Even in that regard, dominant figures like the legendary Mebh (Maeve), St. Margaret, and the very real Grace O'Malley were exceptions. Nevertheless, despite the disadvantage their gender brought to saints such as Non, Íte, Gobnait, and Monenna, who had to contend with secular and clerical misogyny throughout their lives, abbesses such as Brigid and Hilda exercised real power. Children, too, were not only prized, but fostering was widely practiced even among the less-privileged classes, lest orphans or the poor lack access to material and spiritual benefits. It was expected that prisoners and hostages would be treated with sacred respect, and warfare among tribes and kingdoms was conducted with honor and restraint. At least in principle.

In respect to ordinary civil relations, a strong emphasis on kindness and hospitality did in fact pervade early British and Irish literature. Diarmuid Ó Laoghaire describes an ancient series of proverbs which begin with the word *eochair*, "key": " . . . if the key to justice is distribution, the key to miracles is generosity."[3] He then cites two short poems that treat typically of the importance of hospitality:

> O King of Stars!
> whether my house be dark or be bright
> it will not be closed against anybody;
> may Christ not close his house against me.

Conversely, with regard to an unfit guest house,

Great the sorrow!
Christ's guest-house fallen into decay;
if it bears the name of Christ the renowned,
it means that Christ is without a home.[4]

In the richly comic twelfth-century tale *The Vision of Mac Conglinne*, the magical use of satire is brought to bear against a monastery in which hospitality has fallen into serious decline. But the satirist himself is a glutton and wine-bibber, who is almost murdered by his furious hosts. How he escapes their vengeance and, in the process, exorcises a hunger-demon which has been tormenting the king of Munster, illustrates the vagaries of Christian kindness even during a period of relative peace and prosperity.[5]

In short, while noble values were esteemed, life in Christian Ireland had much in common with life in other parts of Europe during the "Dark" and Middle Ages — raids and wars were frequent and brutal, the poor were frequently oppressed by taxation and rapine, women and children were massacred, and hostages were executed. During the Viking era in particular, many of the social accomplishments of the first periods of Christian culture were reversed, as terror reigned along the coasts and often far inland. Achieving peace and justice meant constant struggle and repeated setbacks.

Despite the cultural disaster and the vast human suffering inaugurated by the Viking terror, Celtic society and spirituality emerged from the ordeal purified and, in some respects, stronger. The closest Ireland came to a unified government was under Brian Borumna, whose forces defeated the Danes decisively in 1015 at the Battle of Clontarf. But from the settlements of the Norse invaders grew Ireland's first towns and cities — Dublin, Limerick, Wicklow, Waterford, and the rest. By closing one door on the Celtic past, the Viking era succeeded in opening Ireland to a Europe itself newly awakened from the cultural sleep of the Barbarian Era. And prominent among those who strive to create a new and more civil society were the saints.

Making Peace, Living Justly

Social involvement of an active and even determinative character was a constant feature of Celtic religious life. Like their spiritual forebears in Egypt and Syria, the monks, even the hermits, did not as a rule locate their "cells" so far from human habitation as to be impervious to the spiritual and often material needs of their neighbor.[6] Stories from the

Lives of the saints indicate that they frequently took the initiative in
defending the rights of the poor as well as their own.

One of the earliest traditions concerns St. Patrick himself, who from
his years as a slave knew at first hand the value of human freedom and
dignity. His experience as a teenager undoubtedly lent force to his famous Letter to the soldiers of Coroticus. Less well-known is the forceful
position given Patrick in regard to slavery in later accounts. One of the
stories in the ninth-century *Tripartite Life* concerns the plight of a group
of slaves hewing a yew-tree. When Patrick asks why their hands are
bleeding severely, they explain that they have been forbidden to sharpen
their tools adequately. Patrick accosts the cruel slave-owner, who refuses
even to admit him to his house. So Patrick fasts against him at the gate in
the hallowed tradition. When this fails to move the owner, Patrick spits
on a stone (ritual spitting stones were common features of Celtic monasteries by the ninth century) and curses the intransigent fellow, declaring
that his family would never produce a king or the heir to a king. Later,
the owner is drowned in a lake.[7]

Far from being a simple anecdote, Patrick's intervention is, as Thomas
Cahill claims of the famous Letter, part of a direct attack against slavery
itself: "However blind his British compatriots may have been to it, the
greatness of Patrick is beyond dispute: the first human being in the history of the world to speak out unequivocally against slavery. Nor will
any voice as strong as his be heard again till the seventeenth century."[8]

Promoting justice and instituting and enforcing the "peace of God"
were the chosen tasks of the monastic saints of the first millennium,
much as they would be throughout Europe during the Middle Ages. As
with Patrick, even the saints' characteristic "cursing," the invocation of
divine vengeance, was directed at preserving the peace and preventing
injustice, particularly to the weak and powerless. But the monks were not
without the force of law. Gradually, they developed moral and legal codes
which influenced (and were influenced by) the Brehon laws that regulated
secular affairs. Among the products of this venture into legislation were
the Penitentials and the special laws, or (in Ireland) the *cána*.

The Penitentials

A passion for balance without rigidity animated political life among the
Celts much as it did their art, creating both fluidity and vigor but also
permitting an apparent inconsistency troubling to the Germanic mind
and at variance from the codes of Latinate legalism. In the sphere of
social relationships, this quest for flexible appropriateness can best be
described as the pursuit of poetic justice. In the stories of the saints, the

rewards of the righteous and especially the punishments of the wicked *fit:* kindness is answered by kindness, mercy begets mercy. When the poet Dubhthach and the young noble Erc greet Patrick courteously, they are blessed and ultimately inherit the Kingdom of Christ. But Coroticus, treacherous and evasive, is transformed into a fox; the violently angry Suibne truly becomes mad and is slain by what is, poetically, his own spear.

Nowhere is the penchant for moral proportion more in evidence than in the creation of the monastic Rules and especially the Penitentials, those much-misunderstood manuals designed to balance the penances meted out by confessors and the *anamchara,* avoiding both the harshness and the laxity that might result from temperament or whim. But even the devotional literature carries with it a sense of balance and evenness, as in this passage from the *Alphabet of Piety:*

> When is a person competent to answer for the souls of others? When he is competent to answer for his own soul first. When is he capable of correcting others? When in the first place he can correct himself. A person who corrects his own soul to life everlasting, how many souls could he convert? The people of the whole world: provided that they were tractable, he could convert them to life everlasting so that they would belong to the Kingdom of Heaven. (2, 18)

A major paradigm shift occurred in the late Dark Ages, when the ancient practice of public confession and the imposition of severe penances for sin was gradually replaced by private confession and mitigated penances. This change has been ascribed to the evangelizing efforts of the Celtic monks, who in bringing the light of Christ back to Europe also brought a new appreciation of justice and mercy. These were enshrined in their characteristic manuals which sought to create a more uniform mode of assigning penances, the so-called Penitentials.[9]

The earliest forms appear to have developed in the British church around the time of St. David, to whom is attributed, appropriately enough, the Penitential of David. Also extant are the penitential canons ascribed to the Synods of Brevi and of the "Grove of Victory" from about the same period, and from the next generation, the Penitential of Gildas. Frequent exchange with the Irish monasteries soon brought them to the attention of Irish canonists and confessors. After a period of development in Ireland, *peregrini* and missionaries in turn carried Penitentials and canonical collections to England and the European mainland, where they found great favor. Most of the original manuscripts are now lost, but because of the large number of copies made, the texts have been largely reconstructed.

The Penitentials assign penalties not on the basis of the gravity of the sins considered in themselves as offenses against the divine law or the honor of God, as in later medieval Europe, but in proportion to their disturbance of public peace and order. In this light, as Msgr. Corish explains in regard to the Penitential of Finnian, they "make no concessions to a society accustomed to divorce, remarriage and concubinage," nor do they countenance injury or manslaughter, regardless of their frequency in Celtic society.[10]

The oldest of the Irish Penitentials is likely that attributed to "Vinnian," or Finnian, whom most scholars have assumed was either Finnian of Clonard or Finnian of Moville, although there is no evidence for either attribution. Its antiquity is evident in that the Penitential of Columban draws heavily on it. Kenney and other scholars regard the Penitential of Cummean as the most important, and it, also, dates from sometime in the middle of the seventh century. The probable author is St. Cuimine fota (d. 662). The Paenitentiale Bigotianum (early eighth century) is noteworthy for its schedule of commutations, that is, rules by which lengthy penances may be converted into shorter and more severe ones, or into money payments on the model of secular fines, which are also found in the Old Irish Penitential.

That these and many other Irish Penitentials and canonical writings were welcomed in Europe is evidenced by the large number of copies that were made and the indigenous Penitentials that reveal Irish influence, such as the Paenitentiale Romanum, the Paenitentiale Bobiense, and the Paenitentiale Parisiense, all of which were inspired by the Penitential of Columban.[11] In fact, the widespread provenance of the Irish books and their imitators can only be accounted for by the great missionary effort of the Celtic churches from the sixth to the tenth centuries.

The Cána

Another distinctive Irish innovation, although not widely disseminated on the continent, was the group of laws known as the *cána* (singular, *cáin*), which were as extraordinary in their development as they were in their content. These special laws, and particularly the Cáin Adomnáin, arose from the keenly felt need for a more encompassing form of law that could span the gulf between secular and ecclesiastical spheres and extend beyond the territorial frontiers of tribes and kingdoms.

In Celtic countries, kings normally enacted laws for the secular realm, but jurists (*brehons* in Ireland) also codified decisions and served as consultants or judges in difficult cases. Enforcement of legal decisions was another matter, often left to the discretion of the king or another powerful person who may (or may not) have had the good of the realm as a concern. Ordinary laws thus tended to be limited to the area over which some kind of jurisdiction could be imposed. There was another kind of law, however, as Kenney says, "half-secular, half-ecclesiastical in its origin as well as in its application. Such were the injunctions to which the general term *cáin*, 'law, rule,' was given a peculiar application."[12] Another difference between ordinary laws and the *cána* is that in return for the social benefits resulting from subscription to them, people were bound to make annual payments to the current abbot of the monastic church of the saint who was its author.[13]

Traditionally, at least according to a commentary in the Martyrology of Oengus, there were four of these *cána* of old Ireland which applied anywhere people subscribed to them — Patrick's law, not to kill clerics; Adomnán's law, not to kill women; Dáire's law, not to steal (or, in some versions, kill) cattle; and the Sunday law, prohibiting certain kinds of activity on that day, especially warfare.[14]

The most remarkable and perhaps the earliest of these special laws is the Cáin Adomnáin, also known as the Law of the Innocents or the Law of Women.[15] Its purpose was far broader than the protection of women, but it is in that respect that it was chiefly remembered. The reason, quite simply, was that the situation of women in Ireland by the end of the seventh century had in many respects become intolerable to the Christian conscience, particularly in regard to the question of war and violence.

The Women of Ireland

Despite the strenuous efforts of Mary Condren and other writers to argue for a prepatriarchal, matrilineal society in ancient Ireland, there seems to be little warrant for a strongly proto-feminist interpretation of the pagan sources, much less Christian ones.[16] Rather, there is considerable evidence of the victimization of women in both, such as the tragic story of Deirdre; the legend of Macha, who is forced to race at Emain although near the point of childbirth; and the rape and sometimes murder of Christian virgins that figure in so many Lives of the saints.

In Ireland before the Christian era, as Lisa Bitel shows in her superb investigation, *Isle of the Saints*, "women and children derived their status exclusively from male guardians."[17] Exceptions can be cited, of course, although appealing to mythological sources for evidence of egalitarian social structures and customs favorable to women in general remains perilous. Still, the conventions surrounding the liberties taken by (and given to) Queen Mebh (Maeve) in the Ulster cycle are exploited to effect, and they were accurate enough to be recognized within the world of the Christian Celts and to pass without comment. Clearly, however, the general lot of women in pre-Christian Ireland was precarious.

Christian writings themselves unequivocally testify to the predominance of a male-centered, patriarchal society in which women were in almost every respect subordinated to and controlled by men, whether their fathers, their husbands, or churchmen. Again, exceptions exist, and while they do not disprove the rule, they surely argue for wide latitude in interpreting the evidence. It is also clear that in many respects, in ancient Ireland at least, women fared better in respect to the laws of marriage and divorce than their sisters in other parts of Europe. Legal penalties and penances for adultery, for instance, were far more equitable than the strict Germanic and Latin codes that specified burning.[18]

In the Lives of the saints, the examples of saintly demeanor extended to Christian women often show women not so much as extraordinary members of their gender, but as "manly," sometimes, as with Íte, disparaging the weakness of their own sex. At best, the record is ambiguous:

> In sum, hagiographers created a whole gallery of women whose portraits were didactic, ornamental, or incidental; they were sometimes meant to be taken as honest role models, sometimes meant to warn women, and sometimes simply meant for entertainment or to add color to a dry vita. From these portraits we can deduce much about women's lives in early Ireland, but we cannot extract a coherent theme regarding women's nature or behavior.[19]

It is evident, on the other hand, that in Irish society before and after the advent of Christianity, power was concentrated in the male line. Male heirs inherited land, while female heirs shared only in movable property. If only daughters survived, they had to marry their nearest paternal kinsman.[20] In pre-Christian Ireland, not only was marriage sometimes polygamous, divorce was ordinarily a matter of simple legal renunciation. Surprisingly enough, in early Christian Ireland, polygamous marriages persisted. Katherine Hughes observes, "a man might have a chief wife and a subordinate wife or wives (the usual word — a borrowing — is *adaltrach*), who are all described as 'lawful women.' "[21] And despite claims for matrilineal descent, it is generally recognized that the children of legal marriages belonged to the father's family group, unless an Irish woman had married a foreigner. A woman did not lose her connection to her extended birth family, however, which retained an interest in her well-being as well as that of her children.[22] In cases of divorce, a women could return to her own kindred and, depending on the length of the marriage, take a proportion of her dowry and personal possessions with her.

There was, of course, a "down-side" to even the relative equality women possessed in Christian Celtic culture. Not unlike the warring monks, their recourse to arms exposed them to retribution; both became subject to slaughter. The intensely tribal character of Celtic society also exposed children and the elderly to extreme danger in time of war, not unlike the grim situation found in the historical books of the Hebrew Scriptures. In addition, the position of women had apparently deteriorated in the chaotic period between the sixth and tenth centuries. It is against this background that Adomnán's innovative Law of the Innocents must be evaluated.

The Law of the Innocents

As it has come down to us, the Cáin Adomnáin is a complex document which describes the situation of the women of Ireland in dramatic (and undoubtedly exaggerated) terms, emphasizing in detail the horrors of enforced conscription in which women were made to bear arms in battle and suffered outrageously in consequence. Most likely compiled in its present form in the ninth century, the Cáin Adomnáin also includes a homiletic passage which relates how the mother of the saint Ronnat coerced her son to "save the women of Ireland," despite his understandable reluctance. For the more historically reliable passages detail the opposition his law aroused among the kings and nobility of Ireland, even to the point of murderous threats aimed at the abbot and his monks.

Adomnán prevails by dint of his great skill in the art of malediction, in which he threatens the kings of Ireland with divine vengeance if they fail to subscribe to his law. The Cáin then lists the number of those who sooner or later succumbed to the counter-threat of anathematization. That he succeeded in outlawing the practice of forcing women into combat, and also exacted protection for children and clerics who did not bear arms, is revealed by various Annals that note that Irish, Pictish, and Scottish kings, together with various trial chiefs, abbots, and bishops, solemnly ratified Adomnán's Cáin at the Synod of Birr in 697 and again in 727. And in the Martyrology of Oengus, the holy abbot is celebrated in extraordinary verses:

> To Adomnán of Iona,
> Whose troop is radiant,
> Noble Jesus has granted
> The lasting freedom of the women of the Gaels.[23]

Despite the subscription of a host of kings and religious leaders, the Cáin Adomnáin did not wholly secure the rights of noncombatants, just as the reform movement of the Céli Dé did not wholly succeed in rejuvenating Irish monasticism. For at the very end of the century, a new and terrible threat appeared, waves of Viking pirates who killed and plundered mercilessly throughout Ireland and the coastal areas and waterways of Britain and the northern European mainland for the next two centuries. Nevertheless, the Law of the Innocents first established in principle the immunity of noncombatants in warfare, and as such may be credited as the legal basis for subsequent efforts to achieve their protection up to the present.[24]

The Martyrs of Ireland

Stubbornness characterizes the Celtic temperament and politics no less than do loyalty, vengefulness, and a passion for rightness. The age-old tenacity of Irish, Welsh, and Scots warriors faced with the overwhelming might of those intent on eradicating their freedom, customs, and language at Badon Hill, Bannockburn, the Boyne, and Culloden, as well as the General Post Office on Easter Monday morning, 1916, is echoed in the resistance of the martyrs during the centuries of often bloody oppression that followed.

Whereas the Celtic martyrs of old had died at the hands of pagans, abroad and sporadically, systematic religious persecution began in 1535, when King Henry VIII declared himself supreme head of the church in England, Wales, and Ireland. Hundreds of English, Scottish, and Welsh Catholics died for their faith in the next three hundred years, and, to be sure, about an equal number of Protestants were martyred by Catholics. But in Ireland, thousands of Catholics would perish at the hands of their fellow Christians. Still, duress, material deprivation, enslavement, cultural oppression, and outright martyrdom could not bring the great majority of the Catholic Irish to heel. Most of the victims are known to God alone, killed in massacres such as those at Drogheda and Limerick. Others, particularly priests and religious, were hunted down and executed by hanging, shooting, burning, or the sword. Some were slowly starved to death, and others consigned to slavery in the West Indies, to end their days laboring under the blazing sun of the tropics.[25]

The first martyrdom was recorded in 1572, when Edmund O'Donnell, a Jesuit priest, was hanged, drawn, and quartered in Cork on October 25. The last was Dominic Egan, a Dominican, who died in prison in 1713. Of the many hundreds of known martyrs, 259 were named by a special Vatican commission in 1915. Almost half that number, 112, were Dominican friars and sisters, beginning from around 1600. Before that time, the majority of martyrs were Franciscans, Cistercians, Jesuits, diocesan clergy, and, of course, lay men and women. But under Cromwell in particular, Dominicans seem to have been especially sought out and were killed with exceptional cruelty.

In 1975, the archbishop of Dublin, Dermot Ryan, appointed a special commission to investigate the causes of a number of these men and women. In 1992, seventeen martyrs were solemnly beatified in Rome. Of that number, the Dominican archbishop of Emly, Terence Albert O'Brien, was of considerable interest. Apprehended by Cromwellian forces after the siege of Limerick in 1651 while tending the sick in the city hospital and calmly awaiting arrest, O'Brien was tried before a court martial, which spared the archbishop no indignity. His conviction was certain, and he was executed by slow strangulation. His body was left hanging for three hours while the soldiers hammered it with the butts of their muskets until, as one witness said, it hardly resembled anything human. Finally, his head was hacked off and impaled over St. John's Gate by the river.[26]

In 1653, two Dominican lay women of Mayo, Honoria Magan and Honoria de Burgo (Burke), who had managed to survive the pogroms of Elizabeth, James I, and Charles I, were caught with a younger attendant trying to flee Cromwell's merciless soldiers. Although very aged, the two Dominicans were stripped and beaten, and then left to freeze to death in the harsh winter weather. Their attendant carried Honoria Burke, who was almost a centenarian, back to their little house, leaving her near the foot of a statue of the Virgin Mary. When she returned for Honoria Magan, she found the old woman frozen to death in the hollow of a tree. Returning once more to the house, she discovered the lifeless body of Honoria Burke still kneeling upright in prayer.[27]

Not all the Irish martyrs died in Ireland. A number were emigrant scholars intent on salvaging the ancient Irish manuscripts from the vaults of Europe in order to preserve them for posterity and were killed in Germany and Bohemia, including the Franciscan Patrick Fleming and his deacon, Matthew Hoare (killed by a Lutheran mob in 1631).

Of all the martyred saints of Ireland, few have so captured the attention of their contemporaries and modern Christians as Oliver Plunkett, the archbishop of Armagh (1625–81). Unable to return to Ireland after his ordination in Rome, Plunkett remained in Europe for fifteen years. In 1669, he was secretly consecrated archbishop of Armagh in Ghent before returning to minister to his Irish brothers and sisters. Plunkett made his way through England in disguise and arrived safely in Ireland. Although frequently on the run as an outlaw with a price on his head, for the most part Plunkett was not hindered by the Protestant overlords, to whom he posed no threat. Caught up, however, in the widening dragnet following the "Popish Plot" falsely alleged by Titus Oates in England, Plunkett was seized and tried for treason in Dublin. He was declared innocent by an all-Protestant jury, who stated that the witnesses against him were perjured. Undaunted, the English had the archbishop transferred to London for another trial. On the testimony of false witnesses, he was convicted and sentenced to be hanged, drawn, and quartered at Tyburn, where a number of Jesuit priests had already been executed. In 1918, Oliver Plunkett was declared a "blessed" of the church, a Roman gesture toward Irish independence hard to misunderstand, and on October 12, 1975, he was formally enrolled among the saints. His feast day is celebrated on July 10.

Modern Women Saints

Katherine Hughes pointed out in her groundbreaking study of early Christian Ireland that the place of women's institutions had never been adequately explored, an oversight only barely being corrected at the present time. As for the women saints themselves, whereas the Martyrology of Tallaght lists over 119 Irish women saints or groups of women (and, as she notes, all of November and part of December are missing), there are extant Lives for only four women saints — Brigid, Íte, Monenna, and Samthann.[28] While shamefully true, the fact remains that the elements of women's saintly lives are found in a great number of monks' Lives as well as *legenda,* place names, and inscriptions. (That a resolute women's presence continued in Scotland well into the Reformation is suggested by a grave-slab carving of one of the abbesses of Iona, Anna MacLean [1509–43], "a stout nun with little lapdogs nestling in the folds of her habit.")[29]

Women of the late first millennium and Middle Ages were, of course, not the only saints to be forgotten or neglected in popular and scholarly rolls. Among some of the leaders and founders during the modern period were a number of outstanding women whose achievements surpass those of bishops, priests, and male saints in general yet are rarely mentioned in church histories.

"Nano" Nagle

The most repressive period of persecution and martyrdom in the seventeenth century gave way to the era of the Penal Code in 1704, which deprived Catholics of the right to own property or serve in the military forces. Although many established families were able to circumvent the repressive legislation in Ireland as they did in England, by 1714 Catholics owned only 7 percent of the land.

Honora Nagle (1718–84), one of Ireland's foremost apostles of the poor, was born of the old Anglo-Norman family of De Angulo, which had by wit and wile retained much of their property and wealth. "Nano" was a high-spirited, lively girl apparently destined for a good marriage and life of ease. Sent to be educated in France, Nano was returning home from a ball early one morning when she saw from her carriage a number of poor laborers waiting for the church to open so they could attend mass before reporting for work. Struck by their faith and the opportunity to worship denied Catholics in Ireland, she began to question the direction of her life.

In 1746, Nano's father died. She and her sister Ann returned to Dublin. Touched by a gesture when Ann sold some silk she had bought in Paris in order to provide alms for the poor, Nano resolved to become a nun. She returned to Paris, but her destiny lay in her homeland. Once again in Ireland, where her mother had since died, Nano moved to Cork, where she lived with her brother and his wife near their uncle's house.

Secretly, Nano began a school for the daughters of the Catholic poor — a serious offence under the Penal Laws imposed by the English. Word spread of her schools, and soon other young women offered to assist in teaching and, more dangerously, in catechesis. Nano's clandestine projects, which included caring for Cork's sick and poor, gradually impoverished her family. With her inheritance from her uncle's estate, she founded an Ursuline convent. She did not become a nun, however, recognizing that the strict enclosure would end her active work in the education and care of the poor.

In 1776, Nano and three companions put on the habit of the Sisters of the Presentation, a new congregation intended to devote itself wholly to work with the poor. Nano died in 1784, twenty years before official approval of her order was granted. But with that was also imposed what she had always resisted, the law of strict enclosure.

In time, with the relaxation of the Penal Code in 1782 and 1793, and then the coming of Catholic Emancipation in 1829, social work became possible on a new scale. The Presentation sisters, hindered by the restrictions imposed by Rome, continued and promoted their work in education, as the order extended its activities to England, the United States, Australia, New Zealand, and the Philippines.[30]

Catherine McCauley

Catherine McCauley (1781–1841), whose likeness adorns the last Irish five-pound note of the century, was, like Nano Nagle, born of a well-to-do Catholic family of Dublin which had managed to preserve its wealth and property despite the hardships of the Penal Code. After her parents' deaths, Catherine lived with her uncle, Owen Conway, until his financial ruin forced her to move again to the home of Protestant relatives. Although pressured to renounce Catholicism, Catherine resisted for four years under the guidance of her Jesuit confessor, Thomas Betagh.

For the next twenty years, Catherine found herself residing among the Protestant gentry of the Pale, but they did not interfere directly with her religious practice. Finally, in 1822, Catherine inherited the house and a substantial fortune from the childless couple whom she had been living with and who had become Catholic themselves under her gentle influence.

Selling the house, Catherine was able to use her fortune to establish a school for poor girls on Baggot Street, Dublin, where she was soon joined by several other women committed to teaching and caring for the poor. By 1827, the Sisters of Mercy had come into being in fact if not by official recognition. But that followed in 1835. By then, the religious climate had changed sufficiently in Ireland and Rome to permit approval of an active order of women freed from the restrictions of the monastic cloister.

Mother McCauley died in 1841, having established ten convents in Ireland and another in London. Mary Ryan D'Arcy points out that twenty of Florence Nightingale's thirty-eight nurses who served in the Crimean War were from the Mercy convent there. Now one of the largest orders of women religious in the world, the Sisters of Mercy carry on their apostolate in social work, health care, and education with the assistance of a growing association of lay members.

Edel Quinn

In the twentieth century, the spirit of resolute spirituality that animated the lives and work of Nano Nagle and Catherine McCauley, like the long heritage of women saints before them, found expression in the relatively brief life work of Edel Quinn (1907–44). Her involvement in the Legion of Mary, a lay Catholic service organization founded in Dublin by Frank Duff in 1921, led her first to the Poor Clare monastery in Belfast. Diagnosed with tuberculosis, Edel saw her vocational plans dashed by a prolonged stay in a sanitarium in County Wicklow. On her recovery, she returned to Dublin, where she worked as a secretary and assisted in the main office of the Legion.

In 1936, Edel responded to the invitation of the apostolic delegate, Antonio Riberi, to go to Africa as a missionary in order to spread the work of the Legion of Mary. Her demanding schedule as she traveled from country to country throughout east Africa led to a recurrence of tuberculosis and a long stay in a sanitarium in South Africa. When released, Edel threw herself back into her work, traveling, speaking, and organizing local branches of the Legion of Mary. Struck again with illness, this time fatally, she died on April 12, 1944, in Nairobi and is buried in the missionary cemetery of the Convent of the Sisters of the Precious Blood.[31] Edel Quinn has been beatified by Pope John Paul II. The process of canonization of all three Irish women is well underway in Ireland and Rome.

Saints for Today

Women are not the only modern saints of Ireland, Scotland, Wales, or Brittany, of course. But at the risk of anticipating developments in Rome, it is probably safe to put forward two male candidates, both laymen, both Irish as it happens, whose lives greatly altered the course of spiritual history in the West — Matt Talbot and Frank Duff.

Matt Talbot

Matthew Talbot, considered by many to be a patron saint of alcoholics, lived and died in the obscurity of the teeming Dublin slums, where he was born in 1857 into a culture of extreme poverty and religious oppression.[32] The great potato famine of 1846–50 was still a present reality in the lives of the poor. After minimal schooling, Matt took a job at the age of twelve as a messenger boy for a liquor merchant, exposing himself to the hazards of alcohol. Fifteen years later, addicted to drink, out of work, and without funds, he found his former drinking companions unwilling even to buy him a pint of beer.

Deeply humiliated, Talbot decided "to take the pledge," swearing off drink for three months. He never drank again. Gradually, like one of the monks of the seventh century, Talbot quietly adopted greater and greater personal austerities as his spiritual life developed. He slept on planks with a piece of wood for a pillow, gave what was left of his meager earnings to the poor after supporting his mother and sister, and attended mass daily, kneeling for as long as an hour each morning on the steps until the church was opened, his knees pressed to the cold, wet stone through slits he had cut through his trousers.

Though barely literate, Talbot read church history, the spiritual writings of the saints, and radical Catholic social teaching, through all of which he gained a profound appreciation of the connection between material want and spiritual growth. He managed, during this time, to contribute a surprisingly large amount of money from his wages to help support the newly founded Columban missionaries.

Matt Talbot was stricken by an apparent heart attack on June 7, 1925, on Granby Lane, behind the Dominican church of St. Saviour, where a plaque now commemorates the life and death of this poor man of Christ. It was not until his body was examined at the mortuary that Talbot's austere but hidden spiritual practices became known. Wrapped around his body were large and small chains held together by twine and secured with religious medals. He had also bound himself with knotted cords, which had cut deeply into his flesh. None of this was visible through his street clothes. Surprised by the death that made him famous, Talbot had not been able to remove them, as he had once before when admitted to hospital during a serious illness.

Soon all Dublin knew of this humble saint in their midst, whose devotion, despite his self-chosen obscurity, had not gone unnoticed by those who had seen him daily at mass, praying in the presence of God in a holy ecstasy of adoration. (Among those who as a boy had known Talbot was Sean Kelly, the first president of the Republic of Ireland.) But few had grasped the extent of that holiness. The cause of Matt Talbot's beatification and canonization is currently under consideration by the Vatican.

Frank Duff

Younger by almost a half-century than Talbot, Frank Duff was only in his early thirties when he founded the Legion of Mary in September 1921, in Dublin. Envisioning a lay movement of Catholic men and women eager to engage in active, apostolic endeavor, Duff watched over the Legion for the next sixty years as it grew from a small cell in Dublin to a worldwide organization of some three million members in over fifty countries.

Organized into local groups, or "praesidia," the Legion's members engage in charitable works, missionary activity, and door-to-door evangelization. It has been endorsed by over one thousand bishops and extolled by successive popes. Duff himself lived to attend the Second Vatican Council as a special observer and was applauded by the world's Catholic hierarchy. His vision, as remarked by Msgr. Corish in his history of Irish Catholicism, was that of "personal spirituality rooted in theology."[33] Such a notion coming from a layman in the 1920s and 1930s was enough to earn Duff the abiding distrust of Archbishops Byrne and McQuaid. Nevertheless, the Legion of Mary grew and spread through Ireland, then to Scotland, England, India, and the United States. By 1932 it had reached Australia, and two years later young Edel Quinn brought it to Africa.

Duff died in November 1982, at the age of ninety-one. The promotion of the cause of his beatification and sainthood was signed by Archbishop Desmond Connell in Dublin in 1996.

Kenneth Woodward has cogently argued that since the Middle Ages the tendency in the Roman Catholic Church has been to replace the saint as miracle-worker, heavenly patron, intercessor, and even as spiritual model with the saint as an embodiment not only of general virtues or human moral excellence, but as a representative of authorized policy or ideology.[34] But apart from the political hay harvested by the Vatican in selectively canonizing men and women who symbolize one or another point of politically correct doctrinal or moral currency, and also beyond the perennial desire of the reputedly "simple faithful" for wonder-workers and powerful intermediaries, the question remains, what is the value, if any, of saintliness and sainthood today? What, moreover, can these old (and new) saints of the Celtic churches teach us?

NINE

A Continuing Tradition

The very nature of tradition is that it should constantly change and grow: tradition without renewal quickly becomes obsolescence.
— OLIVER DAVIES[1]

As Celtic spirituality attracted increased attention from the reading public over the last decade, a number of authors addressed various areas of interest: art, literature, music, even the ecological ramifications of developing what might be called a contemporary Celtic vision or way of life. While approaching the subject from different perspectives, most writers seem to agree on at least one thing: in a world gone a bit mad, there is a sane alternative.[2]

The lives of the Celtic saints have a place in this re-visioning, as a number of authors have recognized. Those holy women and men lived in times very different from ours, despite surprising similarities. They are also sometimes remembered in ways that Christians today are likely to find astonishing and even repellent — praying the psalms submerged up to our necks in near-freezing seawater is not the way most of us would choose to spend our early mornings! Nor would the spare diet, fasting, long hours of vigil — prostrate, arms extended in the form of a cross — appeal strongly to those who prefer their Christianity comfortable.

But perhaps that *is* where these old saints (and their later disciples such as Honoria Burke and Matt Talbot) have something to teach us — that a Christianity grown too comfortable is, in the end, no Christianity at all. That to follow the gentle, homeless Christ means to love our enemies and be willing to die at their hands if necessary rather than relinquish the faith that sustains us. That living in the consciousness of God's all-pervading presence calls us to fellowship with the *whole* of

Creation — plants, animals, the rocks, seas, the planet itself, and the very stars and galaxies. That generosity and justice go hand-in-hand, and that it is possible to fight dragons without becoming one.

Being safely in the past, and an alternative to the dominant forms of Christianity that have survived the religious conflicts of the last thousand years, the Celtic churches and their saints often provide a convenient screen on which the desires and hopes of modern Christians can be, and often are, projected. For instance, the interfaith Community of St. Aidán and St. Hilda was founded in 1994 by a group of Anglican clerics and lay persons imbued with admiration for the "apostle of Northumbria" and his English disciple and looking for a kinder, gentler way of promoting the Kingdom of God. According to the community's Guardian, Ray Simpson, "One of the distinctive things about the Celtic church was that it renounced power as a means of extending the Kingdom of God, which did mean that it almost got expunged at Whitby."[3]

Almost. The Celtic churches continued to exist as distinctive communities for another five hundred years, and so far as I can tell, none of them ever remotely considered renouncing power. Wealth, yes. Comfort, yes. But power was something Celtic Christians understood, sought, and used, whether the coercive power of their prayers and curses, as at the Battle of Chester, or the moral power of fasting against their opponents (including God at times), or even the power of armed conflict, as monastery raided monastery in disputes over land, prestige, and prerogatives. The expulsion of St. Mochuda from Rahen was an exercise of blatant power based on nothing much more than tribal jealousies. To be sure the image of St. Patrick striking dead his opponents or riding his chariot three times over the body of his all-too-contrite sister, Lupaid, is not one that is likely to appeal to today's advocates of nonviolence.

Nevertheless, the history of the Celtic churches and the spirituality of its great saints have much to teach us about the promise and pitfalls of discipleship, including the use (and misuse) of power. One of the most important lessons we might learn is the peril of idealizing the past as a means of criticizing the present. At the end of the long history of the Irish church, as Saints Malachy O'More and Lorcan O'Toole struggled to institute reforms and bring Ireland closer into the network of medieval Christendom, they were not betraying the heroes of the past, but continuing a tradition of reform. They looked ahead, not backward. And if they could see farther than many of their contemporaries, it was not least because they, too, stood on the shoulders of giants.

Bede's heavy emphasis on the Synod of Whitby is considered by some historians as an exaggerated interpretation, one consonant, of course, with his own sympathies. But even if the venerable historian's views are accepted as a balanced appraisal, Christopher Bamford's evaluation is surely wide of the mark when he writes, "By 664 and the Synod of Whitby, the Celtic Church as a visible entity was over."[4] In fact, the Celtic church in Ireland was still very much in evidence up to the twelfth century.

Yet the Celtic churches did come to an end then and in that respect may qualify as the only fully extinct major Christian tradition in history. Such a distinction would be seriously misleading, however, if one fails to recognize, first, that the missionaries and scholars from Ireland and Britain who revitalized the continental church after the barbarian invasions thereby set in motion the chain of events that ushered in the great era of Christendom in the High Middle Ages but also doomed their own tradition. Second, the Celtic churches did not simply die out. Guided by leaders both wise and saintly, such as Malachy and Lorcan, they melded fairly smoothly into the mainstream church of Western Europe, now more or less whole and incarnate in a precariously fragile but nonetheless real ecclesial and political body called "The Holy Roman Empire" (although it has been observed that it was neither holy, Roman, nor much of an empire).

If one is prepared to grant so much, the question next arises whether the spirituality of the Celtic saints has anything of particular value to offer the world today that cannot be found among saints of any tradition or place. I think it does, although not by addition so much as emphasis. Among other things, it can teach us much about overcoming terrorism, fostering justice, and conserving the world of nature.[5]

Facing Terrorism

In an age still dominated by war and militarism, increasing global poverty, social oppression, and environmental deterioration, we can learn first of all that no nation or people which relies primarily on military power and the implied threat of violence for its own security will endure long nor leave to coming civilizations a heritage much worth preserving. We will likewise learn that justice for some is ultimately injustice for all. And we will learn that to ignore the intimate implications of the social, biological, and physical systems that constitute our environment and the delicate balance that obtains among them to make this a habitable planet is to court disaster for life on earth.

What can a Celtic spirituality teach us about violence? That it is possible to overcome terror by making peace.

Beginning in 795, coping with terrorism became a recurrent, almost routine challenge for Celtic Christians as, for over two hundred years,

Viking raiders plundered the coasts and navigable river areas. Sometimes the Irish, British, and Christian English were able to repel pirate attacks. The Scandinavian thrust westward was even temporarily halted by military resistance led in Saxon England by Alfred the Great in 878 and again in 895, and in 1014 by Brian Borumna (Boru) in Ireland. However, Christian Celtic and Anglo-Saxon realms still remained prey to raids, whose major targets were usually the monasteries. Overall, thousands of monks and nuns as well as countless lay persons were massacred by the Vikings, for whom terrorism operated as an informal but highly effective colonial policy.

Strangely enough, this terrible period seems to have had little impact on the Lives of the saints themselves. Even in accounts written a century or more after the Viking terror had subsided, it hardly merits a mention. Living with the terror of sporadic night raids, the menace of random violence and wanton killings, cultural oppression, religious persecution, and the ubiquitous presence of fear and dread had become a habit of the heart for the Celts of Ireland, Britain, Scotland, and Brittany for over two hundred years. And helpfully so: even when the Vikings themselves passed into history (and into the society of the Celts and other peoples), the terror was to return in varying measure, especially in Ireland and Scotland, for centuries to come.

In our own time, terrorism has of course become a major, almost formal policy of revolutionary guerillas as well as established and often dictatorial governments throughout the world. Directly or indirectly, major international powers, even while themselves often the target of terrorist attacks, support political terrorism by supplying arms, ammunition, matériel, training, and money to terrorist groups of the right or the left. In Ireland itself, Catholic and Protestant terrorists have contributed disproportionately to the weight of suffering. Similarly, Muslims, Christians, and Jews use terror and counterterror in the Middle East from Algeria to Iran. So widespread and entrenched has terrorism become in world politics that it is not only a major industry, but a professional global network.

The presence of saints among them surely aided the Celts of old to confront and disarm terrorism by the counter-forces of civilization, inculturation, and conversion. Today, the presence of saints — many unnamed and most unheralded — in the midst of the new terror, not of Vikings, but of neighbors and kindred, has enabled Christians in Northern Ireland to inch closer to a moment when peace and justice might at last prevail.[6]

In a word, what we can learn from our Christian brothers and sisters of that far distant time is a lesson far older yet: Do not render evil for evil. For only in patience shall we possess our souls.

Sharing Sufficiencies

The Celtic nations of the ancient world were never wealthy. They had no banks, and even minted coinage was rare. Gold, silver, and precious gems were valued and made into ornaments for human delight and divine worship — to enshrine the Word of God and the real treasures of the saints, old bells, wooden staffs, belts, and bones, as well as to provide liturgical vessels. All were prized not for their worth in trade, but as works of art, for their beauty.

Even the modest luxury of the court and *tuath* (tribe) was suspect to the saints, who never tired of reminding their contemporaries (and us) that "less is more," that voluntary poverty is the surest route to spiritual maturity, that "the key to justice is distribution and that to miracles is generosity." Beginning perhaps with the story of the young Brigid giving away her father's sword, the most consistent themes in the Lives of the saints are the dignity of the poor, the priority of sufficiency in food, clothing, and land, the duty of caring for those who are in need, whether because of illness, misfortune, or just bad judgment. Similarly, the protection of the powerless, as in the Law of the Innocents, expresses the most profound realization of the *human* right to safety and security.

In all of this, the Celtic saints in their teachings and stories recaptured in vivid concreteness the prophetic message of old Israel and the first Christians. They were not unique in that, only prodigiously eloquent.

Restoring Creation

Of equal importance to the quest for peace in the face of terrorism and the achievement of justice in the midst of pervasive poverty and social oppression, the preservation of the integrity of the natural world in the coming decades will continue to be a challenge the next generations cannot and must not neglect. Here, too, the saints have something to teach us.

The literary and political accomplishments of the Celtic saints were matched by their great love of nature, which was brilliantly expressed in a variety of artistic forms. In them the mystical element of Celtic spirituality became especially manifest with its paradoxical tensions between the sense of the nearness and farness of God, the melancholy fleetingness of all life and the vanity of the world, and yet the grandeur and wonder of Creation in all its myriad loveliness.

Unlike many Christian traditions, that of the Celtic saints regarded the world of wildlife, trees, plants, and forces of weather, the sea, and the vast starry sky as manifestations of God's creative nature, a sacrament of divine presence, not a distraction from the obligations of the chapel. The Lives revel in accounts of saints who befriended and protected endangered animals, even wolves and bears (although they could not, in the end, save them from the enmity of farmers). The saints did not romanticize nature, much less allegorize it; they loved and celebrated it.[7]

Reclaiming the ancient contemplative heritage of experiencing nature as theophany could well assist humanity's passage through the next difficult years. For it would at least remind us that the most promising path toward a constructive resolution of our environmental crises begins and ends with the richest sources of creativity available to us: the power of imagination and the sense of God's all-pervading care.

Are there other lessons to be learned from the spirituality of the Celtic saints that will be of benefit to Christians and other peoples of the world in the third millennium of the Common Era? Unquestionably.

With what now seems like amazing prescience, in 1968 the Italian economist and philosopher Roberto Vacca called for a renewal or even rediscovery of the Celtic monastic tradition as a way of preserving civilized values during what he foresaw as the coming of a new dark age.[8] Vacca maintained that if the world managed to avoid the terminal conflagration of nuclear war, the West would still require a host of widespread "conservers of civilization and catalysts of a future renaissance" in order to survive an even deeper crisis, now only in its early stages — a new barbarism in which the most cherished values of the peoples of the world would be confronted by greed, intolerance, and violence. Looking back more than a millennium to the first age dubbed "dark" by Renaissance writers impatient for a return to the glory of classical Rome, Vacca proposed for this role a new kind of monasticism modeled on the Celtic institutions which preserved the learning and culture of the West from the fifth to the tenth centuries.[9] If the Irish saints "saved civilization" once, as Thomas Cahill would have it, perhaps they might do it again.

A Calendar of Celtic Saints
(Much Abbreviated)

The saints are Irish, unless noted otherwise.

Jan. 3   MAINCHIN THE WISE. Bishop. Principal patron of Limerick. Seventh century.

Jan. 7   KENTIGERNA. Wife, mother, and missionary. Scotland. Died in 734.

Jan. 13   KENTIGERN (MUNGO). Bishop. Principal patron of Glasgow. Died in 603.

Jan. 15   ÍTE (ITA) OF KILLEEDY. *Anamchara* of Brendan of Clonfert. Died around 570. Especially remembered in Limerick.

Jan. 16   FURSA (FURSEY). Monk and missionary. Died in 649.

Jan. 19   FILLAN. Monk and missionary. Son of Kentigerna. Scotland. Eighth century.

           BLATHMAC OF IONA. Martyr. Died in 825.

Jan. 25   ST. DWYNWEN. Wales. Considered the patron of true lovers, because he restored a dead suitor to life. Believed to have lived in the fifth century.

Jan. 30   AIDÁN (MAEDOC). Bishop. Principal patron of the Diocese of Ferns. Died in the year 626. Especially remembered in Ferns and Kilmore.

Feb. 1   BRIGID. Secondary patron of Ireland. Principal patron of Kildare and Leighlin. Died about 525.

Feb. 7   MEL. Bishop. Principal patron of Ardagh. Fifth century. Especially remembered in Ardagh and Clonmacnois.

Feb. 9   TEILO. Abbot. Wales. Sixth century.

Feb. 11   GOBNAIT. A nun who lived in Cork. Sixth century.

Feb. 17   FINTAN. Abbot of Clonenagh. Died in 603. Especially remembered in Leighlin.

March 1   DAVID. Abbot and bishop. Principal patron of Wales. Died c. 588. Roman calendar.

March 3   WINWALOE (GUÉNOLÉ, GUIGNOLÉ) OF WALES. Brittany. Died c. 504–532.

NON (NONNA). Wales, Brittany. Mother of St. David. Died c. 550.

March 5   CIARÁN. Bishop. Especially remembered in Ossory.

PIRAN. Patron of Cornwall (Kernow); patron of miners.

KADDROE OF SCOTLAND. Abbot of Metz. Died in 971.

March 8   SÉNÁN. Bishop. Died mid-sixth century. Especially remembered in Killaloe and Limerick.

March 10   KESSOG. Scotland. Invoked by Highlanders when going into battle.

SAINT JOHN OGILVIE. Scottish Jesuit priest and martyr. Died 1615.

March 17   PATRICK. Principal patron of Ireland. A solemn feast. Roman calendar.

March 21   ÉNDA OF ARAN. Abbot. Died in 535.

MOMHANNA (MOVANNA). Very early nun.

March 22   DARERCA OF VALENTIA ISLAND. Mother and widow. The "sister" of St. Patrick.

March 24   MACARTAN. Bishop. Died in 506. Especially remembered in Clogher.

April 1   CEALLACH (CELSUS). Bishop. Died in 1129. Succeeded by Malachy. Especially remembered in Armagh.

April 15   RUADÁN OF LORRHA. Abbot. Died in 584.

April 17   DONNÁN OF EIGG AND HIS COMPANIONS. Martyrs. Scotland. Died in 616.

April 18   LASERIAN (MOLAISE). Bishop. Died about 639. Especially remembered in Leighlin.

April 21   BEUNO OF CYNNOG FAWR. Wales. Abbot. Died c. 640.

MAELRUBHI OF APPLECROSS. Scotland. Abbot. Martyr. Died in 722.

April 23   IBAR OF BEGGERY ISLAND. Abbot. Fourth century.

April 27   ASICUS. Bishop. Fifth century. Especially remembered in Elphin.

May 1   ASAPH OF WALES. Abbot. Died c. 600.

May 2   ULTÁN. Monk and missionary. Brother of Fursa and Faolán. Died in 686.

May 4   CONLAED (CONLETH). Bishop and abbot. Died in 519. Especially remembered in Kildare.

MARTYRS OF ENGLAND AND WALES. 42 canonized by 1976; 160 beatified.

May 10   COMGALL. Abbot of Bangor. Died in 603. Especially remembered in Down and Connor.

May 15   MOCHUDA (CARTHACH, CARTHAGE). Abbot. Bishop. Died in 637. Especially remembered in Lismore.

	DYMPNA (DAMHNAT) OF GHEEL. Patron of the insane. Seventh century.

May 16   BRENDAN "THE NAVIGATOR." Abbot of Clonfert and one of the "Twelve Apostles of Ireland." Died about 580. Especially remembered in Kerry and Clonfert.

June 4   KEVIN. Abbot of Glendalough. Died in 612. Especially remembered in Dublin.

June 6   JARLATH. Bishop. Founder and first bishop of the church of Tuam. Fl. 550. Especially remembered in Tuam.

June 7   COLMÁN OF DROMORE. Bishop. Sixth century. Especially remembered in Dromore.

June 9   COLUMBA (COLUMCILLE). Abbot, one of the "Twelve Apostles of Ireland." Secondary patron of Ireland and Scotland. Principal patron of Derry and Raphoe. Died in 597.

June 17   MOLING OF FERNS. Monk and bishop. Died in 697.

June 20   ALBAN. Protomartyr of Britain. Beheaded at Verulamium c. 287.

          JULIUS AND AARON. Citizens of Caerleon. Executed late in the third century.

July 1   SERF (SERVANUS) OF CULROSS. Scotland. Late sixth century.

July 6   MONENNA OF KILLEEVY. Died c. 517.

July 8   KILIAN. Bishop. Martyred in Franconia, c. 689. Especially remembered in Kilmore.

July 10   OLIVER PLUNKETT. Bishop and martyr. Executed at Tyburn in 1681. Canonized 1975. Especially remembered in Down and Connor.

July 24   DÉCLÁN. Pre-Patrician bishop. Fifth century. Especially remembered in Lismore.

July 28   SAMSON OF DOL. Bishop, monk, and missionary. Wales and Brittany. Died in 565.

Aug. 4   MOLÚA. Abbot of Clonfertmulloe. Died in 608.

Aug. 9   NATHY. Bishop. Especially remembered in Achonry.

          FELIM. Bishop. Principal patron of Kilmore.

Aug. 10   BLANE OF DUNBLANE. Scotland. Monk. Died c. 590.

Aug. 12   ATTRACTA. A nun of the fifth century and convert of Patrick. Especially remembered in Achonry.

          LELIA. A nun of the sixth century. Especially remembered in Limerick.

          MUIREDACH. Bishop. Especially remembered in Killala.

Aug. 14   FACHANAN. Bishop. Principal patron of the church of Ross. Died at the end of the sixth century.

Aug. 23   EOGHAN (EUGENE) OF ARDSTRAW. Died in 618. Especially remembered in Derry.

Aug. 26   NINIAN. Abbot. Britain, Scotland. Believed to have died between c. 432 and 563.

Aug. 30   FIACRA. Monk and missionary. Patron of gardeners. Died c. 670 in France. Especially remembered in Ossory.

Aug. 31   AIDÁN OF LINDISFARNE. Abbot and bishop. Died in 651.

Sept. 4   MAC NISSI. Bishop. Principal patron of Connor. Died in 514.

Sept. 9   CIARÁN. Abbot. Principal patron of Clonmacnois and one of the "Twelve Apostles of Ireland." Died in 548. Especially remembered in Ardagh and Clonmacnois.

Sept. 11   DEINIOL (DANIEL) OF BANGOR FAWR. Wales. Abbot. Died c. 580.

Sept. 12   AILBE. Bishop. Principal patron of Cashel and Emly. Fifth century.

Sept. 23   ADOMNÁN (EUNAN). Abbot of Iona. Principal patron of Raphoe. Died in 704.

Sept. 25   FINBARR. Bishop. Principal patron of Cork. Died in 704.

           CADOC OF LLANCARFAN. Abbot. Wales. Sixth century.

Oct. 11   CAINNECH (or CANICE, "KENNETH") OF AGHABOE. Abbot. Principal patron of Kilkenny City. One of the "Twelve Apostles of Ireland." Died in 600. A solemn feast in Kilkenny City. Also remembered in Scotland. Especially remembered in Ossory.

Oct. 16   GALL. Abbot and missionary. Died in 630. Patron of the Canton of St.-Gallen in Switzerland. Especially remembered in Down and Connor.

Oct. 25   BL. THADDEUS MACCARTHY. Bishop. Died at Ivrea in 1497. Especially remembered in Cork, Cloyne, and Ross.

           CUTHBERT MAYNE, JOHN HOUGHTON, EDMUND CAMPION, RICHARD GWYNN, and thirty-six Welsh and English companions. Martyrs.

Oct. 27   ODRÁN (OTTERAN). Monk and principal patron of Waterford. Probably died on Iona in 549.

           IA (HYA) OF CORNWALL. Patron of St. Ives. Sixth century.

Oct. 29   COLMÁN. Bishop. Principal patron of Kilmacduagh. Died about 632.

Oct. 31   FAOLÁN. Monk and missionary. Brother of Fursa and Ultán. Martyred in France with three companions in 655.

Nov. 2   ERC OF TRALEE. One of Patrick's first converts. Bishop. Fourth century.

Nov. 3   MALACHY (MÁEL MÁEDOC UÁ MORGAIR). Bishop. Principal patron of Armagh. Died in 1148. Especially remembered in Down and Connor.

Nov. 6   ALL THE SAINTS OF IRELAND. Established by indult of Benedict XV.

           ILLTUD. Abbot and missionary. Wales and Brittany. Died in 535.

Nov. 8	JOHN DUNS SCOTUS. Scottish Franciscan theologian. Died at Cologne in 1308.
Nov. 14	LORCAN UÁ TUATHAIL (LAURENCE O'TOOLE). Archbishop. Principal patron of Dublin. Died at Eu in Normandy in 1180.
	DYFRIG (DUBRICIUS). Abbot. Wales. Believed to have died c. 495.
Nov. 16	MARGARET. Queen. Secondary patron of Scotland. Died in Edinburgh in 1093. Roman calendar.
Nov. 23	COLUMBAN. Abbot and missionary. Died in 615. Roman calendar.
Nov. 24	COLMÁN OF CLOYNE. Bishop. Principal patron of Cloyne. Died in 604.
Nov. 27	FERGAL. Bishop of Salzburg, Austria. Died in 784. Especially remembered in Ossory.
Nov. 29	BRENDAN OF BIRR. Abbot. One of the "Twelve Apostles of Ireland." Died c. 572.
Nov. 30	ANDREW. Apostle. Principal patron of Scotland. Roman calendar.
Dec. 7	BUITE (BOITE). Abbot of Monasterboice. Died in 521.
Dec. 12	FINNIAN OF CLONARD. Bishop. "Teacher of the saints of Ireland." Died in the year 549. Especially remembered in Meath.
Dec. 13	COLUM OF TÍR-DÁ-GLAS (TERRYGLASS). Abbot. One of the "Twelve Apostles of Ireland." Died in 549.
Dec. 18	FLANNAN. Bishop. Died about 750. Especially remembered in Killaloe.
	LIOBAN (or LIBANA) OF KILFIAN. An early saint of Mayo.
	SEGHNAT OF DONNYCARNEY. Died in 664.
Dec. 19	SAMTHANN OF CLONBRONEY. Nun and abbess. Died in 739.
	COMMAIGH. Only her name is known of her.
Dec. 20	FACHANAN. Bishop. Principal patron of the diocese of Kilfenora.
Dec. 22	TUA. Only her name is known of her.
Dec. 23	CUMAN (or CUMANIA). Known as "a sister of Columba."
Dec. 29	EALANOR. A woman martyred during the sixteenth century.

Notes

Abbreviations

AA.SS.   *Acta Sanctorum* (Acts of the Saints), published by the Belgian Jesuit
          Bollandist group.

BNE   Charles Plummer, *Bethada Náem nÉrenn,* 2 vols. (Oxford:
          Clarendon Press, 1922, 1968).

HE   Bede, *A History of the English Church and People,* trans. Leo
          Sherley-Price, rev. by R. W. Latham (London and New York:
          Penguin, 1968).

PL   J. P. Migne, *Patrologia Latina.*

VSH   Charles Plummer, *Vitae Sanctorum Hiberniae,* 2 vols. (Oxford:
          Clarendon Press, 1910).

Introduction

1. There are, however, five "Black Letter," or "ordinary," saints in the Anglican
calendar for Wales: Asaph, Deiniol, Dyfrig, Illtud, and Teilo. In the Anglican liturgical calendar "red letter saints" are accorded major honor, while "black letter saints"
are "remembered," much as are ordinary saints in the Roman calendar, i.e., with a
"memorial" rather than a "feast."

2. For a detailed account of this title, see Richard Sharpe, *Medieval Irish Saints'
Lives: An Introduction to Vitae Sanctorum Hiberniae* (Oxford: Clarendon Press,
1991), 3–5.

3. Thomas Cahill, *How the Irish Saved Civilization* (New York: Doubleday,
1995).

4. Robert Ellsberg, *All Saints: Daily Reflections on Saints, Prophets, and
Witnesses for Our Own Time* (New York: Crossroad, 1997).

5. Mary Ryan D'Arcy, *The Saints of Ireland,* foreword by Cardinal Tomás Ó Fiach (Cork: Mercier Press, 1974, 1985). An astonishing compendium of thumbnail
biographies gleaned from over thirty years of research, condensed and arranged
according to nation and calendar date, D'Arcy's book remains a remarkable
achievement and still valuable if scarce resource.

6. Eoin Neeson, *The Book of Irish Saints* (Cork: Mercier Press, 1967). Neeson
lists approximately five hundred saints according to the calendar. Although most
entries are brief, occasionally no more than a name, his introductory comments are
insightful.

7. Aloysius Roche, *The Bedside Book of Irish Saints* (London: Catholic Book Club, 1943).

8. In the late nineteenth and early twentieth centuries, a number of erudite studies of Celtic saints appeared in England, Ireland, and the United States, notably the critical texts of medieval Latin and Old Irish Lives published by Plummer, Baring-Gould and Fisher, Wade-Evans, and Doble, among others. These were followed by scholarly works in a variety of fields — archeology, history, geography, and literature, including contributions by Wendy Davies, Liam and Máire de Paor, Eleanor Duckett, Françoise Henry, Kathleen Hughes, Cardinal Tomás Ó Fiach, and Diarmuid Ó Laoghaire. More recently, Alan Macquarrie, Richard Sharpe, Lisa Bitel, Oliver Davies, and Joseph Nagy have set about updating and extending the work of these outstanding figures.

9. James F. Kenney, *The Sources for the Early History of Ireland: Ecclesiastical,* preface by Ludwig Bieler (Dublin: Four Courts Press, 1997; reprint of Columbia University Press edition, New York, 1929).

10. John O'Donohue, *Anam Chara: Spiritual Wisdom from the Celtic World* (New York: Bantam, and London: Transworld, 1997).

11. For an insightful and still valuable survey of the history of the term, see Jon Alexander, O.P., "What Do Recent Writers Mean by *Spirituality?*" *Spirituality Today* 32, no. 3 (September 1980): 247–56, where he remarks, "In modern English usage, the word *spirituality* has meant primarily a quality or condition rather than an ecclesial state or an incorporeal mode of being. In its recent usages the meaning of *spirituality* has moved from moorings in the dogmas and traditions of particular faith-communities toward a generic and experiential sense" (254).

12. J. A. T. Robinson, *The Body: A Study in Pauline Theology* (Philadelphia: Westminster Press, 1952), 19.

13. Richard Woods, O.P., *Christian Spirituality: God's Presence through the Ages* (Allen, Tex.: Thomas More Press, 1996), 9.

14. Oliver Davies, *Celtic Christianity in Early Medieval Wales: The Origins of the Welsh Spiritual Tradition* (Cardiff: University of Wales Press, 1996), 3. Dr. Davies's book is an excellent introduction to the literary heritage of early Christian Britain and Wales.

15. Ibid., 5.

1. The Celtic Saints

1. Richard Sharpe, *Medieval Irish Saints' Lives: An Introduction to Vitae Sanctorum Hiberniae* (Oxford: Clarendon Press, 1991), v.

2. See Peter O'Dwyer, O.Carm., *Célí Dé: Spiritual Reform in Ireland 750–900* (Dublin: Editions Tailliura, 1981), 171, where he notes that the Lives of Ciarán of Clonmacnoise and Samthann "are much less encumbered with miracles and ascetic practices" and were thus assigned by James Kenney to a date much earlier than the twelfth century (172). The Lives of Berach, Kevin, Moling, and Molúa are believed to emanate from before the tenth century. But note the severe cautions of Richard Sharpe, 1991, 8–12.

3. See Peter Brown, "The Saint as Exemplar in Late Antiquity," in *Saints and Virtues,* ed. John Stratton Hawley (Los Angeles and Berkeley: University of California Press, 1987), 3–14. For a stimulating description of the origin and development of notions of Christian sanctity and the process of canonization, see Kenneth L. Woodward, *Making Saints: How the Catholic Church Determines Who Becomes a*

Saint, Who Doesn't, and Why (New York: Simon & Schuster, 1990), and Robert Ellsberg, *All Saints* (New York: Crossroad, 1997).

4. Concise Oxford Dictionary (1106). The Merriam-Webster Dictionary, tenth edition, is more to the point: "one officially recognized especially through canonization as preeminent for holiness; one of the spirits of the departed in heaven, see *angel*; one of God's chosen and usually Christian people; a member of any of various Christian bodies."

5. See in this regard Robert L. Cohn, "Sainthood on the Periphery: The Case of Judaism," in *Sainthood: Its Manifestations in World Religions,* ed. Richard Kieckhefer and George D. Bond (Berkeley: University of California Press, 1988), 43–68, and the classic work of Samuel H. Dressner, *The Zaddik* (New York: Schocken Books, 1974).

6. I am indebted to Rabbi Samuel Dressner for pointing this out to me.

7. Frederick Denny has compiled a partial list used in Islam that includes over twenty-four titles of holiness in addition to the standard term *wali*. See Frederick M. Denny, " 'God's Friends': The Sanctity of Persons in Islam," in Kieckhefer and Bond, 1988, 69–97. In Asian traditions, holiness is conveyed by a comparably complex set of terms, among them *arahant, rishi, bodhisattva,* and *mahasattva*.

8. See Rudolf Otto, *The Idea of the Holy* (London: Penguin, 1959), and Gerardus Van Der Leeuw, *Religion in Essence and Manifestation,* 2 vols. (New York: Harper and Row, 1963).

9. Kieckhefer and Bond, 1988, viii.

10. For a fuller treatment of this theme, see Richard Woods, "Holy, Healthy, and Whole," *Presence: The Journal of Spiritual Directors International* 3, no. 1 (January 1997): 62–67.

11. See Josef Goldbrunner, *Holiness Is Wholeness* (New York: Pantheon, 1955).

12. Daniel Helminiak, *Spiritual Development: An Interdisciplinary View* (Chicago: Loyola University Press, 1986), 152. He adds, "One may be profoundly holy without ever achieving full spiritual development. A person's authenticity at any stage is the gauge of holiness, and not the stage itself."

13. Woodward, 1990, 223–26.

14. Cf. Kieckhefer and Bond, 1988, 2–3: "The word 'saint' originally meant simply 'holy person' and was used by Greek and Roman pagans for various classes of person: emperors, gods, deceased relatives, and so forth. When Christians adopted the term, they first used it in the plural, in referring collectively to the faithful on earth, those in heaven, the martyrs specifically, or the monks and clergy. When Paul addressed a letter to 'the saints' at Philippi, he meant simply the Christian community there. The term later came to be used commonly in the singular but still with a broad variety of meanings: it could apply to a bishop, priest, abbess, virgin, emperor, martyr, or some other person, living or dead, worthy of honor and veneration."

15. Woodward, 1990, 71.

16. Woodward, 1990, notes, "the [Second Vatican] council specifies, 'the authentic cult of the saints consists not so much in the multiplying of external acts, but rather in the intensity of our active love.' Yet this is not to relegate the saints to a purely exemplary role: the love we bear toward them leads us to seek 'example in their way of life, fellowship in their communion, and aid by their intercession' " (37).

17. See E. G. Bowen, *Saints, Seaways and Settlements* (Cardiff: University of Wales Press, 1977), and especially T. Thornley Jones, *Saints, Knights and Llannau* (Llandysul, Dyfed, Wales: Gomer Press, 1975).

18. E. G. Bowen, from whom I have adapted these characteristics, suggests that since these items are common to all the Lives of the saints, by removing them from the narrative, the "real history" of the saint in question is likely to be what remains (E. G. Bowen, *Dewi Saint, Saint David* [Cardiff: University of Wales Press, 1983], 19). In many cases, however, that would amount to very little.

19. For a concise statement of the relevant scholarly positions and counter-positions, with pertinent references, see Oliver Davies, *Celtic Christianity in Early Medieval Wales: The Origins of the Welsh Spiritual Tradition* (Cardiff: University of Wales Press, 1996), 1–2.

20. Ibid., 1. For an extensive exploration of the common and distinctive aspects of Celtic identity from a variety of perspectives, see Robert O'Driscoll, ed., *The Celtic Consciousness* (New York: George Braziller, 1981), a very large compendium of papers presented by scholars, poets, and artists at an international symposium hosted by St. Michael's College, Toronto, in 1978.

21. The early history of the Celts has been explored in a number of now classic works, including Nora Chadwick, *The Celts* (London and New York: Penguin Books, 1971); Frank Delaney, *The Celts* (Boston: Little, Brown, 1986); Jan Filip, *Celtic Civilization and Its Heritage* (Wellingborth, Norhants.: Collet's; Prague: Academia, 1977); Gerard Herm, *The Celts: The People Who Came Out of Darkness* (New York: St. Martin's Press, 1977); Lloyd Laing, *Celtic Britain* (London and Toronto: Granada, 1981); Jean Markale, *Celtic Civilization* (London and New York: Gordon and Cremonesi, 1978); Robert O'Driscoll, ed., *The Celtic Consciousness* (New York: George Braziller, 1981); T. G. E. Powell, *The Celts* (London: Thames and Hudson, 1983); Joseph Raftery, ed., *The Celts*, The Thomas Davis Lecture Series (Dublin and Cork: Mercier Press, 1964); and Charles Thomas, *Celtic Britain* (London, 1986).

22. Cf. John T. McNeill, *The Celtic Churches* (Chicago: University of Chicago Press, 1974), 1. He adds, with an eye toward understanding the Celtic temperament, "Plato mentions them in a list of nations addicted to drunkenness, and Aristotle notes their reckless indifference to danger, even of earthquakes and raging seas." The references are, first, to *The Laws*, Book I, and, second, to the *Nichomachean Ethics*, Book III. See also Aristotle's *Eudemian Ethics*, Book III, for a similar appraisal. For a synopsis of ancient references to the Celts, see James F. Kenney, *The Sources for the Early History of Ireland: Ecclesiastical*, preface by Ludwig Bieler (Dublin: Four Courts Press, 1997), 118–38.

23. For the sake of convenience, linguists have divided these peoples into major groups based on the fundamental branches of their language, what linguists call "P" Celtic, or Brythonic, spoken in Britain, Cornwall, Brittany, and for a while parts of Scotland, and "Q" Celtic, or Goidelic, the language of Ireland, Man, later Scotland, and for a while the Irish colonies in Wales. Rather than using such categories or the Greek term *Keltoi*, however, these peoples would have known themselves by regional or tribal names, which we know only in their Latin versions: the Scotti, Picti, Catuvellauni, Brigantes, Parisii, Ordovices, Silures, Dumnoni, and so forth. For a history of Celtic language studies, see Martin J. Bell, ed., *The Celtic Languages* (London and New York: Routledge, 1993).

24. "The organization of the Gallic Church of the fourth century was based on the orderly system of Roman civil administration: bishops had their sees in important provincial centres; ecclesiastical law and administration took as their models the imperial legal code and civil service procedure" (J. F. Webb, *Lives of the Saints* [New York: Penguin Books, 1965], 11).

25. See in this regard works cited in the bibliography by Hughes, Laing, Johnson, de Paor and de Paor, Charles Thomas, etc. For the "Glastonbury Legend," see the following chapter.

26. Pockets of Arianism survived among the Visigoths in Spain, and large areas of the West were still under the influence of Constantinople. But, as Philip Sheldrake writes, "To speak of 'the Celtic Church,' in the sense of an entity that rejected the primacy of Rome, is entirely invalid. There is a myth, that still does the rounds occasionally, that 'the Celtic Church' was some kind of British National Church with doctrines and practices that were uncontaminated by association with the Constantinian corruption of Roman Christianity" (Philip Sheldrake, *Living between Worlds: Place and Journey in Celtic Spirituality* [London: Darton, Longman and Todd, 1995], 5).

27. For appraisals of the issues and events surrounding the Synod of Whitby, see John T. McNeill, *The Celtic Churches: A History, A.D. 200 to 1200* (Chicago: University of Chicago Press, 1974), 108–15, further references on 249, and Sheldrake, 1995, 12.

28. Webb, 1965, 13.

29. J. F. Webb writes, "Its mysticism came from the pagan East, had been christianized by the scholars of the Greek Church, and flowered into the severe ascetical ideals of the Desert Fathers of Egypt and Mesopotamia whose way of life John Cassian of Marseilles describes in his *Institutes* and *Conferences*" (ibid., 11).

30. For a concise history of Celtic monasticism, see Jeremiah O'Sullivan, "Old Ireland and Her Monasticism," in *Old Ireland,* ed. Robert McNally, S.J. (New York: Fordham University Press, 1965), 90–119, and Kathleen Hughes and Ann Hamlin, *Celtic Monasticism* (New York: Seabury, 1981). Like the relevant passages in Kenney, 1997, Fr. John Ryan's great work, *Irish Monasticism: Origins and Development* (Dublin: Four Courts Press, 1992), first published in 1931, is still an indispensable resource despite what are, in retrospect, a number of critical lapses. Among recent works, see Lisa Bitel, *Isle of the Saints: Monastic Settlement and Christian Community in Early Ireland* (Ithaca, N.Y.: Cornell University Press, 1990, and Cork: University of Cork Press, 1993.)

31. According to the fragmentary Old Irish Homily in the library of Cambrai, "this is white martyrdom for a man when he leaves everything he loves for the sake of Christ, even though he suffer fasting or labor while so doing. He suffers green martyrdom when by means of fasting and labor he cuts himself off from his desires or suffers toil in penance and repentance. Red martyrdom is the endurance of a cross or death for the sake of Christ as happened to the Apostles while teaching the law of God during the persecution of the wicked. These kinds of martyrdom are to be found in those who turn their backs on their desires, and who shed their blood in fasting and labor for Christ's sake" (cited by Vincent O Maidin, O.C.S.O., "The Ancient Monastic Rules of Ireland," *Religious Life Review* 21, no. 4 [1982]: 7).

32. The Anglo-Saxon Chronicle for the year 891 recounts the story of three Irish *peregrini* who may be taken as an example: "And three Scots came to King Alfred from Ireland in a boat without oars. They had left home bent on serving God in a state of pilgrimage, they cared not where. Their boat was made from two and a half hides and contained enough provisions to last them seven days, and within a week they landed in Cornwall and shortly afterward came to King Alfred. They were called Dubslane, Macbeth and Maelinmum" (Webb, 1965, 19).

33. Nora Chadwick, *The Celts* (New York: Penguin Books, 1971), 255. See

among other versions, H. d'Arbois de Jubainville, *The Irish Mythological Cycle and Celtic Mythology,* trans. from the French with additional notes by Richard Irvine Best (New York: Lemma Publishing Corp., 1970; originally published Dublin, 1903).

34. See Gerard Murphy, ed., *Early Irish Lyrics,* foreword by Tomás Ó Cathasaigh (Dublin: Four Courts Press, 1956, 1998). For examples of early Irish and Welsh religious poems, some of which appear for the first time in translation, see Oliver Davies and Fiona Bowie, eds., *Celtic Christian Spirituality: An Anthology of Medieval and Modern Sources* (London: SPCK, 1995, and New York: Continuum, 1999), 27–56.

35. Cf. Sabine Baring-Gould and John Fisher, *The Lives of the British Saints; The Saints of Wales and Cornwall and Such Irish Saints as Have Dedications in Britain,* 4 vols. (London: C. J. Clark, 1907–13); William W. Heist, *Vitae Sanctorum Hiberniae,* Subsidia Hagiographica 28 (Brussels: Société des Bollandists, 1965); W. M. Metcalfe, *Pinkerton's Lives of the Scottish Saints* (Paisley, 1889; reprint of J. Pinkerton's *Vitae antiquae sanctorum* (London, 1789); and Charles Plummer, *Vitae Sanctorum Hiberniae,* 2 vols. (Oxford: Clarendon Press, 1910), and *Bethada Náem nÉrenn,* 2 vols. (Oxford: Clarendon Press, 1922, 1968).

36. An older Life of Columcille is attributed to the seventh abbot of Iona, Cumméne Ailbe, who died in 669, which may have formed the basis for Adomnán's biography. For the most recent edition with an excellent introduction, see Adomnán of Iona, *Life of St. Columba,* intro. and trans. Richard Sharpe (London and New York: Penguin Books, 1995).

37. G. H. Doble, *Lives of the Welsh Saints,* ed. D. Simon Evans (Cardiff: University of Wales Press, 1971), 82. Prof. Macquarrie observes of Scotland, more circumspectly, "there can be no doubt that, whether as a result of neglect or systematic destruction, the vast bulk of Scotland's liturgical and hagiographic writings have been lost" (Alan Macquarrie, *The Saints of Scotland: Essays in Scottish History AD 450–1093* [Edinburgh: John Donald Publishers, 1997], 10). See also Caroline Bingham, *Beyond the Highland Line: Highland History and Culture* (London: Constable, 1991), 47.

38. In his superb re-visioning of the preface to Charles Plummer's great collections of Latin and Irish Lives, Professor Richard Sharpe has supplied the history, itself fascinating and sometimes thrilling, of how the original collections were assembled by Franciscan and other scholars working under conditions of great difficulty and even mortal danger in the sixteenth and seventeenth centuries. See especially Sharpe, 1991, 39–74.

39. For a view strikingly different yet supportive of the dictum of Carlyle et al., consider Kathleen Hughes, *Early Christian Ireland: Introduction to the Sources* (Ithaca, N.Y.: Cornell University Press, 1972), 219: "Hagiography is not history. The author is not concerned to establish a correct chronology. He is not interested in assembling and examining evidence and coming to a conclusion which takes all the evidence into account. He is rather writing the panegyric of a saint, stressing in particular his holy way of life and the supernatural phenomena which attended it. Sometimes the aim is didactic, sometimes more crudely financial. What he praises will depend on his audience and on the society for which he is writing. Hagiography will thus give reliable contemporary evidence about the aspirations and culture of a people."

40. Róisín Ní Mheara, *In Search of Irish Saints: The Peregrinatio pro Christo* (Dublin: Four Courts Press, 1994). Also see Doble, 1971, 16.

41. For an encompassing overview of the resources for hagiographical research, see Doble, 1971, 16–17.

42. "A gloss on Colmán's hymn reads: The four chief laws of Ireland, the law of Patrick, and of Dáire and of Adamnán, and of Sunday. The law of Patrick, now, not to slay clerics; the law of Dáire, not to steal cattle; of Adamnán, not to slay women; of Sunday, not to travel" (Hughes, 1972, 80–81). There were, in addition, many other laws which, like the major four, were either written by or attributed to saints.

43. Of special importance are the Annals of Innisfallen, the Annals of Ulster, the Annals of Tighernach, and the Annals of Four Masters, which are sometimes supported (and also contested) by entries in the Welsh Annals, "Nennius," Gildas, Bede, and continental sources. For excerpts, see Liam de Paor, *St. Patrick's World: The Christian Culture of Ireland's Apostolic Age* (Dublin: Four Courts Press, 1997).

44. In regard to the Annals and other source material, Kathleen Hughes's masterful *Early Christian Ireland*, 1972, remains indispensable reading for the uninitiated, as does Kenney's monumental *Sources for the Early History of Ireland* and the many volumes edited by Ludwig Bieler. W. W. Heist, Richard Sharpe, Máire Herbert, and other scholars have updated and corrected the work of a previous generation of textual exegetes, while a host of younger scholars has recently appeared on the academic horizon promising renewed vigor and clamor in the critical exploration of early Irish history, among them Bitel, Davies, Nagy, Thomas O'Loughlin, et al. For representative titles, consult the bibliography.

45. Doble, 1971, 207. See note 35 above.

2. The Saints of Celtic Britain

1. For a consideration of the tin trade between the ancient Near East and the British Isles, see James F. Kenney, *The Sources for the Early History of Ireland: Ecclesiastical,* preface by Ludwig Bieler (Dublin: Four Courts Press, 1997), 122–24.

2. The charter of the monastery stated that two missionaries, Phagan and Deruvian, discovered the old church at Glastonbury which had been founded by disciples of St. Philip around the year 63. The Glastonbury Legend has been discussed in detail by Lionel Smithett Lewis, once Vicar of Glastonbury, in *St. Joseph of Arimathea at Glastonbury* (Cambridge: James Clarke, 1922, 1982) and more recently by Geoffrey Ashe in *Avalonian Quest* (London: Metheun, 1982), passim, *Guidebook to Arthurian Britain* (Wellingborough: Aquarian Press, 1983), 111–16, and *Mythology of the British Isles* (London: Metheun, 1992), 145–49 and passim. It also provides the basis of John Cowper Powys's memorable 1933 novel, *A Glastonbury Romance* (London: Picador, 1975).

3. See Richard Barber, *King Arthur in Legend and History* (London: Cardinal Books, 1973), 58–67.

4. See Dom Aelred Watkin, O.S.B., "Last Glimpses of Glastonbury," *Downside Review* (Winter 1948–49): 76–86. John Cowper Powys's father was vicar at Monacute, some ten miles from Glastonbury Tor. According to the legend, St. Joseph also planted his staff, made of native Palestinian thorn, on nearby Wirral Hill, where it took root and grew into a great tree that blossomed every year at Christmastime until felled by Puritans in the seventeenth century. A shoot of the tree was preserved and planted in the church yard of St. John the Baptist in Glastonbury, where its descendants still flourish.

5. See Geoffrey Ashe, *The Glastonbury Tor Maze* (Glastonbury: Gothic Image Publications, 1992).

6. See Sabine Baring-Gould and John Fisher, *The Lives of the British Saints; The Saints of Wales and Cornwall and Such Irish Saints as Have Dedications in Britain*, 4 vols. (London: C. J. Clark, 1907–13).

7. The name "Britain" comes from the Greco-Roman *Brettani*, which was primarily the name of the people of the island as a whole. In time, the land itself came to be known as "Brittania." From about the seventh century, English writers referred to the Celtic western part of Britain as "Wales" and the language as "Welsh," which is correct enough today and for the last thousand years. But *Wealas* (later *Walia*) is an Old English word, as is its cognate "Welsh" (*Wealh*), both of which mean "foreigner" and were applied to the native Christian Britons by their Anglo-Saxon opponents and eventual conquerors. (The German word for "Italian" and "French" is still *welsch*.) From ancient times, and once again, the proper name of western Britain is Cymru, and the language of "the people" or "the community" (which is the meaning of the word) is Cymric.

8. "To an island numb with chill ice and far removed as in a remote nook of the world, from the visible sun, Christ made a present of his rays (that is, his precepts), Christ the true sun, which shows its dazzling brilliance to the entire earth, not from the temporal firmament merely, but from the highest citadel of heaven, that goes beyond all time. This happened first, as we know, in the last years of the emperor Tiberius, at a time when Christ's religion was being propagated without hindrance" (Gildas, *The Ruin of Britain and Other Works*, ed. and trans. Michael Winterbottom, History from the Sources, general ed. John Morris [London and Chichester: Phillimore, 1978], 18).

9. See Bede, *A History of the English Church and People* (HE), trans. Leo Sherley-Price, rev. by R. W. Latham (London and New York: Penguin, 1968), 1:4; 5:24. Charles Thomas observes that the tale has been shown to be "a muddled version of a Papal contact with another Lucius, prince of Edessa, older Birtha or Britio Edessenorum — hence the ascription to Britannia" (Charles Thomas, *Christianity in Roman Britain to AD 500* [Berkeley and Los Angeles: University of California Press, 1981], 48). Moreover, Eleutherius was actually pope from c. 174 to 189. In the *Historia Brittonum* and the Annals attributed to the monk Nennius, c. 829, it is claimed that "Lucius, the British king, received baptism, with all the underkings of the British nation, 167 years after the coming of Christ, after a legation had been sent by the Roman emperors and by Eucharisticus, the Roman Pope" (Nennius, *British History and the Welsh Annals*, ed. and trans. John Morris [London: Phillimore; Totowa, N.J.: Rowman and Littlefield, 1980], 23).

10. Anthony Birley, *The People of Roman Britain* (Berkeley and Los Angeles: University of California Press 1980), 152.

11. See Liam de Paor, *St. Patrick's World: The Christian Culture of Ireland's Apostolic Age* (Dublin: Four Courts Press, 1997), 53–56, and Stephen Johnson, *Later Roman Britain* (London and Toronto: Granada, 1982), 211–20.

12. Birley and John Morris are inclined to place the executions as early as 209. See Birley, 1980, 152.

13. The reference is to Gildas, *The Ruin of Britain*, chapter 10. See Thomas, *Christianity in Roman Britain to AD 500*, 47–48, who comments, "That somewhere, at some date, Christians who were Roman citizens were martyred in Roman Britain is not in doubt. The most probable opinion in fifth-century Britain was that this occurred under Diocletian."

14. Pelagius's major writings consist of biblical commentaries, especially his com-

mentary on St. Paul's Epistles, and a group of letters with notable Christian leaders in Italy. For selections, see Oliver Davies and Fiona Bowie, eds., *Celtic Christian Spirituality: An Anthology of Medieval and Modern Sources* (London: SPCK, 1995, and New York: Continuum, 1999), 61–64. For a sympathetic account of Pelagius's life and teachings, see M. Forthomme Nicholson, "Celtic Theology: Pelagius," in *An Introduction to Celtic Christianity,* ed. James P. Mackey (Edinburgh: T. & T. Clark, 1989), 386–413. Also see relevant passages in John T. McNeill, *The Celtic Churches: A History, A.D. 200 to 1200* (Chicago: University of Chicago Press, 1974), Alan Macquarrie, *The Saints of Scotland: Essays in Scottish History AD 450–1093* (Edinburgh: John Donald Publishers, 1997), and de Paor, 1996.

15. A curious and delightfully sardonic view of Celtic austerity and "Roman" softness can be found in Peter de Rossa's mordant novel, *Pope Patrick* (Dublin: Poolbeg Press, 1995).

16. Garmon is noted in the Welsh Annals attributed to the monk "Nennius." Cf. T. Thornley Jones, *Knights, Saints, and Llanau* (Llandysul, Dyfed, Wales: Gomer Press, 1975), chap. 2, "The Garmon Dedications," 19–25. See also Bede, *HE* 1:17–21.

17. *Vita Sancti Germani,* Monumenta Germaniae Historica 7 (1920), 247ff. Constantius says that Germanus was sent by a council of Gallic bishops, not the pope.

18. For various accounts of the Pelagian-Germanus controversy, see de Paor, 1996, 18–22; Macquarrie, 1977, 16–21; and McNeill, *The Celtic Churches,* 29–32.

19. The *llanau* were not invariably named for saints, however. "Sometimes the word *llan* is found joined with the names of colors, such as Llan Las, Llan Fraith, Llan Ddu, Llan Lwyd or Rhuddlan. There are also other groups of 'topographically descriptive' names like Rhiwlan, Llangoed, Llanole or Llanwern, or 'functional' names like Gwinllan or Llanboidy" (Jones, 1975, 50).

20. Ibid., 46.

21. T. Thornley Jones cites Baring-Gould and Fisher (1907–13, 1:36) to the effect that "the saints of Wales belong to eight great families. The eighth is that of Emyr Llydaw from Armorica [Brittany]. The Welsh pedigrees derive Emyr from Cynan, son of Eudaf and brother of Elen, wife of Maximus" (chapter 3: "The Family of Elen," 26).

22. See Jones, 1975, 46. Bede states, characteristically, that this awful fate came as a result of the monks' resistance to Augustine's demands earlier that year.

23. On May 4 the Roman Catholic Church commemorates the English and Welsh martyrs from the Reformation period, of whom 42 have been canonized and 160 beatified. On October 25 a number of other martyrs are remembered, including Richard Gwynn.

24. Thomas Cahill, *How the Irish Saved Civilization* (New York: Doubleday, 1995), 200. Similarly, Eleanor Duckett observed that "it was Aidán who gave the veil of a nun to Heiu of Hartlepool in Durham, and thus opened the way of the religious life for women in Northumbria. It was Aidán, also, who 'loved devotedly, visited frequently, and diligently taught' Hilda in her earlier years as abbess of Hartlepool, before her rule in Yorkshire over the monastic life of both men and women at Streoneshalh, later known as Whitby" (Eleanor Duckett, *The Wandering Saints of the Early Middle Ages* [New York: W. W. Norton, 1959, 1964], 106). See also McNeill, 1974, 108.

25. Among standard sources for the Lives of the British and Welsh saints, see

Baring-Gould and Fisher, 1907–13; Gilbert H. Doble, *Lives of the Welsh Saints,* ed. D. Simon Evans (Cardiff: University of Wales Press, 1971); Arthur W. Wade-Evans, *Vitae Sanctorum Britanniae et Genealogiae* (Cardiff: University of Wales Press, 1944). Modern studies include Wendy Davies, *Wales in the Early Middle Ages* (Leicester: Leicester University Press, 1982); Elissa R. Henken, *Traditions of the Welsh Saints* (Cambridge and New York: Cambridge University Press, 1987); and Elissa R. Henken, *Welsh Saints: A Study of Patterned Lives* (Cambridge: D. S. Brewer, 1991). In *Celtic Christianity in Early Medieval Wales: The Origins of the Welsh Spiritual Tradition* (Cardiff: University of Wales Press, 1996), Oliver Davies has published a selection of medieval Welsh religious verse and prose, much in English translation for the first time, together with commentary. The chapter on the Lives of the Welsh saints, including synopses of those of Samson, Beuno, and David, is of particular value. See also Davies and Bowie, 1999. The most thorough examination of sources indicating the activity of saints in northern Wales is Molly Miller's *The Saints of Gwynedd,* Studies in Celtic History 1 (Woodbridge, Suffolk: Boydell Press, 1979).

26. In addition to Bede, scattered fragments of a lost Life, possibly in Irish, and other materials were assembled by Aelred of Rievaulx in the twelfth century to fabricate a career. Most likely, Aelred was attempting to establish an early claim to a British church independent of Iona. The historical and archeological information regarding Ninian is addressed by Thomas, 1981, 275–94.

27. Macquarrie, 1997, 66. Also see Duckett, 1964, 47–49.

28. See Baring-Gould and Fisher, 1907–13, vol. 2, for a translation of the *Vita Illtuti,* and Doble, 1971, for a biographical essay.

29. See Jones, 1975, 53–54.

30. See Doble, 1971, for a reconstruction of Dyfrig's *vita.*

31. See Duckett, 1964, 296, and Doble, 1971.

32. McNeill, 1974, 45.

33. See Jones, 1975, 14.

34. For the Latin Life, see Dom François Plaine, O.S.B., ed., *Vita antiqui sancti Samsonis Dolensis episcopi, Analecta Bollandiana* 6 (1887): 77–150, and *Vita S. Samsoni,* ed. R. Fawtier, Bibliothèque de l'École des Hautes Études 197 (1912). An English translation was provided by Thomas Taylor, *The Life of St. Samson* (London, 1925; Felinfach, Lampeter, Wales: Llanerch Publishers, 1991). See also Kenney, 1997, 174 and 359.

35. Doble, 1971, 189.

36. Ibid., 208, 211. For an account of the life of St. Euddogwy see ibid., 1971, and Jones, 1975, 13.

37. An excellent and perhaps the only major study of St. David's life and work is that by E. G. Bowen, *Dewi Sant, Saint David* (Cardiff: University of Wales Press, 1983). See also Doble, 1971, 54–55 and passim. For editions of the Life, see *Buchedd Dewi Sant,* ed. D. Simon Evans (Cardiff: University of Wales Press, 1965); J. W. James, *Rhygyfarch's Life of St. David* (Cardiff: University of Wales Press, 1967); Rhygyfarch, *Life of David,* in Arthur W. Wade-Evans, *Vitae Sanctorum Britanniae et Genealogiae* (Cardiff: University of Wales Press, 1944); and A. W. Wade-Evans, "Rhygyvarch's Life of Saint David," *Y Cymmrodor* 24 (1913): 1–73. MS = BM Nero E1.

38. See Róisín Ní Mheara, *In Search of Irish Saints: The Peregrinatio pro Christo* (Dublin: Four Courts Press, 1994), 33–34.

39. For Gildas's critique of David's Rule see *The Ruin of Britain,* ed. Winterbottom, 1978, 54–55.

40. The tradition that St. Kentigern was at St. Asaph's is supported by Jocelin of Furness. See McNeill, 1974, 48–49.

41. A Life of Cadoc was written in the eleventh century by Lifris, a supposed Archdeacon of Glamorgan, and another in the following century by Caradoc of Llancarfan, which is preserved in the *Codex Gothanus.* See Duckett, 1974, 58; McNeill, 1974, 39; and Jones, 1975, 70–74.

42. McNeill, 1974, 40.

43. Gildas's first Life seems to have been written by the monk Samson around 600. The Breton Life by Vitalis of Rhuys in Brittany dates from about 884, and that by Caradoc of Llancarfan in the 1130s (Baring-Gould and Fisher, *Lives of the British Saints,* 1907–13 [1911]). He is referred to by Giraldus Cambrensis, *Descriptio Cambriae* 2.2. See *The Ruin of Britain,* ed. Winterbottom, 1978; Hugh Williams, trans., *De Excidio Britonum,* the fragments, "Penitential," *Lorica,* and two Lives, *Cymrodorion Record* (Series 3, 1899, 1901); Michael Winterbottom, "Columbanus and Gildas," *Vigiliae Christianae;* also "The Preface of Gildas' *De Excidio,*" *Cymrodorion Transactions* 1974–75: 277–87; "Notes on the Text of Gildas," *Journal of Theological Studies* 27 (1976): 132–40; David Dumville, "Gildas and Uinniau," in *Gildas: New Approaches,* ed. Michael Lapidge and David Dumville, Studies in Celtic History 5 (Woodbridge, Suffolk: Boydell and Brewer, 1984), 207–14; and Richard Sharpe, "Gildas as a Father of the Church," also in *Gildas: New Approaches,* 193–205.

44. Gildas, *The Ruin of Britain,* ed. Winterbottom, 1978, 66.1.

45. The *Lorica* of Gildas is found in several manuscripts, including BM Harl. 2965 (Bk. of Nunnaminster), and Cambridge Univ. Lib. Ll. 1.10 (the Book of Cerne). Kenney suggests that the form was derived from biblical texts, particularly Eph. 6:14 and 1 Thess. 5:8. See Kenney, 1997, 272.

46. Gildas, *The Ruin of Britain,* ed. Winterbottom, 1978, 65.2.

47. The fourteenth-century Welsh Life of St. Beuno (*Buchedd Beuno*) was translated by A. W. Wade Evans in "Beuno Sant," *Archaeology Cambrensis* 75 (1930): 315–41. Also see Davies, 1996, 16–20.

48. A Life of St. Winifred is found in the BM. Cott. Claud. A. 5. Attributed to the monk Elerius, it was supposedly written in the year 660 but is actually a twelfth-century text. Another Life by Robert of Shrewsbury, the abbey to which her remains were transferred, is found at Oxford in the Bodleian MS. Laud. Misc. 114, saec. XII (c. 1139). Both were printed in the *AA.SS.* for November 1 (1887).

49. See Jones, 1975, 13.

50. See ibid., 23–76. Miller, 1979, lists over 170 saints in Gwynedd (North Wales) alone.

51. See Gilbert H. Doble, *The Saints of Cornwall,* ed. Donald Atwater (Truro: Dean and Chapter; London: Chatham, 1960); Thomas Taylor, *The Celtic Christianity of Cornwall: Divers Sketches and Studies* (London and New York: Longman, Green, 1918), and Duckett, 1964, 60.

52. Bede is the only reliable authority for the contest at Streanaeshalch, and his bias is clearly evident. See A *History of the English Church and People,* trans. Leo Sherley-Price, rev. R. W. Latham (London and New York: Penguin, 1968), Book III, chapter 24, 184; and Book IV, chapter 23: "The Life and Death of Abbess Hilda."

53. In his Life of Cuthbert, the usually punctilious Bede is silent about his parent-

age or early childhood (J. F. Webb, *Lives of the Saints* [London and New York: Penguin Books, 1965], 71–129). Skene, Moran, and other older authorities held that Cuthbert was born in Kells. See Mary Ryan D'Arcy, *The Saints of Ireland*, foreword by Cardinal Tomás Ó Fiach (Cork: Mercier Press, 1974, 1985), 106.

54. Hilda died on November 17, 680, at the age of sixty-six, and dutifully appeared to the Irish nun St. Begu (or Bee) at Hackness to establish her sanctity. See Bede, *HE*, 249, and D'Arcy, 1985, 105. Colmán died in Ireland in 676.

55. Bede cannot resist a bit of chauvinism as he tells how the English bishop Ecbert sought to persuade the stubborn monks of Iona to accept the Roman practices. Hearing Ecbert's teaching, "the monks of Iona under Abbot Dunnchad adopted Catholic ways of life about eighty years after they had sent Aidán to preach to the English nation. God's servant Ecbert remained thirteen years on the island, where he restored the gracious light of unity and peace to the Church and consecrated the island anew to Christ" (Bede, *HE*, 329). Appropriately, after celebrating Easter on April 24 in the year 729, Ecbert promptly died.

56. Cf. Philip Sheldrake, *Living between Worlds: Place and Journey in Celtic Spirituality* (London: Darton, Longman and Todd, 1995), 12: "Many people still believe that the Synod marked a definitive victory of the Church of Rome over the native (that is, Celtic) Church of the British Isles. However, the Synod was actually concerned only with the local Church that was dependent on Lindisfarne. Equally, it dealt only with relatively minor matters rather than with the fundamentals of Church organization and authority."

57. See McNeill, 1974, 248, note 15.

58. See D'Arcy, 1985, 19.

59. See ibid., 1985, 92–94. Bede tells us that St. Dicuil also founded a small monastery at Bosham near Chichester around 645. Although the Irish monks were pious, they attracted few converts. But in 656 one of Dicuil's monks was made bishop of Rochester, and in 661 the king of Sussex was baptized in Mercia by the Irish Bishop Jaruman (ibid., 97).

60. Macquarrie, 1997, 65, citing David Dumville, "Gildas and Uinniau," in *Gildas: New Approaches,* ed. M. Lapidge and D. Dumville, 1984, 207–14; and Richard Sharpe, "Gildas as a Father of the Church," in ibid., 196–20.

61. Gerald's Life is found in Bodl. Rawl. B 485 ff. 108–11 it; B 505 ff. 203v–5v. John Colgan's version was printed in the *AA.SS.* for March 11, 599 sqq. and 288–92 for extracts. For comment and sources, see Kenney, 1997, 464.

62. Kenney, 1997, 464. This might be a factual account of the plague years of the sixth century, when a devastating epidemic, probably bubonic plague, was first reported in Constantinople in 542 and quickly spread west. By 547 it had reached Britain and Ireland, carrying off many of the saints of that time. By 594, half the population of Europe had perished from it, a global calamity unsurpassed until the Black Death of 1347.

63. See Doble, 1960, passim; Kenney, 1997, 173; and Jones, 1975, 43.

64. For a representative selection of medieval Welsh religious verse and prose, much in English translation for the first time, together with commentary, see Oliver Davies, *Celtic Christianity in Early Medieval Wales: The Origins of the Welsh Spiritual Tradition* (Cardiff: University of Wales Press, 1996).

65. Ibid., 144.

66. See A. M. Allchin, *God's Presence in the World: The Celtic Vision through the Centuries in Wales* (London: Darton, Longman and Todd, 1997); Davies and Bowie,

1999; D. Simon Evans, "Our Welsh Saints and History," the invaluable introduction to Doble, 1971, 1–55, and below, Chapter 9, "A Continuing Tradition."

3. Early Christian Ireland

1. Triads figure prominently in both Welsh and Irish lore of all kinds. The most thorough exploration I have found is the introduction by Rachel Bromwich to her edition of the *Trioedd Ynys Prydein, The Welsh Triads* (Cardiff: University of Wales Press, 1978). Also see *The Triads of Britain*, compiled by Iolo Morganwg, with an introduction by Malcolm Smith (London: Wildwood House, 1977). A relatively late addition to Irish folklore, the shamrock was introduced as a "model" of the Trinity by patriotic if theologically challenged scribes eager to embellish the legend of Patrick. The first such account seems to have been committed to writing in 1727 by the botanist Caleb Threlkeld. The earliest reference to the *seamrog* itself can be dated only to 1570. St. Patrick and the shamrock were first joined in 1645 on the coins of the Confederate Catholics of Kilkenny, on which Patrick, clad in miter and crosier, holds out a shamrock to the people. Such patriotic coins came to be called "St. Patrick's money." See Kevin Hanlon, "How Ireland Originally Went Green," *The Universe* (Manchester, England), March 15, 1998.

2. See Kenneth L. Woodward, *Making Saints: How the Catholic Church Determines Who Becomes a Saint, Who Doesn't, and Why* (New York: Simon & Schuster, 1990).

3. See John T. McNeill, *The Celtic Churches: A History, A.D. 200 to 1200* (Chicago: University of Chicago Press, 1974), 53.

4. See Joseph Falaky Nagy, *Conversing with Angels and Ancients: Literary Myths of Medieval Ireland* (Ithaca, N.Y.: Cornell University Press, 1997), 200–202.

5. See above, p. 2.

6. The most recent edition is by William W. Heist, *Vitae Sanctorum Hiberniae,* Subsidia hagiographica 28 (Brussels: Société des Bollandists, 1965).

7. Here see James F. Kenney, *The Sources for the Early History of Ireland: Ecclesiastical,* preface by Ludwig Bieler (Dublin: Four Courts Press, 1997), 304–9; Richard Sharpe, *Medieval Irish Saints' Lives: An Introduction to Vitae Sanctorum Hiberniae* (Oxford: Clarendon Press, 1991), 6–7, 34–38, and elsewhere; and Kathleen Hughes, *Early Christian Ireland: Introduction to the Sources* (Ithaca, N.Y.: Cornell University Press, 1972), 221–22.

8. Charles Plummer, *Vitae Sanctorum Hiberniae* (*VSH*), 2 vols. (Oxford: Clarendon Press, 1910), and *Bethada Náem nÉrenn* (*BNE*), 2 vols. (Oxford: Clarendon Press, 1922, 1968). In his *Medieval Irish Saints Lives* (1991), 390–98, Richard Sharpe has appended a list of sixty-six major Latin Lives to his critical reintroduction to Plummer's Latin Lives (*VSH*). John O'Hanlon's *Lives of the Irish Saints*, 10 vols. (Dublin, 1875–1903), is a vast and sometimes useful resource, but both unwieldy and uncritical.

9. *Lives of the Saints from the Book of Lismore*, ed. and trans. Whitley Stokes (Oxford, 1890).

10. *Silva Gadelica*, ed. and trans. Standish H. O'Grady, 2 vols. (London: Williams and Norgate, 1892).

11. Whitley Stokes, ed., *The Tripartite Life of Patrick and Other Documents Relating to the Saint* (London, 1887); Ludwig Bieler, ed., *Patrician Texts in the Book of Armagh* (Dublin, 1979); Donncha Ó hAodha, ed. and trans., *Bethu Brigte: The Life of Brigit* (Dublin: Dublin Institute of Advanced Studies, 1978); Máire Herbert

and Pádraig Ó Riain, eds. and trans., *Betha Adamnáin: The Irish Life of Adamnán* (Cork: Irish Text Society, 1988).

12. See McNeill, 1974, 50, esp. note 1.

13. For an appraisal of Pelagius's theology and influence in the fifth century and afterward and a brief summary of recent scholarship in the field, see M. Forthomme Nicholson, "Celtic Theology: Pelagius," in *An Introduction to Celtic Christianity,* ed. James P. Mackey (Edinburgh: T. & T. Clark, 1989), 386–413; Alan Macquarrie, *The Saints of Scotland: Essays in Scottish History AD 450–1093* (Edinburgh: John Donald Publishers, 1997), 16–18, 28 n. 16; and note 14 above, p. 198.

14. See Eleanor Duckett, *The Wandering Saints of the Early Middle Ages* (New York: W. W. Norton, 1964), 39–40.

15. See McNeill, 1974, 57.

16. Found in the *Codex Kilkenniensis,* and in Plummer, *VSH,* 2:32–59.

17. See Duckett, 1964, 40.

18. Kenney, 1997, 313.

19. For the Life of Ciarán of Saighir (I and II) see *BNE* and *VSH.*

20. How Brother Fox stole Ciarán's shoes is one of the most delightful tales in hagiographical literature. When Ciarán sends Brother Badger to fetch him back, being skilled in tracking and woodlore, Brother Fox begs forgiveness and performs penance by fasting.

21. See D'Arcy, 1985, 4–5. For an account of the gentlemanly debate between Plummer and Baring-Gould and Fisher on this issue, see *BNE* 2:341, note 72.

22. The standard study of the life and writings of Patrick is still R. P. C. Hanson, *St. Patrick: His Origins and Career* (Oxford: Clarendon Press, 1968.) Older studies may still be consulted with profit, especially J. B. Bury, *The Life of St. Patrick and His Place in History* (London: Macmillan, 1905), and D. A. Binchy, "Patrick and His Biographers, Ancient and Modern," *Studia Hibernica* 2 (1962). Especially valuable for the serious scholar are the meticulous editions of Ludwig Bieler, *Libri Epistolarum Sancti Patricii Episcopi,* 2 vols. (Dublin: Stationery Office, 1952); *The Patrician Texts in the Book of Armagh,* Scriptores Latinae Hiberniae 10 (Dublin: Dublin Institute of Advanced Studies, 1979); and his collected essays in *Studies on the Life and Legend of St. Patrick,* ed. Richard Sharpe (London: Variorum Reprints, 1986). Historically, the relevant chapters in Charles Thomas, *Christianity in Roman Britain to AD 500* (Berkeley and Los Angeles: University of California Press, 1981) are exceptionally lucid. Among popular accounts, see Alice-Boyd Proudfoot, *Patrick: Sixteen Centuries with Ireland's Patron Saint* (New York: Macmillan, 1983); Noel Dermot O'Donoghue, O.D.C., *Patrick of Ireland: Aristocracy of Soul* (Wilmington, Del.: Michael Glazier, 1987).

23. The primary sources for the life of Patrick other than his own *Confession* are the *Breviarium* of Tírechán the bishop (c. 675), the Life by Muirchú moccu Machthéni from approximately the same period, and the Book of the Angel, all preserved in the Book of Armagh compiled by Fer-domnach, the abbot of Kells. Also see the ninth-century *Tripartite Life* of St. Patrick (*Bethu Pátric*), edited by Kathleen Mulchrone (Dublin, 1939), and previously by Whitley Stokes (Rolls Series, London 1887). Muirchú's Life is found in Allan B. E. Hood, ed. and trans., *St. Patrick: His Writings and Muirchú's Life,* Arthurian Period Sources 9 (London: Phillimore, 1978). Of some interest but historically doubtful is the twelfth-century Life by Jocelin of Furness.

24. John Morris notes that "the several texts of the Annals give the date of

Patrick's death as 17 March 459, and various texts indicate that he was between 60 and 63 when he died; the latter age is more probable, since he reached Auxerre not later than 418, and he says himself that he was about 22 at the time. He was therefore born not later than 396" (in Hood, 1978, 10). R. P. C. Hanson, following David Dumville, places Patrick's birth around 430, his mission from 457 to 492 or 493, and his death in 493, which is supported by some of the Annals. See David Dumville, *Saint Patrick, AD 493–1993* (Woodbridge, Suffolk: Boydell Press, 1993). For discussion see McNeill, 1974, 56–58.

25. Macquarrie notes that in the Aberdeen Breviary "the *lectiones* for St. Patrick (17 March) allude to his supposed birth at Old Kilpatrick on the Clyde near Dumbarton, and also to traditions relating to 'St. Patrick's Well' and 'St. Patrick's Stone' near the kirkyard. These were important places of pilgrimage in the Middle Ages" (Macquarrie, 1997, 9, 38–39).

26. On deaconesses in the Irish church, see Paul Grosjean, S.J., *Analecta Bollandiana* 73:298, 322.

27. According to the ninth-century *Vita Tripartita,* the rival monasteries of Ard Macha (Armagh), supported by the powerful Uí Néill clans, and Dún Lethglas (Downpatrick), supported by the Airgialla, disputed the right to inter the body of Patrick. By a ruse, as Lisa Bitel relates, "the Uí Néill accepted a false oxcart carrying an imaginary coffin, while Dún Lethglas got the genuine article. Clearly, Dún Lethglas had already legitimated the tradition of Pátraic's burial in its cemetery, despite the envious claims of the more politically powerful community, as even Ard Macha's hagiographers had to admit" (Lisa M. Bitel, *Isle of the Saints: Monastic Settlement and Christian Community in Early Ireland* [Ithaca, N.Y.: Cornell University Press, 1990, and Cork: University of Cork Press, 1993], 69).

28. John Morris, in Hood, 1978, introduction, 10.

29. For editions, see de Paor, 1998, Hood, 1978, and Ludwig Bieler, ed. and trans., *The Works of St. Patrick,* Ancient Christian Writers 17 (Westminster, Md.: Newman Press, and London: Longmans, Green, 1953). For the *Confession,* also see *Patrick in His Own Words,* ed. Joseph Duffey (Dublin: Veritas), 1975.

30. Nora Chadwick, *The Age of the Saints in the Early Celtic Church* (Oxford University Press, 1961), 29, cited in de Paor, 1998, 47.

31. See de Paor, 1998, 19, where she writes, "The literary clichés found in Patrick's writings, *rusticissimis,* very rustic (C 1), and *indoctus,* untaught (C 62:5), must also be evaluated within the literary climate of his era.... Such expressions are, in reality, the mark of polish and literary good taste, an oratorical cliché." Later, she adds, "Given Patrick's manifest gift for oratory, it is likely that the rich and colorful British and Irish idioms found unique expression in his Latin, and that some of his phrases, which defy adequate translation and have baffled scholars from Mohrmann to Bieler and Hanson, may in fact be old Irish or British idioms wearing a Roman toga" (ibid., 20).

32. No. 3. Translated by Hood, 1978, 60.

33. 1.29. The real Coroticus or Ceredig seems to have been a nominally Christian Briton whose capital was at Dumbarton. See Macquarrie, 1997, 42–43. On the symbolism of foxes in Irish hagiography, see Nagy, 1997, 106, n. 110.

34. For a probing and brilliant analysis of the form and intent of these stories, see Nagy, 1997.

35. Hughes, 1972, 239.

36. Ibid.

37. Mary Ryan D'Arcy informs us that "Dabeoc was of Irish blood on his father's side, of the family of Brecan that gave Brecknockshire in Wales its name. The family is reckoned in the Welsh Triads as one of the 'three holy families of Wales' " (Mary Ryan D'Arcy, *The Saints of Ireland* [Cork: Mercier Press, 1974, 1985], 20).

38. Thomas Cahill, *How the Irish Saved Civilization* (New York: Doubleday, 1995), 107.

39. See Kathleen Hughes and Ann Hamlin, *Celtic Monasticism* (New York: Seabury, 1981 [=*The Modern Traveller to the Irish Church* (London: SPCK, 1977)]) and, more recently, Lisa Bitel's superb *Isle of the Saints*, 1993. Although outdated in some respects, John Ryan's *Irish Monasticism: Origins and Development* (Dublin: Four Courts Press, 1992) is still a valuable and even standard resource.

40. In the modern period, Mount Melleray, County Waterford, was reestablished as a Cistercian abbey in 1832; Mount St. Joseph, County Tipperary, was founded in 1878; and Glenstal Abbey, County Limerick, Ireland's only Benedictine abbey, was also founded in the nineteenth century.

41. The most notable are the Rule of Ailbe, the Rule of Columcille, the Rule of Comgall of Bangor, the Rule of Ciarán, the Rule of the Grey Monks, the Rule of Cormac Mac Cuilionáin, the Rule of Patrick, the Rule of Brigid, the Rule of St. Mochta, the Rule of Brendan of Clonfert, the Rule St. Molúa, the Rule of St. Kevin, the Rule of St. Molaise, the Rule of St. Adomnán, the Rule of St. Coman, the Rule of the Célí Dé, the Prose Rule of the Célí Dé, and the Rule of the Monastery of Tallaght. See Vincent O Maidin, O.C.S.O., "The Ancient Monastic Rules of Ireland," *Religious Life Review* 21, no. 94 (January–February 1982): 4–17. The most important Latin rules are the Rule of Columban, the Penitential of Columban, and the Penitentials attributed to Finnian and Cummean. See G. S. M. Walker, ed., *Sancti Columbani Opera* (Dublin: Dublin Institute of Advanced Studies, 1970); Ludwig Bieler, ed., *The Irish Penitentials*, Scriptores Latini Hiberniae 5 (Dublin: Dublin Institute of Advanced Studies, 1975), 74–135; and Peter O'Dwyer, *Towards a History of Irish Spirituality* (Blackrock, County Dublin: Columba Press, 1995), 69–78.

42. The Rule of Ailbe, for instance, was considered very liberal in that fish, honey, mead, milk, curds, and whey were allowed, and bread allowance was a loaf 30 cm. (about 12 inches) in diameter and weighing 850 grams (just over 2 pounds). See O Maidin, 1982, 6. For an insightful discussion of the politics and spirituality of monastic feasting and fasting, see Lisa Bitel, 1993, 207–21.

43. As a prayer form, the *loricae* may have originated in Britain. See the section above on Gildas, p. 39.

44. Ryan, 1992, vii. He adds, with characteristic restraint, "It is true that the monks did add to the disgrace by taking themselves to the use of arms. The miniature armies were drawn from the tenants on the monastic lands."

45. The standard resource is Peter O'Dwyer, O.Carm., *Célí Dé: Spiritual Reform in Ireland 750–900* (Dublin: Editions Tailliura, 1981). See also Patrick Corish, *The Irish Catholic Experience* (Dublin: Gill and Macmillan, 1985), 6–28, passim; John T. McNeill, *The Celtic Churches: A History, A.D. 200 to 1200* (Chicago: University of Chicago Press, 1974); Kathleen Hughes and Ann Hamlin, *Celtic Monasticism* (New York: Seabury, 1981 [=*The Modern Traveller to the Early Irish Church* (London: SPCK, 1977)]); Máire and Liam de Paor, *Early Christian Ireland* (London and New York: Thames and Hudson, 1978). The term was not technical and finds expressions in other monastic rules as *mog dé,* slave of God (Félire Oengusso, 4: O'Dwyer, 1981, 124, n. 2), cf. Welsh *meudwy,* and *mugada dé,* servants of God (O'Dwyer, 1981, 135).

46. Máire and Liam de Paor, 1978, 72.

47. See "Rule of the Célí Dé," ed. E. J. Gwynn, *Hermathena* 64, 2d supplement, 1927.

48. Two manuscript copies survive, both now in the Library of the Royal Irish Academy, Dublin. Translation: *Proceedings of the Royal Irish Academy* 29:115–79.

49. Máire and Liam de Paor, 1978, 72. Citing the various Annals of Ireland, Peter O'Dwyer maintains that "there is no mention in the Annals of any Norse attack on Tallaght or Finglas. [But] it may never have been entered into the Annals. In the case of the other great monasteries, however, all without exception are mentioned" (O'Dwyer, 1981, 29). He goes on to point out, citing the Annals of Innisfallen (Mac Airt ed., Dublin [1951], 824) that "if the monastery of Tallaght escaped from the hands of the Norse it was not so fortunate as to escape from the incursions of other monasteries. In A.D. 824 the community of Kildare plundered Tallaght" (ibid., 32).

50. Ibid., 34.

51. Ryan, 1992, vii.

52. See Conleth Manning, *Early Irish Monasteries* (Dublin: Country House, 1995), 44.

53. Brigid's name has enjoyed various spellings — Brigit, from the Irish, and Brigid, from the Latin *Brigida*. In English, her name was commonly shortened to Bride. (The legend that medieval knights called their new wives "brides" in her honor, as mentioned by D'Arcy, Wallace, and others, is specious. The English word "bride" comes from an ancient Teutonic term. The modern Irish *brídeach* is itself a loan-word.)

54. Once believed to have been the oldest account of her life, the poem *Ni car Brigit* attributed to St. Broccán Cloen, who died around 650, cannot be earlier than the ninth century. See Kenney, 1997, 360. Cogitosus's Life of Brigid was written about 650. The original manuscript is in the Dominican Priory in Eichstadt, Bavaria. Editions: Migne, *PL* 72:775–90. John Colgan, *Trias Thaumaturga* (Louvain, 1647), 518–26. English translation, Liam de Paor, *St. Patrick's World: The Christian Culture of Ireland's Apostolic Age* (Dublin: Four Courts Press, 1997), 207–24. For the Latin Life of Brigid (*Vita Brigidae* IV), see Sharpe, 1991, 139–208, with comment. Others: Whitley Stokes, *Lives of the Saints from the Book of Lismore; Three Middle Irish Homilies;* O'Hanlon, *Lives of the Irish Saints* (February 1), II; Mario Esposito, "On the Earliest Latin Life of St. Brigid of Kildare," *Proceedings of the Royal Irish Academy* 30, 100 (Dublin, 1912): 307–26. For recent editions and studies, see Donncha Ó hAodha, ed. and trans., *Bethu Brigte* (Dublin: Dublin Institute of Advanced Studies, 1978); Donál Ó Cathasaigh, "The Cult of Brigid: A Study of Pagan-Christian Syncretism in Ireland," in James J. Preston, ed., *Mother Worship: Theme and Variation* (Chapel Hill: University of North Carolina Press, 1982), 75–94; Nagy, 1997, 232ff., 151. For the later Latin Lives of Brigit, the verse Life of Chilienus (Coelan), the Life attributed to Animosus (Anmchad), and Colgan's third Life, see Kenney, 1997, 361.

55. "A Cogitosus is noticed under April 18 in the Martyrology of Tallaght and the Martyrology of Gorman" (Kenney, 1997), 359.

56. See de Paor, 1997, 47–48.

57. "Since many of the stories told about her are to be found in the Lives of the handful of other female saints who attracted the attention of the hagiographers, we are almost forced to conclude that these are stories told originally about the goddess, or goddesses, of whom the most widespread name is Brigid but who is known by different names in different localities" (ibid., 47).

58. Kathleen Hughes, *Early Christian Ireland: Introduction to the Sources* (Ithaca, N.Y.: Cornell University Press, 1972), 228.

59. See de Paor, 1997, 215.

60. See Macquarrie, 1997, 177.

61. Róisín Ní Mheara points out that although devotion to St. Brigid was introduced into Belgium by St. Faolán around 650, the custom of making St. Brigid's Crosses is still active there today. See *In Search of Irish Saints: The Peregrinatio pro Christo* (Dublin: Four Courts Press, 1994), 67–68.

62. See Adomnán of Iona, *Life of St. Columba*, intro. and trans. Richard Sharpe (London and New York: Penguin Books, 1995); Ian Finlay, *Columba* (Glasgow: Richard Drew Publishing, 1990; originally published London: Victor Gollancz, 1979); Máire Herbert, *Iona, Kells and Derry: The History and Hagiography of the Monastic Familia of Columba* (Oxford: Clarendon Press, 1988); Cormac Burke, ed., *Studies in the Cult of St. Columba* (Dublin: Four Courts Press, 1997); Lesley Whiteside, *In Search of Columba* (Dublin: Columba Press, 1995); and Francis MacManus, *Saint Columba* (New York: Sheed and Ward, 1962). The sections on Columba in Kenney, 1997, 422–42, are still essential for source work.

63. Finlay, 1979, 53.

64. Other Irish monasteries attributed to Columba include Boyle, Drumcliff, Kilmore, Swords, Raphoe, and Rechra. The surviving form of the Rule is a metrical guide for hermits, composed of twenty-seven ascetic maxims and precepts which center on the life of prayer, silence, and poverty. O Maidin writes, "Two of the maxims of this rule of Colmcille introduced a well-known idea: 'have a mind steadfast and fortified for white martyrdom. Have a mind ready for red martyrdom.'" The extant manuscripts are found in the Bibliothèque Royale, Brussels, and the Rawlinson Collection in the Bodleian Library, Oxford. See O Maidin, 1982, 6–7.

65. William Reeves, *The Life of St. Columba, Founder of Hy, Written by Adamnan Ninth Abbot of That Monastery* (Dublin: Irish Archaeological and Celtic Society; Edinburgh: Bannatine Club, 1857). See Kenney, 1997, 424.

66. Kenney explains that the name "Iona" was derived by a later misreading of Adomnán's Latin adjective "Ioua" (Kenney, 1997, 423, n. 169).

67. See Thomas Owen Clancy and Gilbert Márkus, O.P., *Iona: The Earliest Poetry of a Celtic Monastery* (Edinburgh: Edinburgh University Press, 1995). Several poems attributed to Columba can be found in Gerard Murphy, ed., *Early Irish Lyrics* (Dublin: Four Courts Press, 1998).

68. In the later Old Irish Life, Columba is able to attend, despite his (wholly legendary) vow neither to look upon Ireland nor set foot on its soil, by wearing a hood over his head and by standing on a piece of sod specially imported from Iona for that purpose.

69. See Bede, *HE*, Book III, ch. 4.

70. Found in several collections, including the *Leabhar Breac*, 29–34; the *Book of Lismore*, the National Library of Scotland MS Gael. XL s XV/XVI PP. 13–28. It has been edited by Whitley Stokes in *Three Middle-Irish Homilies* (Calcutta, 1877) and translated by W. M. Hennessy, *The Old Irish Life of St. Columba*, in W. F. Skene, *Celtic Scotland* II (Edinburgh, 1877), 467–507. See Kenney, 1997, 433.

71. There is a manuscript in Oxford's Bodleian Museum, Rawl. B 502 s XII ff–54–59v. Extracts appear in the old Irish Life of Columcille, fragments in Bodl. Laud Alisc. 615 s XIII/XIV, etc. See Whitley Stokes, "The Bodleian *Amra Choluimb Chille*," *Revue Celtique* 20 (1899): 30–55, 132–83, 248–89, 400–437, 21 (1900):

133–36, text of Rawl. B 502, trans., notes, with several poems attributed to Columba, or referring to him. Kenney notes that the obscure and artificial character of the language "makes it impossible that the *Amra* as we have it is a composition of the sixth century. Nevertheless it may be that all our copies depend on a reediting, perhaps in the eighth century, of an original text of the sixth" (Kenney, 1997, 427). On the early Latin poems attributed to Columba, see Kenney, 1997, 380 and 425.

72. Manuscripts in the Library of St. Omer, 716 s XIII vol. v ff. 160–63; the Royal Library of Brussels, 7460 s XIII ff. 167–69. It has been edited by John Colgan, *Trias Thaumaturga* (1647), 321–24, and by Mabillon in *AA.SS.* (Paris, 2d ed.; Venice, 1733), 342–49. See J. F. Kenney, "The Earliest Life of St. Columcille," *Catholic Historical Review* (January 1926): 636–44.

73. Manuscripts include the Schaffhausen Stadtbibliothek Msc. Generalia i; British Museum Cotton Tiberius D. III s XII/XIII ff. 192–217; and BM Addit. 35110 s XII (1154–65) ff. 96–143. Several editions exist: John Colgan, 1647, 336–72; *AA.SS.* for June 11 (1698): 197–236; Reeves, 1857; and Alan O. Anderson and Marjorie O. Anderson, *Adomnan's Life of Columba* (London and Edinburgh: Thomas Nelson and Sons, 1961, 1991). See especially Richard Sharpe, 1995.

74. See Kenney, 1997, 432.

75. A. O Kelleher and G. Schoepperle, *Betha Colaim Chille* (Urbana, 1918), 60–61. The same story is in Colgan, *Trias Thaumaturga,* 396. See Kenney, 1997, 423.

4. The Saints of Ireland

1. The major sources for the Lives of the Irish saints are William W. Heist, *Vitae Sanctorum Hiberniae,* Subsidia Hagiographica 28 (Brussels: Société des Bollandists, 1965); Charles Plummer, *Vitae Sanctorum Hiberniae* (*VSH*), 2 vols. (Oxford: Clarendon Press, 1910) and *Bethada Náem nÉrenn* (*BNE*), 2 vols. (Oxford: Clarendon Press, 1968); and James F. Kenney, *The Sources for the Early History of Ireland: Ecclesiastical* (Dublin: Four Courts Press, 1997). John O'Hanlon's unfinished *Lives of the Irish Saints,* 10 vols. (Dublin, 1875–1903) remains a vast but unreliable resource. A number of popular works, some of them simply digests of legendary material, can be found in the bibliography. For both the interested browser and dedicated scholar, Mary Ryan D'Arcy's *The Saints of Ireland,* 3d ed. (Cork: Mercier Press, 1985) provides a vast treasury of saints' lives. Also worthy of note is the small book by Eoin Neeson, *The Book of Irish Saints* (Cork: Mercier Press, 1967).

2. Other methods of cataloguing saints have been used, even by the saints themselves, e.g., alphabetically, thematically, or according to the annual calendar for the dates on which they are remembered.

3. See Liam de Paor, *St. Patrick's World: The Christian Culture of Ireland's Apostolic Age* (Dublin: Four Courts Press, 1997), 227–43, and Joseph Falaky Nagy, *Conversing with Angels and Ancients: Literary Myths of Medieval Ireland* (Ithaca, N.Y.: Cornell University Press, 1997), 228–32, who comments on 228, "because he supposedly spread Christianity even before the arrival of Patrick, [Ailbe] poses a threat to *the* monopolizing reputation of the missionary to the Irish."

4. See Paul Grosjean, *Analecta Bollandiana* 77 (1959): 439–41. Manuscript references and other critical apparatus regarding the following saints' Lives will be found in Plummer, *VSH* and *BNE,* Kenney, 1997, and Richard Sharpe, *Medieval Irish Saints' Lives: An Introduction to Vitae Sanctorum Hiberniae* (Oxford:

Clarendon Press, 1991), among other sources, and will not be repeated in this chapter.

5. Kenney reports that Auxilius and Iserninus are noted in the Annals, where their deaths are listed for 459 and 468. "Auxilius is commemorated in the church of Cell-Usailli, or Auxili, now Killossy or Killashee, near Naas. To Iserninus, whose Irish name is given as Fith, are ascribed the foundations of Cell-Chuilind (Kilcullen) in Kildare and Ath-Fithot (Ahade) in Carlow" (Kenney, 1997, 169–70). The names of Auxilius and Iserninus appear in the penitential decree of the so-called "First Synod of St. Patrick" (Ludwig Bieler, ed., *The Irish Penitentials* [Dublin Institute of Advanced Studies, 1975], 55). To Sechnall, who is remembered on November 27, a hymn to Patrick was attributed. A short lectionary Life was published by Paul Grosjean, *Analecta Bollandiana* 60 (1942): 26–34.

6. See D'Arcy, 1985, 18.

7. See ibid., 17.

8. Ibid.

9. See Plummer, *VSH* 2.

10. According to an implausible etymology in the Martyrology of Oengus (*Félire Oengusso*), she received her hypocoristic (pet) name when a poet fasted against her in order to regain his speech. The miracle took place in due course, and at first he was only able to mumble "Nin, Nin." Thus Edana was called Mo-ninne and the poet Ninine (*Félire Oengusso*, ed. Whitley Stokes [London: Harrison, 1905], 166–67).

11. For a wry commentary on this episode, see Lisa M. Bitel, *Land of Women* (Ithaca, N.Y.: Cornell University Press, 1996), 175.

12. For Monenna's Life see Heist, 1965, and also the Ulster Society for Medieval Latin Studies edition, vol. 1. For a translation of the Life from the Salamanca Codex, see de Paor, 1997. See also Mario Esposito, "The Sources of Conchubranus' Life of St. Monenna," *English Historical Review* 35 (January 1920): 71–78.

13. William F. Skene, *Celtic Scotland: A History of Ancient Alban* (Edinburgh: David Douglas, 1886–90), vol. 2, 36.

14. See D'Arcy, 1985, 28–29, and Bitel, 1996, 201.

15. D'Arcy, 1985, 23, and John T. McNeill, *The Celtic Churches* (Chicago: University of Chicago Press, 1974), 45.

16. Ludwig Bieler, ed., *The Irish Penitentials* (Dublin: Dublin Institute of Advanced Studies, 1975), 74–95. It has also been attributed to Finnian of Magh Bile. See below.

17. Kenney remarks wryly, "almost every saint living within a century of his time is represented to have been a pupil of the founder of Clonard."

18. As Mary Ryan D'Arcy points out, Ciarán of Saighir is too early to be included in the Twelve, and Comgall of Bangor is sometimes added, as is Finnian himself. Membership was apparently somewhat flexible. See D'Arcy, 1985, 35.

19. Plummer, *BNE* 2:93–98; discussion in *BNE* 1:xxiv–xxv.

20. Two early Lives exist, the Latin *Vita Brendani* and the Irish *Betha Brenáinn*, as well as the later *Navigatio Brendani* (*Muiridecht Brenáinn*). Another version of the latter is found in "The Twelve Apostles of Ireland (Brendan II)," in Plummer, *BNE*. The earlier, Latin work more likely represents something of Brendan's actual life and adventures. See *The Voyage of St. Brendan*, trans. J. J. O'Meara (Portlaoise, Ireland: Dolmen Press, 1985), and "The Voyage of St. Brendan," trans. J. F. Webb, *Lives of the Saints* (London and New York: Penguin Books, 1965), 33–68.

21. On the possibility of constructing ocean-going craft in sixth-century Ireland,

E. G. Bowen writes, "Pliny, quoting the 4th century B.C. writer Timaeus, says that people of Britain sailed abroad in vessels of wickerwork covered with hide, and Avienus also mentions vessels of this type. These are clearly vessels of the coracle or curragh type. In spite of their frailty it is said that such craft were able to withstand seas that would be fatal to boats of a more solid construction. From an early time there was undoubtedly a larger boat of this kind possessing a wicker framework and covered by many thicknesses of hide. It would be capable of transporting a crew of twenty men and carrying a mast. Such large craft were certainly known in Ireland in later times, for in the ninth century A.D. Dicuil [in *De memoria orbis terrae*] speaks of large seafaring coracles sailing to Iceland. Vessels of even stronger build were certainly known in Ireland toward the close of the Iron Age, as indicated by the elaborate gold ship-model from Broighter in County Derry" (E. G. Bowen, *Saints, Seaways and Settlements* [Cardiff: University of Wales Press, 1977], 19). Tim Severin's reconstruction of "the Brendan," a hide-covered currach on which he sailed from Ireland to America in 1976, is now on display at the Craggaunowen Project, north of the city of Limerick.

22. Plummer notes that "the word *luchurpán* (lit. little body) occurs in many forms, and is the Anglo-Irish 'Leprechaun,' a kind of fairy. In Rawl. B. 502 f. 41c. 5, these beings are said to be the offspring of the unlawful intercourse of the children of Seth with those of Cain; but according to ibid. F. 42b. 47 (= LU 2a 45) they are the descendants of Ham after he had been cursed by his father [Noah]" (Plummer, *BNE* 2:332–33, note 95, from the Life of Brendan [I]).

23. See Plummer, *BNE* 2:63–64.

24. See D'Arcy, 1985, 41.

25. Kenney, 1997, 392. Also see D'Arcy, 1985, 45–46.

26. The Missal is now in the Royal Irish Academy (Stowe D. II. 3 *s* VIII/IX). The best modern edition is still George F. Warner, ed., *The Stowe Missal,* 2 vols. (London: Henry Bradshaw Society, 1906, 1915). See D. Fitzgerald, "Irish Missals," *The Academy* 17 (1880): 48, and B. MacCarthy, "On the Stowe Missal," trans. *Royal Irish Academy* 27 (1886): 135–268. Controversies over translation and interpretation aired in a number of letters by F. E. Warren, Whitley Stokes, and B. MacCarthy in *The Academy,* from 15 (1879) to 46 (1894). See Kenney, 1997, 692–99 and Peter O'Dwyer, O.Carm., *Célí Dé: Spiritual Reform in Ireland 750–900* (Dublin: Editions Tailliura, 1981), 151–59.

27. See Ryan, 1992, 122, 124.

28. See D'Arcy, 1985, 35 and John Ryan, S.J., *Irish Monasticism: Origins and Development* (Dublin: Four Courts Press, 1992), 124.

29. Three versions exist, the Kilkenny Codex and manuscripts in Oxford and Dublin.

30. It is found in the *Félire Oengusso* (Stokes ed., 1905, 2:44–45), the *Leabhar Breac,* and a manuscript in the British Museum. There is a translation by Gerard Murphy, ed., *Early Irish Lyrics* (Dublin: Four Courts Press, 1998), and by Whitley Stokes in David H. Green, ed., *An Anthology of Irish Literature* (New York: Modern Library, 1954).

31. Plummer, *VSH* 2:28.

32. See Eleanor Duckett, *The Wandering Saints of the Early Middle Ages* (New York: W. W. Norton, 1964), 67.

33. Abbán's Life is found in Plummer, *BNE* 1.

34. D'Arcy, 1985, 35.

35. See ibid., 37.

36. See ibid., 36.

37. See David Dumville, "Gildas and Uinniau," in *Gildas: New Approaches,* ed. Michael Lapidge and David Dumville (Woodbridge, Suffolk: Boydell and Brewer, 1984), 207–14; and Richard Sharpe, "Gildas as a Father of the Church," in ibid., 196–201, and Alan Macquarrie, *The Saints of Scotland: Essays in Scottish History AD 450–1093* (Edinburgh: John Donald Publishers, 1997), 65.

38. See Sharpe, 1991, 11, and Duckett, 1964, 67.

39. Latin Lives are found in the Kilkenny and Salamanca Codices, and several Irish texts survive. For the former, see Plummer *VSH* 1:234–57, and Heist, 1965, 361–65. Three Irish Lives are translated by Plummer in *BNE* 2 (cf. *BNE* 1:159–60). Two late Irish manuscripts exist from 1725 and 1765.

40. For a general description of the monastic site and its heritage, see Michael Rodgers and Marcus Losack, *Glendalough: A Celtic Pilgrimage,* foreword by Esther de Waal (Blackrock, County Dublin: Columba Press, 1996).

41. Plummer, *BNE* 2:155.

42. For the Irish Life of Mochuda and other supporting manuscripts, including "The Expulsion of Mochuda from Rahen," see Plummer, *BNE* 2:282–302.

43. See Macquarrie, 1997, 9, 134–35. Constantine II did in fact abdicate his throne in 943 and join the Culdees at St. Andrews, at least three hundred years after Mochuda's death. Constantine mac Fergus of the Cenel nGabráin died in 820, still two centuries too late to have been a contemporary of Mochuda. Although several Constantines are connected with royal families of Scotland during the ninth and tenth centuries, it is otherwise a rare name.

44. See Plummer, *BNE* 1:xxix, and *VSH* 1:xlvi.

45. See Kenney, 1997, 453.

46. Ibid., 451.

47. See Nagy, 1997, 281–84.

48. See D'Arcy, 1985, 74–75.

49. See Kenney, 1997, 450–51. For a full-length study, see Colum Kenny, *Molaise: Abbot of Leighlin and Hermit of Holy Island* (Killala, Ireland: Morrigan, 1998).

50. See Kenny, 1998, ix.

51. See D'Arcy, 1985, 109.

52. Several medieval Latin Lives of Moling are found in the Kilkenny and Salamanca Codices and exist in manuscripts in Oxford and Dublin. An independent eleventh- or twelfth-century Irish Life is found in the Royal Irish Academy and a number of Irish poems in various manuscripts have been attributed to him. See Kenney, 1997, 461–63, and D'Arcy, 1985, 62.

53. See Murphy, 1998, 32–33 (no. 13), and notes on 112–13 (nos. 43 and 44) for connections with the *Suibne Geilt* poems.

54. See note 52 above and Nagy, 1997, 194–95.

55. The Life of Molúa is found in the Salamanca and Kilkenny Codices and the *AA.SS.* for August, among other sources, which possess elements of historical value for the times in which they were written. See Kenney, 1997, 397–98.

56. Cited by Ryan, 1992, 128–29.

57. Plummer, *BNE* 2:172. Colmán Elo's Life is found in four manuscripts, the Salamanca and Kilkenny Codices located in Dublin and London and in Brussels.

58. See Kenney, 1997, 399–400, and Ryan, 1992, 129.

59. See ibid., 455–56, and Duckett, 1964, 72–73.

60. For details of his life and ministry, see above, pp. 42 and 95.

61. For a decidedly biased account of the controversies, see Bede, *A History of the English Church and People*, trans. Leo Sherley-Price, rev. R. W. Latham (London and New York: Penguin, 1968), chapter 15: "Adomnán and the Easter Controversy."

62. Manuscripts exist in the Bodleian Museum (Rawl. B 512 ff–48–S IV) and the Royal Library in Brussels (2324–40 76–85), which was copied in 1627 by Michael O'Clery from a manuscript written by his cousin. Kenney mentions that the O'Clery manuscript, and probably the Rawlinson, goes back to the monastery of Raphoe, of which Adomnán was patron (Kenney, 1997, 245). Editions exist by Kuno Meyer, *Cáin Adomnáin: An Old-Irish Treatise on the Law of Adamnán* (Anec. Oxon. Med. & Mod. Ser. XII, Oxford 1905) and Gilbert Márkus, O.P., trans., *Adomnán's "Law of the Innocents," Cáin Adomnáin* (Glasgow: Blackfriars Books, 1997).

63. Neeson, 1967, 171.

64. The most reliable edition is that found in the *AA.SS.* for May, III (1866 ed.), 475–84. See Kenney, 1997, 510; Róisín Ní Mheara, *In Search of Irish Saints: The Peregrinatio pro Christo* (Dublin: Four Courts Press, 1994), 75–78; and D'Arcy, 1985, 135–36.

65. Kenney, 1997, 450. Several versions of the Life of Fintan exist, ultimately derived from a single source which contained enough historically reliable material to reveal the character of the individual, but not reliable with regard to the Easter controversies.

66. Ryan, 1992, 127, citing Plummer, *VSH* 2:98.

67. Ibid., 127–28.

68. Her Life, one of the four major Lives of women saints (the others being Brigid, Íte, and Monenna), is found in manuscripts in the Bodleian Museum, Oxford, and the Franciscan Convent in Dublin. Although a late manuscript, Kenney thought it may go back "to a good and early text" (Kenney, 1997, 465). See also Plummer, *VSH* 2:253; D'Arcy, 1985, 64; Hughes, 1972, 233; and Neeson, 1967, 216–17.

69. See Duckett, 1964, 64.

70. Kenney, 1997, 695, note 164.

71. For a concise account of Malachy's life, see Kenney, 1997, 764–67 and Bitel, 1993, 238–40.

72. Kenney, 1997, 767.

73. Lorcan's Life is found in late manuscripts, including the Kilkenny Codex and the panegyric by Jean Halgrin, the bishop of Besançon, found in the National Library of Paris (BN 14364 s XIII), and others. See Kenney, 1997, 770–71; John O'Hanlon, *The Life of St. Laurence O'Toole Archbishop of Dublin* (Dublin, 1877), and A. Legris, *Saint Laurent O'Toole (Saint Laurent d'Eu), Archevêque de Dublin* (Rouen: Eu, 1914).

5. The Scottish Saints

1. For a summary account of early Christian inscriptions and artifacts, see Alan Macquarrie, *The Saints of Scotland: Essays in Scottish History AD 450–1093* (Edinburgh: John Donald Publishers, 1997), 21–27, with extensive references, 27–30.

2. The Picts, or *Picti* (the "Painted People" according to the Romans), were known as Pretani or Cruithni to the British and Irish. A Celtic people of mixed ancestry distinct culturally from both the Irish and British, they occupied most of the area north of Hadrian's Wall until pushed back by incursions of colonizing forces

from northern Wales and the Dál Riada of Ulster in the late fifth century. Picts also figured prominently in Ulster itself, where their realm was known as the Dál Araidi for Fiacha Araide, an eponymous Pictish ancestor. Although eventually engulfed by the Scots and Northumbrians, the Picts exercised a profound and lasting influence on late Irish art, particularly in the Book of Kells and other masterpieces of the golden age. See Isabel Henderson, *The Picts* (London: Thomas and Hudson, 1967), and Caroline Bingham, *Beyond the Highland Line: Highland History and Culture* (London: Constable, 1991), 35–42, 49–50.

3. Although resource materials for the early church in Scotland are fewer than those for Britain and Ireland, excellent resources have been assembled since the late nineteenth century. W. M. Metcalfe's edition of Pinkerton's 1789 *Lives of the Scottish Saints* (Paisley, 1889) and W. F. Skene's great three-volume collection, *Celtic Scotland: A History of Ancient Alban* (Edinburgh: David Douglas, 1886–90), remain valuable sources. Recent scholarship has significantly increased the number of useful materials, including works by John MacQueen, Alan Macquarrie, Caroline Bingham, Máire Herbert, and others. See bibliography.

4. In most accounts, the Convention at Druim Cett was held in 574, but Alan Macquarrie makes a strong case for the later date. See Macquarrie, 1997, 78–80, and 113–15.

5. See Bingham, 1991, 48–50.

6. Ibid., 50.

7. See ibid., 1991, 60.

8. Printed by W. F. Skene in *Chronicles of the Picts: Chronicles of the British Islands* (1867), 138–40, 183–93. See Macquarrie, 1997, 10, note 9.

9. Macquarrie notes that the death of Tuathalán, the abbot of Cinrighmona (Ceannríghmonadh), is recorded in the Annals of Ulster for 747, "indicating that St. Andrews was in existence by that date" (Macquarrie, 1997, 181–82). (Rigmond, Kill-Rigmonaig, Kylrimont, and Ceannríghmonadh are variants of "royal mount.")

10. See Macquarrie, 1997, 6–9. For a résumé of other source material, see 3–6.

11. See ibid., 145–59, and Alan Macquarrie, "Vita Sancti Servani: the Life of St. Serf," *Innes Review* 44 (1993): 122–52.

12. Macquarrie, 1997, 156.

13. Ibid., 152.

14. John T. McNeill, *The Celtic Churches: A History, A.D. 200 to 1200* (Chicago: University of Chicago Press, 1974), 45–47.

15. Mary Ryan D'Arcy relates that St. Enoch's Square in Glasgow, also known as St. Thanog's, was named for a church built there in her honor but destroyed in the Reformation (D'Arcy, 1985, 82).

16. Despite the Welsh and Scottish accounts, the claim that Kentigern fled to Wales and founded Llanelwy lacks all historical support. St. Asaph's was in fact established many years later. See McNeill, 1974, 46.

17. McNeill, 1974, 45.

18. See D'Arcy, 1985, 23.

19. Adomnán, *Life of Columba*, 2, 13.

20. See D'Arcy, 1985, 72–73, and McNeill, 1974, 97.

21. See Macquarrie, 1997, 171.

22. See D'Arcy, 1985, 84–85, and McNeill, 1974, 97.

23. McNeill, 1974, 97. Also see D'Arcy, 1985, 82–83.

24. See Bingham, 1991, 47–48, and McNeill, 1974, 91.

25. See Macquarrie, 1997, 98–100.

26. See ibid., 232.

27. Ibid., 81.

28. Adomnán, *Life of Columba,* ll. 655ff.

29. See Bede, *A History of the English Church and People (HE)* (London and New York: Penguin, 1968), 3:3.

30. Begun during the Great Depression in the slums of Glasgow under the inspired leadership of Rev. MacLeod, the Iona Community symbolized the "rebuilding of the common life" by reconstructing the medieval monastery, once the source of the spiritual vitality of Scotland. Today, the community includes over 3,400 members, associates, and friends throughout the world who are committed to spiritual and social renewal through communal worship and the promotion of justice and peace, concern for the poor, environmental protection, ecumenical cooperation, and healing. The Iona Community Web Page can be found at www. iona.org.uk/community.

31. See below, p. 115.

32. See Bingham, 1991, 56. Also see McNeill, 1974, 207.

33. Kenney, 1997, 286, note 416.

34. Bede, *HE,* 299.

35. Ibid. See Kenney, 1997, 284.

36. Kenney notes that at this great gathering of church leaders, the northern delegates met with Ecbert, supporting the view that the adoption of the new paschal regulations was effected at that time. He also points out that the participation of the Armagh delegates Aed of Sletty and Muir-chúi maccu Machthéni (Patrick's biographer) could support the theory that the development of Patrick's story in the seventh century was part of the effort to win the northerners over to the paschal reform. See Kenney, 1997, 246.

37. See D'Arcy, 1985, 85–87.

38. Walafrid Strabo, *Life of Blathmac,* Monumenta Germaniae Historica, Poetae Latini Aevi Carolini, 2:299–301. Walafrid's 180-line poem has often been printed. It can also be found in Migne's *Patrologia Latina.* On Walafrid himself and the relationship between Reichenau and St. Gall, see Eleanor S. Duckett, "Walafrid Strabo of Reichenau," in *Carolingian Portraits: A Study in the Ninth Century* (Ann Arbor: University of Michigan Press, 1969), 121–60.

39. See D'Arcy, 1985, 87–88; McNeill, 1974, 207; and Bingham, 1991, 54, note 2, citing Alfred Smyth's *Warlords and Holy Men,* 147–48.

40. McNeill, 1974, 47; D'Arcy, 1985, 79.

41. Macquarrie, 1997, 199–210. Also see D'Arcy, 1985, 159–60. The *Vita Kaddroe Abbatis Metis in Lotharingia* was edited with commentary in *AA.SS.* for March, 1 (1865), 468–80, and translated in part by Alan O. Anderson, in *Early Sources of Scottish History, AD 500–1286* (London: Oliver and Boyd, 1922, 1990), 431–43.

42. Her Life was written by her chaplain, the bishop Turgot. See J. Pinkerton, *Lives of the Scottish Saints,* rev. and enlarged by W. M. Metcalfe, 2 vols. (Paisley, 1889), 159–82. Also translated by Anderson, 1922. See Alan Macquarrie, "St. Margaret of Scotland," in *The Saints of Scotland: Essays in Scottish History AD 450–1093* (Edinburgh: John Donald Publishers, 1997), 211–29, and Bingham, 1991, 61–63. Also see Derek Baker, " 'A Nursery of Saints': St. Margaret of Scotland Reconsidered," *Medieval Women,* ed. Derek Baker, Studies in Church History, Subsidia I (Oxford: Basil Blackwell, 1978), 119–41.

43. Macquarrie, 1997, 215.

44. Macquarrie notes that "the story about Queen Margaret is a contemporary account written while the queen was still alive or very shortly after her death; although written in distant Canterbury, and perhaps suitably exaggerated for hagiographical purposes, its primary authority cannot be doubted" (ibid., 219).

45. Baker, 1978, 155. McNeill similarly concludes, "Her reforms were broadly wholesome for the life of the church, while at the same time conducive to its coordination with English and continental practice" (McNeill, 1974, 210).

46. See Richard of St. Victor, *The Twelve Patriarchs, The Mystical Ark, Book Three of the Trinity,* trans. Grover A. Zinn (New York: Paulist Press, 1979).

6. Brittany and Beyond

1. E. G. Bowen, *Saints, Seaways and Settlements* (Cardiff: University of Wales Press, 1977).

2. Sources for the Lives of Celtic saints in Brittany are even fewer than for those of Scotland and other Celtic realms. The quest for the historical origins of the Breton churches was begun in earnest in the mid-nineteenth century by Arthur le Moyne la Borderie in his *Histoire de Bretagne* (Rennes, 1896). Later historians such as Louis Duchesne and Ferdinand Lot greatly refined Borderie's theories. More recent assessments are found in René Largillière, *Les saints et l'organisation chrétienne primitive dans l'Armorique Bretonne* (Rennes: Plihon et Hommay, 1925), and Armand Rébillon, *Histoire de Bretagne* (Paris: A. Collin, 1957). For a concise history of ancient and Christian Brittany, see John T. McNeill, *The Celtic Churches: A History, A.D. 200 to 1200* (Chicago: University of Chicago Press, 1974), 137–54, and Nora Chadwick, *Early Brittany* (Cardiff: University of Wales Press, 1969). For an excellent overview of the work of the Irish missionaries in Brittany, France, the Low Countries, Germany, Austria, and Switzerland, see Eleanor Duckett, *The Wandering Saints of the Early Middle Ages* (New York: W. W. Norton, 1964), and especially Róisín Ní Mheara, *In Search of Irish Saints: The Peregrinatio pro Christo* (Dublin: Four Courts Press, 1994).

3. See McNeill, 1974, 137–38.

4. For a concise history of early Christian Brittany, see ibid., 138–50.

5. Ibid., 141. Other Breton ecclesiastical prefixes include *tre,* "oratory" or "hermitage," and *lan,* "monastery."

6. For a number of these saints, see above, pp. 36–38, 39–41, and 45.

7. See above, p. 37.

8. McNeill, 1974, 144.

9. Ibid.

10. See above, p. 34.

11. See McNeill, 1974, 144.

12. See above, p. 35.

13. The Welsh version of the primitive Life in the Book of Llandaff was compiled about 1132. See Kenney, 1997, 174, especially note 74.

14. McNeill, 1974, 146.

15. See above, p. 37.

16. See above, p. 45.

17. Versions of the ninth-century Latin Life by Wrdisten are found in *AA.SS.* March I, 256–61 [incomplete] and the *Analecta Bollandiana* 7 (1888) 172–249, ed. C. De Smedt (which includes an additional metrical Life).

18. See McNeill, 1974, 146.

19. Kenney, 1997, 175. A curious addendum to the fervent devotion shown St. Guénolé in Brittany concerns his intercession for relief from infertility and impotence. Apparently one of the old churches in Brest features an anatomically complete statue of the saint. Although generations of devotees have chipped off slivers of the saint's relevant body part to take with them as a charm, the statue has remained miraculously unimpaired. I am indebted for this anecdote to Jeffrey Kacirk's *Forgotten English* calendar for Tuesday, March 2, 1999 (Rohnert, Calif.: Pomegranate, 1998).

20. McNeill, 1974, 143, and D'Arcy, 1985, 117–18.

21. Ní Mheara, 1994, 34–35.

22. See Kenney, 1997, 181–82.

23. In Breton lore, dragons are also associated (usually coweringly) with Paul Aurelian, Tugdual (Tudwal), Non, and German. See Ní Mheara, 1994, 20, 25, 29, 33, and 58.

24. See ibid., 26–28.

25. Ibid.

26. Among Irish saints for whom place names and both oral and written history offer some likelihood of historical verifiability are Disibod, Erhard (Iorard), Goar, Landelin, Rupert, Trudpert, and Wendalin. See Ní Mheara, 1994, passim. Mary Ryan D'Arcy provides biographies of eighty-two Irish saints who traveled to the European mainland as missionaries between 450 and the tenth century. Corish points out that an Irish monastery was founded in Rome by the eleventh century: "the Annals of Inisfallen record the death of its abbot, Eógan, in 1095, and a manuscript in the Vatican library has two lists of its monks from about the same date. There are five names on one list and four in the other" (Patrick J. Corish, *The Irish Catholic Experience: A Historical Survey* [Dublin: Gill and Macmillan, 1985], 29).

27. While accepting the general outline of Fridolin's Life, Kenney argues for a date abut one hundred years later. See Kenney, 1997, 496.

28. See Ní Mheara, 1994, 16–18, 117–20; D'Arcy, 1985, 116; Kenney, 1997, 496.

29. He called himself Columba, like his namesake of the sixth century, but to distinguish him from his more famous fellow Irishman, writers have called him Columban, Columbanus, and sometimes Columba the Younger.

30. Jonas of Susa, *Vita Sancti Columbani*, ed. Bruno Krusch, Monumenta Germaniae Historica, Scriptores Rerum Merovingicarum 4 (1902), 1–52. See also Migne, *PL* 87:1011–84. The critical edition of Columbanus' writings is G. S. M. Walker, ed., *Sancti Columbani Opera* (Dublin: Dublin Institute of Advanced Studies, 1970). See also Michael Lapidge, ed., *Columbanus: Studies in the Latin Writings,* Studies in Celtic History 17 (Woodbridge, Suffolk: Boydell and Brewer, 1997), Tomás Ó Fiach, *Columbanus in His Own Words* (Dublin: Veritas, 1990), McNeill, 1974, 155–68, and Mary Ryan D'Arcy, *The Saints of Ireland,* 3d ed. (Cork: Mercier Press, 1985), 118–24.

31. For a summary of Columban's involvement in the "Three Chapters" controversy, see McNeill, 1974, 164–65.

32. D'Arcy, 1985, 122.

33. St. Columban, *Instructions on Faith,* 1:3–5.

34. Kenney, 1997, 175, citing Louis Gougaud, *Chrétientés celtiques,* 123. Landévennec remained the most "Irish" of the Breton monasteries.

35. Ibid.

36. The Life of St. Gall was written by the abbot of Reichenau, Walafrid Strabo: *Vita Sancti Galli,* Monumenta Germaniae Historica, Scriptores Rerum Merovingi-

carum 4, and Migne, *PL* 114. Trans. by Maud Joynt: *The Life of St. Gall* (London: SPCK, 1927).

37. See D'Arcy, 1985, 126–28; McNeill, 1974, 168–69; and Duckett, 1964, 131–39.

38. The seventh-century Life of Fursa was edited by Bruno Krusch, Monumenta Germaniae Historica, Scriptores Rerum Merovingicarum 4 (1902), 423–49 (excluding the visions). The *Vita et miracula S. Fursei* was edited by W. W. Heist, *Vitae Sanctorum Hiberniae,* Subsidia Hagiographica 28 (Brussels: Société des Bollandists, 1965), 37–55. The Irish Life, edited by Whitley Stokes, is found in the *Revue Celtique* 25 (1904): 385–404.

39. Bede, *HE,* 3:19.

40. See Ní Mheara, 1994, 53.

41. See D'Arcy, 1985, 92–94, 129–32, 139–40; and Ní Mheara, 1994, 52–68.

42. See Ní Mheara, 1994, 68.

43. See Duckett, 1964, 151–53; D'Arcy, 1985, 133–35; Ní Mheara, 1994, 36–37, 46–49.

44. Ní Mheara, 1994, 46.

45. As bishop of Meaux, Faron, who with his little sister, St. Fara, the founder of the abbey of Faremoutier, had been blessed as children by Columban, greatly favored the Irish *peregrini.* He also befriended St. Kilian of Artois, related by blood to Fiacre, who went on to become a missionary in the region of Cambrai. See Duckett, 1964, 151.

46. Ní Mheara, 1994, 47.

47. Martin Wallace, *Celtic Saints* (Belfast: Appletree Press, and San Francisco: Chronicle Books, 1995), 55. He adds that the curved stone on which Fiacra had once awaited judgment attracted pilgrims seeking relief from hemorrhoids. It was preserved for centuries next to his tomb.

48. D'Arcy, 1985, 134.

49. Ibid., 90–91.

50. Ní Mheara, 1994, 18.

51. Ibid., 77–79.

52. D'Arcy, 1985, 142–43. Among other Irish martyrs are found the names of Boetien (Boethius), German (St.-Germain), Grimona, Mona, Proba (Preuve), and Rumold. See Ní Mheara, 1994, and D'Arcy, 1985, passim.

7. The Blessing and the Curse

1. In this chapter, I have drawn in places on my earlier article "The Spirituality of the Celtic Church," *Spirituality Today* 37, no. 3 (1985): 243–55.

2. Recent anthologies and explorations of Celtic spirituality have focused on the poetry and religious prose of both monastic and secular writers. See, for instance, Oliver Davies and Fiona Bowie, eds., *Celtic Christian Spirituality: An Anthology of Medieval and Modern Sources* (London: SPCK, 1995, and New York: Continuum, 1999) and Peter O'Dwyer, O.Carm., *Towards a History of Irish Spirituality* (Blackrock, County Dublin: Columba Press, 1995).

3. See Martin MacNamara, "The Bible in Irish Spirituality," in *Irish Spirituality,* ed. Michael Maher (Dublin: Veritas Publications, 1979), 35.

4. For Patrick's use of Scripture, even as a structural element in the *Confession,* see Máire B. de Paor, P.B.V.M., ed. and trans., *Patrick the Pilgrim Apostle of Ireland: St. Patrick's* Confessio *and* Epistola (Dublin: Veritas, 1998).

5. The following marginal protest usefully reminds us, on the other hand, that by the eighth century most people could neither read nor write, particularly Latin, but were not for that reason to be despised by the learned: " 'Tis sad to see the sons of learning / In everlasting Hellfire burning / While he that never read a line / Doth in eternal glory shine" (Robin Flower's translation, in *An Anthology of Irish Literature*, ed. David Greene [New York: Modern Library, 1954], 14).

6. Early British liturgical documents are almost wholly lacking. Irish liturgical sources include the Stowe Missal, the Book of Armagh, the Book of Deer, the Book of Dimma, and the Book of Mulling. One of the treasures of the continental church is the famous Sacramentary of Rheinau, c. 800 (St. Gall 1305, Rheinau Library, Zurich). Less a source for the Irish liturgy, it testifies to Celtic influence on the development of liturgy elsewhere, mainly through the work of missionaries such as Columban and Gall. On the *Cathach,* the "Battler" Psalter attributed to St. Columba, see above, p. 111. Cf. also J. H. Bernard and R. Atkinson, eds. and trans., *The Irish Liber Hymnorum,* 2 vols. (London: Harrison and Sons, 1898), Hugh Jackson Lawlor, ed., *The Rosslyn Missal* (London: Harrison, 1899), and Bruno Stablein, "Two Melodies of the Old Irish Liturgy (*Zwei Melodien der altirischen Liturgie*)," *Fellerer Festscrift* (RILM74 1645): 590–97. For an overview of this subject, see John Hennig, "Old Ireland and Her Liturgy," in Robert McNally, S.J., ed., *Old Ireland* (New York: Fordham University Press, 1965), 60–89.

7. Some of the earliest sources of devotional material, all from about the year 800, include the Book of Nunnaminster (British Library, Harley 2965), the Book of Cerne (Cambridge Univ., LI.I.1), the Harleian Prayer Book (British Library, Harley 7653), the Royal Library Prayer Book (British Library, Reg. 2A, XX), and the Durham Ritual.

8. See below, p. 147.

9. Patrick Corish observes in their regard, "The devotional literature of the Culdees is very distinctively Irish, with its imaginative freshness and its constant repetition of phrases expressing trust and abandonment, as in the 'Broom of Devotion,' or the 'Alphabet of Piety': 'O holy Jesu, O gentle friend, O morning Star, O midday Sun adorned.... O Son of the Merciful Father without mother in heaven, O Son of the true Virgin maid Mary without father on earth, O true and loving brother...' " (Patrick J. Corish, *The Irish Catholic Experience: A Historical Survey* [Dublin: Gill and Macmillan, 1985], 23).

10. A number of these fascinating books have been edited and translated since the late nineteenth century, including the *Martyrology of Oengus (Félire Oengusso),* ed. Whitley Stokes (London: Harrison, 1880, 1905); the *Martyrology of Gorman, (Félire Húi Gormáin),* ed. Whitley Stokes (London: Harrison, 1895); the *Psalter and Martyrology of Ricemarch (Rhygyfarch),* ed. H. J. Lawlor, 2 vols. (London: Harrison, 1914); the *Martyrology of Tallaght,* ed. R. I. Best and H. J. Lawlor (London: Harrison, 1931); and the *Martyrology of St. Jerome,* ed. Dom Henri Quentin, O.S.B. (London: Harrison, 1931). There are, additionally, the Martyrology of Donegal and several others.

11. In the language of the gospels, being blessed does not mean "following your bliss" in the way Joseph Campbell's self-regarding slogan has become the battle cry of New Age groupies. The word "bliss" comes from the Old English *bliths,* which means complete happiness or contentment. It is related to *blithe,* and has about as much depth. Both are not only independent of the ancient meaning of *bless* but, from a Christian perspective, its antithesis.

12. Kuno Meyer, trans., *Selections from Ancient Irish Poetry* (London, 1911), 25. Text: *Thesaurus Paleohibernicus: A Collection of Old Irish Glosses, Scholia, Prose and Verse,* ed. Whitley Stokes and John Strachan (Cambridge, 1901–3), 2:354. Although considered by scholars today to be from the eighth century, according to Eugene O'Curry, the nineteenth-century founder of Old Irish studies, St. Patrick's Breastplate was composed in 1477. See Kenney, 1997, 272ff.

13. Dan. 3:56–88 (the Greek addition to Daniel, found in the Apocrypha, vv. 28–68).

14. For "women" I have substituted "witches," which more accurately catches the meaning.

15. Noel Dermot O'Donoghue, *The Mountain behind the Mountain* (Edinburgh: T. & T. Clark, 1993), 13.

16. After Carmichael's death, three more volumes were published at intervals, followed by a sixth volume of notes. See Alexander Carmichael, *Carmina Gadelica: Hymns and Incantation,* 2 vols. (Edinburgh: T. & A. Constable, 1900). Vols. 3 and 4, ed. James Carmichael Watson (Edinburgh: Oliver & Boyd, 1940–41). Vol. 5, ed. Angus Matheson (Edinburgh: Oliver & Boyd, 1954). Vol. 6, Notes and Indices (Edinburgh: Scottish Academic Press, 1971). All were reprinted by the Scottish Academic Press between 1984 and 1988. For selections, see Esther de Waal, *The Celtic Vision: Prayers and Blessings from the Outer Hebrides* (London: Darton, Longman and Todd, 1988), and also Oliver Davies and Fiona Bowie, eds., *Celtic Christian Spirituality: An Anthology of Medieval and Modern Sources* (London: SPCK, 1995, and New York: Continuum, 1999), 89–142, and 238–39, for additional information on the history of Carmichael's publishing project. Another short, finely illustrated collection was published in 1981: *Celtic Prayers,* selected by Avery Brooke, calligraphy by Laurel Casazza (New York: Seabury, 1981; originally published as Alexander Carmichael, *Celtic Invocations* [Noroton, Conn.: Vineyard Books, 1977]). For a contemporary spiritual and theological commentary on a number of prayers in Carmichael's *Carmina Gadelica,* see O'Donoghue, 1993, 16–17, 46–80.

17. Carmichael, 1900, 1:183. Further references will be to the volumes as indicated in footnote 16.

18. 1:236–37.

19. 1:293.

20. 1:319–21.

21. 4:65.

22. 1:73.

23. 1:110

24. 1:125.

25. 1:55.

26. 1:5.

27. In one account noted in the Annals of the Four Masters, in 847 the savage bishop-king of Munster, Fedlimid mac Crimthainn, died from what was alleged to be a wound inflicted on him in a visitation by the long-dead Ciarán, who stabbed him with his pastoral staff in punishment for his many crimes. See Lisa M. Bitel, *Isle of the Saints: Monastic Settlement and Christian Community in Early Ireland* (Ithaca, N.Y.: Cornell University Press, 1990, and Cork: University of Cork Press, 1993), 153.

28. Patrick Power relates that the English word "curse" may itself have come

from the Irish *cúrsachadh,* "abuse," which has long since fallen out of use. See Patrick C. Power, *The Book of Irish Curses* (Cork: Mercier Press, and Springfield, Ill.: Templegate Publishers, 1974), 10.

29. See 1 Cor. 16:22: "If any one has no love for the Lord, let him be accursed [*anathema*]." Other references include Mark 11:21, Gal. 3:10 and 13, Heb. 6:8, James 3:8, and 2 Pet. 2:14 [*kataromai* and *katara*]

30. See Pss. 12, 58, 59, 69, 129, and especially 109.

31. Cf. Rom. 12:14: "Bless those who persecute you; bless and do not curse them," and also Matt. 5:22 and 1 Pet. 3:9.

32. Oliver Davies, *Celtic Christianity in Early Medieval Wales: The Origins of the Welsh Spiritual Tradition* (Cardiff: University of Wales Press, 1996), 17. Conversely, Davies notes that Beuno "is capable also of bringing the dead to life, which he does on three occasions." Ibid.

33. See Exod. 22:21–24, Deut. 10:17–18, Ps. 68:5, Isa. 1:17, Jer. 7:5–7, Mark 12:38–40, James 1:27, etc.

34. See Power, 1974, 91.

35. Ibid., 49–50.

36. Ibid., 51.

37. See above, p. 85.

38. See above, p. 93.

39. Power, 1974, 59.

40. Peter O'Dwyer points out that "The custom of fasting to settle a dispute or to force an adversary to do one's will was quite common in Ireland. The Penitential [of Tallaght] assumes that it is the normal way of deciding an issue. Maelruain fasted three times since he came to Tallaght and this was undertaken against Artrí son of Faelmaire. The matter in dispute affected the monastery. After the first fast Artrí's leg broke in two. As a result of the second, fire fell from heaven and burned him from top to toe and after the third fast he died" (Peter O'Dwyer, O.Carm., *Céli Dé: Spiritual Reform in Ireland 750–900* [Dublin: Editions Tailliura, 1981], 80).

41. G. H. Doble observes in regard to Teilo, one of the principal Welsh saints, that the threat of a curse, whether divine, human, or both, reinforces the authority of the saint over agreements made in "his" church and recorded in "his" gospel book. See Gilbert H. Doble, *Lives of the Welsh Saints,* ed. D. Simon Evans (Cardiff: University of Wales Press, 1971), 163.

8. The Struggle for Justice

1. In this chapter, I have again drawn at times on my article "The Spirituality of the Celtic Church," *Spirituality Today* 37, no. 3 (1985): 243–55.

2. As Philip Sheldrake observes, "[monastic] spirituality was not something detached from social values and organization but was intimately entwined with them" (Philip Sheldrake, *Living between Worlds: Place and Journey in Celtic Spirituality* [London: Darton, Longman and Todd, 1995], 30–31).

3. See Diarmuid Ó Laoghaire, S.J., "Old Ireland and Her Spirituality," in *Old Ireland,* ed. Robert McNally, S.J. (New York: Fordham University Press, 1965), 47.

4. Ibid., 48.

5. For a probing discussion of "the politics of hospitality," see the chapter by that name in Lisa M. Bitel's *Isle of the Saints: Monastic Settlement and Christian Community in Early Ireland* (Ithaca, N.Y.: Cornell University Press, 1990, and Cork:

University of Cork Press, 1993), 194–221. The *Aislinge meic Conglinne* was edited by Kuno Meyer and published in London in 1992.

6. Lisa Bitel points out, "The *dísert* (wasteland) of the saints was rarely far from clustered settlements.... Even the stone cells of the western shores, once thought to be the solitary retreats of hermits, were actually quite close to farms" (Bitel, 1993, 37).

7. See Patrick C. Power, *The Book of Irish Curses* (Cork: Mercier Press, and Springfield, Ill.: Templegate Publishers, 1974), 49.

8. Thomas Cahill, *How the Irish Saved Civilization* (New York: Doubleday, 1995), 114.

9. At present the standard work on the Irish Penitentials is still Ludwig Bieler, ed., *The Irish Penitentials,* with an appendix by D. A. Binchy, Scriptores Latini Hiberniae 5 (Dublin: Dublin Institute of Advanced Studies, 1975). Kenney references and discusses over a dozen principal Penitentials and canonical rules: the Penitential of Columban, the Penitential of Vinnian, the Penitential of Cummean, the Paenitentiale Bigotianum, the Penitential of Theodore, the Old-Irish Penitential, the Old-Irish Treatise on Commutations, the Penitential of Pseudo-Cummian, the Canones Hibernenses, the Pseudo-Patrician Synod: Synodus II Patricii, the Canones Adomnani, the Law of Adomnán (Cáin Adomnáin), and the Collectio Canonum Hibernensis (James F. Kenney, *The Sources for the Early History of Ireland: Ecclesiastical,* preface by Ludwig Bieler [Dublin: Four Courts Press, 1997], 235–49). See also J. T. McNeill, "The Celtic Penitentials," *Revue Celtique* 39 (1922): 257–300, and 40 (1923): 51–103, 320–24.

10. Patrick J. Corish, *The Irish Catholic Experience: A Historical Survey* (Dublin: Gill and Macmillan, 1985), 16.

11. For an extended discussion of the influence of the Penitentials, see Kenney, 1997, 243–44.

12. Ibid., 237.

13. The living representative of the saint, his *comarba,* usually made an annual circuit of the areas protected under the *cáin* to collect the duty or "cess." Today, the ordinary Irish word for "tax" is still *cáin.*

14. Kenney, 1997, 237, where Kenney remarks that there are in fact more than four *cána,* as the annalists mention enforcement of the "laws" of many saints.

15. Manuscripts exist in the Bodleian Museum (Rawl. B 512 ff–48–S IV) and the Royal Library in Brussels (2324–40 76–85), which was copied in 1627 by Michael O'Clery. See above, p. 213, n. 62.

16. The range of literature on women in Celtic countries is already vast and still growing. See, for example, Lisa M. Bitel, *Land of Women: Tales of Sex and Gender from Early Ireland* (Ithaca, N.Y.: Cornell University Press, 1996); Mary Condren, *The Serpent and the Goddess: Women, Religion, and Power in Celtic Ireland* (New York and London: Harper and Row, 1989); Christopher McAll, "The Normal Paradigms of a Woman's Life in the Irish and Welsh Law Texts," in *The Welsh Law of Women: Studies Presented to Professor David A. Binchy,* ed. Dafydd Jenkins and Morfydd E. Owen (Cardiff: University of Wales Press, 1980), 7–22; Jean Markale, *Women of the Celts,* trans. A. Mygind, C. Hauch, and P. Henry (Rochester, Vt.: Inner Traditions International, 1986); also published in England by Gordon and Cremonesi; originally published as *La Femme Celte* (Editions Payot, 1972); Donnchadh Ó Corráin, "Women in Early Irish Society," in *Women in Irish Society: The Historical Dimension,* ed. D. Ó Corráin and Margaret MacCurtain (Westport,

Conn.: Greenwood Press, 1980, 1–20); Patrick C. Power, *Sex and Marriage in Ancient Ireland* (Cork: Mercier Press, 1972). For a personal reflection on the changing situation of women in contemporary Ireland, see Rosemary Mahoney's *Whoredom in Kimmage* (Boston: Houghton Mifflin, 1993).

17. Bitel, 1993, 5.

18. See Bitel, 1996, 39–110. In an important article, however, Katherine Simms has shown that in medieval Ireland, divorce did not work to women's advantage. Cited by Bitel, 1996, 237, referring to Katherine Simms, "The Legal Position of Irishwomen in the Later Middle Ages," *Irish Jurist,* n.s. 10 (1975): 96–111.

19. Bitel, 1996, 31.

20. Kathleen Hughes, *Early Christian Ireland: Introduction to the Sources* (Ithaca, N.Y.: Cornell University Press, 1972), 46–47, where she notes, however, "Later the laws were modified so that if a man had no sons, and if male heirs failed within the *gelfine* [the descendants of a man's grandfather], his daughters inherited the land."

21. Ibid., 47. The term *adaltrach,* it should be noted, also means "adulteress." Moreover, "the *adaltrach* with sons enjoyed a higher status than the one without" (ibid., 48).

22. Ibid.

23. Cited by Márkus, p. 2 (Whitley Stokes's translation).

24. Peter O'Dwyer points out that the Law of Adomnán was not the only legislation that sought to protect clerics from military duty and reprisal. In 804, the high king of Ireland, Aed Oirdnide, was similarly pressured by Connmach, the bishop of Armagh and St. Patrick's successor, to exempt them from combat. Aed deferred to a Céle Dé, Fothad, who was highly regarded for the wisdom of his judgments. Fothad (d. 818) decided that all clerics should be exempt from "hostings and expeditions." See Peter O'Dwyer, O.Carm., *Céli Dé: Spiritual Reform in Ireland 750–900* (Dublin: Editions Tailliura, 1981), 124–31, 138–39.

25. See D'Arcy, 1985, 190–209.

26. For the life of Terence O'Brien and Peter Higgins, the prior of Naas, who was hanged in 1642, see Augustine Valkenburg, O.P., with Hugh Fenning, O.P., *Two Dominican Martyrs of Ireland* (Dublin: Dominican Publications, 1992).

27. D'Arcy, 1985, 196–97.

28. Hughes, 1972, 234, where she notes that "there is also a list of abbesses drawn up in the early ninth century." See Mario Esposito, *Proceedings of the Royal Irish Academy* 12, C (1910): 202–51."

29. Caroline Bingham, *Beyond the Highland Line: Highland History and Culture* (London: Constable, 1991), 64g.

30. See D'Arcy, 1985, 211–14. For a brief biography, also see Urban Flanagan, O.P., "Nano Nagle: 1718–1784," *Religious Life Review* 23, no. 107 (March–April 1984): 91–98.

31. See D'Arcy, 1985, 224–25.

32. See ibid., 221–22, and Sir Joseph Glynn, *The Life of Matt Talbot* (Dublin: Catholic Truth Society, 1925).

33. Patrick J. Corish, *The Irish Catholic Experience: A Historical Survey* (Dublin: Gill and Macmillan, 1985), 252.

34. Kenneth L. Woodward, *Making Saints: How the Catholic Church Determines Who Becomes a Saint, Who Doesn't, and Why* (New York: Simon & Schuster, 1990), 69–72, 117–19, 334–39, etc.

9. A Continuing Tradition

1. Oliver Davies, *Celtic Christianity in Early Medieval Wales: The Origins of the Welsh Spiritual Tradition* (Cardiff: University of Wales Press, 1996), 145.

2. Among them, let me mention A. M. Allchin, *God's Presence in the World: The Celtic Vision through the Centuries in Wales* (London: Darton, Longman and Todd, 1997); Christopher Bamford and William Parker Marsh, eds., *Celtic Christianity: Ecology and Holiness* (Edinburgh: Floris Press, 1986); Esther de Waal, *The Celtic Vision: Prayers and Blessings from the Outer Hebrides* (London: Darton, Longman and Todd, 1988); Noel Dermot O'Donoghue, *The Mountain behind the Mountain* (Edinburgh: T. & T. Clark, 1993); Timothy Joyce, *Celtic Christianity: A Sacred Tradition, a Vision of Hope* (Maryknoll, N.Y.: Orbis Books, 1998); Michael Minton, *The Soul of Celtic Spirituality in the Lives of Its Saints* (Mystic, Conn.: Twenty-Third Publications, 1996); originally published as *Restoring the Woven Cord* (London: Darton, Longman and Todd); John O'Donohue, *Anam Chara: Spiritual Wisdom from the Celtic World* (New York: Bantam, and London: Transworld, 1997); John J. Ó Ríordáin, C.SS.R., *The Music of What Happens: Celtic Spirituality, a View from the Inside* (Dublin: Columba Press, and Winona, Minn.: Saint Mary's Press, 1996); Edward C. Sellner, *The Wisdom of the Celtic Saints,* illustrated by Susan McLean-Keeney (Notre Dame, Ind.: Ave Maria Press, 1993); Philip Sheldrake, *Living between Worlds: Place and Journey in Celtic Spirituality* (London: Darton, Longman and Todd, 1995); Ray Simpson, *Exploring Celtic Spirituality: Historic Roots for Our Future* (London: Hodder and Stoughton, 1995); and Richard Woods, O.P., *Symbion: Spirituality for a Possible Future* (Santa Fe, N.Mex.: Bear and Co., 1983).

3. Cited by Eldred Willey, "The Jewel and the Flame," *The Month* (March 1995): 102.

4. Christopher Bamford, "The Heritage of Celtic Christianity: Ecology and Holiness," *The Celtic Consciousness,* ed. Robert O'Driscoll (New York: George Braziller, 1982), 182.

5. I have drawn some of these concluding remarks from earlier writings, especially "Environment as Spiritual Horizon: The Legacy of Celtic Monasticism," in *The Cry of the Environment: Rebuilding the Christian Creation Tradition,* ed. Philip Joranson and Ken Butigan (Santa Fe, N.Mex.: Bear and Co., 1984), 62–84; and "The Spirituality of the Celtic Church," *Spirituality Today* 37, no. 3 (1985): 243–55. This is mainly because my thinking on the matter has not altered. If anything, I am even more convinced that dis-covering the spirit of Celtic Christianity can assist coming generations in meeting the demands and challenges of living in a world dominated by technology, materialism, and violence.

6. For a recent account of the struggle for peace and justice in Northern Ireland, especially on the part of women, see *The Vision of Peace: Faith and Hope in Northern Ireland,* ed. John Dear (Maryknoll, N.Y.: Orbis Books, 1999), a collection of essays and letters by Nobel Laureate Mairead Corrigan Maguire, founder of the Community of Peace People.

7. For a more thorough treatment of this theme, see my article, "Environment as Spiritual Horizon," 1984.

8. Roberto Vacca, *The Coming Dark Age* (Garden City, N.Y.: Doubleday Anchor, 1978).

9. Ibid., 210–11. In the summer of 1999, a Methodist-Benedictine monastery for women was established on the grounds of St. John's Abbey in Collegeville, Min-

nesota. Named in honor of St. Brigid of Kildare, the monastery will follow the Rule of St. Benedict, but will be in accord with "the spirit of St. Brigid." See *United Methodist Review* 16, no. 20 (September 17, 1999): 1. Further information may be obtained from Dr. Mary Ewing Stamps at *mestamps@juno.com.*

Bibliography

Adomnán of Iona. *Life of St. Columba.* Intro. and trans. Richard Sharpe. London and New York: Penguin Books, 1995.

Allchin, A. M. *God's Presence in the World: The Celtic Vision through the Centuries in Wales.* London: Darton, Longman and Todd, 1997.

———. *Songs to Her God: Spirituality of Ann Griffiths.* Cambridge, Mass.: Cowley Publications, 1987.

Anderson, Alan O. *Early Sources of Scottish History, AD 500–1286.* London: Oliver and Boyd, 1922, 1990.

Baker, Derek. " 'A Nursery of Saints': St. Margaret of Scotland Reconsidered." In *Medieval Women,* ed. Derek Baker, Studies in Church History, Subsidia I, 119–41. Oxford: Basil Blackwell, 1978.

Bamford, Christopher. "The Heritage of Celtic Christianity: Ecology and Holiness." In *The Celtic Consciousness,* ed. Robert O'Driscoll, 169–84. New York: George Braziller, 1982.

Bamford, Christopher, and William Parker Marsh, eds. *Celtic Christianity: Ecology and Holiness.* Edinburgh: Floris Press, 1986.

Baring-Gould, Sabine, and John Fisher. *The Lives of the British Saints; The Saints of Wales and Cornwall and Such Irish Saints as Have Dedications in Britain.* 4 vols. London: C. J. Clark, 1907–13.

Bede. *A History of the English Church and People.* Trans. Leo Sherley-Price. Rev. R. W. Latham. London and New York: Penguin, 1968.

Bell, Martin J., ed. *The Celtic Languages.* London and New York: Routledge, 1993.

Bernard of Clairvaux. *The Life and Death of Saint Malachy the Irishman.* Trans. Robert T. Meyer. Cistercian Fathers series 10. Kalamazoo, Mich.: Cistercian Publications, 1978.

Bieler, Ludwig, ed. *The Irish Penitentials.* With an appendix by D. A. Binchy. Scriptores Latini Hiberniae 5. Dublin: Dublin Institute of Advanced Studies, 1975. *Paenitentiale S. Columbani,* 96–107.

Bingham, Caroline. *Beyond the Highland Line: Highland History and Culture.* London: Constable, 1991.

Bitel, Lisa M. "Women's Monastic Enclosures in Early Ireland: A Study of Female Spirituality and Male Monastic Mentalities." *Journal of Medieval History* 12 (1986): 15–36.

———. *Isle of the Saints: Monastic Settlement and Christian Community in Early Ireland.* Ithaca, N.Y.: Cornell University Press, 1990, and Cork: University of Cork Press, 1993.

———. *Land of Women: Tales of Sex and Gender from Early Ireland.* Ithaca, N.Y.: Cornell University Press, 1996.

Bowen, E. G. *Saints, Seaways and Settlements.* Cardiff: University of Wales Press, 1977.

———. *Dewi Sant, Saint David.* Cardiff: University of Wales Press, 1983.

Brown, Peter. "The Saint as Exemplar in Late Antiquity." In *Saints and Virtues,* ed. John Stratton Hawley, 3–14. Los Angeles and Berkeley: University of California Press, 1987.

Burke, Cormac, ed. *Studies in the Cult of St. Columba.* Dublin: Four Courts Press, 1997.

Bryce, Derek. *Symbolism of the Celtic Cross.* Rev. ed. Felinfach, Lampeter, Wales: Llanerch Publishers, 1994.

Cahill, Thomas. *How the Irish Saved Civilization.* New York: Doubleday, 1995.

Caldecott, Mary. *Women in Celtic Myth.* Rochester, Vt.: Destiny Books, 1988, 1992.

Carey, John. *King of Mysteries: Early Irish Religious Writings.* Dublin: Four Courts Press, 1998.

Carmichael, Alexander. *Celtic Invocations.* Noroton, Conn.: Vineyard Books, 1977. Greatly abridged version of the *Carmina Gadelica.* Also published as *Celtic Prayers.* Selected by Avery Brooke. Calligraphy by Laurel Casazza. New York: Seabury, 1981.

Chadwick, Nora. *The Celts.* London and New York: Penguin Books, 1971.

Clancy, Joseph P., ed. and trans. *The Earliest Welsh Poetry.* London: Macmillan, and New York: St. Martin's Press, 1970.

Clancy, Thomas Owen, and Gilbert Márkus, O.P. *Iona: The Earliest Poetry of a Celtic Monastery.* Edinburgh: Edinburgh University Press, 1995.

Corish, Patrick J. *The Irish Catholic Experience: A Historical Survey.* Dublin: Gill and Macmillan, 1985.

Dales, Douglas. *Light to the Isles: Missionary Theology in Celtic and Anglo Saxon Britain.* Cambridge: Lutterworth Press, 1998.

D'Arcy, Mary Ryan. *The Saints of Ireland.* Foreword by Cardinal Tomás Ó Fiach. Cork: Mercier Press, 1974, 1985.

Davies, Oliver. *Celtic Christianity in Early Medieval Wales: The Origins of the Welsh Spiritual Tradition.* Cardiff: University of Wales Press, 1996.

Davies, Oliver, and Fiona Bowie, eds. *Celtic Christian Spirituality: An Anthology of Medieval and Modern Sources.* London: SPCK, 1995, and New York: Continuum, 1999.

Davies, Wendy. *Wales in the Early Middle Ages.* Leicester: Leicester University Press, 1982.

Davis, Courtney. *The Book of Celtic Saints.* Text by Elaine Gill. London: Blandford, and New York: Sterling, 1995.

Delaney, Frank. *The Celts.* Boston, Little, Brown, 1986.

de Paor, Liam. *St. Patrick's World: The Christian Culture of Ireland's Apostolic Age.* Dublin: Four Courts Press, 1997.

de Paor, Máire B., P.B.V.M., ed. and trans. *Patrick the Pilgrim Apostle of Ireland: St. Patrick's Confessio and Epistola.* Dublin: Veritas, 1998.

de Paor, Máire and Liam. *Early Christian Ireland.* London and New York: Thames and Hudson, 1978.

Doble, Gilbert H. *The Saints of Cornwall.* Ed. Donald Atwater. Truro: Dean and Chapter, and London: Chatham, 1960.

———. *Lives of the Welsh Saints.* Ed. D. Simon Evans. Cardiff: University of Wales Press, 1971. Biographical essays on Saints Dubricius, Iltyd, Paulinus, Teilo, and Oudoceus.

Duckett, Eleanor. *The Wandering Saints of the Early Middle Ages.* New York: W. W. Norton, 1959, 1964. Includes short biographies of Patrick, Ninian, Columba, Kenneth, Kentigern, Oswald, Aidán, Cuthbert, Columban, Gall, Ouen, Fursey, Amand, Willibrord, and other saints woven into a superb historical overview.

Finlay, Ian. *Columba.* Glasgow: Richard Drew Publishing, 1990; originally published London: Victor Gollancz, 1979.

Flanagan, Urban, O.P. "Nano Nagle: 1718–1784." *Religious Life Review* 23, 107 (March–April 1984): 91–98.

Forristal, Desmond. *Man in the Middle: St. Laurence O'Toole, Patron Saint of Dublin.* San Francisco: Ignatius Press, 1988.

Gildas. *The Ruin of Britain and Other Works.* Ed. and trans. Michael Winterbottom. London and Chichester: Phillimore, 1978. (2) Text: ed. Theodore Mommsen, MGH AA xiii = *Chronica minora* iii, 25–88.

Hanson, R. P. C. *St. Patrick, His Origins and Career.* Oxford: Clarendon Press, 1968.

Heffernan, Thomas J. *Sacred Biography: Saints and Their Biographers in the Middle Ages.* Oxford and New York: Oxford University Press, 1988.

Heist, William W. *Vitae Sanctorum Hiberniae.* Subsidia Hagiographica 28. Brussels: Société des Bollandists, 1965.

Henken, Elissa R. *Traditions of the Welsh Saints.* Cambridge and New York: Cambridge University Press, 1987.

———. *Welsh Saints: A Study of Patterned Lives.* Cambridge: D. S. Brewer, 1991.

Herbert, Máire. *Iona, Kells and Derry: The History and Hagiography of the Monastic Familia of Columba.* Oxford: Clarendon Press, 1988.

Herm, Gerard. *The Celts: The People Who Came Out of Darkness.* New York: St. Martin's Press, 1977.

Hood, Allan B. E., ed. and trans. *St. Patrick: His Writings and Muirchu's Life.* Arthurian Period Sources 9. London: Phillimore, 1978.

Howlett, D. R. *The Book of Letters of Saint Patrick the Bishop.* Dublin: Four Courts Press, 1993.

Hughes, Kathleen. *Early Christian Ireland: Introduction to the Sources.* Ithaca, N.Y.: Cornell University Press, 1972.

Hughes, Kathleen, and Ann Hamlin, *Celtic Monasticism.* New York: Seabury, 1981. (=*The Modern Traveller to the Irish Church.* London: SPCK, 1977.)

Iohannis Scotti Eriugenae. *Periphyseon (De Divisione Naturae).* Ed. I. P. Sheldon-Williams and Ludwig Bieler. 3 vols. Dublin: Dublin Institute for Advanced Studies, 1968.

Jackson, Kenneth. *Studies in Early Celtic Nature Poetry.* Cambridge University Press, 1935; Felinfach, Lampeter, Wales: Llanerch Publishers, 1995.

James, J. W. *Rhygyfarch's Life of St. David.* Cardiff: University of Wales Press, 1967.

Johannes Scottus Eriugena. *Treatise on Divine Predestination.* Trans. Mary Brennan. Notre Dame Texts in Medieval Culture 5. Notre Dame, Ind.: University of Notre Dame Press, 1999.

Johnson, Stephen. *Later Roman Britain.* London and Toronto: Granada, 1982.

Jones, T. Thornley. *Saints, Knights and Llannau.* Llandysul, Dyfed, Wales: Gomer Press, 1975.

Joyce, Timothy. *Celtic Christianity: A Sacred Tradition, a Vision of Hope.* Maryknoll, N.Y.: Orbis Books, 1998.

Kennedy, Conan. *Ancient Ireland: The User's Guide.* Killala, Ireland: Morrigan Books, 1997.

Kenney, James F. *The Sources for the Early History of Ireland: Ecclesiastical.* Preface by Ludwig Bieler. Dublin: Four Courts Press, 1997; originally published New York: Columbia University Press, 1929.

Kieckhefer, Richard, and George D. Bond, eds. *Sainthood: Its Manifestations in World Religions.* Berkeley: University of California Press, 1988.

Lacey, Brian. *Colum Cille and His Legacy.* Dublin: Four Courts Press, 1997.

Lapidge, Michael, and David Dumville, eds. *Gildas: New Approaches.* Woodbridge, Suffolk: Boydell and Brewer, 1984.

Lehane, Brendan. *Early Celtic Christianity.* London: Constable, 1968, 1994.

Low, Mary. *Celtic Christianity and Nature.* Edinburgh: Edinburgh University Press, 1996.

McCone, Kim. "An Introduction to Early Irish Saints' Lives." *Maynooth Review* 11 (1984): 26–59.

McDonald, R. Andrew. *The Kingdom of the Isles: Scotland's Western Seaboard c. 1100–c. 1336.* Scottish Historical Review Monographs Series. East Lothian: Tuckwell Press, 1997.

Mackey, James P., ed. *An Introduction to Celtic Christianity.* Edinburgh: T. & T. Clark, 1989.

McNally, Robert, S.J., ed. *Old Ireland.* New York: Fordham University Press, 1965.

MacNamara, Martin. "The Bible in Irish Spirituality." In *Irish Spirituality,* ed. Michael Maher, 35. Dublin: Veritas Publications, 1979.

McNeill, John T. *The Celtic Churches: A History, A.D. 200 to 1200.* Chicago: University of Chicago Press, 1974.

Macquarrie, Alan. *The Saints of Scotland: Essays in Scottish History AD 450–1093.* Edinburgh: John Donald Publishers, 1997.

MacQueen, John. "Myth and the Legends of Lowland Scottish Saints." *Scottish Studies* 24 (1980): 1–21.

Maher, Michael, ed. *Irish Spirituality.* Dublin: Veritas Publications, 1979.

Markale, Jean. *Women of the Celts.* Trans. A. Mygind, C. Hauch, and P. Henry. Rochester, Vt.: Inner Traditions International, 1986. Orig.: *La Femme Celte.* Editions Payot, 1972.

Márkus, Gilbert, O.P., trans. *Adomnán's "Law of the Innocents," Cáin Adomnáin.* Glasgow: Blackfriars Books, 1997.

Metcalfe, W. M. *Pinkerton's Lives of the Scottish Saints.* Paisley, 1889. Reprint of J. Pinkerton's *Vitae antiquae sanctorum* (London, 1789).

Mheara, Róisín Ní. *In Search of Irish Saints: The Peregrinatio pro Christo.* Dublin: Four Courts Press, 1994.

Minton, Michael. *The Soul of Celtic Spirituality in the Lives of Its Saints.* Mystic, Conn.: Twenty-Third Publications, 1996; originally published as *Restoring the Woven Cord.* London: Darton, Longman and Todd, 1996.

Murphy, Gerard, ed. *Early Irish Lyrics.* Foreword by Tomás Ó Cathasaigh. Dublin: Four Courts Press, 1956, 1998.

Nagy, Joseph Falaky. *Conversing with Angels and Ancients: Literary Myths of Medieval Ireland.* Ithaca, N.Y.: Cornell University Press, 1997.

Neeson, Eoin. *The Book of Irish Saints.* Cork: Mercier Press, 1967.

Nennius, *British History and the Welsh Annals*. Ed. and trans. John Morris. London: Phillimore, and Totowa, N.J.: Rowman and Littlefield, 1980.

Nicholson, M. Forthomme. "Celtic Theology: Pelagius." In Mackey, 1989, 386–413.

O Cróinín, Dáithí. *Early Medieval Ireland 400–1200*. London: Longman, 1995.

O'Donoghue, Noel Dermot. *Patrick of Ireland: Aristocracy of Soul*. Wilmington, Del.: Michael Glazier, 1987.

———. *The Mountain behind the Mountain*. Edinburgh: T. & T. Clark, 1993.

O'Driscoll, Robert, ed. *The Celtic Consciousness*. New York: George Braziller, 1981.

O'Dwyer, Peter, O.Carm. *Céli Dé: Spiritual Reform in Ireland 750–900*. Dublin: Editions Tailliura, 1981.

———. "Celtic Monks and the Culdee Reform." In Mackey, 1989, 140–71.

———. *Towards a History of Irish Spirituality*. Blackrock, County Dublin: Columba Press, 1995.

Ó Fiach, Tomás. "Irish Monks on the Continent." In Mackey, 1989, 101–39.

———. *Columbanus in His Own Words*. Dublin: Veritas, 1974, 1990.

O Fiannachta, Pádraig. "The Spirituality of the Céli Dé." In *Irish Spirituality*, ed. Michael Maher, 22–32. Dublin: Veritas, 1979.

Ó Laoghaire, Diarmuid, S.J. "Celtic Spirituality." In *The Study of Spirituality*, ed. Cheslyn Jones, Geoffrey Wainwright, and Edward Yarnold, 216–25. Oxford and New York: Oxford University Press, 1986.

———. "Soul Friendship." In *Traditions of Spiritual Guidance*, ed. Lavinia Byrne. Collegeville, Minn.: Liturgical Press, 1990.

O Maidin, Vincent, O.C.S.O. "The Ancient Monastic Rules of Ireland." *Religious Life Review* 21, no. 94 (January–February 1982): 4–17.

Ó Ríordáin, John J., C.S.S.R. *Irish Catholics: Tradition and Transition*. Dublin: Veritas, 1980.

———. *The Music of What Happens: Celtic Spirituality, a View from the Inside*. Dublin: Columba Press, and Winona, Minn.: Saint Mary's Press, 1996.

———. *A Pilgrim in Celtic Scotland*. Blackrock, County Dublin: Columba Press, 1997.

Pennick, Nigel. *The Celtic Saints*. London: Thorson, 1997.

Plummer, Charles. *Bethada Náem nÉrenn*. 2 vols. Oxford: Clarendon Press, 1922, 1968.

———. *Vitae Sanctorum Hiberniae*. 2 vols. Oxford: Clarendon Press, 1910.

Power, Patrick C. *Sex and Marriage in Ancient Ireland*. Cork: Mercier Press, 1972.

———. *The Book of Irish Curses*. Cork: Mercier Press, and Springfield, Ill.: Templegate Publishers, 1974.

Raftery, Joseph, ed. *The Celts*. The Thomas Davis Lecture Series. Dublin and Cork: Mercier Press, 1964.

Rodgers, Michael, and Marcus Losack. *Glendalough: A Celtic Pilgrimage*. Blackrock, County Dublin: Columba Press, 1996.

Ryan, John, S.J. *Irish Monasticism: Origins and Development*. Dublin: Four Courts Press, 1931, 1992.

Sellner, Edward C. *The Wisdom of the Celtic Saints*. Illustrated by Susan McLean-Keeney. Notre Dame, Ind.: Ave Maria Press, 1993.

Sharpe, Richard. *Medieval Irish Saints' Lives: An Introduction to Vitae Sanctorum Hiberniae*. Oxford: Clarendon Press, 1991.

Sheehy, M. P. "Concerning the Origins of Early Medieval Irish Monasteries." *Irish Theological Quarterly* 29 (1962): 136–44.

Sheldrake, Philip. *Living between Worlds: Place and Journey in Celtic Spirituality.* London: Darton, Longman and Todd, 1995.

Skene, William F. *Celtic Scotland: A History of Ancient Alban.* 3 vols. Edinburgh: David Douglas, 1886–90.

Simpson, Ray. *Exploring Celtic Spirituality: Historic Roots for Our Future.* London: Hodder and Stoughton, 1995.

Taylor, Thomas, trans. *The Life of St. Samson.* London, 1925; Felinfach, Lampeter, Wales: Llanerch Publishers, 1991.

Thesaurus Paleohibernicus: A Collection of Old Irish Glosses, Scholia, Prose and Verse. Ed. Whitley Stokes and John Strachan, 2 vols. Cambridge, 1901–3.

Thomas, Charles. *Christianity in Roman Britain to AD 500.* Berkeley and Los Angeles: University of California Press, 1981.

Travis, James. *Early Celtic Versecraft.* Ithaca, N.Y.: Cornell University Press, 1973.

Tripartite Life of St. Patrick (Bethu Pátric). Ed. Kathleen Mulchrone. Dublin, 1939. Also ed. and trans. Whitley Stokes (Rolls Series, London, 1887).

Valkenburg, Augustine, O.P., with Hugh Fenning, O.P. *Two Dominican Martyrs of Ireland.* Dublin: Dominican Publications, 1992.

Waal, Esther de. *The Celtic Vision: Prayers and Blessings from the Outer Hebrides.* London: Darton, Longman and Todd, 1988. Based on Alexander Carmichael's *Carmina Gadelica.*

Wade-Evans, Arthur W. *Vitae Sanctorum Britanniae et Genealogiae.* Cardiff: University of Wales Press, 1944.

Walker, G. S. M., ed. *Sancti Columbani Opera.* Dublin: Dublin Institute of Advanced Studies, 1970.

Wallace, Martin. *Celtic Saints.* Illustrated by Ann MacDuff. Belfast: Appletree Press, and San Francisco: Chronicle Books, 1995.

Walsh, John R., and Thomas Bradley. *A History of the Irish Church 400–700 AD.* Dublin: Columba Press, 1991.

Webb, J. F. *Lives of the Saints.* New York: Penguin Books, 1965.

Whiteside, Lesley. *In Search of Columba.* Dublin: Columba Press, 1995.

Woods, Richard, O.P. "Environment as Spiritual Horizon: The Legacy of Celtic Monasticism." In *The Cry of the Environment: Rebuilding the Christian Creation Tradition,* ed. Philip Joranson and Ken Butigan, 62–84. Santa Fe, N.Mex.: Bear and Co., 1984.

———. "The Spirituality of the Celtic Church." *Spirituality Today* 37, no. 3 (1985): 243–55.

Woodward, Kenneth L. *Making Saints: How the Catholic Church Determines Who Becomes a Saint, Who Doesn't, and Why.* New York: Simon & Schuster, 1990.

Index

Aaron (protomartyr), St., 28, 29, 187
Abáin. *See* Abbán
Abbán, 10, 87
Aberdeen, 115
Aberdeen Breviary, 104
Abernathy, 70
abortion. *See* termination of pregnancy
Achonry, 187
Acta, 24
adaltrach, 66, 168, 223n.21
Adhracht. *See* Attracta (Adhracht)
Adomnán (Eunan), St.: accepting Whitby reforms, 75; biography of Columcille and, 196n.36; Cainnech and, 107; on Cogitosus's Life of Brigid, 22; on Columba, 73–74, 110; feast day of, 188; overview of, 95–96; Scotland and, 112–14; Serf of Fife and, 105; social justice and, 161; on women, 169–70
Aedán mac Gabráin, 109
Aedh, King, 158
Aed Oirdnide, 223n.24
Aelred of Rievaulx, 200n.26
Aghaboe, 59, 84, 115
Aidán (Maedoc), St., 185
Aidán of Lindisfarne, St.: Columba and, 75; feast day of, 188; mission to the English church, 42, 43; in Northumbria, 41; overview of, 95; the Picts and, 44; as true "Apostle of England," 33; women and, 199n.24
Ailbe of Emly, 50, 56, 76–77, 188, 209n.3
Alba, 107–8
Alban (protomartyr), St., 28–29, 187
Alcuin, 21
Aldfrith, 113
Aleth (Malo), St., 124
Alexander, Jon, 192n.11
Alphabet of Piety, 165

Altus, 49
Anam Chara (O'Donohue), 3
anamchara (soul-friends), 62, 64, 84, 86, 113, 165
Andrew, St., 2, 103–4, 189
Angus, King, 103–4
animals: Brigid and, 68, 69–70; Celtic poets on, 143; Ciarán of Clonmacnois and, 82; Ciarán of Saighir and, 51, 204n.20; Columba and, 74; Gall (St.) and, 134; Kevin and, 89; Moling and, 93; Molúa and, 94
Annegray, 128
Anselm, 46
Anthony of Egypt, 143
Applecross, 107–8
Aran Islands, 78
Ardagh, 185, 188
Ard Macha. *See* Armagh
Ardmore, 50
Ardstraw, 87
Arianism, 195n.26
Aristotle, 194n.22
Armagh: Ceallach and, 186; Malachy and, 99; Monenna and, 79; Patrick and, 50, 51, 53, 56, 59, 205n.27; Plunkett and, 171; relation of town to monastery, 65
Arthur, King, 26–27, 39, 125–26
Artrí son of Faelmaire, 221n.40
Asaph, St., 40, 186
asceticism: of the Célí Dé, 144–45; David of Menevia's extreme, 37–38; in early Irish monasticism, 20, 60, 62. *See also* green martyrdom; hermits
Asicus. *See* Assic (Asicus)
Assic (Asicus), 77, 186
Athala, 131
Attracta (Adhracht), 77, 187
Augustine of Canterbury, 33, 41–42
Augustine of Hippo, St., 18, 29

233

Energy, Chaos, and Chemical Change

By the same authors

By A. H. Johnstone and T. I. Morrison
Chemistry Takes Shape, Books 1–5

By A. H. Johnstone and Iain Duncan
Chemistry Check-up

By A. H. Johnstone, T. I. Morrison, and J. T. McCarron
Test Your Chemistry

Energy, Chaos, and Chemical Change

Concepts and Applications of Chemical Thermodynamics

A. H. Johnstone, B.Sc., Ph.D., F.R.I.C.
G. Webb, B. Sc., Ph.D., M.R.I.C.
Senior Lecturers in Chemistry, University of Glasgow

Heinemann Educational Books
London and Edinburgh

Heinemann Educational Books
22 Bedford Square, London WC1B 3HH
London Edinburgh Melbourne Auckland
Hong Kong Singapore Kuala Lumpur New Delhi
Ibadan Nairobi Johannesburg
Exeter (NH) Kingston Port of Spain

ISBN 0 435 65525 6
© A. H. Johnstone and G. Webb 1977
First published 1977
Reprinted 1979

Filmset and printed Offset Litho in Great Britain by
Fakenham Press Ltd

Preface

Writing a book can be at the same time an exhilarating and an exhausting experience. The excitement of tossing ideas around, hitting upon new ideas, and discovering new approaches can sometimes blunt the authors' critical faculties.

It is especially important, therefore, to have the helpful and critical advice of colleagues who have not been directly involved in the writing. We have been particularly fortunate in having comments from a group of experienced teachers and we should like to offer our thanks to Professor D. W. A. Sharp, Professor S. J. Thomson, and Mr N. Reid of the University of Glasgow; Mr J. Smart of Dundee High School; and Mr J. Freeman of Gracemount School, Edinburgh.

1977   A.H.J.
                                                                        G.W.

Contents

Introduction for Teachers

From our experience of learning and teaching thermodynamics over many years, it has become clear that the subject can be 'understood' on more than one level. It is possible to understand the mathematics and equate this with an understanding of the concepts, but most chemists would confess to having undergone an undergraduate course in thermodynamics without really understanding what it was all about.

This book is about the basic concepts of thermodynamics. Mathematics has been replaced by what we hope is an accurate pictorial approach. We believe that no student will have to do any unlearning when he approaches the more advanced mathematical treatments of the subject and a sound conceptual basis will make it easier for him to pursue the subject further if required.

It is intended that this book should find a place both in sixth form work and in the early part of college and university courses, but it has been written with no particular syllabus in mind. It is our sincere conviction that a book of this kind is necessary to introduce young scientists, not only chemists, to the elegance of the methods and applications of this fascinating branch of science – a branch so often totally misunderstood and dreaded.

The book has been written in a personal style so that it can function as a self-instructional text, with fairly lengthy consolidation sections at regular intervals throughout. Fully worked answers to the problems in the consolidation sections are given at the end of the book.

There is no reason, however, why the book should not be used as a companion to any elementary course in thermodynamics and be a bridge book between senior school and university.

Introduction for Students

This book is about a very important area of science called thermo-dynamics. It is not the province solely of the physicist or chemist but has important things to say for all branches of science.

It is possible to approach the subject mathematically. This puts many people off and so we have chosen to teach the basic concepts in a pictorial fashion, which will form the basis for a possible mathematical treatment later in your studies.

The book can be used as a text in conjunction with normal lessons, but it can also be used as a self-instructional book. At the end of every few chapters there is a consolidation section, which we strongly urge you to work through before proceeding to the next piece of work. At the back of the book, the answers to the questions are fully worked out so that you can check your reasoning thoroughly.

It is our sincere hope that you will enjoy this introduction to a topic which has often earned for itself a poor image, not because of its subject matter, but because of the way in which it has been presented.

1 Why study Thermodynamics?

The idea of energy is basic to our way of living. We use the term frequently in all sorts of contexts, ranging from 'energy' to play games to the world 'energy' crisis. But what is energy? In what forms does it occur? Are there any rules by which we can rationalize our ideas of energy and its behaviour?

Energy and history

Let us go back into history to see how closely man's use of energy is bound up with the development of civilization. We shall then see the growth of ideas about energy and be in a better position to answer the questions posed in the previous paragraph.

One fact that primitive man learned was that energy can be converted into work. A man's personal capacity for doing work using the energy from his food and the 'machine' of his body is about 1/30 horsepower – about 25 watts ($J s^{-1}$). As long as man was solely dependent on his own unaided muscle power, the tasks he could perform were severely limited. Most kinds of building in wood or stone were outside his scope and he had to be content with the shelter which nature provided in caves or in simple forest cover.

The design of hand tools and weapons provided the means for the more effective use of man's muscle power. A club became the extension of his arm to allow him to deliver more effective blows. An axe was really a sharp edged club by which his arm was lengthened and his muscle power concentrated on a small area, allowing him to cut and chop. The sharp point of a spear or knife made it possible for him to focus his energies on to a very small area indeed and penetrate effectively. The possible range of work which man could do with his 1/30 horsepower was now very much extended.

Domestication of animals for their work energy, as well as for food, increased man's scope for work enormously. One horse or bullock could do the work of thirty men. Each man could effectively have the equivalent of the energetic services of thirty others.

As civilization has developed, man has been able to call upon more and more energy to do his work. In fact, the availability of energy has been a precondition for every material advance in our

Table 1.1

Energy source	Rate of energy delivery	
	Horsepower	$J\,s^{-1}$ (watts)
Man	1/30	25
Horse	1	750
Waterwheel	5	3750
Windmill	8	6000
First steam engines	100	75 000
Hydro-electric power station	3×10^6	2250×10^6

society (Table 1.1). In advanced countries today, an average hour's salary is enough to buy electricity equivalent to the work output of about 2000 men!

In our discussion we must not forget our food, the biological sources of energy which ultimately are the stored energy of the sun. When man learned to cultivate crops systematically, he was improving the efficiency by which he tapped the sun's energy. He had moved from a random, food-gathering, even nomadic existence to a settled existence and reliable food source. Similar considerations applied to animal farming, by which he no longer expended his energy hunting but had his 'prey' on hand in enclosed fields. Animals were converting the energy in plants into other forms which man could use at will.

Large energy sources

At present the world's sources of energy are almost all chemical in nature. As a result of chemical changes (almost all combustion) we obtain energy for our industrial, locomotive, and domestic uses (Figure 1.1).

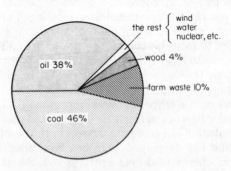

Figure 1.1

Our energy food sources are, of course, all chemical in nature and ultimately all of our energy sources (food and fuel) are derived from the sun, with the possible exception of·nuclear power.

Chemistry and energy

Bearing in mind this vital connection between chemistry and energy, it is important that chemists should spend time in the study of this aspect of their subject to understand how energy is released and how it can be used most effectively ; to discover the laws governing energy transfers and the consequences for the direction of chemical change.

This study is the province of *chemical thermodynamics* which is of importance not only to the chemist but also to the biologist, the engineer, the geologist, and the nutritionist to mention but a few.

The name *thermodynamics* implies that it has something to do with *heat* and *movement*. This is largely true in practice, but not exclusively so. The ideas and principles of thermodynamics are applicable to all other forms of energy, but historically the study began with heat and heat engines and the name has remained.

Forms of energy

Energy appears in many forms such as heat, light, electricity, sound, kinetic energy (the energy of movement), potential energy (the energy of position), and chemical energy. At first sight these may seem to be distinctly different forms of energy, but in reality some of them are the same. For example, heat is kinetic energy at a molecular level in which molecular motion as a whole or internal vibrations of the molecule's bonds are involved. The chemical energy associated with bond-making and bond-breaking is a form of potential energy, a consequence of the position of atoms relative to each other in a molecule.

Two very important rules have arisen from the study of energy in its different forms.

(a) *Energy can be converted from one form to another.* This is our everyday experience. The chemical energy in our food is converted into heat, maintaining our temperature, and also into kinetic energy as we move about. The potential energy of a clock spring changes into the mechanical movement of the hands and creates sound energy when the alarm rings.

(b) *The amount of energy in the universe is constant.* Another way of saying this is that 'energy can be neither created nor destroyed'.

A proviso must be added here because it is possible to convert matter into energy during a nuclear reaction (Chapter 13, page 77) and so, strictly speaking, we should say that 'the amount of mass and energy in the universe is constant'. From a chemical point of view we can stick to our original statement in (b).

The two ideas in (a) and (b) took a long time to become generally accepted. In the 1840s men like James Joule and Julius Mayer were convinced that there was an equivalence between one form of energy and another. Joule was particularly interested in the conversion of mechanical work into heat and, by patient experiment, established a numerical relationship between them. His contemporaries dismissed him as an eccentric, particularly when he suggested that the water at the bottom of the Niagara Falls should be 0.2 °F warmer than at the top because of the decrease in potential energy. Joule lived long enough to see his ideas accepted, but Mayer suffered a mental breakdown in face of the scepticism in his own country.

First Law of Thermodynamics

We can now arrive at a statement which combines both of the ideas above – 'In any process, energy can be changed from one form to another, but it is neither created nor destroyed.' This is the *First Law of Thermodynamics*.

This all looks very tidy, but somewhere at the back of your mind there may be a suspicion that everything is not so cut and dried. Steam locomotives run at only about 5 per cent efficiency, that is, only 5 per cent of the energy in the fuel is converted into work. Cars are rather better at 30 per cent efficiency, and power stations can reach about 30 to 35 per cent efficiency of conversion. Where does the rest of the energy go if the First Law holds? During the fuel crisis of 1974, an eminent politician was heard to say that power stations would have to become 100 per cent efficient to save fuel. He could have done with a course in thermodynamics! As we shall see later in this book, there are good and logical reasons why 100 per cent conversion of heat into work is not possible, and yet the First Law still holds good.

We intend to treat the subject in a practical way, which we hope you will see as having relevance to your future work and which will help your understanding of the energy changes vital to our bodies, our economy, and our civilization.

2   Agreeing the Terms

What is heat?

In almost every example of chemical change which you have met, heat has been involved. In some cases heat has been released, for example during the burning of metals or hydrocarbons, or the displacement of one metal from its compounds by another. Other reactions have required the addition of heat to make them take place – the decomposition of carbonates and nitrates are examples.

It would be a good idea to clear our minds about the nature of heat. As suggested in Chapter 1, it is a form of kinetic energy, the energy of motion, but at a molecular level. In a solid there is kinetic and potential energy involved in the vibration of molecules around a mean position and there may even be a slight amount of rotation. Any migration of molecules through a solid is very limited. In liquids, molecules vibrate and rotate and to some extent move bodily from place to place. Molecules in gases vibrate, rotate, and move quite rapidly from place to place (translate). Heat is this kinetic energy at molecular level. As the temperature decreases the motion diminishes until, at the absolute zero of temperature (0 K), the motion ceases.

The important thing about this motion is that it is quite randomly arranged among the molecules. The statistical chance of two neighbouring molecules moving perfectly in parallel is so low as to be nearly an impossibility.

Now compare this with the kinetic energy of a falling brick. In this case, all the particles which make up the brick are moving downwards together. Admittedly, they have some micro-random motion as they vibrate internally because of the brick's temperature, but the overriding direction is downwards (Figure 2.1).

When the brick lands on the bench its falling kinetic energy is destroyed and turned into heat and sound. That is, the random molecular vibrations increase in both the bench and the brick. The important thing to notice is that the 'parallel' kinetic energy of the particles in the falling brick has been converted to the random molecular kinetic energy we call heat. We can never persuade all the molecules to vibrate in parallel and lift the brick back up into the air again. This random nature of heat energy will keep on

predominant
kinetic
movement

kinetic energy at micro-level
because of temperature
of the brick

BENCH

BENCH

kinetic energy at micro-level
because of temperature of the bench

Figure 2.1

appearing in this book and will help us to understand some of the problems raised at the end of the last chapter.

What is enthalpy?

We have to clear up some terminology before we go much further and so let us begin with a term you may have used earlier without fully understanding it.

Imagine that we are carrying out a chemical reaction in a measuring cylinder (Figure 2.2 (a)). The cylinder is full of air down to the

air

(a)   (b)

Figure 2.2

surface of the reactants. During the reaction energy is released, mainly by the net effect of bond-making and bond-breaking processes. Let us call this internal energy change ΔE. If the reaction is releasing a gas, this gas has to fight its way out into the atmosphere by pushing back the air (Figure 2.2 (b)). To do this, some of the energy produced by the reaction will be diverted into doing work –

the work of pushing back a volume of air (ΔV) against atmospheric pressure (P). Since this is work coming *out* of the system, it has a negative sign.

If we try to measure ΔE, we cannot get its true value because of the work expended on pushing back the atmosphere. The value we obtain is usually indicated by ΔH and is called the **enthalpy change**.

We can sum this up in an equation

$$\Delta E = \Delta H - P\Delta V$$

Since chemists, for most practical purposes, do reactions in open vessels exposed to the air and any gases are allowed to go off into the air, it is usual to work with the enthalpy change (ΔH) and ignore the $P\Delta V$ part. These are constant pressure reactions.

ΔE	=	ΔH	−	$P\Delta V$
internal energy change		enthalpy change		'entrance fee' into the atmosphere

For reactions in which no gases are involved (and so the volume changes are tiny), ΔE and ΔH are the same for all practical purposes.

Another look at the First Law of Thermodynamics

You may already have met the First Law under a different guise and different name when it was called Hess's Law. This is really a particular example of the First Law. It says that 'the enthalpy change between reactants (in a specified state) and products (in a specified state) is independent of the route taken'. Look at this diagrammatically (Figure 2.3).

Let us suppose that the enthalpy change in going from substance A to substance B is ΔH_1 and that there is an alternative route to

Figure 2.3

get from A to B via substance C, in which there are two enthalpy changes, ΔH_2 and ΔH_3. Now if ΔH_1 is greater than the sum of ΔH_2 and ΔH_3, it would be possible to *create energy* by going from A to B directly and then going back to A via C. This violates the First Law and the only condition which satisfies the First Law is that

$$\Delta H_1 = \Delta H_2 + \Delta H_3$$

Hess's Law is a very powerful tool in helping us to unravel some of the energy problems in chemistry (see Chapter 3).

In the statement of Hess's Law above there were two parentheses referring to 'state'. Let us now deal with this word.

Standard state

It is important that when we do energy calculations we should agree upon some standards, otherwise our measurements are meaningless in relation to each other. For example, in the reaction

$$H_2 + \tfrac{1}{2}O_2 \rightarrow H_2O$$

there is no indication (a) of the amount of water formed, (b) if it is in the liquid or gaseous state, or (c) at what pressure it exists.

To avoid confusion, a common *Standard State* is defined as *1 mole of the substance at 1 atmosphere pressure* and the physical state is specified by (g), (l), or (s); the temperature is then specified by a subscript. For the reaction above the ΔH value, taking the Standard State into account, is written as ΔH_T°. In most books of tables the temperature is fixed at 25 °C or 298 K, but it need not be so long as the value of T is specified. We can now get all the necessary information from the equation

$$H_2(g) + \tfrac{1}{2}O_2(g) \rightarrow H_2O(l); \; \Delta H_{298}^\circ = -286 \, kJ$$

By common usage, it is assumed that if T is not specified it is 298 K. The equation, in words, now says that when one mole of hydrogen gas and half a mole of oxygen gas react to give one mole of liquid water at one atmosphere pressure and 298 K the enthalpy change is $-286 \, kJ$.

Throughout this book we shall use the *Standard Enthalpy Change*, ΔH°, in our calculations.

As a consequence of the First Law, enthalpy changes can be added and subtracted, multiplied and divided as ordinary numbers and so the arithmetic associated with enthalpy calculations is very simple indeed. We shall use this in the next chapter to solve apparently complex chemical energy problems.

3   Calculating the Impossible

In this chapter we shall spend some time using Hess's Law (a special case of the First Law of Thermodynamics) to solve some chemical problems.

Sign convention
There are two ways of looking at an enthalpy change in a reaction – from the point of view of the observer or from the point of view of the contents of the reaction vessel. If we are receiving heat from the reaction, it follows that the reactants are losing heat, and conversely if the contents of the reaction vessel become cold during the reaction, heat will flow from the surroundings (of which we are part) to warm the reactants.

By convention, enthalpy changes are viewed **from the reactants** and the sign applied to the ΔH value fits accordingly.

For a reaction which is giving out energy to its surroundings (an **exothermic reaction**) the enthalpy change, ΔH, is given a *negative* sign.

For a reaction which is taking in energy from its surroundings (an **endothermic reaction**) the enthalpy change, ΔH, is given a *positive* sign.

Hess's Law at work
Here is an equation for an apparently simple reaction

$$C \text{ (graphite)} + 2H_2(g) \rightarrow CH_4(g)$$

But in practice, if carbon and hydrogen react together, many carbon–hydrogen compounds can be formed and so methane is by no means the only product. How then can we find the enthalpy change when one mole of methane is made from its elements; in other words how can we find the heat of formation, ΔH_f°, of methane? ('Formation' is denoted by the subscript f.)

By definition, the *Standard Heat of Formation* of a substance is the enthalpy change when one mole of the substance is made from its elements in their Standard State. Heats of Formation must be measured from some arbitrary zero in the same way as the height of a mountain is taken from 'sea level'. In this chemical situation, all elements in their Standard States are assigned a zero value for their Heats of Formation, giving a base line from which to measure the ΔH_f° of the substances made from them.

Hess's Law can help us to solve the 'methane problem' if we know the enthalpy changes involved in a number of related reactions.

For instance, it is possible to measure the following enthalpy changes experimentally:

1.　　$CH_4(g) + 2O_2(g)$ 　　$\rightarrow CO_2(g) + 2H_2O(l)$; $\Delta H^{\circ} = -890 \, kJ$
2.　　$C \, (graphite) + O_2(g) \rightarrow CO_2(g)$;　　　$\Delta H^{\circ} = -394 \, kJ$
3.　　$H_2(g) + \tfrac{1}{2}O_2(g)$　　$\rightarrow H_2O(l)$;　　　$\Delta H^{\circ} = -286 \, kJ$

They are the Standard Heats of Combustion of methane, graphite, and hydrogen respectively.

When we compare our original 'unmeasurable' equation with the three 'measurable' equations we can see similarities. For example, one mole of carbon appears on the left of the original and also on the left of equation 2. Two moles of hydrogen gas appear on the left of the original equation. The same would apply to equation 3 if we doubled it throughout. In the original equation, a mole of methane appears on the right and the same would apply to equation 1 if we wrote it in reverse. Let us make these amendments and see how far this takes us.

New equation 1 now reads

$$CO_2(g) + 2H_2O(l) \rightarrow CH_4(g) + 2O_2(g); \; \Delta H^{\circ} = +890 \, kJ$$

Note that the value of ΔH° remains the same, but its sign changes.

Equation 2 remains unchanged as

$$C \, (graphite) + O_2(g) \rightarrow CO_2(g); \; \Delta H^{\circ} = -394 \, kJ$$

New equation 3 now reads

$$2H_2(g) + O_2(g) \rightarrow 2H_2O(l); \; \Delta H^{\circ} = -572 \, kJ$$

Note that the value of ΔH° is now doubled to allow for the making of *two* moles of water.

If we now add all these equations together algebraically we get

$$\left. \begin{array}{l} CO_2(g) + 2H_2O(l) + C \, (graphite) \\ + O_2(g) + 2H_2(g) + O_2(g) \end{array} \right\} \rightarrow \left\{ \begin{array}{l} CH_4(g) + 2O_2(g) + CO_2(g) \\ + 2H_2O(l); \; \Delta H^{\circ} = -76 \, kJ \end{array} \right.$$

Some substances appear on both sides of this equation. If we remove those that are common, we are left with

$$C \, (graphite) + 2H_2(g) \rightarrow CH_4(g); \; \Delta H^{\circ} = -76 \, kJ$$

and so we have been able to calculate a value which was impossible to achieve directly by experiment.

Here is another example, but with less explanation this time.

If we want to find ΔH_f° for $ICl(g)$ we first write the equation

$$\tfrac{1}{2}I_2(s) + \tfrac{1}{2}Cl_2(g) \rightarrow ICl(g)$$

Given the following information we can calculate the result.

1. $Cl_2(g) \rightarrow 2Cl(g);$ $\Delta H^\circ = +242\,kJ$
2. $I_2(g) \;\; \rightarrow 2I(g);$ $\Delta H^\circ = +151\,kJ$
3. $I_2(s) \;\; \rightarrow I_2(g);$ $\Delta H^\circ = +\;\;63\,kJ$
4. $ICl(g) \rightarrow I(g) + Cl(g);$ $\Delta H^\circ = +211\,kJ$

If we halve equations 1 and 3, we have the makings of the left-hand side of the original equation and if we reverse 4, we have the right-hand side of the original equation.

New equation 1. $\tfrac{1}{2}Cl_2(g)$ $\rightarrow Cl(g);$ $\Delta H^\circ = +121\,kJ$

New equation 3. $\tfrac{1}{2}I_2(s)$ $\rightarrow \tfrac{1}{2}I_2(g);$ $\Delta H^\circ = +\;\;31.5\,kJ$

New equation 4. $I(g) + Cl(g) \rightarrow ICl(g);$ $\Delta H^\circ = -211\,kJ$

Let us add these together to give equation 5.

5. $\tfrac{1}{2}Cl_2(g) + \tfrac{1}{2}I_2(s) + I(g) + Cl(g) \rightarrow Cl(g) + \tfrac{1}{2}I_2(g) + ICl(g);$ $\Delta H^\circ = -58.5\,kJ$

or, more simply,

$$\tfrac{1}{2}Cl_2(g) + \tfrac{1}{2}I_2(s) + I(g) \rightarrow \tfrac{1}{2}I_2(g) + ICl(g); \quad \Delta H^\circ = -58.5\,kJ$$

We still have not arrived at the original equation. $I(g)$ and $I_2(g)$ still have to be eliminated. This can easily be done by using half of equation 2 and adding it to equation 5.

New equation 2. $\tfrac{1}{2}I_2(g) \rightarrow I(g);$ $\Delta H^\circ = +75.5\,kJ$

Equation 5. $\tfrac{1}{2}Cl_2(g) + \tfrac{1}{2}I_2(s) + I(g) \rightarrow \tfrac{1}{2}I_2(g) + ICl(g);$ $\Delta H^\circ = -58.5\,kJ$

This gives

$$\tfrac{1}{2}Cl_2(g) + \tfrac{1}{2}I_2(s) \rightarrow ICl(g); \quad \Delta H^\circ = +17\,kJ$$

or the heat of formation, ΔH_f°, of $ICl(g)$ is $+17\,kJ\,mol^{-1}$.

At the end of this chapter there are a few more examples to give you the opportunity to improve your skill.

Another way of using Hess's Law

On page 3 it was suggested that the energy associated with bonds was a form of potential energy. It would be interesting and useful to get some idea of how much energy is associated with a bond. We cannot take an isolated molecule and pluck an atom from it like plucking a petal from a flower. We must be content with handling molecules in bulk, millions of them at a time, and arriving indirectly at the values we want. To do this we can visualize the bonding processes in a step-by-step fashion and so obtain the required energy values. This is where Hess's Law comes into its own.

Suppose that we want to find the average energy associated with a nitrogen–hydrogen bond in ammonia. Beginning with nitrogen gas and hydrogen gas, what steps take place in the formation of ammonia?

1. The nitrogen molecules will have to break to give nitrogen atoms

$$\tfrac{1}{2}N_2(g) \rightarrow N(g)$$

2. The hydrogen molecules will have to break to give hydrogen atoms

$$\tfrac{3}{2}H_2(g) \rightarrow 3H(g)$$

3. The nitrogen and hydrogen will have to combine to give ammonia

$$N(g) + 3H(g) \rightarrow NH_3(g)$$

The enthalpy change when half a mole of nitrogen gas is split into separate atoms is known experimentally to be +472 kJ. The enthalpy change when 3/2 moles of hydrogen gas split into separate

Figure 3.1

atoms is known experimentally to be $+654\,kJ$. Notice that both of these values are positive because bonds are being broken.

   N.B. – bond breaking *always* costs energy and *never* releases energy. There are no magical 'high-energy bonds' which release energy when they are broken.

Let us set this out in a cyclic diagram called a Born–Haber cycle (Figure 3.1).

One other piece of information required to complete the cycle is the heat of formation of ammonia, which is $-46\,kJ$.

We have now made a Hess's Law type of diagram. The enthalpy change (x) between ammonia and its constituent atoms ($N+3H$) must be the same as the sum of the enthalpy changes in the multistage process represented by the left-hand side of the diagram.

$$x = 46 + 472 + 654 \, kJ$$

$$= 1172 \, kJ$$

If we are thinking about the energy required for

$$NH_3(g) \rightarrow N(g) + 3H(g)$$

the value of x will be *positive* because this is a *bond-breaking* process.

On the other hand if we are interested in the energy released for

$$N(g) + 3H(g) \rightarrow NH_3(g)$$

the value of x will be *negative* because a *bond-making* process gives out energy.

We are now within sight of our original goal; to find out the average energy associated with one mole of nitrogen–hydrogen bonds in ammonia. The value of x corresponds to three moles of N–H bonds and so the average N–H bond enthalpy is one third of $1172\,kJ\,mol^{-1}$

$$= \frac{1172}{3} kJ \, mol^{-1}$$

$$= 391 \, kJ \, mol^{-1}$$

This is a considerable amount of energy – more than enough to bring a litre of water at room temperature to the boil! It is important to stress that these are *average* bond enthalpies because an N–H bond has slightly different enthalpy values depending upon the compound in which it exists. For example, by similar calculations it is possible to compile a set of values for the average enthalpy associated with a range of bonds (see page 93).

Let us try a more complicated example, although arithmetically it is very simple if we reason it out step by step.

What is the average enthalpy associated with a C–C bond in propane?

$$3C \text{ (graphite)} + 4H_2(g) \rightarrow H-\underset{\overset{|}{H}}{\overset{\overset{H}{|}}{C}}-\underset{\overset{|}{H}}{\overset{\overset{H}{|}}{C}}-\underset{\overset{|}{H}}{\overset{\overset{H}{|}}{C}}-H \text{ (g)}$$

List the *bond-breaking steps* required to produce the pieces from which the propane molecule will be made.

1.   3 moles of solid carbon will have to be broken into separate carbon atoms, that is, $3 \times$ Sublimation Energy of Carbon (obtainable from the table on page 93).

Figure 3.2

2. 4 moles of hydrogen gas molecules will have to be broken to give 8 moles of hydrogen atoms, i.e. $4 \times$ H–H bond energy (see table on page 93).

Now for the bond-making steps:

1. 8 moles of C–H bonds have to be made (see page 93).
2. 2 moles of C–C bonds have to be made (to be found from our calculation).

By plotting the bond-breaking (endothermic) processes on the left of the cycle and the bond-making (exothermic) processes on the right we get a Born–Haber diagram like Figure 3.2.

The enthalpy change in making a mole of $C_3H_8(g)$ from 3 moles of $C(g)$ and 8 moles of $H(g)$ must be the same whether we go down the left or down the right of the diagram (Hess's Law).

$$3296 + x = 1744 + 2145 + 104$$

$$x = 697 \, kJ$$

But x corresponds to the formation of two moles of C–C bonds. Therefore the enthalpy associated with one mole of C–C bonds

$$= \frac{697}{2} kJ$$

$$= 348 \, kJ$$

Using the tables on pages 92–94, try the examples in the following Consolidation Section for yourself. This is not difficult work, but it needs practice. Please do not miss out this Consolidation Section – it contains useful extra material and some calculations to try. The answers are worked out fully for you on page 95.

Consolidation of Chapters 1 to 3

In Chapter 1 we saw the importance of a study of energy to the understanding of much that is basic to science and to society.

1. Here is a popular statement of the First Law of Thermodynamics. 'In energy terms you can't get something for nothing.' Go back to the more formal statement and satisfy yourself that the statements are identical.

Chapter 2 spent some time on the essential nature of heat as kinetic energy at molecular level.

2. Satisfy yourself that you understand why the 'falling kinetic energy' of the brick, when turned into heat, can never again be organized to raise the brick. It has been said that 'the difference between the macro (or large scale) kinetic energy of the brick and the micro kinetic energy (heat) into which it is converted, is the difference between a bump on the head and burnt fingers'!

3. Make sure that you understand the need for a Standard State and be able to explain clearly what it means.

Chapter 3 was devoted to the use of Hess's Law as an elegant means of obtaining information which was not available from direct experimental measurement. A few extra examples are added now for you to try using the data on page 92. Full answers are available for these calculations on page 95, but you should try the calculations yourself before comparing your results with ours.

4. Calculate the energy required to break a mole of C–Cl bonds in the compound $CH_3Cl(g)$. The Standard Enthalpy of Formation, ΔH_f°, of $CH_3Cl(g)$ from solid carbon, hydrogen gas, and chlorine gas is $-82\,\mathrm{kJ\,mol^{-1}}$.

5. By definition, the Standard Heat of Formation of a substance, ΔH_f°, is the enthalpy change when one mole of the substance is made from its constituent elements in their Standard States. It follows, therefore, that *for elements themselves* in their Standard States, ΔH_f° must be zero. Look at Figure C.1 and then use it for the calculation following.

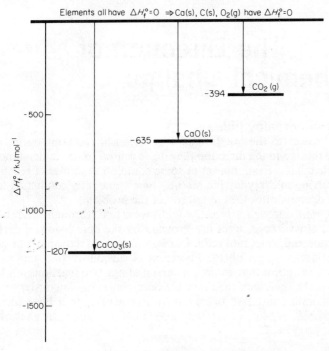

Figure C.1

Find ΔH° for the reaction

$$CaCO_3(s) \rightarrow CaO(s) + CO_2(g)$$

6. Given that

$$2P(s) + 3Cl_2(g) \rightarrow 2PCl_3(l); \quad \Delta H^\circ = -635 \, kJ \text{ (per equation)}$$

$$PCl_3(l) + Cl_2(g) \rightarrow PCl_5(s); \quad \Delta H^\circ = -137 \, kJ$$

Calculate the Standard Heat of Formation of solid PCl_5.

7. Calculate the Standard Enthalpy of Formation of $Ca(OH)_2(s)$ from the following data.

A $H_2(g) + \frac{1}{2}O_2(g) \rightarrow H_2O(l);$ $\Delta H^\circ = -285 \, kJ$

B $CaO(s) + H_2O(l) \rightarrow Ca(OH)_2(s);$ $\Delta H^\circ = -64 \, kJ$

C $Ca(s) + \frac{1}{2}O_2(g) \rightarrow CaO(s);$ $\Delta H^\circ = -635 \, kJ$

4   The Direction of Chemical Change

Down enthalpy hills

An answer to the question of why chemical reactions occur, and why they go in the direction they do, is central to our understanding of chemistry. Examination of some common examples of reactions occurring in everyday life reveals some apparently conflicting facts and demonstrates the complexity of the problem.

A walk through a forest would reveal that, through the process of photosynthesis, trees are growing by the conversion of carbon dioxide and water into cellulose (wood), while at the same time dead trees are rotting with the liberation of carbon dioxide and water. It would appear that, in similar surroundings, two reactions in which one is the reverse of the other are occurring simultaneously.

A similar situation occurs at an iron works. In a blast furnace iron oxide is being converted into iron at the same time as the iron

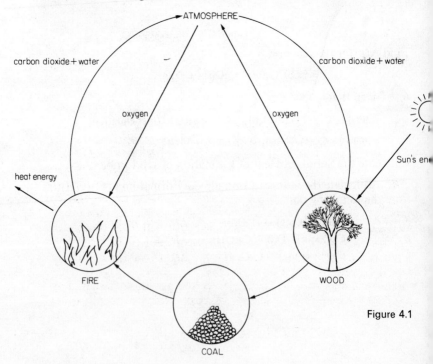

Figure 4.1

walls on the outside of the furnace are rusting to give iron oxide. The carbon cycle involving the formation and combustion of coal provides us with yet another example of a similar phenomenon (Figure 4.1).

Clearly the situation is much more complex than a simple consideration of the reactants and the products would reveal. We must look for other factors which are involved in determining the direction of change in a reaction. Let us take as an example the combustion of carbon (coke).

$$C(s) + O_2(g) \rightarrow CO_2(g)$$

We know that this reaction proceeds quite readily and that it is accompanied by the liberation of large amounts of energy as heat. The reaction is exothermic, since the enthalpy content of one mole of carbon and one mole of oxygen is greater than the enthalpy content of one mole of carbon dioxide and since

$$\Delta H^\circ = \Delta H_f^\circ \text{ (products)} - \Delta H_f^\circ \text{ (reactants)}$$

ΔH° will be negative.

ΔH_f° (products) and ΔH_f° (reactants) refer to the Enthalpies of Formation of the products and reactants respectively, relative to the Enthalpies of Formation of the elements.

It follows that if we consider the reverse reaction

$$CO_2(g) \rightarrow C(s) + O_2(g)$$

then, since $\Delta H_f^\circ(CO_2)$ is less than $(\Delta H_f^\circ(C) + \Delta H_f^\circ(O_2))$, this reaction must be endothermic. We are also aware that there is no tendency for this reaction to occur.

On the basis of this example it would seem that we might form a hypothesis that reactions which are exothermic are likely to occur whereas endothermic reactions are not. This seems quite reasonable since, by analogy with things in a physical world, we would expect that any process in which there is a decrease in energy will tend to occur. For example, a man standing at the top of a ladder will have a higher potential energy than when he is standing at the bottom of the ladder; there is a tendency for the man to fall from the top of the ladder to the bottom, but no tendency to fall from bottom to top. The direction of change is towards a lower energy state. Similarly, water tends to flow from the mountain side (high potential energy) down to the sea (low potential energy).

Let us examine our hypothesis further by considering the enthalpy changes of some other reactions which we know to occur quite readily.

$$\Delta H^\circ \text{ (kJ)}$$

$H_2(g) + \frac{1}{2}O_2(g)$	$\rightarrow H_2O(l)$	-286
$\frac{1}{2}H_2(g) + \frac{1}{2}Cl_2(g)$	$\rightarrow HCl(g)$	-92
$HCl(g) + NH_3(g)$	$\rightarrow NH_4Cl(s)$	-177
$Mg(s) + \frac{1}{2}O_2(g)$	$\rightarrow MgO(s)$	-602
$Na(s) + H_2O(l)$	$\rightarrow NaOH(aq) + \frac{1}{2}H_2(g)$	-184
$NaOH(aq) + HCl(aq)$	$\rightarrow NaCl(aq) + H_2O(l)$	
(or $OH^-(aq) + H^+(aq) \rightarrow H_2O(l)$)		$\bigg\} -57$

It appears that the liberation of heat is an important factor in determining the direction of change in a reaction.

We must now ask whether it is possible for endothermic reactions to occur of their own accord. We know that, for example, we can carry out the endothermic reaction

$$H_2O(l) \rightarrow H_2(g) + \frac{1}{2}O_2(g); \quad \Delta H^\circ = +286\,kJ$$

by continuously supplying electrical energy to overcome the enthalpy increase, i.e. by electrolysis. This reaction is not going of its own accord, but is having to be forced to take place by the applied electrical potential. Can we find endothermic reactions which occur without this continuous input of energy?

Up enthalpy hills

Let us examine the following experiment.

Equal bulks of hydrated barium hydroxide solid and ammonium thiocyanate solid are placed in a conical flask, which is then stoppered and shaken. The flask is set on a block of wood which has a layer of water on it. After a short time we find that the temperature of the flask and its contents has dropped appreciably, sometimes sufficient to freeze it to the block of wood and, on removing the stopper, we can detect a strong smell of ammonia.

$$Ba(OH)_2 \cdot 8H_2O(s) + 2NH_4SCN(s) \rightarrow Ba(SCN)_2(s) + 2NH_3(g) + 10H_2O(l)$$

Clearly we have an example of a reaction which proceeds quite readily of its own accord, but at the same time has taken in heat from the surroundings. In other words the reaction is endothermic.

We can find other examples of endothermic reactions which proceed readily at room temperature. The addition of thionyl chloride ($SOCl_2$) to hexaaquacobalt(II) chloride ($Co(H_2O)_6Cl_2$) results in an immediate decrease in temperature of the reaction mixture and the liberation of hydrogen chloride and sulphur dioxide gas.

$$Co(H_2O)_6Cl_2(s) + 6SOCl_2(l) \rightarrow CoCl_2(s) + 12HCl(g) + 6SO_2(g)$$

A similar cooling effect is observed during the addition of propanoic acid to ammonium carbonate.

$$2CH_3CH_2COOH(l) + (NH_4)_2CO_3(s) \rightarrow$$
$$2CH_3CH_2COONH_4(aq) + CO_2(g) + H_2O(l)$$

Here we have examples of reactions which run up enthalpy hills of their own accord. Obviously the fact that a reaction is exothermic is not the key to determining the direction in which it will go. Our hypothesis is incorrect and we must look for yet other factors. By examining the examples of exothermic and endothermic reactions which we have considered above, can you see any other features which we should consider?

You should be able to see that in each of the endothermic reactions there is a common factor, namely the liberation of a gas. More accurately, in each of the endothermic reactions there is a change in state when we go from reactants to products in the direction which turns solid to liquid to gas. This is not necessarily the case with exothermic reactions, where the change in state appears to be of less importance.

We have then two factors which may play a role in determining the direction of change: (a) the enthalpy change and (b) the physical state of reactants and products. The effects of the enthalpy change we can understand by analogy with energy changes in physical systems such as the man on the ladder, or a ball rolling down a hill but never up a hill of its own accord. We must now ask the question 'what has the change in state to do with determining the direction of change?'

The arguments so far are summarized in Figure 4.2.

Figure 4.2

5 Change, and the Direction of Change

Solid, liquid, and gas

Before we can understand how the physical states of reactants and products can influence the direction of chemical change, it is important that we have a clear picture of the nature and behaviour of matter in its various states.

We know that the atoms or molecules in a solid occupy approximately fixed positions. The solid is usually crystalline, having a fixed shape, and for all practical purposes we can assume that there is no net movement of the atoms or molecules within the solid. Although a liquid, like a solid, possesses a surface, the atoms or molecules do move relative to each other as demonstrated by Brownian movement or the diffusion of a soluble solid throughout the bulk of a liquid. By comparison, the atoms or molecules of a gas are not confined to any fixed boundaries other than the walls of the container, and the gas is characterized by complete freedom of molecular movement.

From this simple kinetic picture we can see that, whereas a solid is a highly ordered array of atoms, ions, or molecules, there is virtually no order in a gas. In other words, as we move from solid to liquid to gas the *degree of disorder* within the system is increasing. As we shall see later this idea of disorder is of extreme thermodynamic importance.

Order or chaos?

Given a free choice, in which direction will any system tend to move? Will it move towards a state of more order, or more disorder, or will it remain the same?

We can find an answer to this question simply by observing the chemical reactions which occur around us. Each day thousands of gallons of relatively ordered liquid petrol are burned in cars to produce vast volumes of disordered, mixed-up, exhaust gases. Solid coal is being burned in power stations with the production of large quantities of smoke and gases. Although each of these reactions is producing energy, the tendency is clearly to move from an ordered

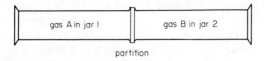

partition

Figure 5.1

to a disordered state. We can also observe this tendency even when there is no energy change, as in the following examples.

Let us suppose we have two non-reacting gases, A and B, in gas jars arranged as shown in Figure 5.1.

We have a system which possesses a degree of order in that gas A is confined to jar 1 and gas B is confined to jar 2. What happens when we remove the partition? We know from experience that the two gases will mix by diffusing into each other. You should be able to see that, as the gases mix, the degree of order in the system is reduced in that each jar now contains both A and B. Since the temperature remains constant throughout the diffusion process, there is no energy change.

A similar situation occurs if a drop of liquid in a sealed glass vessel is placed in an evacuated container (Figure 5.2). Immediately the glass vessel is broken the liquid evaporates, although the

Figure 5.2

total energy of the container and contents remains constant. Again the system has moved from a state of order to one of disorder of its own accord.

You should now realize that changes tend to occur in the direction which produces a state of chaos rather than a state of order and we must now ask why this is so.

The answer to this question is quite simply that statistically there is a greater probability of a system being arranged in a disordered than in an ordered manner. We can see that this is the case by doing the following 'thought experiment'.

Imagine a box containing three balls and having two compartments as in Figure 5.3.

What is the probability of finding all three balls in compartment

A after the box lid has been closed and the box shaken? To find this we need to consider all the possible arrangements of the balls in the two compartments. Figure 5.4 shows these possible arrangements. Since there is a total of four, only one of which is the desired ordered arrangement, the probability of obtaining this arrangement would appear to be 1 chance in 4.

Figure 5.3

Figure 5.4

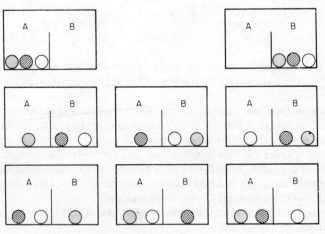

Figure 5.5

But think of the possibilities if we have three balls each of a different colour. The possible arrangements are shown in Figure 5.5.

The chance of obtaining all three balls in compartment A is not 1 in 4 but 1 in 8.

Write down for yourself all possible arrangements for four balls between the two compartments. You should find that there are 16 possible arrangements. The more balls we introduce, the lower is the probability of obtaining an ordered arrangement of all the balls in compartment A. In fact if we have n balls each of a different colour, the probability of obtaining a particular arrangement is 1 in 2^n.

We can apply exactly the same arguments at a molecular level. Suppose we have two flasks each of one litre capacity as shown in Figure 5.6.

Figure 5.6

Flask A contains a gas at s.t.p. and flask B is evacuated. We know from experience that, on opening the tap, the gas will diffuse from A to B until the pressure is the same in both flasks. Our system has again moved to a state of greater disorder. By analogy with the balls in the box we can calculate the probability that, at any future time, *all* the gas molecules will be in flask A. We have $\dfrac{6 \times 10^{23}}{22.4} = 2.7 \times 10^{22}$ ($\sim 10^{22}$) molecules in one litre of gas at s.t.p. and the probability of finding all the molecules in flask A will be 1 in $2^{10^{22}}$, that is, 1 chance in $2^{10\,000\,000\,000\,000\,000\,000\,000}$ The likelihood of this happening is so negligibly small as to be an impossibility.

Statistically there is a much greater probability of creating disorder than of creating order. We can also use statistical probability arguments to show that the degree of disorder increases as we go from the solid to liquid to gaseous state.

We have already seen (Chapter 2, page 6) that one of the fundamental properties of any substance is that it possesses internal energy, E. We also saw how the heat energy of a substance is related to the microkinetic energies of the particles within the substance. How is the energy stored within the atoms or molecules of the substance?

If we examine any individual particle (atom or molecule) in a substance it may possess three forms of molecular motion. It may vibrate, rotate, or move from place to place – known as translational motion. Each of these types of motion will have energy associated with it. The total energy of the substance will be made up of a potential energy term, which is a consequence of the positions of the particles within the substance, and a kinetic energy term due to the translational, rotational, and vibrational motions of the particles themselves. The actual motions which the particle possesses will depend upon whether it is in the gaseous, liquid, or solid phase, as shown in Table 5.1.

Table 5.1

| | | Molecular Motion | |
Phase	Translation	Rotation	Vibration
Gas	Free	Free	Free
Liquid	Restricted	Less free than in gas	Free
Solid	Absent	Extremely limited	Free

If we are to consider how a molecule changes its energy, it is important at this stage that we understand one of the fundamental properties of energy – *changes in energy occur only by separate individual energy packets of definite size.* Each packet is called a *quantum* of energy and we say that energy is *quantized.*

The idea of quantization of energy leads us to the concept of fixed energy levels within atoms and molecules; the quanta of energy exactly fit the gaps between these levels. We can liken the energy levels within the atom or molecule to a staircase, with each step representing a fixed energy level. We cannot climb the staircase in units of less than one step; we cannot take half a step at a time. Similarly, we can change the energy of our atom or molecule only in unit steps, each step representing one quantum of energy. Using this analogy, if we represent the vibrational energy levels by a normal staircase, then in comparison we would need to represent the rotational energy levels by a staircase in which the steps were sufficiently small for a small child to climb without difficulty; the rotational energy levels are much closer together than the vibrational energy levels. By comparison the translational energy levels are so small that we can consider our staircase as an inclined plane with no more than a faint ripple to serve as steps. We can represent the various energy levels as in Figure 5.7:

We are now in a position to examine how an individual molecule or atom stores its energy. Let us consider a molecule with a certain energy, E. If the molecule is part of a solid, for practical purposes this energy E will be distributed as a number of individual energy quanta among the various vibrational energy levels only. If the

Figure 5.7

molecule is in the gas phase, in addition to the vibrational energy levels, the translational and rotational energy levels are freely available for the distribution of energy. In changing from solid to gas, the number of available levels over which the *same total amount of energy* can be distributed has increased markedly.

Furthermore, the size of the energy quanta decreases in the order: vibrational > rotational > translational (see Figure 5.7). In changing from solid to gas, vibrational energy quanta are effectively being transformed into smaller rotational and yet smaller translational energy quanta.

Thus in changing the physical state of the molecule from solid to gas two effects are apparent. First, there is a large increase in the number of levels over which the total energy may be distributed. Second, there is a large increase in the number of energy quanta which may be distributed among the various energy levels.

By analogy with our statistical model of the balls in a box we can see that, in the transformation solid to liquid to gas, we are increasing the number of balls to be distributed among the various compartments and, at the same time, we are increasing the number of compartments in the box. We have already seen (page 25) the effect of increasing the number of balls (with a fixed number of compartments in the box) upon the total number of possible arrangements. The effect of increasing the number of compartments over which a number of balls can be distributed can be seen by considering the number of possible arrangements of four similar balls between two compartments (Figure 5.8) and between four compartments (Figure 5.9).

From these statistical arguments we can see that the probability of obtaining a *particular* arrangement of the energy quanta is greater for a solid than for a liquid, which in turn is greater than for a gas. Statistically, the number of possible arrangements of the

Figure 5.8 A total of 16 ways

Figure 5.9 A total of 88 ways

energy quanta increases, and hence the degree of order decreases, in changing from solid to liquid to gas. Conversely, the degree of disorder increases in changing from solid to liquid to gas.

From the arguments used above we can see that if we have, for example, one mole of a substance, i.e. 6.02×10^{23} particles, and each particle possesses a large number of quanta of energy, then there must exist an extremely large number of possible arrangements of the energy within the substance. Each of these possible arrangements is called a *microstate*, and we assume that each microstate is as probable as any other microstate.

Entropy

We have seen (Chapter 4, page 20) that one of the factors which determines the direction of a chemical change is the creation of a less ordered state of affairs by converting solid reactants to liquid or gaseous products. The degree of disorder within any system is of considerable thermodynamic importance and leads us to a new thermodynamic quantity called *entropy*, S, which is *related* to and is a measure of the degree of disorder as determined by both the arrangement of the available energy quanta within the particles and the actual arrangement of the particles themselves within the system.

The entropy of a system is related to the total number (w) of the microstates, that is

$$S \propto \text{function of } w$$

in fact

$$S \propto \log_e w$$

$$S = \text{constant} \times \log_e w$$

Second Law of Thermodynamics

The concept of entropy leads us to the Second Law of Thermodynamics. We are all familiar with the observation that if we place a block of ice cream on the table, it will melt by taking heat from the surroundings. Similarly, if you touch a hot piece of metal you do not heat the metal, the metal burns your hand. In other words, heat flows from the hot object to the cold object and not in the reverse direction. Why is this the case? The answer is that this is the direction of change in which the entropy increases. We can illustrate this as follows.

Suppose that we have two blocks of metal, A and B, at different temperatures, T_1 and T_2, where T_1 is greater than T_2. Block A will have a certain energy E_1 which will be distributed among the various microstates. Block B will have an energy E_2 again distributed among the various microstates. Since E_1 is greater than E_2, the number of quanta accommodated in the various energy levels of block A will be greater than the number of quanta accommodated in block B.

When the two blocks are placed together heat energy, as quanta, will flow from A to B until both blocks are at the same temperature.

This will result in an increase in the total number of possible arrangements of the energy quanta in the system of the two blocks A and B together. We can see that this is the case if we represent block A as a box containing two compartments and three balls and block B as a box containing two compartments and one ball (Figure 5.10).

Figure 5.10

When the blocks are together, that is, when they attain the same temperature, we have to distribute the four balls over four compartments (two compartments from A and two from B), which gives us a total of eighty-eight possible arrangements (microstates) (Figure 5.9). The process of transfer of energy quanta (heat flow) goes in the direction which gives the greater possibility of creating more microstates, that is, from hot to cold. In other words, the entropy of the two metal blocks, when regarded as a single unit, increases as heat flows from hot to cold. If on the other hand heat was to flow of its own accord from the cold block to the hot block, this would result in a decrease in the possible number of microstates in the system. Such a situation does not occur according to the laws of probability and certainly does not occur in practice.

By reference to any example we may care to choose, we find that in every case when the system is left to its own devices the direction of heat flow is *always* from a hot body to a cold body, *never* in the reverse direction. This is in effect a statement of the *Second Law of Thermodynamics*. More usefully, we may formulate the Second Law as follows:

'Any system of its own accord will always undergo change in such a way as to increase the entropy.'

A sobering thought!
From the Second Law we can see that entropy and time are interconnected in the sense that as time progresses so the entropy, or the degree of disorder of which the entropy is a measure, increases.

If we consider our own world then, according to thermodynamics, we must conclude that in spite of all the technological innovation leading to the creation of apparent order (such as buildings, cars, and spaceships) nature is gradually moving towards a state of disorder. It is perhaps not quite so surprising that mountains are gradually disappearing as they are eroded by the weather, or that the world's resources of oil and coal are being gradually exhausted. Such events are clearly examples of the Second Law of Thermodynamics at work.

6   Surroundings matter

A narrow view

We have noticed so far that the sign of the enthalpy change in a reaction does not really help us to decide the likely direction of a chemical change. There are plenty of exothermic and endothermic reactions which take place quite readily of their own accord at room temperature.

We suggested in the last chapter that the driving force might be the relentless statistical probability that disorder will occur. The direction which increases disorder should therefore be the direction which the chemical change will take. When we consider changes in general we can probably think of many examples to support this idea.

Things burn but don't unburn.

A sugar lump, when eaten, ends up as carbon dioxide and water vapour.

No matter how hard we try to prevent it, cars rust away.

A household generates a surprising quantity of mixed rubbish in a week.

A single packet of cigarettes generates the chaos of scattered butts, smoke, tar, and an empty packet.

This may all sound very convincing but you are almost certainly feeling uneasy about the argument. Without too much effort you can think of many examples in which changes produce order rather than disorder.

Is our Second Law of Thermodynamics (page 30) to be short-lived? Can it rightly carry the title 'Law'?

Order from chaos?

In plants, orderly sugar molecules are formed from relatively disordered carbon dioxide gas and water during photosynthesis (Chapter 13, page 88).

Houses are built as an ordered structure from disordered piles of bricks, sand, cement, and timber.

The orderly structure of animals, including ourselves, emerges from the jumble of amino acid molecules in our mother's food and later in our own food.

Crystals of amazing regularity and order emerge from a solution in which the molecules and ions are fairly randomly distributed.

The equations below represent a number of common chemical reactions in which gases (disordered) are consumed rather than released and relatively ordered substances are produced. All of these reactions happen quite readily of their own accord.

$$Mg(s) + \tfrac{1}{2}O_2(g) \rightarrow MgO(s)$$

$$CuO(s) + H_2(g) \rightarrow Cu(s) + H_2O(l)$$

$$NH_3(g) + HCl(g) \rightarrow NH_4Cl(s)$$

$$2H_2S(g) + SO_2(g) \rightarrow 2H_2O(l) + 3S(s)$$

Where is the Second Law now? Is it true that in any change which happens of its own accord there is an increase in disorder?

The Law is the Law!

Strange as it may seem, the Second Law does hold for all changes which happen of their own accord (spontaneously). While all the statements in the last section are true, we have been short-sighted in our view of them. We have been looking at the changes in isolation from their surroundings, but the surroundings are as much part of the material universe as are the reactants in the vessel. The Second Law applies to the *sum* of the changes taking place in the 'reaction vessel' (called the *system*) and the changes taking place in the surroundings.

The words 'reaction vessel' appear in inverted commas because their meaning can range from a beaker in the corner of a laboratory to the 'cauldron' of the sun itself.

Now let us apply this wider idea beginning with the first of the reactions listed in the previous section.

$$Mg(s) + \tfrac{1}{2}O_2(g) \rightarrow MgO(s) \; ; \; \Delta H° = -602 \, kJ$$

Inside the dashed box we have the *system* in which half a mole of gas has been consumed to produce the *ordered* solid MgO. In the system the entropy has decreased, but outside the dashed box is information about what has happened to the *surroundings*. The *system* has lost to the *surroundings* 602 kJ of heat energy. This heat is the net effect of the bond-breaking and bond-making processes in the reaction, which has been located in a fairly restricted situation.

The number of possible ways of arranging that energy when it is locked in bonds is fairly small (Chapter 5, page 22) but now the heat energy has been released into the atmosphere, where the number of ways of arranging the energy is vastly increased (Chapter 5, page 28). This corresponds to a large increase in disorder of the *surroundings*. If we make quantitative measurements of the entropy change within the reaction vessel and in the surroundings we find that the entropy increase in the surroundings far outweighs the entropy decrease in the system, and so the net effect is a total entropy *increase* in accordance with the Second Law.

A similar argument applies to all four reactions listed in the previous section, because all of them are exothermic and so affect the surroundings, causing a net increase in entropy. Notice in passing that when there is a decrease in entropy in a system, that system (reaction) is exothermic. This idea will be developed further in Chapter 8, page 40.

Before we endorse the Second Law, let us look at some of the other changes mentioned above – changes which profoundly affect our lives.

Entropy and life
The growth of a young animal from the egg to birth, its growth after birth, and the maintenance of its adult living are a series of inter-locked chemical reactions. The constant addition of amino acids to the protein structure of the animal is rapid during growth but less so during adult life. The formation of protein is an exothermic

Table 6.1

Example	Enthalpy change	Entropy change in system	Entropy change in surroundings	Net entropy change
Burning coal	Exothermic	Increase	Increase	Increase
Growing crystals	Exothermic	Decrease	Increase	Increase
Propanoic acid and ammonium carbonate	Endothermic	Increase	Decrease	Increase
Life	Exothermic	Temporary decrease	Increase	Increase

process accompanied by a decrease in entropy of the system; the arguments applying to other exothermic processes apply equally well here.

When we consider the system (body) and the surroundings together we can see that the Second Law is being obeyed. The body creates disorder around it during its lifetime by giving off heat to the atmosphere, by breaking down foodstuffs such as carbohydrates into small gas molecules such as carbon dioxide and water, and by using up some of the world's resources. Even the order of the body is only a temporary thing and immediately after death the rapid process of decay takes over and returns the body to a highly disordered state.

Taken all together the system and the surroundings show an increase in entropy during the life cycle of the animal.

Let us sum up the various changes in Table 6.1 and see that the Second Law applies to them all.

A compromise sought

The Second Law holds when seen in the wide context of both system and surroundings, and so far no process has been found which violates this law. In practical terms though, this is not very helpful in deciding the direction of change. It is easy enough to make measurements on the system in the reaction vessel, but it is often impossible to make measurements on the surroundings, which may include the universe! If only we could apply some test to the system *alone* which would predict the direction of change.

A measurement of the enthalpy change in the system also applies to the surroundings because the heat which the reaction gains or loses is gained from or lost to the surroundings, and so the enthalpy measurement can have a dual role. A measurement of the entropy change in the system is related to the entropy change of the surroundings, since both together must obey the Second Law.

It seems possible then that a method can be devised by which measurements on the system *alone* will give us enough information to decide on the direction of change. How this is done will appear in Chapters 7 and 8.

7 Enthalpy, Entropy, or both?

The problem of surroundings

At the end of Chapter 4 we saw that we have to take account of both enthalpy and entropy changes when considering the direction of change in a chemical reaction. We have also seen (Chapter 6) that in order to satisfy both the First and Second Laws of Thermodynamics we must always consider *both* the reaction 'system' and the 'surroundings'. This gives rise to some difficulties when we consider a practical situation. What should we specify as the 'surroundings' when we consider the reduction of iron oxide to iron in a blast furnace, or what are the 'surroundings' when we carry out a reaction in an open beaker on the laboratory bench? We can see immediately that our approach to understanding chemical reactions through enthalpy and entropy changes is severely limited. Is there some thermodynamic quantity which we can use in a practical situation without having to define what we mean by system and surroundings?

Energy and work

You should already be familiar with the idea that energy and work can be interconverted; for example, we can use the energy liberated by the combustion of petrol to drive an engine. We must now ask how much work we can get from the heat liberated – the enthalpy change – during a chemical reaction.

We know that when zinc reacts with dilute acid in a beaker the reaction mixture gets hot; the reaction is strongly exothermic.

$$Zn(s) + 2H^+(aq) \rightarrow Zn^{2+}(aq) + H_2(g); \ \Delta H^\circ = -152 \, kJ$$

However, if we carry out this reaction in an electrochemical cell

$$Zn(s) \mid Zn^{2+}(aq) \mid H^+(aq) \mid H_2(g)$$

we can harness the energy and use it to do useful work by providing an electric current. We find that the maximum amount of useful work which can be obtained from the reaction of one mole of zinc with two moles of hydrogen ions is 146 kJ. The enthalpy change during a reaction is *not* an indication of the possible work obtainable from the reaction. As we shall see later, some of the enthalpy of reaction is involved in the creation of disorder. How then can we relate a reaction's capacity for doing work to the energy changes during reaction?

Only part of the enthalpy change is available for doing work and that part is called the **free energy**, to which we give the symbol G. (G is used in recognition of the contribution made by Willard Gibbs to our understanding of thermodynamics.) The free energy is a thermodynamic quantity and we define it simply as the energy *available to do useful work*. The free energy change associated with a reaction is a measure of the capability of that reaction to do useful work. When we consider the efficiency of a power station, we should take into account the free energy changes rather than the enthalpy changes in order to evaluate the true capacity of the combustion reactions to do work.

Standard free energy change ($\triangle G^\circ$)

As with all thermodynamic quantities we need to specify the conditions under which changes occur. We define the Standard Free Energy Change as the free energy change for a reaction involving one mole of a substance at one atmosphere pressure. Again it is necessary to specify the temperature separately as this is *not* implied in the Standard State condition. We write ΔG°_T, where T is the *absolute* temperature (K).

$\triangle G$ or $\triangle G^\circ$?

Whereas the free energy change (ΔG) for a reaction gives us a measure of the energy which is actually available to do work, the Standard Free Energy Change (ΔG°) is a measure of the *maximum* amount of work which it is *possible* to obtain from a system, when operated under standard conditions. What do we mean by the *maximum* amount of work and how do we obtain it?

In order to answer this question we need to digress a little and consider some mechanical systems.

Let us suppose we have a mass of 1 kg suspended at a height of one metre above the bench (Figure 7.1).

Relative to the bench, the mass will have a potential energy of 10 J. If the mass is released it will fall to the bench with the loss of this energy to the surroundings as heat and sound.

Now suppose that we connect the mass by a rope and pulley to another mass of 0.5 kg as shown in Figure 7.2.

As the 1 kg mass falls it will lift the 0.5 kg mass to a height of one metre. In other words, if we assume that no energy is lost as the rope passes over the pulley, the 1 kg mass will again lose 10 J of energy, but 5 J of this will appear as work performed in lifting the

Figure 7.1

Figure 7.2

0.5 kg mass to a height of one metre. The remaining 5 J will be lost as 'useless' heat to the surroundings. What is the maximum work which we can obtain from this system? You should see that if we replace the 0.5 kg mass by a mass fractionally less than 1 kg, then we have a system where we convert the whole of the potential energy of the falling mass into work. You should also be able to see something else of considerable thermodynamic importance, namely that in the first situation (Figure 7.2) the change will occur in one direction only, that is, mass A will fall and mass B will rise. The change will be *irreversible* of its own accord. However, when masses A and B are the same, our system will effectively be in balance and the changes will be easily reversed; a touch on one or the other will reverse the direction of movement. Such a change will occur *reversibly* and at the same time the rate of change will be extremely slow; so slow that, if the two masses are exactly the same, we can regard any change as occurring *infinitely slowly*. For practical purposes no change at all will occur.

From our mechanical system we can see that, in order to obtain the *maximum* amount of work, we must carry out the change *reversibly* and, in consequence, *infinitely slowly*. It follows that in practice, since observable and useful changes do not occur infinitely slowly, the maximum work corresponding to the Standard Free Energy Change ($\Delta G°$) is never available. A car deriving the maximum work from the combustion of petrol would never move!

We can obtain a parallel between the mechanical system and a chemical reaction by considering an electrochemical cell. If we set up the cell

$$\text{Zn(s)} \left| \begin{array}{c} \text{Zn}^{2+}\text{(aq)} \\ \text{(1 M)} \end{array} \right| \left. \begin{array}{c} \text{Cu}^{2+}\text{(aq)} \\ \text{(1 M)} \end{array} \right| \text{Cu(s)}$$

we can measure the e.m.f. (E) when the cell is doing no useful work, that is when no current is being drawn from the cell and the reaction is occurring reversibly and infinitely slowly. This e.m.f. (E) is a measure of the maximum capability of the cell–the reaction–to do work. The maximum work which can be obtained from the cell (w_{max}) is given by

$$w_{max} = nFE$$

where n is the number of electrons transferred per equation and F is the Faraday constant (one mole of electrons). nFE is the amount of work required to raise a charge of n moles of electrons through a potential difference of E volts. By measuring the e.m.f. of a cell we have a means of determining ΔG of the reaction because

$$w_{max} = -\Delta G = nFE$$

Since the cell is giving out energy, ΔG has a negative sign.

In the special case when the cell is operating under standard conditions (1 molar solutions at 1 atmosphere pressure) $E = E°$ and

$$w_{max} = -\Delta G° = nFE°$$

8 Putting the Pieces Together

Where does the energy go?

You are perhaps still puzzled about why it is the free energy change, rather than the enthalpy change, which is a measure of the ability of a reaction to do work.

Let us go back to the 1 kg mass again (Figure 8.1). As shown in this sketch, it has 10 J of potential energy which will be converted into 10 J of kinetic energy as it falls. But this is not the whole story of its energy content. Since the mass is at room temperature, the molecules within it will be moving with microkinetic energy (heat). As we saw in Chapter 2, page 5, this microkinetic energy is randomized within the mass and contributes nothing to the ability of the

Figure 8.1

mass to do work in lifting another mass. Its total energy content, as it stands in Figure 8.1, is made up of 10 J of potential energy plus internal random kinetic energy (x J).

When the block lands on the bench the 10 J of potential energy will be released as heat (and possibly sound) and, if the bench is colder than the block, some of the microkinetic energy (heat) will also be transferred to the bench. If the bench is massive compared with the mass and is at zero on the absolute temperature scale, all the microkinetic energy of the block can be transferred from the block to the bench, provided that this extra heat makes virtually no difference to the temperature of the bench.

This is analogous to the chemical situation. The total energy change when the block lands on the bench at 0 K will be $10\,J + x\,J$ and this corresponds to the enthalpy change (ΔH). However, only $10\,J$ will be available to do work in raising another block and this corresponds to the free energy change (ΔG). The $x\,J$ of random microkinetic kinetic energy is related to the entropy change (ΔS). Under standard conditions, we have

$$\Delta H^\circ \equiv 10\,J + x\,J$$

$$\Delta G^\circ \equiv 10\,J$$

$$\Delta S^\circ \text{ is related to } x\,J$$

Entropy is not energy

Notice that in the last line above it has been carefully stated that ΔS° 'is related to' $x\,J$. If you refer back to Chapter 5, page 29, you will find that the entropy (S) was given as

$$S = \text{constant} \times \log_e w$$

where w was a probability term. The logarithm of a probability term is not an energy term and would not carry the unit joule. Although ΔS° is related to this quantity of microkinetic energy we have called $x\,J$, it cannot be equal to it. We must seek some mathematical relationship which will allow us to make direct connection between the entropy term and the 'unusable' part of the enthalpy term.

Heat, temperature, and entropy

In Chapter 5, page 25, we saw that when we were trying to calculate the number of possible arrangements of balls in a box, the number of arrangements rose dramatically as the number of balls was increased. Similarly, if we substitute 'quanta of energy' for the 'balls' and the 'number of arrangements' for 'disorder' we can see that the more energy supplied to a situation the more we increase the disorder.

If we use q to represent the amount of heat supplied to a body, then

$$\Delta S \propto q$$

A second factor which must be considered is the temperature at which this heat is supplied to the body. Let us take an extreme case to illustrate the point.

At zero on the Kelvin scale a body has for all practical purposes zero entropy. This is an approximate statement of the Third Law of Thermodynamics. The precise statement is that 'for a perfect crystal at zero kelvin the entropy is zero'. If this body is given one unit of heat energy, its new entropy compared with its original entropy (zero) is infinitely larger.

If the same body is now considered at 300 K and one unit of heat energy is added to what is already a disordered system, the entropy increase is much less than in the first case. At 1000 K, the addition of one unit of heat energy would give an increase in entropy of even less than before.

There is, therefore, an inverse relationship between the entropy change and the absolute temperature and so we can write

$$\Delta S \propto \frac{1}{T}$$

If we now put both of these relationships together we have

$$\Delta S \propto \frac{q}{T}$$

If all the heat being supplied to a system is to be used to create disorder, none of it must go to raising the temperature. This is the kind of situation we find at the boiling point of a liquid or the melting point of a solid. At the boiling point or melting point of a substance, the addition or subtraction of a small quantity of heat energy will reverse the direction of the physical change. Such changes are said to be carried out reversibly and the heat supplied is q_{rev}.

Our expression now becomes

$$\Delta S \propto \frac{q_{rev}}{T}$$

By choosing our units, and by operating on one mole of the substance under standard conditions, the relationship can be written as

$$\Delta S^{\circ} = \frac{q_{rev}}{T}$$

Testing the relationship

To show that this relationship is reasonable and is in accord with practical observation, let us examine the behaviour of a range of liquids at their boiling points. At one atmosphere pressure benzene boils at 80 °C (353 K). The heat supplied at 353 K does not alter the temperature of the benzene but is used to drive off benzene molecules from the liquid into the gas phase. This heat is the Molar Heat of Vaporization of benzene (ΔH°_{vap}) in which 30.8 kJ are required to vaporize one mole of benzene. This is a reversible situation in that the momentary withdrawal of the heat source will cause vapour molecules to return to the liquid phase and vice versa. In this case $\Delta H^{\circ}_{vap} = q_{rev}$.

According to our relationship in the previous section the Standard Entropy Change during this vaporization process will be given by

$$\Delta S^{\circ} = \frac{30\,800}{353} \text{ J K}^{-1} \text{ mol}^{-1}$$

$$= 87 \text{ J K}^{-1} \text{ mol}^{-1}$$

Notice the units of ΔS°, which are usually quoted in joules (not kJ) per mole and also per kelvin.

The results of similar calculations for a range of liquids are shown in Table 8.1.

Table 8.1

Liquid	Molar heat of vaporization (kJ mol^{-1})	b.p.(K)	ΔS° (J K^{-1} mol^{-1})
Benzene	30.8	353	87
Bromine	30.0	332	90
Tetrachloromethane	30.5	350	87
Phosphorus trichloride	30.5	347	88
Hydrogen sulphide	18.7	212	88
Hydrogen chloride	16.2	188	86

The relationship $\Delta S^{\circ} = \frac{q_{rev}}{T}$ has given rise to an almost constant value for ΔS°, around 88 J K^{-1} mol^{-1}. This is not unreasonable because in each case, one mole of liquid molecules has been converted into one mole of vapour molecules at a fixed temperature. The average speed of the liquid and vapour molecules is the same at the boiling point of a liquid and the only thing which has changed is that, in going into the vapour phase, the possible number of ways of distributing the energy has increased, i.e. the entropy value has increased.

If our relationship is now rearranged, we have an energy change which is related to the entropy change and which can fit into an energy equation.

$$\Delta S^{\circ} = \frac{q_{rev}}{T}$$

or

$$q_{rev} = T\Delta S^{\circ}$$

This corresponds to the energy difference between ΔG° and ΔH° and is the energy which was not available to do work (page 41).

Completing the equation

We can now arrive at an equation which links mathematically ΔH°, ΔG°, and ΔS°.

$$\Delta H^{\circ} \quad = \quad \Delta G^{\circ} \quad + \quad T\Delta S^{\circ}$$

The overall enthalpy change $=$ The free energy change available to do work $+$ The energy used to create disorder

Rearranging this equation gives

$$\Delta G^{\circ} = \Delta H^{\circ} - T\Delta S^{\circ} \quad \text{(the Gibbs–Helmholtz equation)}$$

We now have an equation in which all the terms are measurable *within the system*, but which take the surroundings into account as well. This equation will enable us to make predictions about the direction of change.

Our first idea was that reactions 'ran down enthalpy hills', but this was shown to be false when we saw the number of spontaneous endothermic reactions. From the point of view of the system only there are cases where there are entropy decreases as well as increases, and so the entropy change was not an infallible guide to the direction of change.

At last we have the key – the Standard Free Energy Change (ΔG°). Reactions tend to go in the direction which will result in a decrease in free energy, that is, they tend to 'run down free energy hills' of their own accord (spontaneously).

In Figure 8.2 (a) the Standard Free Energy Content of the reactants (G_1°) is greater than the Standard Free Energy Content of the products (G_2°) and so ΔG° will, by convention, have a negative sign.

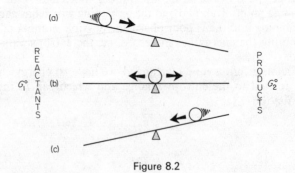

Figure 8.2

The reaction will tend to go in the direction which favours the formation of products.

Figure 8.2 (b) is a case in which G_1^o is equal to G_2^o and so $\Delta G^o = 0$. Products and reactants are equally likely.

Figure 8.2 (c) is a case in which G_1^o is less than G_2^o and so ΔG^o will have a positive sign. Reactants are more likely than products or, in other words, the direction of change will tend to be that in which ΔG^o is negative (right to left).

The point at which the products are just about to be favoured more than the reactants is when $\Delta G^o = 0$.

A reaction for which ΔG^o is zero or negative is said to be *feasible*. Here an ordinary English word is given a special meaning; do not confuse it with the normal English usage of 'feasible'. Here the word does not mean that the reaction will definitely go spontaneously in favour of the products, it merely states that if the reaction does proceed, it will tend towards the products rather than the reactants. In Chapter 11 you will see that even if a reaction is feasible it may not readily yield the products.

If the Gibbs–Helmholtz equation is correct, it should be possible to use it to explain the variety of apparently conflicting data we found in Chapters 4 and 5. Both exothermic and endothermic reactions were found to proceed spontaneously and so also did reactions in which the entropy change *of the system* either increased or decreased.

What combinations of ΔH^o and ΔS^o will make ΔG^o negative and thus make the reaction feasible? All the possibilities are set out in Table 8.2.

Table 8.2

$$\Delta G^o = \Delta H^o - T\Delta S^o$$

ΔH^o	ΔS^o	ΔG^o	Feasibility
1. Negative (exothermic)	Positive (increase)	Negative	Yes
2. Negative (exothermic)	Negative (decrease)	Negative if $T\Delta S^o < \Delta H^o$	Yes
3. Positive (endothermic)	Positive (increase)	Negative if $T\Delta S^o > \Delta H^o$	Yes
4. Positive (endothermic)	Negative (decrease)	Positive	No

Reactions of the type described in 1, 2, and 3 are capable of going spontaneously down the free energy hill. Type 4 cannot occur spontaneously.

Temperature and reaction

From the Gibbs–Helmholtz equation we can see that the value and sign of ΔG° is dependent upon the value of T and this helps us to understand why a source of heat is one of the chemist's basic tools. No laboratory is complete without a Bunsen burner or its modern equivalent. Heat is often necessary for kinetic reasons which we shall meet in Chapter 11, but it has thermodynamic importance as well.

Here is a very simple example.

$$CaCO_3(s) \rightarrow CaO(s) + CO_2(g)$$

First we shall calculate the Standard Enthalpy Change (ΔH°_{298}) for the reaction at room temperature (25 °C) from the Standard Heats of Formation (see data on page 92).

Substance	$\Delta H^\circ_f (kJ\ mol^{-1})$
$CaCO_3(s)$	−1207
$CaO(s)$	−635 ⎫
$CO_2(g)$	−394 ⎬ −1029

In going from reactants to products,

$$\Delta H^\circ = +178\ kJ\ mol^{-1}$$

Now let us do a similar operation to find the Standard Entropy Change, ΔS°_{298}.

Substance	$\Delta S^\circ (J\ K^{-1}\ mol^{-1})$
$CaCO_3(s)$	93
$CaO(s)$	40 ⎫
$CO_2(g)$	214 ⎬ 254

Notice that we can find Absolute Entropies for substances because the Third Law gives us an absolute zero from which to work.

In going from reactants to products there has been a gain in entropy of $(254 - 93)\ J\ K^{-1}\ mol^{-1}$, that is $\Delta S^\circ_{298} = +161\ J\ K^{-1}\ mol^{-1}$

Using the Gibbs–Helmholtz equation, we can now calculate ΔG°_{298} for the reaction.

$$\Delta G^\circ_{298} = \Delta H^\circ_{298} - T\Delta S^\circ_{298}$$

$$= 178 - 298 \times \frac{161}{1000} \text{ kJ mol}^{-1}$$

$$= +130 \text{ kJ mol}^{-1}$$

This very positive value for ΔG°_{298} shows that the decomposition of chalk or limestone at room temperature is not feasible (in the thermodynamic sense) although it does not mean that no CaO or CO_2 is ever formed at room temperature. This fits in with our everyday experience; the Pennines don't decompose to any extent on a warm day, nor do egg shells decompose during boiling!

However, it is important industrially to make quicklime, CaO, from limestone, $CaCO_3$. How are we going to make the value of ΔG° negative and so make the reaction feasible?

ΔH° changes very little with temperature – only by about 1 per cent for every 100 degrees increase in temperature. ΔS° is a little more susceptible to temperature change, but not sufficiently to make any major difference to the value of ΔG°. The $T\Delta S^\circ$ term, however, will change markedly with temperature and it might be possible to use this to alter the sign of ΔG°. It is a matter of simple arithmetic to find the value for T at which ΔG° is zero and the reaction just becomes feasible.

When $\hspace{3cm} \Delta G^\circ = 0$

then $\hspace{3cm} \Delta H^\circ = T\Delta S^\circ$

or $\hspace{3cm} T = \dfrac{\Delta H^\circ}{\Delta S^\circ}$

$$= \frac{178}{(161/1000)} \text{ K}$$

$$= 1106 \text{ K}$$

$$= 833 \,^\circ\text{C}$$

(Notice that both ΔH° and $T\Delta S^\circ$ are now in the same units, kJ.) A manufacturer must have a kiln which will operate well above 830 °C. Do not be misled into thinking that at 833 °C suddenly $CaCO_3$ begins to decompose; it does decompose to some extent at lower temperatures, but about 830 °C is the temperature at which the products are beginning to be favoured more than the reactant.

Further examples of the working of similar calculations will be encountered in Chapter 13.

Now work through the consolidation exercises. Answers, fully worked out, can be found on page 95.

The arguments so far are summarized in Figure 8.3.

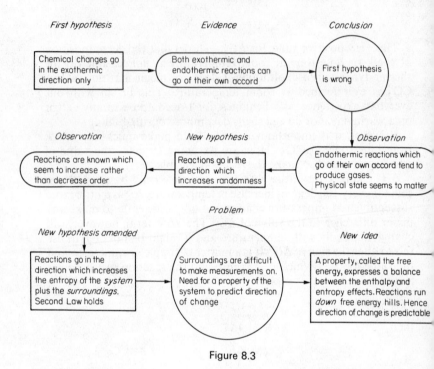

First hypothesis

Chemical changes go in the exothermic direction only

Evidence

Both exothermic and endothermic reactions can go of their own accord

Conclusion

First hypothesis is wrong

Observation

Reactions are known which seem to increase rather than decrease order

New hypothesis

Reactions go in the direction which increases randomness

Observation

Endothermic reactions which go of their own accord tend to produce gases.
Physical state seems to matter

Problem

New hypothesis amended

Reactions go in the direction which increases the entropy of the *system* plus the *surroundings*.
Second Law holds

Surroundings are difficult to make measurements on. Need for a property of the system to predict direction of change

New idea

A property, called the free energy, expresses a balance between the enthalpy and entropy effects. Reactions run *down* free energy hills. Hence direction of change is predictable

Figure 8.3

Consolidation of Chapters 4 to 8

In these chapters we have spent a great deal of time on the question of the direction of chemical change and it may seem to have been a fuss about nothing. We have raised a succession of theories and then discarded or modified them. We hope, however, that you have been able to see the way in which scientific theory is built and also we hope you have appreciated the intellectual elegance of the chemists and physicists who developed these arguments over the last century or so. However, this has not been for intellectual stimulus alone, but also to lay the basis for many industrial, biological, and ecological decisions upon which the solution to many of our future problems will depend.

Before we proceed further it would be a good idea to consolidate what has been done in the previous chapters.

1. Select the endothermic reactions from this list, explaining why you place each of them in this category. (No calculations are required.)

A	$C_6H_6(l) + 7\tfrac{1}{2}O_2(g) \rightarrow 6CO_2(g) + 3H_2O(g)$
B	$4Na(s) + TiO_2(s) \rightarrow 2Na_2O(s) + Ti(s)$
C	$CaO(s) + H_2O(l) \rightarrow Ca(OH)_2(s)$
D	$CaCO_3(s) \rightarrow CaO(s) + CO_2(g)$
E	$N_2(g) + O_2(g) \rightarrow 2NO(g)$
F	$N_2O_4(g) \rightarrow 2NO_2(g)$
G	$Zn(s) + Cu^{2+}(aq) \rightarrow Zn^{2+}(aq) + Cu(s)$
H	$Al_2O_3(s) \rightarrow 2Al(s) + \tfrac{3}{2}O_2(g)$
I	$KNO_3(s) \rightarrow KNO_2(s) + \tfrac{1}{2}O_2(g)$

2.   The density of water is $1.00 \, \text{g cm}^{-3}$ and the density of ethanol is $0.79 \, \text{g cm}^{-3}$. If a cylinder is set up as shown in Figure C.2 and the partition is removed, ethanol and water will mix spontaneously and after a while the composition of the mixture will be the same throughout. Explain this in terms of what you learned from Chapter 5.

Figure C.2

3.   On a really cold day clothes on a washing line may freeze solid and yet, given time, they will dry. Explain this.

4.   Turn to the Table of Absolute Entropies on page 94 and retabulate them under the headings *solid, liquid,* and *gas.* What pattern now emerges? In the column of solids, look for a relationship between hardness and entropy.

5.   A colloquial version of the Second Law of Thermodynamics says, 'If you think things are mixed up now, just wait!' How far is this in accord with the two statements of the Second Law given in Chapter 5?

6.   Make sure that you understand that 'entropy is not disorder, but it is a measure of the degree of disorder'.

7.   A philosophical thought to ponder. If the entropy of the universe is increasing, does this imply that there must have been an initial ordered state from which everything has come?

8.   Look back at the list in Question 1 and select the reactions in which you think there has been an increase in disorder *of the system.*

9.   As you are sitting reading this question, list the ways in which you are obeying the Second Law, taking into consideration both the system (yourself) and the surroundings.

10.   When solid ammonium chloride is dissolved in water the temperature of the solution falls. Try to explain this spontaneous change in terms of the Second Law.

11.   When NaOH pellets are being dissolved in water the temperature of the solution rises. Try to explain the spontaneous change in terms of the Second Law.

12. Sea water contains vast amounts of heat energy (that is, its temperature is well above 0 K). Why has no one designed a ship which uses this energy to propel it? How does the Second Law help us to explain this?

13. Make quite sure that you could explain to someone else the meaning of the following statements. If not, go back and revise Chapter 7.
(a) It is impossible to use all of the enthalpy in a reaction to do useful work. (You may have to look into Chapter 8 to answer this fully.)
(b) The maximum amount of useful work available from a system is the free energy change.
(c) In practice we can never use this maximum amount of useful work.
(d) The consequence of obtaining the maximum amount of work from a system is that the reaction must go infinitely slowly.
(e) A 100 per cent efficient power station is an impossibility.

14. For the cell below, the E° value is 1.1 volts.

$$Zn(s) \left| \begin{array}{c} Zn^{2+}(aq) \\ 1\ M \end{array} \right| \left| \begin{array}{c} Cu^{2+}(aq) \\ 1\ M \end{array} \right| Cu(s)$$

Calculate ΔG° for the cell. A Faraday is 96 500 coulombs.

15. From the results of Question 14 decide upon the feasibility of the reaction

$$Cu(s) + ZnSO_4(aq) \rightarrow CuSO_4(aq) + Zn(s)$$

16. The value of ΔS° for the reaction $H_2O(l) \rightarrow H_2O(g)$ at 373 K is 118 J K^{-1} mol^{-1}. How do you explain this when compared with the results in Table 8.1, page 43?

17. (a) If 1000 J of heat are added to a body and this increases its entropy by 10 J K^{-1}, what is the temperature of the substance?
(b) If the same amount of heat was added to the same body at room temperature (298 K) what increase would this cause to its entropy?

18. What is meant when a reaction is said to be (a) *spontaneous* and (b) *feasible*?

19. Using the data on page 92, calculate
(a) the temperature at which the decomposition of $MgCO_3(s)$ to $MgO(s) + CO_2(g)$ would become feasible;
(b) by further use of the data find out why this reaction stops at $MgO(s)$ and does not proceed to $Mg(s) + \frac{1}{2}O_2(g)$.

9 Free Energy and Equilibrium

$\triangle G$ and $\triangle G^{\circ}$

We have seen in Chapter 8 that the free energy change is related to the enthalpy and entropy changes occurring during a reaction,

$$\Delta G = \Delta H - T\Delta S$$

or
$$\Delta G^{\circ} = \Delta H^{\circ} - T\Delta S^{\circ}$$

It was stated that reactions for which ΔG° is less than or equal to zero are said to be feasible, i.e. the products are favoured compared with the reactants. In this chapter we take a closer look at the free energy changes which occur during a chemical reaction.

Taking the synthesis of ammonia as an example, we can write

$$N_2(g) + 3H_2(g) \rightarrow 2NH_3(g); \quad \Delta G^{\circ}_{298} = -33 \text{ kJ}$$

Since ΔG° is negative, the reaction is feasible and the formation of ammonia is favoured. We must now ask if thermodynamics can tell us how much ammonia will be formed when we allow a mixture of one mole of nitrogen and three moles of hydrogen to react.

We begin by considering a simple reaction

$$A \rightarrow B$$

for which ΔG° is negative, i.e. G°_A is greater than G°_B, and examine the free energy changes as the reaction proceeds from reactants to products. What will be the free energy of our reaction system when half of A has been converted to B? The answer you will probably give is that the free energy at this point will be the average G° between G°_A and G°_B However, we must be careful. Remember that G° refers to a Standard State of one mole of substance at one atmosphere pressure. If we start out with one mole of A, as soon as the reaction commences we no longer satisfy our Standard State conditions because we will have less than one mole of reactant or product. It follows that we must consider ΔG rather than $\Delta G°$ *during* the reaction. At any composition of reactants and products between 100 per cent A and 100 per cent B the free energy G will be less than the expected value calculated from the $G°$ values of A and B (Figure 9.1).

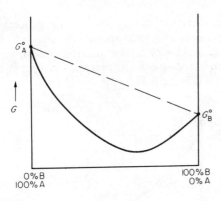

Figure 9.1

Mixing products and reactants

There is another factor which we must also take into account. During the conversion of A to B the molecules of A and B will be mixed in random fashion in the same vessel. This mixing will be present at all stages of the reaction between the limits of pure reactant A and pure product B, and will have an effect upon the total free energy content of the reaction system.

Think about the following situation (Figure 9.2).

Figure 9.2

We know from experience that when the partition between the two gas containers is removed, the gases will diffuse into each other spontaneously. From the arguments we used in Chapter 6, we also know that this diffusion results in an increase in the degree of disorder. In other words, in moving from situation 1 to situation 2 there is an increase in entropy; ΔS is positive. Since the gas diffusion occurs without any change in temperature, ΔH for the process must be zero. It follows that since $\Delta G = \Delta H - T\Delta S$ and $\Delta H = 0$,

$$\Delta G = -T\Delta S$$

ΔS is positive, therefore during the mixing process ΔG must be negative; the process will occur spontaneously.

Applying this conclusion to the reaction system, you can see that this will tend to decrease even further the free energy content of the reaction mixture (Figure 9.3).

Figure 9.3

Equilibrium – the free energy minimum

From Figure 9.3 we can see that the reaction will reach a point when the free energy content, G, will be at a minimum. You should also be able to see that we can reach this position of minimum free energy either by converting reactants to products or products to reactants. We can demonstrate this using the following experiment.

Take 100 cm^3 of tetrachloromethane containing 0.1 g of iodine (this will be a purple solution) and add 100 cm^3 of aqueous potassium iodide solution. If we shake this mixture, the colour of the tetrachloromethane solution will decrease in intensity as some of the iodine moves into the potassium iodide solution, which will develop a brown coloration.

Now take 100 cm^3 of potassium iodide solution containing 0.1 g of iodine (this will be a brown solution) and add 100 cm^3 of tetrachloromethane. On shaking, the tetrachloromethane layer will become coloured as the iodine moves into this layer (Figure 9.4).

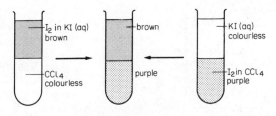

Figure 9.4

Eventually we will reach a point when the intensity of colour of the tetrachloromethane layer is the same in both experiments. This point corresponds to the minimum free energy of the system $CCl_4/KI(aq)/I_2$. You should be able to see that the minimum in the free energy curve corresponds to the point at which the free energy of the reactants, $G_{reactants}$, has become the same as the free energy of the products, $G_{products}$, and

$$\Delta G = G_{products} - G_{reactants} = 0$$

In other words, at this point the reaction has reached a stalemate situation, where energetically there is no net tendency for the reactants to become products or for products to become reactants. **The minimum in the free energy curve corresponds to the position of equilibrium in the reaction system and it follows that this position of** *equilibrium* **will be reached when $\Delta G = 0$.** Be careful not to confuse this with $\Delta G° = 0$.

There is a considerable difference between ΔG of a reaction and $\Delta G°$ of that reaction. A casual examination of a free energy diagram (Figure 9.5) would suggest that reactions can occur, even though $\Delta G°$ is positive, in the sense that we can approach the position of equilibrium either from the reactant side or from the product side. Again it must be emphasized that we can apply $\Delta G°$ only to systems in their Standard States and it is impossible to have pure reactants, pure products, and an equilibrium mixture all in their Standard States simultaneously in the same vessel. What then does $\Delta G°$ of a reaction tell us? If we remember that $\Delta G°$ applies *only* to the initial and final states of a reaction (i.e. pure reactants and pure products) this allows us to say whether or not the products will predominate over the reactants in that reaction. If $\Delta G°$ is greater than 0, then it is impossible to obtain a predominance of products over reactants. In other words, $\Delta G°$ allows us to stand outside the reaction system and to *predict* whether products or reactants will be favoured; it allows us to *predict* where the *position of equilibrium* will lie, as illustrated in Figure 9.5.

$\Delta G°$ large and −ve; equilibrium
lies on side of products

$\Delta G°$ large and +ve; equilibrium
lies on side of reactants

$\Delta G°\sim 0$; reactants and products
equally favoured

Figure 9.5

Once inside the reaction vessel, however, we can no longer use $\Delta G°$. We *must* then consider the actual free energy change, ΔG.

10   The Position of Equilibrium

Equilibrium - where precisely does it lie?

In the previous chapter we established that equilibrium occurs when a point is reached in a reaction at which $\Delta G = 0$. We now ask the question, can we predict exactly where the position of equilibrium will be?

We have stated earlier that the position of equilibrium of a reaction will be dependent upon $\Delta G°$ as shown in Table 10.1.

Table 10.1

$\Delta G°$	Position of equilibrium
<0	Nearer to products than reactants
~ 0	At neither extreme
>0	Nearer to reactants than products

We can see by analogy that this is the case, using a sliding weight on a string fixed at both ends. If the two ends of the string are fixed at different heights, the weight will come to rest at a position nearer the lower end (Figure 10.1).

The two fixed ends of the string correspond to $G°$ for reactants and products, and the difference in heights is equivalent to $\Delta G°$ of the reaction. The position at which the weight comes to rest corresponds to the position of equilibrium in the reaction.

Figure 10.1

It is worth noting at this point that, using this thermodynamic approach to determine the position of equilibrium, we have not been obliged to make any assumptions regarding the actual molecular nature of either reactants or products. We can, however, use the concept of molecules to help us in our understanding of equilibrium in a reaction system.

$\triangle G°$ and the equilibrium constant (K)

Imagine a reaction, which we can represent as

$$A + B \rightarrow C + D$$

Assuming that reactants and products are composed of molecules, there will be no reaction between A and B until the molecules come in contact with each other. In other words, molecular collisions between reactants are necessary before reaction can occur (Figure 10.2).

reaction   no reaction

Figure 10.2

The amount of reaction will depend upon the number of molecular collisions which, in turn, will depend upon the number of molecules present (the concentration). Now think about what happens during the course of a reaction. Initially, the reaction mixture will consist entirely of reactant molecules which will collide and produce product molecules. However, as the reaction proceeds, the concentration of product molecules will increase and so the number of collisions between product molecules will increase. Consequently, the amount of product which reacts to re-form reactants will increase. Eventually we will reach a point at which the number of product molecules being formed from reactants will be equal to the number of reactant molecules being re-formed from products. At this point equilibrium will be established.

You should be able to see that, according to this collision theory, the position of equilibrium will be related to the concentrations of reactants and products in the reaction mixture. We can define the position of equilibrium in terms of an equilibrium constant, K.

$$K = \frac{\text{concentration of products}}{\text{concentration of reactants}} = \frac{[\text{products}]}{[\text{reactants}]}$$

The [ ] are commonly used to denote 'concentration of'.

The size of K will depend upon the position of equilibrium. If the equilibrium lies towards the product side then [products] is greater than [reactants] and K is greater than one. Conversely, if [reactants] is greater than [products] then K is less than one and the equilibrium will lie on the side of the reactants. The limiting case will be when $K = 1$, when [reactants] = [products].

We will now compare our thermodynamic approach to equilibrium with the molecular collision approach and examine together the conclusions from each (Table 10.2).

Table 10.2

Position of equilibrium	K	$\triangle G^\circ$
[products] > [reactants]	>1	negative
[products] = [reactants]	1	0
[products] < [reactants]	<1	positive

You should be able to see that there is a relationship between ΔG° and the equilibrium constant, K. Can you see what the relationship is?

When $K = 1$, $\Delta G^\circ = 0$; this indicates a logarithmic relationship. When K is greater than one, ΔG° is negative. This indicates that the relationship is

$$-\Delta G^\circ \propto \log_e K$$

or

$$-\Delta G^\circ = \text{constant} \times \log_e K$$

We know that ΔG° is susceptible to temperature; K must also be so since increasing the temperature of the reaction mixture will increase the number of molecular collisions. The constant term must therefore contain the temperature T (absolute), and we write

$$-\Delta G^\circ = RT \log_e K$$

$$= 2.3 \, RT \log_{10} K$$

R is the gas constant ($8.3 \text{ J K}^{-1} \text{ mol}^{-1}$) and 2.3 converts natural logarithms ($\log_e$) to the more convenient logarithms to base 10.

Given that we can find ΔG° for a reaction, we can now calculate the value of the equilibrium constant K and predict the precise position of equilibrium. It follows from the relationship between ΔG° and K that, *for a reaction to be feasible*, and for the products to be favoured over the reactants,

ΔG° must be less than or equal to zero;
K must be greater than or equal to one

11   The Rate of Attainment of Equilibrium

Why only 'maybe'?

In Chapter 8 we stated that a reaction is feasible when ΔG° is less than or equal to zero. However, you may have noticed that we immediately added a rider that, although ΔG° is negative, this does not necessarily mean that the reaction will proceed at a measurable rate. In other words, thermodynamics says 'maybe'.

Let us examine, from a purely thermodynamic point of view, the reaction

$$H_2(g) + \tfrac{1}{2}O_2(g) \rightarrow H_2O(l); \quad \Delta G^\circ_{298} = -237 \, kJ$$

Using the equation

$$-\Delta G^\circ = 2.3 \, RT \log_{10} K$$

we can calculate the value of K to be 3.4×10^{41}. Clearly, very little hydrogen and oxygen will be present in the equilibrium mixture.

Now let us take a look at the practical situation. If we took a mixture containing one mole of hydrogen and half a mole of oxygen at 298 K it would take something like one million years for 1 cm^3 of water to be formed. Our thermodynamic arguments tell us **nothing** about the **rate** of attainment of equilibrium. ΔG° of the reaction tells us which state of the system is most stable from an energetic stand-point; however, that state is not automatically attained. What other factors must we consider before we can definitely say that a reaction will proceed at a measurable rate?

In the example we quoted above, we can rapidly attain the equilibrium state by applying a single spark to the hydrogen–oxygen mixture, or by adding a piece of platinum foil. In both cases the reaction proceeds violently to the equilibrium position predicted by thermodynamics. Let us look at a few more examples to see if we can find the clue.

A mixture of iron filings and sulphur, when dry, is stable at room temperature, although ΔG° for the reaction

$$Fe(s) + S(s) \rightarrow FeS(s)$$

is negative ($-98 \, kJ \, mol^{-1}$). However, if we heat the mixture a little or add a few drops of water, the mixture reacts vigorously and may even become incandescent as heat is liberated. Similarly, we know that a mixture of petrol and air is stable until either heated to a high temperature or sparked.

From these examples we can see that the reactions are feasible in the thermodynamic sense, in that they proceed with a reduction in free energy, but before reaction can occur we have to supply some energy to the system. This indicates that there must be some form of energy barrier to be overcome before reaction can occur, even though the reaction then proceeds with the evolution of energy. The energy profile for the reaction will be as shown in Figure 11.1.

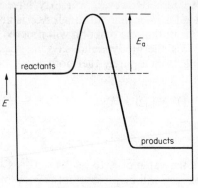

Figure 11.1

This energy barrier is called the Activation Energy (E_a) for the reaction.

We must note that this activation energy is in no way related to the thermodynamic energies. We must also differentiate clearly between two possible reasons why a reaction mixture must be heated to persuade reaction to occur.

(a) We saw in Chapter 8 that, in order to decompose calcium carbonate to quicklime, it is necessary to *maintain* a temperature in excess of 830 °C for the reaction to become feasible and ΔG to become less than or equal to zero. This heat is required to make the $T\Delta S$ term sufficiently large so that ΔG becomes negative. In such cases, once the supply of heat is stopped the reaction ceases because it is no longer thermodynamically feasible.

(b) On the other hand, heat must be supplied to magnesium before it will react with oxygen. However, in this case, once the reaction is started, we can immediately remove the source of heat without stopping the reaction. The energy liberated by the reaction itself is sufficient to overcome the activation energy barrier and allow the reaction to continue.

What is the activation energy?

You should now be aware that thermodynamic quantities such as changes in Standard Free Energy, Enthalpy, and Entropy depend only upon the initial and final states in the reaction. The activation energy, however, depends upon the actual route taken by the reactants in order to become products. This point becomes clearer if we compare values for the activation energy for a reaction in the presence and absence of a catalyst, as in Table 11.1.

Table 11.1

Reaction	$E_a(kJ\,mol^{-1})$	
	uncatalysed	catalysed
$H_2 + \frac{1}{2}O_2 \rightarrow H_2O$	280	56
$HI \rightarrow \frac{1}{2}H_2 + \frac{1}{2}I_2$	176	56
$N_2O \rightarrow N_2 + \frac{1}{2}O_2$	236	132

The presence of a catalyst lowers the activation energy because it provides an easier route by which reactants may be converted into products. You should see from Figure 11.2 that the presence of a catalyst does not alter the energy content of reactants or products; ΔH°, ΔG°, and ΔS° are unaltered. A catalyst does not, therefore, alter

Figure 11.2

the *position* of equilibrium in a reaction, but only the *rate* at which equilibrium is attained.

We can see that, if we wish to say whether or not a reaction will occur at a measurable rate, we first have to consider the thermodynamics and in particular the free energy changes in the reaction. We will then be able to say whether or not a reaction is feasible, i.e. whether the position of equilibrium will be nearer to the products than to the reactants. If we established that a reaction is feasible, we must then ask the question, 'at what rate will equilibrium be attained?' To answer this question we need to consider the 'mechanism' by which reactants are converted to products.

Activation energies are often regarded as a nuisance since they may prevent us from proceeding easily from reactants to products. However, we should be thankful that they exist – if all thermodynamically feasible reactions were deprived of their activation energy barriers, we would be in a very sorry state! Just think what would happen – all hydrocarbons would burn on contact with air; wood would do likewise, and all metals would instantly revert to their ores; all carbohydrates would break down into carbon dioxide and water. These are but a few examples of where thermodynamics would lead us if the activation energy barriers were not there to hold thermodynamics in check.

Consolidation of Chapters 9 to 11

In Chapters 9 to 11 we have emphasized the differences between ΔG and $\Delta G°$. Satisfy yourself that you clearly understand these differences, and then examine each of the following statements to find out in what respect each statement is *incorrect*.

1. (a) '$\Delta G°$ for a reaction is positive, therefore the reaction will not go.'
    (b) '$\Delta G°$ for a reaction is large and negative, therefore the reaction will occur spontaneously, i.e. it will proceed very quickly.'
    (c) 'At equilibrium the value of $\Delta G° = 0$.'

2. Using the data on page 92, decide which of the following reactions are feasible. Calculate values for the equilibrium constants, and state the values of the free energy changes at equilibrium, at 298 K.

A	$C_2H_6(g) + Cl_2(g) \rightarrow C_2H_5Cl(g) + HCl(g)$
B	$2HCl(g) \rightarrow H_2(g) + Cl_2(g)$
C	$CO(g) + H_2O(g) \rightarrow CO_2(g) + H_2(g)$
D	$C_2H_4(g) \rightarrow C_2H_2(g) + H_2(g)$

3. The following results were obtained for the composition of the equilibrium mixture during the hydrolysis of ethyl ethanoate at 298 K (concentrations shown in the table are in $mol\,l^{-1}$).

$$CH_3COOCH_2CH_3(l) + H_2O(l) \rightarrow CH_3COOH(l) + CH_3CH_2OH(l)$$

ethyl ethanoate	water	ethanoic acid	ethanol
0.155	0.725	0.185	0.185

What is the value of $\Delta G°$ for the reaction?

4. In a reaction

$$A + B \rightarrow C$$

at 298 K, the concentrations of reactants and products at equilibrium are $[A] = 0.35 \, \text{mol} \, l^{-1}$; $[B] = 0.70 \, \text{mol} \, l^{-1}$; and $[C] = 0.50$ $\text{mol} \, l^{-1}$. What is the Standard Free Energy Change of the reaction at 298 K?

5. The equilibrium constants for the following reactions have been measured at 823 K

A $CoO(s) + H_2(g) \rightarrow Co(s) + H_2O(g)$; $K = 67$

B $CoO(s) + CO(g) \rightarrow Co(s) + CO_2(g)$; $K = 490$

Calculate the equilibrium constant and the Standard Free Energy Change at 823 K for the reaction

$$CO_2(g) + H_2(g) \rightarrow CO(g) + H_2O(g)$$

12 Thermodynamics at Work in the Laboratory

In the foregoing chapters we have been largely concerned with establishing the principles of thermodynamics. In this chapter we take a look at some of the processes which we perform in the laboratory and examine how thermodynamics can help us to interpret them.

Diffusion

We have already seen in Chapter 10 that when two gases, A and B, are allowed to mix they do so spontaneously, i.e. the process of diffusion is associated with a decrease in free energy of the system of the two gases in the container. We also deduced that the ability of the gases to mix was related to probability, since the entropy content of the mixture (S_{A+B}) was greater than the total entropy content of the gases in separate containers ($S_A + S_B$)

$$S_{A+B} > (S_A + S_B)$$

A similar situation to the diffusion of gases is the distribution of a solute between two solutions. If we take a concentrated solution and place it in contact with a dilute solution, the concentration of the former inevitably decreases, whilst the dilute solution becomes more concentrated. Equilibrium will be established when the two solutions are of the same concentration. We can represent this process of diffusion in the following way (Figure 12.1).

The diffusion, or equalizing of concentrations, can be regarded

Figure 12.1

as a flow down two concentration hills – one involving the solvent, the other the solute. Relative to B, the concentrated solution A has too high a concentration of solute and too low a concentration of solvent. Conversely, relative to A, dilute solution B has too low a concentration of solute and too high a concentration of solvent. The equalizing of the concentrations is achieved by a net flow of solute molecules from A to B and by a net flow of solvent molecules from B to A. The effect of these two processes is to maximize the disorder (Second Law) within the total system of A and B together and to make the free energy a minimum, i.e. when the concentration is the same in both compartments the free energy of mixing is zero. Since no heat is generated or lost during the diffusion process, the enthalpy change is zero, and the diffusion is a direct consequence of the increase in entropy.

Osmosis
Another example of a process in which we can see the Second Law of Thermodynamics at work is the phenomenon of osmosis. Consider again two solutions of different concentrations. However, instead of placing them in direct contact as in the diffusion process, we separate the two solutions by a membrane which allows solvent molecules through it, but which blocks the flow of solute molecules (Figure 12.2).

semi-permeable
membrane

Figure 12.2

The system of solution A and solution B together will show the same tendency to attain a state of maximum disorder (equal concentration) as in diffusion. However, since the semipermeable membrane blocks the flow of solute from A to B, the solvent must flow through the membrane from B to A in an effort to dilute the concentrated solution and at the same time to concentrate the dilute solution. This tends to increase the degree of disorder within the system as a *whole*. This process, in which there is a *net* flow of solvent from the dilute solution to the more concentrated solution, is the process of osmosis.

The net flow of solvent will result in a pressure difference being established between the two sides of the membrane (Figure 12.3).

The pressure difference between the two sides at equilibrium is called the osmotic pressure, which may be of the order of several atmospheres.

Figure 12.3

Since the process of osmosis occurs spontaneously, it must be accompanied by a decrease in free energy of the overall system. Remembering that

$$\Delta G = \Delta H - T\Delta S$$

we can see that the process must be accompanied by either a negative enthalpy change or a positive entropy change. The enthalpy changes will be associated with bond-breaking and bond-making processes. For the molecules of solvent to pass through the membrane it will be necessary to break relatively weak solvent–solvent bonds. Once through the membrane these bonds will be reformed, or slightly stronger solute–solvent bonds may be formed. The net enthalpy change will be zero or very slightly negative. As the solvent passes into the solution, the degree of disorder will increase; ΔS for the process will be positive and ΔG will be negative. Equilibrium will be reached when the flow of the solvent from the pure solvent compartment to the solution compartment will be equal to the flow of solvent from the solution compartment to the pure solvent compartment. ΔG will be zero when the pressure difference between the two sides of the membrane is such that the potential energy difference between the two sides is equal to the energy $(T\Delta S)$ associated with the entropy change.

The process of osmosis is of great importance in biological systems, both in plants and animals, since most biological membranes such as cell walls are semipermeable. The human kidney is a particularly effective example. In the kidney we have the situation where on one side of a semipermeable membrane we have blood, which is an aqueous solution containing impurities and an almost colloidal suspension of blood particles, and on the other side a dilute aqueous solution. The membrane prevents the passage of blood into the dilute aqueous solution, but allows the passage of impurities, such as urea, which are then carried away to the bladder as urine. The process of dialysis using artificial kidney machines is in effect a process of osmosis. In such machines, blood on one side of a semipermeable membrane and sodium chloride on the other flow counter to each other (Figure 12.4) and the impurities flow from the blood stream to the aqueous salt solution.

Figure 12.4

Osmosis is also responsible, at least in part, for the transport of water from the roots to the leaves of plants and trees. Here we see examples of the operation of the Second Law of Thermodynamics in Nature.

Concentration cells

In the preceding two sections we have seen that when we have two solutions of different concentration in contact, or separated by a semipermeable membrane, there is a natural tendency for the system to move in such a way as to equalize the concentrations of the two solutions. This tendency is still present even if the solutions are not in *direct* contact. For example, if we have two beakers, one containing a $1M$ Cu^{2+} solution and the other a $0.1M$ Cu^{2+} solution linked by a salt bridge, the Cu^{2+} ions will gradually diffuse from the concentrated to the dilute solution.

There is another way in which the two solutions can attain equilibrium without coming into direct contact. If we set up the following cell

$$Cu(s) \left| \begin{array}{c} Cu^{2+}(aq) \\ 0.1\ M \end{array} \right| \left. \begin{array}{c} Cu^{2+}(aq) \\ 1\ M \end{array} \right| Cu(s)$$

Cu^{2+} can be taken from the more concentrated solution and by electron transfer an equivalent amount of Cu^{2+} can be released into the more dilute solution. In the left-hand half-cell the reaction

$$Cu(s) \rightarrow Cu^{2+} + 2e^-$$

will occur. Electrons will be transferred through the external circuit to the right-hand half-cell, where the reaction

$$Cu^{2+} + 2e^- \rightarrow Cu(s)$$

will take place.

This is an example of a concentration cell, and the voltage will depend upon the ratio of the concentrations in the two half-cells. Since

$$-\Delta G = nFE$$

we can see that the operation of the cell is associated with a negative free energy change.

Since these cells operate at constant temperature, $\Delta H = 0$, and so

$$\Delta G = -T\Delta S = -nFE$$

The tendency for the system, represented by the cell, to attain a state of maximum disorder according to the Second Law of Thermodynamics gives rise to the e.m.f.

Separation processes

In Chapter 9 we mentioned that if a solution of iodine in aqueous potassium iodide is shaken with tetrachloromethane, some of the iodine will move from the aqueous solution into the tetrachloromethane. We also saw that an equilibrium was established between the iodine concentration in the two layers. This experiment is an example of the process of partition of a solute between two immiscible solvents. Such processes can be used to separate mixtures of substances and we now examine the thermodynamics of partition using the iodine/aqueous potassium iodide/tetrachloromethane system as our example.

When iodine is dissolved in aqueous iodide solution, iodine reacts with $I^-(aq)$ to form $I_3^-(aq)$ anions. On addition of tetrachloromethane, some of the iodine will be transferred from the aqueous layer to the tetrachloromethane layer. This process will be endothermic, since relatively strong I_2–I^- bonds are broken and only weak iodine–tetrachloromethane bonds are formed. There will be an increase in entropy of the system, since iodine will move from a relatively ordered I_3^- state to a less ordered state when dissolved in tetrachloromethane. Equilibrium will be established when $\Delta H = T\Delta S$, i.e. when $\Delta G = 0$. The partition process will depend upon both enthalpy and entropy changes. We should note that if we considered the reverse process of iodine in tetrachloromethane solution with aqueous potassium iodide the partition will be exothermic, but the overall entropy change will be positive. In either case the position of equilibrium will be the same and will be given by the value of the equilibrium constant (K), defined as

$$K = \frac{\text{(concentration of } I_2 \text{ in } CCl_4)}{\text{(concentration of } I_2 \text{ in KI (aq))}}$$

K is called the partition or distribution coefficient.

The process of partition can be used to separate a mixture of substances provided suitable pairs of immiscible liquids can be found. Let us suppose we have a mixture containing equal amounts of two compounds, A and B, which is to be partitioned between equal volumes of two solvents, X and Y. A has a partition coefficient of 10 between X and Y, while B has a partition coefficient of 0.1,

$$\frac{[A] \text{ in X}}{[A] \text{ in Y}} = 10 \quad \text{and} \quad \frac{[B] \text{ in X}}{[B] \text{ in Y}} = 0.1$$

If we take 22 g of the mixture and shake it with equal volumes of X and Y then, at equilibrium, X will contain 10 g of A and 1 g of B, while Y will contain 1 g of A and 10 g of B. If the two layers are now separated and the X layer is shaken with an equal volume of pure solvent Y, a new equilibrium will be established; layer X will now contain 9.1 g of A and 0.1 g of B. By repeating this process a number of times you should be able to see that we can get almost pure A in X, although we shall never achieve complete separation of A and B without very many successive equilibria (Figure 12.5).

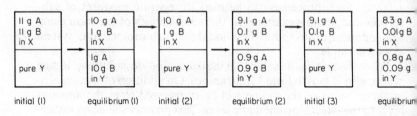

initial (1)   equilibrium (1)   initial (2)   equilibrium (2)   initial (3)   equilibrium

Figure 12.5

The process of partition chromatography permits several thousands of partition equilibria to be achieved in one operation. In partition chromatography one of the solvents, usually water, is adsorbed on the surface of a solid such as silica gel or alumina. The solid is packed into a column and a solution of the mixture to be separated is introduced at the top of the column. The second solvent, the eluant, which is immiscible with water, is *slowly* run through the column carrying the mixture with it. As the material moves down the column, it will partition itself between the moving phase, the eluant, and the stationary adsorbed water. As the mixture passes down the column a whole series of partition equilibria, on a microscopic scale, will be established. We should note that although these equilibria will be established, they will only be instantaneous equilibria. Since the eluant is flowing through the column it is continuously changing the system.

The rate at which the individual components pass through the column will depend upon their individual partition coefficients. Provided these partition coefficients are sufficiently different and provided that the system is *never allowed to settle* at equilibrium by allowing the eluant to flow slowly but *continuously* through the column, complete separation of a mixture can be achieved (Figure 12.6).

Figure 12.6

Ion exchange

Ion exchange is essentially chromatography of ionic substances. In the ion exchange process a solution containing the 'undesirable' ions is passed through a column containing an ion exchange resin. The 'undesirable' ions are removed and replaced by other ions. Cation exchange resins are commonly organic polymeric materials containing free sulphonic acid groups (Figure 12.7(a)), while anion exchangers are polymers with 'free' quaternary ammonium groups (Figure 12.7(b)).

Figure 12.7

Let us suppose we have a solution containing Na^+ ions which we wish to replace by H^+ ions. In solution, Na^+ ions will be surrounded in a fairly ordered manner by solvent water molecules. H^+ ions will be bonded to SO_3^- groups of the resin. To obtain ion exchange, we will have to break $H^+-SO_3^-$ bonds and Na^+–water bonds and form $Na^+-SO_3^-$ bonds and H^+–water bonds. The difference between these quantities will give rise to an enthalpy term. We shall also have an entropy term since the degree of solvation, i.e. the number of water molecules surrounding the ion, will be different for Na^+ ions and H^+ ions. Both enthalpy and entropy effects may be present in the ion exchange process and equilibrium will be reached, at any point in the column, when the ΔH and $T\Delta S$ terms are equal.

Although, as in partition chromatography, we can regard ion exchange as occurring through a series of 'mini' equilibria down the column, we must realize that for the efficient operation of an ion exchange column in achieving complete replacement of one ion by another, the system must never be allowed to reach overall equilibrium. The process must be operated under irreversible conditions by continuously removing one of the components of the system. Complete ion exchange would not be achieved if the ion exchange resin was simply placed in a beaker of the solution containing the 'unwanted' ions. In this case the solution and ion exchange resin would eventually reach an equilibrium in which solution and resin would each contain both ions.

Solution processes
In this section we take a look at the thermodynamic factors involved in dissolving a substance in a solvent. We shall take as our example the dissolving of an ionic solid in water, although the arguments are equally valid for other systems. For a solid to dissolve in a solvent the free energy change accompanying the dissolving must be negative. Since

$$\Delta G = \Delta H - T\Delta S$$

we must again consider both the enthalpy and the entropy changes.

Let us take as our example the dissolving of sodium chloride in water. We can represent the overall process as

$$NaCl(s) + H_2O(l) \rightarrow Na^+(aq) + Cl^-(aq)$$

Figure 12.8

We can most conveniently represent the enthalpy changes in this process by writing a Born–Haber cycle (Figure 12.8).

For the dissolving process we need to break down the sodium chloride crystal lattice. Since this is a bond-breaking process it will be endothermic. The free ions will then become solvated and bonds will be formed between the ions and water molecules; this will be an exothermic process. From the Born–Haber cycle

$$\Delta H_{solution} = U - \Delta H_{solvation}(Na^+) - \Delta H_{solvation}(Cl^-)$$

The process of solution may be endothermic or exothermic, depending upon the relative magnitudes of the lattice energy, U, and the heats of solvation (or solvation energies) of the ions.

In the process of breaking the lattice, we are producing gaseous ions from a solid and so there will be a large increase in entropy. In the solvation process the ions are surrounded by water molecules (Figure 12.9), which will tend to increase the order in the liquid relative to that in pure water.

H₂O disordered   H₂O more ordered

Figure 12.9

The process of dissolving involves both enthalpy and entropy terms. For substances which dissolve endothermically, such as sodium nitrate, potassium chloride, and ammonium bromide, the entropy change must be sufficiently large so that $T\Delta S$ is greater than ΔH, for the dissolving to occur spontaneously.

For those substances which dissolve exothermically, such as sodium carbonate, lithium chloride, and calcium chloride, both enthalpy and entropy factors will tend to favour the dissolving process.

13 Thermodynamics and Everyday Things

The work in this book will remain largely an academic exercise unless we can see it operating in the world at large. We have tried throughout to keep in touch with the real world, but we shall devote the whole of this chapter to the applications of thermodynamics in industry and in everyday life.

The efficiency of heat engines

It is now possible to see in perspective why heat engines must be less than 100 per cent efficient. We now know that the heat energy associated with an enthalpy change is not all available to do work; only the free energy can do useful work. If we attempt to obtain the maximum work (ΔG^o) from free energy, we have the consequence that the process will have to occur infinitely slowly or not at all. It is inevitable that the conversion of chemical energy via heat into work can never be 100 per cent efficient, or anywhere near it.

In a power station (or any heat engine) heat has to flow. The molecular motions of heat are random kinetic energy; to obtain work from heat, a direction has to be superimposed on it. This directional flow can be caused by having a hot area and a relatively cold area within the engine. As heat flows the cold area gets hotter, and eventually the flow will stop when the two areas achieve the same temperature. This would stop the engine, and the only way to maintain its operation is to keep the cold area cold by some cooling system such as river water or by cold air cooling the condenser water. This is what is done in practice and results in large volumes of warm air or warm water, both high in entropy. This low temperature heat is low grade heat in the sense that it is almost entirely occupied in creating disorder. In this chaotic state it is no longer fit to do work (Figure 13.1).

In moving vehicles the problem of efficiency is even more acute than in a static power station. For instance of the actual power generated by a car engine, some 20 per cent is lost in pushing the car against the air. This loss is additional to those suffered in a power station; vehicles also have cooling problems, and a great deal of heat is lost through the radiator and through the exhaust gases.

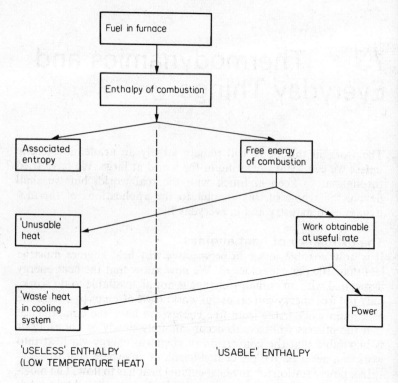

Figure 13.1

Metal extraction processes

None of the metals in common use is found to any extent in the metallic state in Nature. The vast bulk of metal has to be extracted from ores which are mainly oxides, or compounds which are readily converted to oxides such as sulphides and carbonates.

The reduction processes are not numerous and you may recall some of them from your earlier chemistry. Some of these processes are listed below; M stands for a metal.

(a) *Reduction with hydrogen* $MO + H_2 \rightarrow M + H_2O$

(b) *Reduction with carbon* This can operate in several ways.

$$\text{(i)} \qquad 2MO + C \rightarrow 2M + CO_2$$

$$\text{(ii)} \qquad MO + C \rightarrow M + CO$$

(iii) $\begin{cases} C + \frac{1}{2}O_2 \rightarrow CO \\ MO + CO \rightarrow M + CO_2 \end{cases}$

(iv) $\begin{cases} C + O_2 \rightarrow CO_2 \\ CO_2 + C \rightarrow 2CO \\ MO + CO \rightarrow M + CO_2 \end{cases}$

(c) *Reduction by electrolysis* There are several possibilities.

(i) $\begin{cases} MO(s) \quad \rightarrow \quad MO(l) \\ MO(l) \xrightarrow{\text{electrolysis}} M \text{ (at cathode)} + \frac{1}{2}O_2 \text{ (at anode)} \end{cases}$

(ii) $\begin{cases} MO(s) \quad \rightarrow \quad M \text{ salt(s)} \rightarrow M \text{ salt(l)} \\ M \text{ salt(l)} \xrightarrow{\text{electrolysis}} M \text{ (at cathode)} \end{cases}$

Hydrogen reduction is usually employed on a relatively small scale for specialist situations, such as the extraction of tungsten metal for making the filaments in light bulbs. Electrolysis, though very important, will not be discussed here. We shall concentrate upon carbon reductions. Reduction by carbon (or carbon monoxide) is responsible for the largest tonnage of metal, in particular iron. Probably the simplest way to approach the thermodynamics of these processes is to examine a series of graphs, in which the Standard Free Energy Changes in a large number of oxidation processes are plotted against temperature. Remember that ΔG° requires that we standardize on one mole of a reactant (or product) and one atmosphere pressure. Temperature appears as a suffix T in ΔG_T° and can vary. Such graphs are called *Ellingham diagrams*.

Ellingham diagrams
The common reactant in all of these reactions is oxygen and so the ΔG° values are standardized on one mole of oxygen gas. Examine the diagram shown in Figure 13.2.

Characteristics of the diagrams
1. The top of the scale is the horizontal line corresponding to $\Delta G^\circ = 0$, so that all the *oxidation* reactions below this line are

feasible. It follows, however, that any reaction above this line will become feasible in the opposite direction, namely *reduction*.

As you can see, the graph for the oxidation of silver crosses the $\Delta G° = 0$ line and so, above the temperature at which they intersect, the reaction will tend to go in reverse and the oxide will revert to the metal.

2.   The general trend is for graphs to rise to less negative values of $\Delta G°$ as temperature increases. There are two notable exceptions.

$$2C + O_2 \rightarrow 2CO$$

becomes more negative with temperature rise and

$$C + O_2 \rightarrow CO_2$$

is almost unaffected by temperature change. This means that both of these graphs tend to intersect the metal plus oxygen graphs. This gives us the key to the extraction processes.

How can we explain these trends? Most oxidation processes are strongly exothermic, i.e. the enthalpy term is large and negative making it likely that the free energy term will be negative. In the case of metal oxidations, a mole of gas is being consumed to give a solid product and so the entropy of the *system* is decreasing.

$$\Delta G° = \underset{\text{negative}}{\Delta H°} - \underset{\text{negative}}{T\Delta S°}$$

The *negative* $T\Delta S°$ term is being *subtracted* from the *negative* $\Delta H°$ term. As T increases this will have the effect of making $\Delta G°$ less negative.

For the reaction

$$C(s) + O_2(g) \rightarrow CO_2(g)$$

the volume of gas is remaining constant and so the $\Delta S°$ term will be very small (almost zero). As the temperature rises, $\Delta G°$ will not change much.

The reaction

$$2C(s) + O_2(g) \rightarrow 2CO(g)$$

is generating more gas than it is consuming. The $\Delta S°$ term is positive and so, as temperature rises, the value of $\Delta G°$ will become more negative.

These arguments assume that the $\Delta H°$ and $\Delta S°$ values remain constant with temperature change, and this is substantially true. For a 100 K rise in temperature, $\Delta H°$ values vary only by about 1 per cent and $\Delta S°$ values by about 5 per cent.

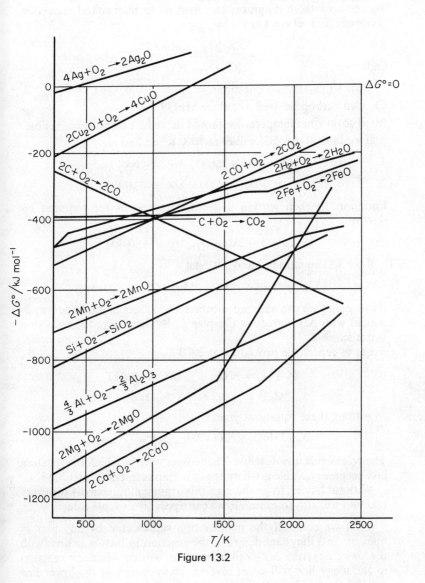

Figure 13.2

Ellingham diagrams working

To see how these diagrams can help us to understand reduction processes look at the graphs for

$$2Mn + O_2 \rightarrow 2MnO$$

and

$$2C + O_2 \rightarrow 2CO$$

Now let us ask two questions.

(i)   Can carbon be used to reduce MnO?

(ii) If so, at what temperature should the reduction become feasible?

If we look at the $\Delta G°$ values at 1000 K, we find

1. $2Mn + O_2 \rightarrow 2MnO$; $\Delta G° = -600\,kJ$

2. $2C + O_2 \rightarrow 2CO$; $\Delta G° = -380\,kJ$

Equation 1, when written in reverse, represents the required reduction.

3. $2MnO \rightarrow 2Mn + O_2$; $\Delta G° = +600\,kJ$

If we add equations 2 and 3 we get

$$2C + 2MnO \rightarrow 2CO + 2Mn; \ \Delta G° = +220\,kJ$$

(Notice that we can add and subtract $\Delta G°$ values in the same way as we did with $\Delta H°$ values in Chapter 3.) By definition, the reduction is not feasible.

Let us repeat the procedure at 2000 K.

$$2C + O_2 \rightarrow 2CO; \qquad \Delta G° = -560\,kJ$$

$$2MnO \rightarrow 2Mn + O_2; \ \Delta G° = +450\,kJ$$

Adding these equations gives

$$2C + 2MnO \rightarrow 2CO + 2Mn; \ \Delta G° = -110\,kJ$$

The reaction is now feasible. The temperature at which the reaction just becomes feasible is where the two graphs intersect, at 1700 K.

Without having to go through this argument repeatedly for every reaction we wish to examine, we can apply two simple rules:

(a) If we consider the net reaction represented by any pair of lines on an Ellingham diagram, the reaction in the *lower* line (with the more negative $\Delta G°$) will proceed as written while the reaction in the *upper* line will go in reverse. The reaction in the lower line will be the oxidation; the reaction in the upper line, written in reverse, will be the reduction.

(b) If the lines cross each other, the oxidation and reduction roles

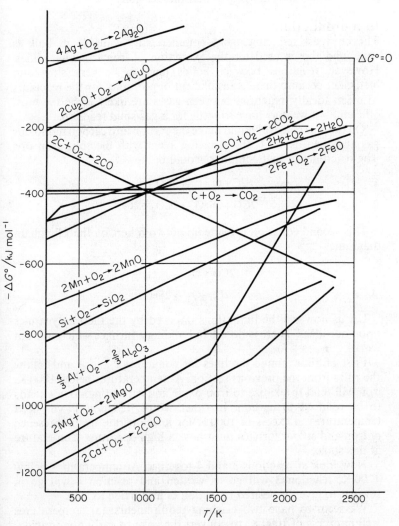

Figure 13.2 (repeat)

will be reversed, because the upper line has now become the lower one. The temperature corresponding to this crossing will be the point at which the changeover becomes feasible.

Iron production

The cheapest reducing agent commercially available in bulk is coke, and this is used for the extraction of iron from its oxides. However, reactions between solids tend to be very slow and inefficient because there is insufficient opportunity for the reactants to meet. Ideally, reactions between gases are likely to be the most efficient, but we may have to settle for a gas/solid reaction.

On the face of it, we should make the carbon into carbon monoxide gas and then use it as the reducing agent with the solid iron ore. The reactions, at their simplest, would be

1. $$2C + O_2 \rightarrow 2CO$$

2. $$2CO + 2FeO \rightarrow 2CO_2 + 2Fe$$

This second equation is made up of two others on the Ellingham diagram.

3. $$2CO + O_2 \rightarrow 2CO_2$$

4. $$2Fe + O_2 \rightarrow 2FeO$$

Let us now see the limitations imposed by the thermodynamics upon our ideas. There is no use in building a furnace which will not work!

First of all, examine the lines for equations 1 and 4 and follow the rules from the previous section. At temperatures below 1000 K, iron will tend to oxidize to iron oxide and carbon monoxide tends to be reduced to carbon. In other words, reaction 1 will need temperatures in excess of 1000 K for it to operate in the presence of iron and so our furnace must have a high operating temperature at this stage.

Now look at reactions 3 and 4 together. At temperatures below 1200 K, reaction 3 will go as written and reaction 4 will go in reverse, to give the desired reduction of iron oxide to iron.

We seem to have two clashing requirements: (a) temperatures well in excess of 1000 K, to convert the coke to carbon monoxide; (b) temperatures well below 1200 K, to allow the reduction of iron oxide to take place.

These limitations dictate the design of the blast furnace (Figure 13.3) in which iron is made. It is built to have very high temperatures at the bottom and a strongly oxidizing atmosphere, caused by a

Figure 13.2 (repeat)

Figure 13.3

blast of hot air at around 2000 K. This turns carbon into carbon monoxide. As they rise into the reduction zone, the gases cool to about 1000 K to meet the thermodynamic requirements for iron oxide reduction. The heat left in the gases after the reduction is over is used to heat the incoming materials and, at about 500 K, the gases containing some carbon monoxide are led off. These exhaust gases are then burnt in stoves to heat the incoming air up to about 2000 K ready to repeat the cycle.

The actual process is more complex than is shown above, but the argument serves to illustrate how thermodynamics has a part to play in industrial design.

Similar considerations can be made for the extraction of other metals and, in the Consolidation Section on page 90 you will have the opportunity of trying an example for yourself.

Pollution problems
The full statement of the First Law says that 'the amount of mass and energy in the universe is a constant'. We have said a great deal

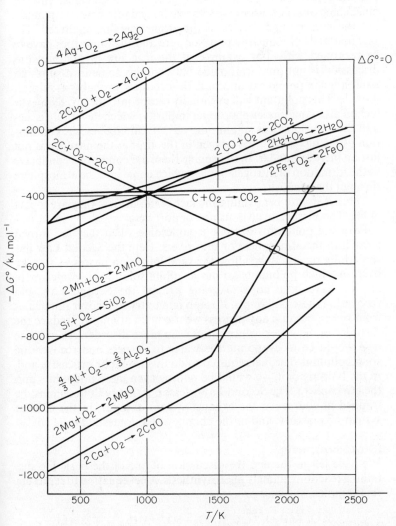

Figure 13.2 (repeat)

about energy being constant, but the 'mass' part of the statement cannot be ignored. This has consequences for a discussion of pollution problems, because what goes into a chemical process must come out. The atoms may be rearranged into new compounds, but the number and species of the atoms remains unaltered. The raw materials of industry are never pure and the impurities have to be reckoned with. For example, if the iron ore in our previous discussion is not pure iron oxide but contains some iron sulphide, a sulphur compound will appear in the products, probably as sulphur dioxide. This pollutant will eventually escape into the air. Domestic fuel oil also contains sulphur as an impurity, which inevitably issues into the atmosphere as sulphur dioxide. In car engines, the combustion of the fuel is with the oxygen in the air, but the nitrogen is not just an inert bystander. In the engine there are conditions conducive to the formation of nitrogen oxides, which come into the atmosphere through the exhaust.

There is no use bemoaning the fact of impurities; they are a part of life. The First Law gives us no comfort here.

Potential pollutants become troublesome when they are turned loose into the atmosphere or into rivers. Here the Second Law has something to say. If we allow the randomization processes to take over, in which pollutants go out as dilute solutions in water or in air, we have little hope of going against the Second Law and recovering these pollutants. It is too late to try to recover impurities from rivers, because any process we use in an attempt to reduce the disorder in the water will result in even more disorder. An extreme case would be to evaporate the water to dryness and recover the solid pollutant. The fuel required to do this would be expensive and, in the burning of it, we would be putting even more pollutants into the atmosphere. The Second Law's lesson is that pollutants must be trapped at source; in the exhaust system of a car, in the effluent system of a factory, and in the chimney of a domestic fire.

Photosynthesis

We have left to the end the discussion of one of the basic life-sustaining reactions, namely photosynthesis. A net equation to represent this complex, stepwise process is

$$6CO_2 + 6H_2O \xrightarrow{\text{light}} \underset{\text{glucose}}{C_6H_{12}O_6} + 6O_2; \quad \begin{aligned} \Delta H^\circ_{298} &= +2814\,\text{kJ} \\ \Delta G^\circ_{298} &= +2867\,\text{kJ} \end{aligned}$$

It can be seen from these energy values that this is very much an uphill process. It is certainly not feasible, by our definition, nor is it spontaneous. It must be driven by some external force to keep it going and yet it certainly proceeds, converting in a year about

35×10^9 tonnes of carbon into glucose! The energy requirement for this has been estimated at 10^{18} kJ per year.

It is helpful here to return to our idea of system and surroundings and to see the sun as the system and the photosynthesizing plants as part of the surroundings.

In the sun there is a fantastically exothermic reaction taking place.

$$4H \rightarrow He + 2e \quad ; \quad \Delta H = -24 \times 10^8 \, kJ \, mol^{-1} \text{ of He}$$

Mass (0.029 g) is being converted into energy (Chapter 1, page 3) in this reaction. This is accompanied by a massive decrease in free energy, which becomes available to the surroundings to do work, such as the work of driving photosynthesis up its free energy hill. When plants are not exposed to the sun or when they die, the process has to stop, or even go in its spontaneous direction to CO_2 and H_2O (Chapter 3, page 10). Not all of the sun's energy reaches the earth and only a fraction of that landing on the earth is used by plants. In a year plants store for useful purposes about 100 times more energy than is used by man to drive all of his machines.

Most animals have no mechanism within their bodies for storing the energy of the sun. We could sunbathe all day and every day in a futile attempt to absorb and store energy. We are, ultimately, entirely dependent upon plants for our energy supply and attempts which have been made to copy the plant processes have not yet met with real success. Any solution to this problem will be found only by careful observation and application of the Laws of Thermodynamics.

Consolidation of Chapters
12 and *13*

1. The starch and iodine solutions in Figure C.3 are of the same concentration in water. Describe and explain the situation you would expect to see after one hour.

aqueous starch solution

semi-permeable membrane

aqueous I_2 solution

Figure C.3

2. In a cubic kilometre of sea water there is 6.3 kg of gold in gold compounds (worth \$2225 at 1976 prices). In terms of the Second Law try to explain why this 'gold mine' has not been economically exploited.

3. There is a water purification system called reverse osmosis. Impure water is forced into a semipermeable tube and pure water comes through the walls of the tube. Is this going against the Second Law?

4. Chromatography is a process whereby mixtures are *separated spontaneously*. By considering *all* the processes at work during the separation, show how chromatography conforms to the Second Law.

5. What is the commercial possibility of reducing aluminium oxide with hydrogen?

6. Use the Ellingham diagram (Figure 13.2) for 'magnesium to magnesium oxide' to answer the following questions.

(a) By reference to the physical properties of magnesium, suggest why the slope of the graph changes so suddenly at about 1380 K.

(b) Show why, when magnesium is burned in a jar of carbon dioxide, black specks of carbon are deposited.

(c) What is the lowest temperature at which magnesium oxide could be reduced to magnesium by carbon compounds?

(d) On balance, what might be the most efficient way of reducing magnesium oxide?

(e) When the metallic magnesium is produced, what will be its physical state and what hazards will be associated with it?

7. Steam blown through hot coke gives water gas, an industrial fuel

$$C(s) + H_2O(g) \rightarrow CO(g) + H_2(g)$$

(a) From ΔH_f° data (page 92), find out if this reaction is exothermic or endothermic.

(b) From the Ellingham diagram (Figure 13.2), calculate the temperature at which the coke must be maintained for the reaction to be feasible.

(c) How can the results from (a) and (b) be reconciled?

8. Can you see at least two examples in Figure 13.2 in which the Reactivity Series does not apply at high temperatures? List them.

9. Try now to explain the apparent contradiction which was stated in Chapter 4, page 18. 'In a blast furnace iron oxide is being converted into iron at the same time as the iron walls of the furnace are rusting to iron oxide.'

Thermodynamic Data

Standard Enthalpies of Formation, ΔH_f^o, and Standard Free Energies of Formation, ΔG_f^o, of Compounds at 298 K

By definition all pure elements have $\Delta H_f^o = 0$ and $\Delta G_f^o = 0$.

Substance	$\Delta H_f^o (kJ\ mol^{-1})$	$\Delta G_f^o (kJ\ mol^{-1})$
$Al_2O_3(s)$	-1669	-1576
$CaO(s)$	-635	-604
$Ca(OH)_2(s)$	-987	-897
$CaCO_3(s)$	-1207	-1129
$CH_4(g)$	-75	-51
$C_2H_6(g)$	-85	-33
$C_3H_8(g)$	-104	-24
$C_6H_6(g)$	83	130
$C_6H_6(l)$	49	125
$C_2H_4(g)$	52	68
$C_2H_2(g)$	227	209
$CH_3Cl(g)$	-82	-59
$C_2H_5Cl(g)$	-105	-53
$CO(g)$	-111	-137
$CO_2(g)$	-394	-395
$FeO(s)$	-266	-244
$FeS(s)$	-95	-98
$HCl(g)$	-92	-95
$H_2O(g)$	-242	-229
$H_2O(l)$	-286	-237
$KNO_2(s)$	-370	
$KNO_3(s)$	-493	-393
$MgO(s)$	-602	-570
$MgCO_3(s)$	-1113	-1030
$NH_3(g)$	-46	-17
$NH_4Cl(s)$	-315	-204
$NO(g)$	90	87
$NO_2(g)$	34	52

Substance	$\triangle H_f^o (kJ\,mol^{-1})$	$\triangle G_f^o (kJ\,mol^{-1})$
$N_2O_4(g)$	10	98
$Na_2O(s)$	-416	-377
$NaOH(s)$	-427	-377
$PCl_3(l)$	-339	
$PCl_5(l)$	-463	
$TiO_2(s)$	-912	-853

Standard Enthalpies of Combustion at 298 K

Substance	$\triangle H^o(kJ\,mol^{-1})$
$H_2(g)$	-286
C (graphite)	-394
$CH_4(g)$	-882
$C_3H_8(g)$	-2202
$CO(g)$	-293
$C_6H_{12}O_6(s)$ (glucose)	-2816

Standard Enthalpies of Sublimation at 298 K

Substance	$\triangle H^o_{sub}(kJ\,mol^{-1})$
C (graphite)	715
I_2	62
Mg	168
Na	109

Average Bond Enthalpies at 298 K

Bond	$\triangle H(kJ\,mol^{-1})$
C——C	348
C══C	612
C═══C (benzene)	518
C≡══C	837
C——H	412
C——Cl	338
Cl——Cl	242
H——H	436
I——Cl	211
N≡══N	944
N——H	388
O══O	496
O——H	463

Absolute Entropies of Substances at 298 K

Substance	$S°(J K^{-1} mol^{-1})$
$Br_2(g)$	245
$Br_2(l)$	152
$Ca(s)$	42
$CaO(s)$	40
$CaCO_3(s)$	93
C (graphite)	6
$C_6H_6(g)$	269
$C_6H_6(l)$	173
$CO(g)$	198
$CO_2(g)$	214
$Cl_2(g)$	223
$H_2(g)$	131
$HCl(g)$	187
$H_2O(g)$	189
$H_2O(l)$	70
$H_2S(g)$	206
$Mg(s)$	33
$MgO(s)$	27
$MgCO_3(s)$	66
$N_2(g)$	192
$O_2(g)$	205
$PCl_3(g)$	312
$NH_3(g)$	193

Answers to Problems in Consolidation Sections

Chapters 1 to 3

4. The enthalpy of formation of $CH_3Cl(g)$ is given as $-82\,kJ$ mol^{-1}. This means that

$$C(s) + \tfrac{3}{2}H_2(g) + \tfrac{1}{2}Cl_2(g) \rightarrow CH_3Cl(g); \quad \Delta H^\circ = -82\,kJ$$

We shall have to set up a Born–Haber cycle (Figure A.1) for the indirect route to the formation of CH_3Cl.

Figure A.1

There are two routes from $C(g) + 3H(g) + Cl(g)$ to $CH_3Cl(g)$, both of which must be energetically the same. Therefore

$$(3 \times 412) + x = (\tfrac{1}{2} \times 242) + (3 \times 218) + 715 + 82$$
$$1236 + x = 121 + 654 + 715 + 82$$
$$x = 336\ kJ$$

Energy required to break a C–Cl bond is $+336\,kJ$, or energy released when a C–Cl bond forms is $-336\,kJ$.

5.   In this case we are measuring everything from the Standard Enthalpy of Formation line for all elements, taken as zero.

To make a mole of $CaCO_3(s)$ from its elements releases $1207\,kJ$ of energy.

To make a mole of $CaCO_3(s)$ and a mole of $CO_2(g)$ from their elements releases $635+394\,kJ$ of energy $= 1029\,kJ$. In the equation

$$CaCO_3(s) \rightarrow CaO(s)+CO_2(g)$$

the products, relative to the reactant, are less negative (that is, more positive) by

$$1207-1029\,kJ = +178\,kJ$$
$$CaCO_3(s) \rightarrow CaO(s)+CO_2(g); \; \Delta H^\circ = +178\,kJ$$

6.   The equation for the Standard Heat of Formation, ΔH°_f, of $PCl_5(s)$ is

$$P(s)+\tfrac{5}{2}Cl_2(g) \rightarrow PCl_5(s)$$

Of the given equations, the first one must be halved to give $P(s)$ on the left-hand side.

$$P(s)+\tfrac{3}{2}Cl_2(g) \rightarrow PCl_3(l); \; \Delta H^\circ = -318\,kJ$$

This can now be added to the second equation given to provide the required result.

$$P(s)+\tfrac{3}{2}Cl_2(g)+PCl_3(l)+Cl_2(g) \rightarrow PCl_3(l)+PCl_5(s); \; \Delta H^\circ = -455\,kJ$$

or $P(s)+\tfrac{5}{2}Cl_2(g) \rightarrow PCl_5(s); \; \Delta H^\circ = -455\,kJ$

7.   The equation for the formation of $Ca(OH)_2(s)$ from its elements is

$$Ca(s)+H_2(g)+O_2(g) \rightarrow Ca(OH)_2(s)$$

Of the equations, **B** gives us $Ca(OH)_2(s)$ on the right and **C** gives $Ca(s)$ on the left, while **A** gives $H_2(g)+O_2(g)$ on the left. If all three equations are added as they stand, we should arrive at the required equation.

$$H_2(g)+O_2(g)+CaO(s)+H_2O(l)+Ca(s) \rightarrow H_2O(l)+Ca(OH)_2(s)+CaO(s);$$
$$\Delta H^\circ = -984\,kJ$$

or $Ca(s)+H_2(g)+O_2(g) \rightarrow Ca(OH)_2(s); \; \Delta H^\circ = -984\,kJ$

Chapters 4 to 8

1.   Endothermic reactions are:

D   Decompositions into smaller molecules are generally endothermic. Because of the generation of gas, the entropy term is positive, making it possible for the ΔG term to be negative.

E $N \equiv N$ is the strongest among the common bonds ($944\,kJ$

mol^{-1}). This bond-breaking energy is unlikely to be compensated for in the formation of nitrogen–oxygen bonds. In the atmosphere, this reaction occurs only during thunderstorms.

F Bonds must be broken and no new ones are made.

H As for **D**.

I As for **D**.

2. Density has nothing to do with this. The controlling factor is that, in the mixed state, the entropy of the system has increased. Liquids of different density remain as two distinct layers only if the bonding between molecules is sufficiently strong to oppose the entropy increase. In the water/alcohol situation, hydrogen bonding is available in both the mixed and separate states. This does not oppose the tendency for the entropy to increase.

3. Above a piece of dry ice there are always molecules of water vapour. Since the water vapour is being constantly carried away into the atmosphere, more ice will turn to vapour (direction of increasing entropy) until the clothes are dry.

4. The bulk of solids have a Standard Molar Entropy below 40 J K^{-1}, liquids about 140 J K^{-1}, and gases about 200 J K^{-1}. In the solids column, the hardest materials tend to have the lowest entropy values. Belloc, in one of his poems, reinforces this: 'I shoot the Hippopotamus with bullets made of platinum, Because if I use leaden ones his hide is sure to flatten 'em.'

5. See pages 29 and 30.

6. See page 30.

7. This is a possible interpretation but, although the general trend is towards chaos, there is a finite statistical chance of order. Among the billions of events happening every second in the universe, some must be creating order, even if it is a temporary order of the kind we find in living things. It would seem that the 'big bang' theory and the 'steady state' theory of astronomy are both possible.

8. **A** More gas has been created than consumed.

D More gas has been created than consumed.

E Although the number of gas molecules remains the same, diatomic molecules containing dissimilar atoms tend to have a higher entropy than simple diatomic molecules.

F Two moles of gas have been created from one mole of gas.

H Gas created from solid.

I Gas created from solid.

In all the other cases there is no significant change or, in **C**, a mole of liquid has been consumed.

9. See page 35.

10. The process of spontaneous dissolution can be seen as two sets of competing forces.

(a) *Enthalpy* – the energy required to break the crystal lattice versus the energy released by the arrangement of water molecules round the ions (hydration energy). In this case the former seems to be bigger than the latter. The process is endothermic.

(b) *Entropy* – the increase in disorder caused by the release of the ions from the lattice versus the decrease in disorder as the water molecules form an orderly pattern around the free ions. In this case the former must be the greater to make $T\Delta S$ greater than ΔH and therefore make ΔG negative and the dissolution spontaneous.

11. The argument is similar to that of Question 10.

12. To attempt to do so would be to go against the Second Law. For a heat engine to operate there must be a hot area and a cold area to give a direction to the heat flow. The water could be pumped aboard, but the low temperature heat in it could not flow spontaneously to the hot end of the engine.

After the heat was extracted, the water would be thrown over the stern as blocks of ice. Once more, we would be going against the Second Law by creating order (ice) from relative disorder (liquid water).

13. (a) See page 39.
(b) See page 37.
(c) See page 39.
(d) See page 39.
(e) See page 39.

14. $\Delta G^\circ = -nFE^\circ$ joules (notice the unit which comes out of this equation is J).

$n = 2$ because two electrons are transferred whenever an atom of Zn becomes Zn^{2+}

$$\Delta G^\circ = -2 \times 96\,500 \times 1.1\,\text{J}$$

$$= -2.2 \times 96.5\,\text{kJ}$$

$$= -212\,\text{kJ}$$

15. The reaction in reverse would have $\Delta G^\circ = +212\,\text{kJ}$. This reaction would not be feasible and the equilibrium would be very much to the left (Chapter 11). You already know that in practice copper does not displace zinc from its salts.

16. Water(l) changing to water(g) seems to have an unusually high value for ΔS°. The state of disorder in gases is much the same for all gases at the same temperature. The difference must lie in the state of order in the liquid. Water, because of hydrogen bonding, is a fairly well-ordered liquid.

17. (a)

$$\Delta S^\circ = \frac{q_{rev}}{T}$$

$$T = \frac{q_{rev}}{\Delta S^\circ} = \frac{1000}{10} \, K = 100 \, K$$

(b)

$$\Delta S^\circ = \frac{q_{rev}}{T} = \frac{1000}{298} \, J \, K^{-1} \, mol^{-1}$$

$$= 3.4 \, J \, K^{-1} \, mol^{-1}$$

18. (a) Spontaneous means capable of going in the direction as written of its own accord.

(b) A reaction is feasible if ΔG° is equal to or less than zero, or K is equal to or more than one (Chapter 11).

19. (a)

Substance	$\Delta H_f^\circ (kJ \, mol^{-1})$	$S^\circ (J \, K^{-1} \, mol^{-1})$
$MgCO_3(s)$	-1113	66
$MgO(s)$	$-602 \left.\right\} -996$	$27 \left.\right\} 241$
$CO_2(g)$	-394	214

$$\Delta H^\circ = +117 \, kJ \, mol^{-1}$$

$$\Delta S^\circ = +175 \, J \, K^{-1} \, mol^{-1}$$

When $\Delta G^\circ = 0$, the reaction just becomes feasible.

$$\Delta H^\circ = T\Delta S^\circ$$

$$T = \frac{\Delta H^\circ}{\Delta S^\circ} = \frac{117\,000}{175} \, K$$

$$= 669 \, K$$

$$= 396\,^\circ C$$

(b)

Substance	$\Delta H_f^\circ (kJ \, mol^{-1})$	$S^\circ (J \, K^{-1} \, mol^{-1})$
$MgO(s)$	-602	27
$Mg(s)$	$0 \left.\right\} 0$	$33 \left.\right\} 136$
$\frac{1}{2}O_2(g)$	0	103

For the reaction

$$MgO(s) \rightarrow Mg(s) + \tfrac{1}{2}O_2(g)$$

$$\Delta H^\circ = +602 \text{ kJ mol}^{-1}$$

$$\Delta S^\circ = 109 \text{ J K}^{-1} \text{ mol}^{-1}$$

$$\Delta G^\circ = 602 - 669 \times \frac{109}{1000} \text{ kJ}$$

$$= +529 \text{ kJ}$$

At 669 K when $MgCO_3$ is decomposing, the MgO decomposition is not feasible. The temperature at which it becomes feasible is calculated as follows

$$T = \frac{\Delta H^\circ}{\Delta S^\circ} = \frac{602 \times 1000}{109} \text{ K}$$

$$= 5523 \text{ K}$$

$$= 5250\,^\circ\text{C}$$

It is not surprising that magnesia (MgO) is used to make high temperature crucibles!

Chapters 9 to 11

1. (a) ΔG° greater than zero for a reaction tells us that the equilibrium position will lie on the reactants' side. The reaction will go to the equilibrium position.

(b) ΔG° large and negative tells us that the products will be favoured. However, thermodynamics tells us *nothing* about the rate at which equilibrium will be attained.

(c) At equilibrium $\Delta G = 0$, not $\Delta G^\circ = 0$.

$\Delta G^\circ = 0$ is the limiting condition for a reaction to be *feasible*, i.e. for the equilibrium to lie on the side of the products.

2.

A $\Delta G_f^\circ \text{ (reactants)} = \Delta G_f^\circ(C_2H_6) + \Delta G_f^\circ(Cl_2) \quad = -33 + 0 \text{ kJ}$

$\Delta G_f^\circ \text{ (products)} = \Delta G_f^\circ(C_2H_5Cl) + \Delta G_f^\circ(HCl)$

$$= (-53) + (-95) \qquad = -148 \text{ kJ}$$

$$\Delta G^\circ = \Delta G_f^\circ \text{ (products)} - \Delta G_f^\circ \text{ (reactants)}$$

$$= -148 - (-33)$$

$$= -115 \text{ kJ } \textit{The reaction is feasible.}$$

$$-\Delta G^\circ = 2.303 \, RT \log_{10} K$$

$$\log_{10} K = \frac{115\,000}{2.303 \times 8.314 \times 298} = 20.15$$

$$K = 1.4 \times 10^{20}$$

B $\qquad \Delta G^\circ = 2 \times 95.3 = +190.6\,\text{kJ}$

(Note that we are dealing with 2 moles of HCl.)

$$\log_{10} K = -33.4 \equiv \overline{34}.60$$

$$K = 4 \times 10^{-34} \quad \textit{The reaction is not feasible.}$$

C $\qquad \Delta G^\circ = -29\,\text{kJ} \quad \textit{The reaction is feasible.}$

$$\log_{10} K = 5.08$$

$$K = 12 \times 10^4$$

D $\qquad \Delta G^\circ = +141\,\text{kJ} \quad \textit{The reaction is not feasible.}$

$$\log K = -24.71 \, (\overline{25}.29)$$

$$K = 2.0 \times 10^{-25}$$

In all cases, at equilibrium $\Delta G = 0$.

3. $\qquad K = \dfrac{[\text{products}]}{[\text{reactants}]}$

$$K = \frac{[\text{acid}] \times [\text{alcohol}]}{[\text{ester}] \times [\text{water}]}$$

$$= \frac{0.185 \times 0.185}{0.155 \times 0.725}$$

$$= 0.305$$

$$-\Delta G^\circ = 2.30 \, RT \log_{10} K \; (\log_{10} K \equiv \overline{1}.484 \equiv -0.516)$$

$$-\Delta G^\circ = 2.30 \times 8.31 \times 298 \times (-0.516)\,\text{J}$$

$$\Delta G^\circ = 2939\,\text{J}$$

$$= +2.94\,\text{kJ}$$

4.
$$A + B \rightarrow C$$

$$K = \frac{[C]}{[A][B]} = \frac{0.50}{0.35 \times 0.70}$$

$$K = 2.04$$

$$-\Delta G^\circ = 1767\,J$$

5. For reaction **A**,

$$K_A = \frac{[H_2O][Co]}{[H_2][CoO]}$$

For reaction **B**,

$$K_B = \frac{[CO_2][Co]}{[CO][CoO]}$$

For the reaction

$$CO_2(g) + H_2(g) \rightarrow CO(g) + H_2O(g)$$

$$K = \frac{[H_2O][CO]}{[H_2][CO_2]}$$

$$K = \frac{K_A}{K_B} = \frac{67}{490}$$

$$= 0.137$$

$$-\Delta G^\circ = 2.30 \times 8.31 \times 823 \log_{10} K$$

$$\left[\begin{array}{l} \log_{10} K = \bar{1}.137 \\ \qquad = -0.863 \end{array} \right]$$

$$-\Delta G^\circ = -13579\ J$$

$$\Delta G^\circ = 13.6\ kJ$$

N.B. For reactions involving solids, the [solid] is not included in the expression for the equilibrium constant. Strictly speaking, for reaction **A**

$$K_A = \frac{[H_2O]}{[H_2]}$$

and for reaction **B**

$$K_B = \frac{[CO_2]}{[CO]}$$

Chapters 12 and 13

1. Assuming that starch molecules are too large to go through the semipermeable membrane and that I_2 molecules are small enough to do so, the result should be as shown in Figure A.2.

— blue starch / I_2 complex solution

— semi–permeable membrane

— aqueous I_2 solution

Figure A.2

2. The disorder of gold within sea water means that, for the process to be reversed (i.e. an increase in free energy), there must be an even greater decrease in free energy somewhere else. This could happen when fuel is consumed to evaporate the sea water to dryness. If gold were the only impurity in the water the task would be daunting enough, but the evaporation of a cubic kilometre of sea water to dryness would result in a dry mixture of about 32×10^6 tonnes of mixed salts!

3. The clue lies in the word 'forced'. If the osmosis process is reversed, it must go up a free energy hill. For this to happen something else must descend a free energy hill. The pump and engine forcing the water into the tube are operating by a decrease in free energy greater than the increase caused by the reverse osmosis.

4. Chromatography is a process by which substances equilibrate themselves between two phases, such as two immiscible liquids, many times over. When a substance is distributing itself between two phases it is moving down a free energy hill or, in other words, increasing in entropy. The process of distribution is controlled by both entropy and enthalpy factors (Chapter 12, page 71). The components of the mixture separate because the entropy and enthalpy factors for any pair of substances are unlikely to be identical. No infringement of the Second Law occurs.

5. From the Ellingham diagram, the aluminium and hydrogen lines are unlikely to cross at any temperature within the industrial range; this method of reduction is therefore very unlikely.

6. (a) The increase in slope suggests that the entropy term is becoming even more important. This could happen only if more gas is consumed, i.e. if magnesium as well as oxygen is in the gas state. From tables you will find that the boiling point of magnesium is 1110 °C (1383 K).

(b) At temperatures up to about 2000 K the magnesium line is below the C to CO_2 line, and so CO_2 will be reduced while magnesium is oxidized. The same argument will apply to the reduction of steam by magnesium. Neither CO_2 nor water are good extinguishers for a magnesium fire!

(c) The lowest temperature would be at the point where the magnesium line and the C to CO line cross, at about 1900 K.

(d) The reaction between CO(g) and MgO(s) would probably be the most efficient and might warrant the higher temperature of 2600 K.

(e) It will be magnesium vapour which will be very susceptible to oxidation. Even when it is cooled to room temperature, it will probably be so finely powdered as to be a fire hazard.

Magnesium is now produced by electrolysis, but carbon reduction was used at one time. Silicon is used to some extent as a reducing agent for magnesium production.

7. (a)

Substance	ΔH_f° (kJ mol^{-1})	
CO(g)	-111	$\left.\begin{array}{c}\end{array}\right\} -111$
H_2(g)	0	
C(s)	0	$\left.\begin{array}{c}\end{array}\right\} -242$
H_2O(g)	-242	

$$\Delta H^{\circ} = +131 \text{ kJ mol}^{-1}$$

The reaction is endothermic.

(b) The C to CO line crosses the H_2 to H_2O line at 800 K. But at that temperature there is a tendency for CO to oxidize to CO_2 and so higher working temperatures will, in practice, be necessary (about 1000 °C to keep the amount of CO_2 down to a minimum).

(c) Because the main reaction is so endothermic there will be a tendency for the temperature to drop below the feasibility level. To compensate for this, air is blown through with the steam to give the exothermic reaction

$$2C + O_2 \rightarrow 2CO$$

By balancing the air and steam flow, the temperature can be maintained above the feasibility level.

8. Part of the reactivity series was the ability of metals high in the series to displace metals lower in the series from their compounds.

(i) Mg can displace Al from Al_2O_3 at low temperatures, but above 1600 K the reverse is true.

(ii) Mg can displace Fe from FeO, but at about 2250 K the reverse is true.

(iii) At about 2300 K hydrogen can displace magnesium from MgO.

9. The Ellingham diagram shows us that Fe to FeO is feasible ($\Delta G°$ is negative) over a very wide temperature range. This is what happens on the outside of the furnace. If this reaction is to be put into reverse it must be coupled with another reaction so that the *combined* free energy change is negative. This happens inside the furnace when CO to CO_2 is coupled with FeO to Fe.

Index